Lecture Notes in Computer Science 9382

Commenced Publication in 1973
Founding and Former Series Editors:
Gerhard Goos, Juris Hartmanis, and Jan van Leeuwen

Editorial Board

More information about this series at http://www.springer.com/series/7409

Manfred A. Jeusfeld · Kamalakar Karlapalem (Eds.)

Advances in Conceptual Modeling

ER 2015 Workshops, AHA, CMS, EMoV,
MoBiD, MORE-BI, MReBA, QMMQ, and SCME
Stockholm, Sweden, October 19–22, 2015
Proceedings

 Springer

Editors
Manfred A. Jeusfeld
University of Skövde
Skövde
Sweden

Kamalakar Karlapalem
Indian Institute of Technology
Gujarat
India

ISSN 0302-9743   ISSN 1611-3349   (electronic)
Lecture Notes in Computer Science
ISBN 978-3-319-25746-4   ISBN 978-3-319-25747-1   (eBook)
DOI 10.1007/978-3-319-25747-1

Library of Congress Control Number: 2015952755

LNCS Sublibrary: SL3 – Information Systems and Applications, incl. Internet/Web, and HCI

Springer International Publishing AG Switzerland is part of Springer Science+Business Media
(www.springer.com)

Preface

Welcome to the proceedings of the workshops held during the 34th International Conference on Conceptual Modeling (ER conference 2015) in Stockholm, Sweden. Workshops offer an incremental exploration of cutting-edge research issues that become prominent in the future. The ER conference has a long tradition of thought-provoking and state-of-the-art workshops. This year we had a rich combination of seven workshops and a special symposium on conceptual modeling education.

We attracted 52 paper submissions for all the workshops, of which 26 were accepted. These workshops also have invited papers along with papers from the symposium on conceptual modeling education.

This volume comprises contributions from the following workshops:

AHA 2015 – Conceptual Modeling for Ambient Assistance and Healthy Ageing
CMS 2015 – Conceptual Modeling of Services
EMoV 2015 – Event Modeling and Processing in Business Process Management
MoBiD 2015 – Modeling and Management of Big Data
MORE-BI 2015 – Modeling and Reasoning for Business Intelligence
MReBA 2015 – Conceptual Modeling in Requirements Engineering and Business Analysis
QMMQ 2015 – Quality of Modeling and Modeling of Quality
SCME 2015 – Symposium on Conceptual Modeling Education

Each of these workshops deal with different aspects of conceptual modeling issues. Technology impacts conceptual modeling, and the workshops EMoV 2015, CMS 2015, and MoBiD 2015 explore these aspects. Applications play a key role in showing the deficiencies of state-of-the-art conceptual modeling methodologies – the workshops AHA-2015, MORE-BI, and MReBA-2015 discuss some of these issues. Quality is difficult to define in the context of conceptual modeling, and QMMQ-2015 identifies research problems in this area.

The workshop program of ER 2015 thus provided a place for participants to discuss, deliberate, and provoke to set an agenda for future research in these areas.

August 2015

Manfred A. Jeusfeld
Kamalakar Karlapalem

ER 2015 Workshop Organization

General Conference Chairs

Paul Johannesson	Stockholm University, Sweden
Andreas Opdahl	University of Bergen, Belgium

Workshops Co-chairs

Manfred Jeusfeld	University of Skövde, Sweden
Kamalakar Karlapalem	Indian Institute of Technology, Gandhinagar, India

Publicity Co-chairs

Ilia Bider	Stockholm University, Sweden
Erik Perjons	Stockholm University, Sweden

Organization Co-chairs

Maria Bergholtz	Stockholm University, Sweden
Jelena Zdravkovic	Stockholm University, Sweden
Eric-Oluf Svee	Stockholm University, Sweden

Treasurer and Registration Chairs

Martin Henkel	Stockholm University, Sweden

Technical Chair

Iyad Zikra	Stockholm University, Sweden

Conceptual Modeling for Ambient Assistance and Healthy Ageing

Organizing and Program Committee

Heinrich C. Mayr	Alpen-Adria-Universität Klagenfurt, Austria (Co-chair)
Ulrich Frank	Universität Essen-Duisburg, Germany (Co-chair)
Fadi Al Machot	Alpen-Adria-Universität Klagenfurt, Austria
Vadim Ermolayev	Zaporozhye National University, Ukraine
Hans-Georg Fill	Universität Wien, Austria
Athula Ginige	University of Western Sydney, Australia
Marion A. Hersh	University of Glasgow, UK

Dimitris Karagiannis	Universität Wien, Austria
Gerhard Lakemeyer	RWTH Aachen, Germany
Stephen Liddle	Brigham Young University, Provo, USA
Elisabeth Métais	Laboratory CEDRIC, Paris, France
Judith Michael	Alpen-Adria-Universität Klagenfurt, Austria
Yuichi Kurita	Hiroshima University, Japan
Oscar Pastor	Valencia University of Technology, Spain
Wolfgang Reisig	Humboldt-Universität Berlin, Germany
Elmar Sinz	Universität Bamberg, Germany
Vladimir Shekhovtsov	National Technical University Kharkiv, Ukraine
Josefine Sullivan	The Royal Institute of Technology, Stockholm, Sweden
Markus Stumptner	University of South Australia, Australia
Tatjana Welzer	University of Maribor, Slovenia

Conceptual Modeling of Services

Organizing and Program Committee

Karoly Bosa	Johannes Kepler University Linz, Austria (Co-chair)
Thomas Ziebermayr	Software Competence Center Hagenberg, Austria (Co-chair)
Dagmar Auer	Johannes Kepler University, Austria
Karoly Bosa	CDCC, Johannes Kepler University, Austria
Andreea Buga	CDCC, Johannes Kepler University, Austria
Roxana-Maria Holom	CDCC, Johannes Kepler University, Austria
Paul Johannesson	DSV, Stockholm University, Sweden
Harald Lampesberger	CDCC, Johannes Kepler University, Austria
Hui Ma	Victoria University of Wellington, New Zealand
Tania Nemes	CDCC, Johannes Kepler University, Austria
Dana Petcu	West University Timisoara, Romania
Mariam Rady	CDCC, Johannes Kepler University, Austria
Wolfgang Schreiner	RISC, Johannes Kepler University, Austria
Qing Wang	University of Otago, New Zealand
Yan Zhu	Southwest Jiaotong University Chengdu, China
Thomas Ziebermayr	Software Competence Center Hagenberg, Austria

Event Modeling and Processing in Business Process Management

Organizing and Program Committee

Nico Herzberg	SAP, Germany (Co-chair)
Falko Kötter	Fraunhofer-Institut IAO, Germany (Co-chair)
Stefan Appel	Siemens AG, Germany (Co-chair)
Nenad Stojanovic	FZI, Germany (Co-chair)
Darko Anicic	Siemens AG, Germany
Dimitris Apostolou	University of Piraeus, Greece
Anne Baumgraß	University of Potsdam, Germany

Opher Etzion	Academic College of Emek Yezreel, Israel
Dirk Fahrland	Technical University of Eindhoven, The Netherlands
Christoph Fehling	University of Stuttgart, Germany
Holger Giese	University of Potsdam, Germany
Georg Grossmann	University of South Australia, Adelaide, Australia
Christian Janiesch	University of Würzburg, Germany
Maximilien Kintz	Fraunhofer IAO Stuttgart, Germany
Stefan Krumnow	Signavio GmbH, Germany
Matthias Kunze	University of Potsdam, Germany
Frank Leymann	University of Stuttgart, Germany
Andre Ludwig	University of Leipzig, Germany
Jan Mendling	Vienna University of Economics and Business, Austria
Adrian Paschke	Freie Universität Berlin, Germany
Stefanie Rinderle-Ma	University of Vienna, Austria
Stefan Sackmann	University of Halle, Germany
Sigrid Schefer-Wenzel	FH Campus Wien, Austria
Stefan Schulte	Vienna University of Technology, Austria
Stefan Sobernig	Vienna University of Economics and Business, Austria
Mark Strembeck	Vienna University of Economics and Business, Austria
Walter Waterfeld	Software AG, Germany
Barbara Weber	University of Innsbruck, Austria
Matthias Weidlich	Imperial College London, UK
Mathias Weske	University of Potsdam, Germany
Uwe Zdun	University of Vienna, Austria

Modeling and Management of Big Data

Organizing and Program Committee

Il-Yeol Song	Drexel University, USA (Co-chair)
Juan Trujillo	University of Alicante, Spain (Co-chair)
David Gill	University of Alicante, Spain (Co-chair)
Alejandro Mate	University of Alicante, Spain (Co-chair)
Yuan An	Drexel University, Philadelphia, USA
Marie-Aude Aufaure	Ecole Centrale Paris, France
Rafael Berlanga Llavori	Universitat Jaume I, Spain
Sandro Bimonte	National Research Institute of Science and Technology for Environment and Agriculture, France
Michael Blaha	Yahoo!, Inc.
Gennaro Cordasco	Università di Salerno, Italy
Dickson Chiu	University of Hong Kong, SAR China
Alfredo Cuzzocrea	University of Calabria, Italy
Gill Dobbie	University of Auckland, New Zealand
Jose Luis Fernández-Alemán	University of Murcia, Spain

Eduardo Fernández-Medina Patón	Universidad de Castilla-La Mancha, Spain
Pedro Furtado	Universidade de Coimbra, Portugal
Matteo Golfarelli	University of Bologna, Italy
Magnus Johnsson	University of Lund, Sweden
Nectarios Koziris	National Technical University of Athens, Greece
Jiexun Li	Drexel University, Philadelphia, USA
Stephen W. Liddle	Brigham Young University, USA
Alexander Löser	Beuth University of Applied Sciences Berlin, Germany
Antoni Olivé	Universitat Politècnica de Catalunya, Spain
Jeffrey Parsons	Memorial University of Newfoundland, Canada
Oscar Pastor	Universidad Politécnica de Valencia, Spain
Nicolas Prat	ESSEC Business School, France
Sudha Ram	University of Arizona, USA
Carlos Rivero	University of Idaho, USA
Colette Rolland	Université Paris, Panthéon Sorbonne, France
Keng Siau	Missouri University of Science and Technology, USA
Alkis Simitsis	Hewlett-Packard Co., USA
Alejandro Vaisman	Universidad de la República, Uruguay
Panos Vassiliadis	University of Ioannina, Greece

Modeling and Reasoning for Business Intelligence

Organizing and Program Committee

Ivan J. Jureta	FNRS and University of Namur, Belgium (Co-chair, Steering Committee)
Corentin Burnay	FNRS and University of Namur, Belgium (Co-chair)
Stéphane Faulkner	University of Namur, Belgium (Co-chair, Steering Committee)
Sarah Bouraga	University of Namur, Belgium (Co-chair)
Ivan J. Jureta	FNRS and University of Namur, Belgium (Co-chair)
Esteban Zimányi	Université Libre de Bruxelles, Belgium (Steering Committee)
Alberto Abelló	Universitat Politècnica de Catalunya, Spain
Ladjel Bellatreche	Ecole Nationale Supérieure de Mécanique et d'Aérotechnique, France
Sandro Bimonte	Irstea Clermont Ferrand, France
Olivier Corby	Inria, France
Alfredo Cuzzocrea	ICAR-CNR and University of Calabria Italy
Marin Dimitrov	Ontotext
Neil Ernst	University of British Columbia, Canada
Cécile Favre	Université Lyon 2, France
Paolo Giorgini	University of Trento, Italy
Jennifer Horkoff	University of Trento, Italy
Dimitris Karagiannis	University of Vienna, Austria

Alexei Lapouchnian	University of Trento, Italy
Sotirios Liaskos	York University, Canada
Isabelle Linden	University of Namur, Belgium
Patrick Marcel	Université François Rabelais de Tours, France
Jose-Norberto Mazón	University of Alicante, Spain
Anna Perini	Fondazione Bruno Kessler, Italy
Stefano Rizzi	University of Bologna, Italy
Catherine Roussey	Irstea Clermont Ferrand, France
Monique Snoeck	Katholieke Universiteit Leuven, Belgium
Thodoros Topaloglou	University of Toronto, Canada
Juan-Carlos Trujillo Mondéjar	University of Alicante, Spain
Robert Wrembel	Poznań University of Technology, Poland

Conceptual Modeling in Requirements and Business Analysis

Organizing and Program Committee

Jennifer Horkoff	City University London, UK (Co-chair)
Renata Guizzardi	Universidade Federal do Espírito Santo (UFES), Brazil (Co-chair)
Jelena Zdravkovic	Stockholm University, Stockholm (Co-chair)
Colette Rolland	Université Paris 1 Panthéon – Sorbonne, France (Steering Committee)
Eric Yu	University of Toronto, Canada (Steering Committee)
Thomas Alspaugh	University of California, Irvine, USA
Daniel Amyot	University of Ottawa, Canada
Claudia Cappelli	NP2TEC/Universidade Federal do Estado do Rio de Janeiro, Brazil
Jaelson Castro	Universidade Federal de Pernambuco, Brazil
Fabiano Dalpiaz	Utrecht University, The Netherlands
Sergio España	Universitat Politècnica de València, Spain
Aditya Ghose	University of Wollongong, Australia
Aneesh Krishna	Curtin University, Australia
Paul Johannesson	KTH Royal Institute of Technology, Sweden
Gustaf Juell-Skielse	Stockholm University, Sweden
Ivan Jureta	University of Namur, Belgium
Sotirios Liaskos	York University, Canada
Lin Liu	Tsinghua University, China
Lidia Lopez	Universitat Politècnica de Catalunya, Spain
Pericles Loucopoulos	University of Manchester, UK
Luiz Olavo Bonino da Silva Santos	Bizzdesign, The Netherlands
Andreas Opdahl	University of Bergen, Norway
Anna Perini	Fondazione Bruno Kessler, Italy
Jolita Ralyté	University of Geneva, Switzerland

Bill Robinson	Georgia State University, USA
Samira Si-Said Cherfi	Conservatoire National des Arts et Métiers, France
Pnina Soffer	University of Haifa, Israel
Vitor Souza	Universidade Federal do Espírito Santo, Brazil
Sam Supakkul	Sabre Travel Network, USA
Lucineia Thom	Universidade Federal do Rio Grande do Sul, Brazil
Roel Wieringa	University of Twente, The Netherlands

Quality of Models and Models of Quality

Organizing and Program Committee

Samira Si-Said Cherfi	Conservatoire National des Arts et Metiers, France (Co-chair)
Charlotte Hug	Université Paris 1 Pantheon, Sorbonne, France (Co-chair)
Oscar Pastor	Valencia University of Technology, Spain (Co-chair)
Jacky Akoka	CNAM, France
Said Assar	Telecom Ecole de Management, France
Laure Berti-Equille	Institut de Recherche pour le Développement, France
Lotfi Bouzguenda	ISMIS, Tunisia
Cristina Cachero	Universidad de Alicante, Spain
Isabelle Comyn-Wattiau	CNAM-ESSEC, France
Rebecca Deneckere	University of Paris 1 Panthéon-Sorbonne, France
Sophie Dupuy-Chessa	UPMF-Grenoble 2, France
Virginie Goasdoue-Thion	University of Rennes I, France
Cesar Gonzalez-Perez	Spanish National Research Council, Institute of Heritage Sciences, Spain
Roberto E. Lopez-Herrejon	Johannes Kepler Universität, Austria
Wolfgang Maass	Saarland University, Germany
Raimundas Matulevicius	University of Tartu, Estonia
Jeffrey Parson	University of Newfoundland, Canada
Verónika Peralta	University of Tours, France
Erik A. Proper	CRP Henri Tudor, Luxembourg
Jolita Ralyte	University of Geneva, Switzerland
Sudha Ram	University of Arizona, USA
Farida Semmak	UPEC, Université Paris-Est Créteil, France
Guttorm Sindre	Norwegian University of Science and Technology, Norway
Pnina Soffer	University of Haifa, Israel

Conceptual Modeling Education

Organizing and Program Committee

Ernest Teniente — Universitat Politecnica de Catalunya, Spain (Co-chair)

Giancarlo Guizzardi — Federal University of Espirito Santo, Brazil (Co-chair)

Contents

Conceptual Modeling in Requirements and Business Analysis

Quality of Models and Models of Quality

Conceptual Modeling Education

Conceptual Modeling for Ambient Assistance and Healthy Ageing

Preface: Conceptual Modeling for Ambient Assistance and Healthy Ageing

The European Commission defined "Health, demographic change and wellbeing" as one of the six "Grand Challenges" of the European Union. But a look at demographic statistics shows that this is or will become a challenge of the entire world. Endeavors are made in various directions to meet that challenge, amongst which the fields of "Active and Assisted Living (AAL)" and "Healthy Ageing (HA)" are rather prominent. The design of innovative and beneficial IT solutions in these domains recommends "thinking out of the box", i.e. looking beyond current ways of living in the older age. For innovation to work, it is also important to get various stakeholders of future assistance systems involved in time, i.e. to offer them comprehensible representations of possible solutions that enable them to express their concerns and demands. Therefore, the realization of advanced systems to support "Active and Assisted Living (AAL)" and "Healthy Ageing (HA)" recommends powerful abstractions, or, in other words, the design and use of conceptual models.

Although most projects dealing with AAL and HA use models in some way, only few systematic approaches to modeling methods for these fields have been reported so far. Therefore, the workshop "Conceptual Modeling for Ambient Assistance and Healthy Ageing, AHA2015" was designed to reveal the existing and potential contributions, which can be made by the modeling community to AAL and HA. A particular emphasis was on Conceptual Modeling within the context of designing and developing systems for assisting humans in their everyday live and in healthy ageing.

Questions to be discussed at the workshop were, among others, which modeling method might be useful for which purpose, how the requirements of the end users could be met by using (conceptual) modeling techniques, and how to relate modeling tools to common standards in the fields of Ambient Assistance, Ambient Assisted Living and Healthy Ageing.

All submitted papers have been peer reviewed by members of the program committee. This chapter contains those papers, which have been accepted by the program committee, and carefully revised following the reviewers' comments.

The paper *"PersonLink: An Ontology Representing Family Relationships for the CAPTAIN MEMO Memory Prosthesis"* by Noura Herradi Faycal Hamdi, Elisabeth Métais, Fatma Ghorbel, and Assia Soukane dicusses an ontology for modeling, storing and reasoning on "family relationships" links. This ontology is used as backbone of the "CAPTAIN MEMO memory prosthesis", which is intended to support an older person as a memory-aid.

Alencar Machado, Leandro Krug Wives, and José Palazzo Moreira de Oliveira propose in their paper "*A Semantic Model for Proactive Home Care Systems*" semantic models, which are to support the interoperability between the physical environments and different software levels in a Home Care environment by allowing the identification of the particular user context.

Process models are focused on by the paper "*Understanding Care Work and the Coordination of Care Process Conglomerations*" by Monica Winge, Erik Perjons, Benkt Wangler: The authors introduce the notions of patient-centered care process and a conglomeration of such. The latter is defined as a set of patient care processes that all concern the same patient, are overlapping in time, and are all sharing the overall goal of improving or maintaining the health and social well-being of the patient. Generic models of such processes are presented.

Finally, the paper "*A Method to Analyze, Diagnose and Propose Innovations for Complex Ecosystems: the InnoServ Project*" by Mario Cortes-Cornax, Dominique Rieu, Christine Verdier, Agnès Front, Fabrice Forest, Annabelle Mercier, Anne Marie Benoit, Aurélien Faravelon reports on a project that aimed at understanding and supporting innovation strategies and services around a fragile person. A method for analyzing complex ecosystems is presented, the application of which lead to organizational innovations to improve efficiency and quality to take care of fragile people.

We thank all authors for submitting to AHA2015 as well as the members of our renowned program committee for their careful and intensive collaboration to make AHA2015 a success.

Heinrich C. Mayr, Alpen-Adria-Universität Klagenfurt, Austria (chair)
Ulrich Frank, Universität Essen-Duisburg, Germany (co-chair)

PersonLink: An Ontology Representing Family Relationships for the CAPTAIN MEMO Memory Prosthesis

Noura Herradi[1,2], Fayçal Hamdi[1], Elisabeth Métais[1(✉)], Fatma Ghorbel[3], and Assia Soukane[2]

[1] Cedric Lab, Conservatoire National des Arts Et Métiers (CNAM), Paris, France
{faycal.hamdi,elisabeth.metais}@cnam.fr
[2] Ecole Centrale d'Electronique (ECE), Paris, France
{herradi,soukane}@ece.fr
[3] Laboratoire MIRACLE, Université de Sfax, Sfax, Tunisia

Abstract. In the context of the CAPTAIN MEMO memory prosthesis for elderly, we propose the PersonLink ontology for modeling, storing and reasoning on "family relationships" links. Rules are provided to infer new links and/or check inconsistencies in the inputs. On the one hand PersonLink is as generic as possible and is integrated in the linked data formalisms; on the other hand a prosthesis has to be adaptable to users. Thus the PersonLink ontology defines rigorously and precisely family relationships, and takes into account the differences that may exist between cultures/languages, including new relationships emerging in our societies nowadays. The transition from one culture/language to another one cannot be solved with a simple translation of terms, but refers to a meta-ontology and associated mechanisms.

Keywords: Vocabulary · Family relationships · Memory prosthesis · Multilingual ontology · Linked data

1 Introduction

In 2050, 30 % of people from the European countries will be at least 65 years old. Memory troubles will be one of the major disabilities these people will suffer from. A survey of literature suggests that cognitive decline begins averagely before the age of 60 [16]. The prevalence of diseases involving memory impairment such as Alzheimer Disease is directly correlated with age, increasing to 50 % in people older than 90 years; memory loss is very progressive and the first symptoms begin many years before the person becomes dependent.

According to [15], participants with memory impairment who have used a PDA[1] had their independence in daily tasks increased, with a benefit reminding even if they stopped using the PDA. Ergonomic aspect study and "Design for

---

[1] Personal Digital Assistant.

© Springer International Publishing Switzerland 2015
M.A. Jeusfeld and K. Karlapalem (Eds.): ER 2015 Workshops, LNCS 9382, pp. 3–13, 2015.
DOI: 10.1007/978-3-319-25747-1_1

All" orientation will allow the use of the assistant by elderlies. It is the episodic memory of the elderly that becomes first failing; while the implicit memory - based on routines and automatisms - remains longer preserved, that enable the possibility of creating new connections for durably use of a numeric assistant.

In this context, we are currently developing the CAPTAIN MEMO memory prosthesis that acts as a memory-aid application for elderly people. This prosthesis stores personal data and can be connected to the pervasive environment, using various sensors and localisation systems in order to supply a set of services indoor and outdoor. Among these services, one is devoted to "remember things about people", i.e. retrieving a person by navigation in the family/entourage tree, retrieving a person according to criteria, retrieving a person facing the camera, retrieving information about a person (name, family or conviviality relationship, age, preferences, gifts exchanged, favourite meals, recent events, shared events, etc.).

The CAPTAIN MEMO memory prosthesis aims at taking into consideration incomplete and inconsistent data. Rules are used either for checking or for deducing. Based on ontologies and semantic web languages, it can (i) store and semantically organize the information; (ii) deduces new facts from the given ones; (iii) check inconsistencies in the input data due to mnesic discordance. In order to store the family and entourage of the user, the modeling is endorsed to an ontology of family and convivial links, which constitutes the backbone of personal information storage.

The works presented in this paper consist in the definition of the PersonLink new ontology for representing and reasoning on the family relationships, that is adaptable to the culture of the person and aware of new concepts of this area. PersonLink gives a precise description of family relationships (e.g., parent/child, grandparents, uncles, cousins, etc.).

The paper is organized as follows. In the next section, we present motivating examples. In Sect. 3 we present some related works and in Sect. 4 the PersonLink ontology. In Sects. 5 and 6 we present experiments on the Captain Memo prosthesis and others performed in the context of linked data. Finally, we conclude and give some perspectives in Sect. 7.

2   Motivating Examples

The memory prothesis has to be adaptable to its users. However family links are completely dependent on the culture and the language [1].

For instance, the surrogate mother carries the child of a couple who gave its embryos. In the United States, there is no federal legislation for Surrogacy. Each state has its own rules, based on jurisprudence. So the Surrogacy is licensed in 14 states. The term used in English for this mother is "*Surrogate*". In France, the law n° 94–653 of 29 July 1994 prohibits surrogacy. However there exists a term in French which is "*Mère porteuse*".

Some concepts may not exists in certain languages, for example "*Godmother*" does not exist in some cultures/languages. Even if concepts are similar in different languages/cultures, they may differ in their constraints. For instance, depending on the culture, the "spouse" relationship may be defined between 1 man and 1 woman, or between 1 man and several women, etc.

Thus, it is not possible to carry out a translation of terms to switch from a language/culture to another one, since the concept could not exist or could have another definition in the target culture.

3   Related Works

Different ontologies have been proposed to describe family relationships in the web. The most famous one is FOAF [4]. It defines relationships through the predicate *"foaf:knows"* that links together two individuals; we can see the UML[2] Class Diagram on Fig. 1[3]. However, this representation is very limited because it does not provide the nature (e.g., family, friendship, etc.) of these links.

The Relationship[4] ontology [5] which extended FOAF, introduced several sub-properties to the property *"foaf:knows"*, that provide some terms representing parenthood, childhood, siblinghood and a generic term representing marriage *"SpouseOf"*. The Agrelon[5] (Agent Relationship Ontology) ontology [9], presents a more precise set of terms that distinguish between the different types of relationships. For example, siblings and half siblings can be distinguished by the two distinct properties *"hasSibling"* and *"hasHalfSibling"*. The Relationship and Agrelon ontologies bring more clarity to the relationships. Nevertheless, they remain very generic, lack precision, and they do not support multiculturalism. In [10], Yutaka Matsuo et al. describe the human relationships by considering that every relationship between persons is either belonging to one or more specific events or sharing common properties. In [13], the relationships depend on the context. The authors propose an ontology based on the D & S (Descriptions and Situations) framework. It defines context-specific relationships. This is an interesting solution for making flexible the representation of the relationships, but it cannot permit logic reasoning on interpersonal relationships. The Bio[6] ontology, aims to describe biographical information about people.There are some relationships that may be interesting, such as *"Father"*, *"Mother"*, etc. However, the Bio ontology is intended to store events (e.g. birth, marriage, etc.) and not links (e.g. father, wife, niece, etc.) since the persons are stored as partners of the same event and do not have a direct link.

To conclude, the current ontologies offer very short and generic definitions to describe interpersonal relationships. In addition to the lack of precision, the majority of existing ontologies are in English. However, ontologies should be used in different cultures. The PersonLink ontology that we propose deals with these issues by considering the culture/language aspect.

---

[2] http://www.uml.org/.
[3] http://creately.com/diagram/example/hmayq484/FOAF.
[4] http://vocab.org/relationship/.html.
[5] http://www.contentus-projekt.de/fileadmin/download/agrelon.owl.
[6] http://vocab.org/bio/0.1/.html.

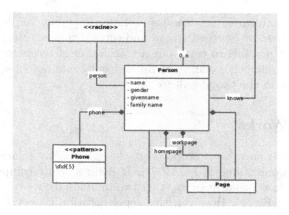

Fig. 1. FOAF (class diagram (UML))

4   The PersonLink Ontology

Our main objective is to represent interpersonal relationships in a precise manner. The Fig. 2 shows an excerpt of the class diagram of the PersonLink ontology with English concepts. However, in the full version there are 12 links between two Person classes, 23 links between the Female class and the Person one, 2 links between two Female classes, 6 links between Female class and Male Class, 22 links between Male class and Person class, 6 links between Male class and Female one and 2 links between two Male classes.

Furthermore the PersonLink ontology represents and defines the concepts according to the considered culture, and expresses them by using terms of the appropriate language. To do this, the first step consists on considering culture in the definition of the concept. For each culture, we look at whether the concept exists or not. If it exists, we describe it using its definition in this culture/language. So, for our ontology, if the concept exists in the culture, a term is assigned to it using the language related to this culture. If the concept does not exist, the term is $\emptyset$. Note that synonyms might exist in a same language, in this case all the terms are represented. We obtain as a result a kind of sparse ontology that we have called "*lace* ontology" because it contains many null values as we show in Fig. 3. Then, from this precise definition of concepts related to culture, we proceed to the formal representation of these relationships using the fragments of OWL2 [6] corresponding to the description logic $\mathcal{SROIQ}(\mathcal{D})$ [7]. Finally, we enrich these relationships by a set of DL-safe rules [14] (ensuring decidability) to have more inference possibilities.

4.1   The Lace Meta-ontology

The problem that arises in the representation of properties that describe interpersonal relationships, lies in the description of the property in two different languages/cultures.

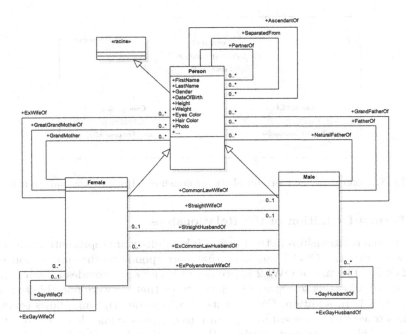

Fig. 2. Excerpt of PersonLink (class diagram (UML))

Taking the example of the property defining cousins, in French there exist two specific terms that represent this relationship according to the gender of cousin. However only a generic term exists to define this relationship in the English language/culture.

In the PersonLink ontology, we define each concept with a unique number, so each number represents a concept defining a relationship. This will allow us to have a hierarchy with multiple levels of accuracy which combines different languages/cultures. We can move from one concept to another in the level of accuracy (vertically), and therefore from a culture/language to another. Besides, the true meaning of the concept represented by a term for each language (obviously, if it exists in the associated culture) is preserved. We get as a result a *lace* meta-ontology (because of the null values it may have) of concepts with their representations in different cultures/languages.

The concepts represented in the lace meta-ontology for the cousinhood relationship of a person, shown in Fig. 3, have the following definitions:

- *Concept #2*: the descendant (regardless of gender) of the uncle or of the aunt (both mother's or father's side);
- *Concept #2.1*: the female descendant of the uncle or of the aunt (both mother's or father's side);
- *Concept #2.2*: the male descendant of the uncle or of the aunt (both mother's or father's side).

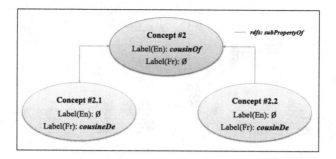

Fig. 3. Excerpt of the meta-ontology for cousinhood in English and French.

4.2 Formal Definition of the Relationships

Interpersonal relationships in the PersonLink ontology are represented in a structured way with the OWL2 language that corresponds to the description logic $\mathcal{SROIQ(D)}$. The use of OWL2 is privileged because it provides a high expressiveness and allows us to represent relationships that we were not able to represent in OWL1. In addition, OWL2, with this logic description, allows semantic reasoners to verify the consistency of data, to derive new knowledge or to extract information already present. Besides, the reasoning in OWL2 is complete and decidable. In predicate logic, the hierarchy represented in Fig. 3 means that:

$$2(?x, ?y) \Leftrightarrow 2.1(?x, ?y) \vee 2.2(?x, ?y)$$

In order to have more precision about the relationship going from the most generic concept ("*cousinOf*" in our example) to a specific one ("*cousineDe*") (which means: a female cousin), we have to get more information about the instance (female in our example) from the knowledge base of the CAPTAIN MEMO Memory Prosthesis. The specific concept would be inferred from the SWRL [8] (DL-Safe) rules that we would have previously created:

$$2(?x, ?y) \wedge Female(?x) \Rightarrow 2.1(?x, ?y)$$

We note that we need the information $Female(?x)$, to deduce that the type of the relationship $2(?x, ?y)$ ("*cousinOf*") is, in this case, the $2.1(?x, ?y)$ relationship (in French "*cousineDe*"). We define these relationships in the description logic $\mathcal{SROIQ(D)}$, with a set of constraints $\mathcal{K}$. For example, the definition of the cousinhood relationship is the following:

$$\mathcal{K} = \{\exists cousinOf.\top \sqsubseteq Person, Sym(cousinOf), Irr(cousinOf),$$
$$cousinDe \sqsubseteq cousinOf, Irr(cousinDe),$$
$$cousineDe \sqsubseteq cousinOf, Irr(cousineDe), cousineDe \equiv cousinDe-, \}$$

We applied the same method to define all the other relationships. The PersonLink ontology is available through a dereferenceable URI (and thus, would be referenced by the Linked Open Vocabulary) at: http://cedric.cnam.fr/~hamdif/ontologies/PersonLink.owl.

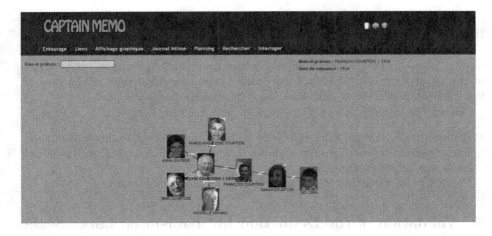

Fig. 4. Graphic editor using PersonLink

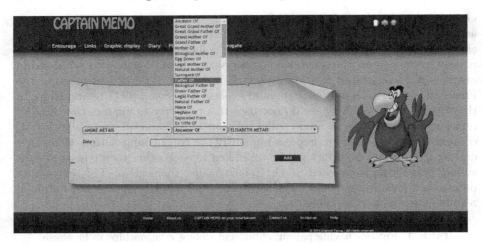

Fig. 5. Inputs through menu

5   Validation of PersonLink with Captain Memo

The CAPTAIN MEMO prosthesis [11,12] has been developed to help elderly to palliate mnesic problems. It acts as a memory-aid application for elderly people. This prosthesis stores personal data and can be connected to the pervasive environment using various sensors and localization systems in order to supply a set of services indoor and outdoor.

PersonLink is used for modeling, storing and reasoning on "family relationships" links. Figure 4 shows the graphical editor, used for display and search. On Fig. 5 we can see a part of the menu for textual input. The user can also input persons and family relationships through a vocal interface.

In spite of a unified internal representation, a language has to be chosen for the interfaces (we have chosen French for Fig. 4 and English for Fig. 5).

Rules are provided to infer new links and/or check inconsistencies in the inputs. Deducing new facts from ones given by users, and checking inconsistencies in the input data due to mnesic discordance are very important in the case of the CAPTAIN MEMO application targeting elderly persons.

Given the input graph of Fig. 4, the system will for example:

- Automatically deduce that Jad Cane is the grand-child of François Courtois;
- Suggest and confirm through a dialog that Marie-Madeleine Courtois could be Jean Courtois's daughter;
- Prevent from inputting that Jad is François Courtois's brother.

6   Validation of the Deduction Mechanism on Large Scale Linked Data

On a larger scale, to test the validity of our reasoning approach, we have taken as a sample persons described in context of the Linked Open Data (LOD). We chose as dataset Freebase, which is a large collaborative knowledge base built mainly from data provided by its community members. We show as relationship example, the cousinship relation presented in Sect. 4. First, we searched in the Freebase ontology, properties that could express the *"cousinOf"* relationship. In the current versions, Freebase do not uses this property to express that kind of relationship. However, we found other relationships (parental and sibling) that, combined, could be used to express implicitly the cousinship relation. Hence, we extract from Freebase, entities that are linked to each other by a parent and/or sibling relationships, as well as the relationships themselves. This extraction process is done automatically using scripts running MQL[7] queries. The obtained results are presented in Table 1:

Table 1. Entities having parent, child, and sibling relationships in Freebase

Relationship	Freebase relationship	Number of entities
Parent	/people/person/parents	2000
Child	/people/person/children	5155
Sibling	/people/sibling_relationship/sibling	1815
Sibling's child	–	0
Cousin	–	0

We extracted 2000 entities "person" that have parent relationship. From theses entities, 5155 children and 1815 siblings are generated. There too, no sibling's child or cousin relationships were found. In the result of this test, we note that the sibling's children and the person children could be candidates

---

[7] http://wiki.freebase.com/wiki/MQL.

Table 2. Inferred relationships using Freebase properties

FreeBase relationship	Number of entities	Inferred relationship	Number of entities	Null gender value
/people/person/parents	2000	motherOf	717	8
		fatherOf	1275	
/people/person/children	5155	daughterOf	2100	269
		sonOf	2786	
–	5117	nieceOf	2069	230
		nephewOf	2818	

to be cousins. Thus, we integrated entities and relationships that we obtained, on the PersonLink ontology to populate our knowledge base, then we applied automated reasoning to get new relationships. The reasoner is able to infer much more rigorous relationships. For instance, the *"fatherOf"* and *"motherOf"* relationships are inferred by exploiting the "parent" and "gender" properties describing Freebase entities. The *"daughterOf"* and *"sonOf"* relationships are inferred by exploiting the "children" and "gender" properties. We note that there are some people with null gender values. The results we got are presented in Table 2:

7 Conclusion and Future Works

In this paper we have presented a new ontology called PersonLink, that enables to represent family relationships in the context of a memory prosthesis. PersonLink provides a precise definition for each relationship and takes into consideration the culture/language aspect.

We also presented the notion of lace meta-ontology that facilitates the expression, in multiple cultures/languages of each relationship and allows to switch between languages and find the right terms expressing the relationships. A set of inference rules allow to deduce new links from the given ones, and to check the consistency of inputs, that is particularly useful in the case of a memory prosthesis for users having memory impairments. The current version of PersonLink includes 3 classes (Person, Male and Female), 86 properties, and 582 SWRL rules.

Representing and dealing with family relationships is an important issue on the web; in the context of Linked Data [2,3], a huge and growing number of data representing persons and relationships between them are published (e.g., data available in DBPedia[8], Freebase[9], Yago[10], etc.). Tests of Personlink conducted on the Freebase dataset show that the use of PersonLink enables inferring

---

[8] http://dbpedia.org/.
[9] https://www.freebase.com/.
[10] http://www.mpi-inf.mpg.de/yago/.

much more rigorous relationships than those already present in these datasets. Moreover these tests ensure the scalability of our reasoning mechanism.

Future works will be mainly devoted:

- To enrich the ontology with convivial links between people (neighbours, friends, care givers, etc.);
- To enhance deducing rules with context;
- To take into account time variance.

Acknowledgments. This research has been partially funded by the *"Ville de Paris"* under the VIVA project ("Vivre à Paris avec Alzheimer en 2030 grâce aux nouvelles technologies").

The authors wish to thank the reviewers for their evaluable comments.

References

1. Barry, L.: La parenté. Folio essais (2008)
2. Berners-Lee, T.: Design Issues: Linked Data. 1 March 2012. http://www.w3.org/DesignIssues/LinkedData.html
3. Bizer, C., Heath, T., Berners-Lee, T.: Linked data - the story so far. Int. J. Semant. Web Inf. Syst. **5**(3), 1–22 (2009)
4. Brickley, D., Miller, L.: FOAF vocabulary specification 0.97. Namespace document, January 2010. http://xmlns.com/foaf/spec/20100101.html
5. Davis, I., Vitiello, E.J.: RELATIONSHIP: a vocabulary for describing relationships between people. Technical report, vocab.org (2005)
6. Hitzler, P., Krötzsch, M., Parsia, B., Patel-Schneider, P.F., Rudolph, S.: OWL 2 Web ontology language primer (Second Edition). W3C Recommendation, World Wide Web Consortium (December 2012). http://www.w3.org/TR/owl2-primer/
7. Horrocks, I., Kutz, O., Sattler, U.: The even more irresistible SROIQ. In: Doherty, P., Mylopoulos, J., Welty, C.A. (eds.) KR, pp. 57–67. AAAI Press (2006)
8. Horrocks, I., Patel-Schneider, P.F., Boley, H., Tabet, S., Grosof, B., Dean, M.: SWRL: a semantic web rule language combining owl and ruleml. W3c member submission, World Wide Web Consortium (2004). http://www.w3.org/Submission/SWRL
9. Litz, B., Löhden, A., Hannemann, J., Svensson, L.: AgRelOn – an agent relationship ontology. In: Dodero, J.M., Palomo-Duarte, M., Karampiperis, P. (eds.) MTSR 2012. CCIS, vol. 343, pp. 202–213. Springer, Heidelberg (2012)
10. Matsuo, Y., Hamasaki, M., Mori, J., Takeda, H., Hasida, K.: Ontological consideration on human relationship vocabulary for FOAF. In: Proceedings of the 1st Workshop on Friend of a Friend, Social Networking and Semantic Web (2004)
11. Metais, E., Ghorbel, F., Herradi, N., Hamdi, F., Lammari, N., Nakache, D., Ellouze, N., Gargouri, F., Soukane, A.: Memory Prosthesis. In: Non-pharmacological Therapies in Dementia, p. 4 (2015) (To appear)
12. Metais, E., Nakache, D., Herradi, N., Ghorbel, F.: Rapport final du projet VIVA: Vivre à Paris avec Alzheimer en 2030 grâce aux nouvelles technologies. Technical report, CEDRIC-14-3246, CEDRIC laboratory, CNAM-Paris, France
13. Mika, P., Gangemi, A.: Descriptions of social relations. In: 1st Workshop on Friend of a Friend, Social Networking and the (Semantic) Web, September 2004

14. Motik, B., Sattler, U., Studer, R.: Query answering for OWL-DL with rules. J. Web Sem. **3**(1), 41–60 (2005)
15. Sainath, R.: Use of Personal Digital Assistants (PDAs) by Individuals with Acquired Brain Injury: Does it Improve Their Adaptive Function?. Alliant International University, San Diego (2007)
16. Salthouse, T.A.: When does age-related cognitive decline begin? Neurobiol. Aging **30**(4), 507–514 (2009)

A Semantic Model for Proactive Home Care Systems

Alencar Machado[1,2(✉)], Leandro Krug Wives[1],
and José Palazzo Moreira de Oliveira[1]

[1] Instituto de Informática, PPGC, UFRGS, Porto Alegre, Brazil
alencar.machado@ufsm.br, {wives,palazzo}@inf.ufrgs.br
[2] Colégio Politécnico, Universidade Federal de Santa Maria, Santa Maria, Brazil

Abstract. In proactive computing, systems can act to eliminate, mitigate or take advantage of previous knowledge to manipulate situations of interest in advance. Such behavior is critical for Ambient Assisted Living Systems. In this paper, we present semantic models to design and implement proactive systems to Home Care environments implemented with devices and sensors. These models support semantic interoperability between the physical environments and different software levels allowing the identification of the user context. Proactivity is then obtained by the construction of the most suitable action´s plan that results from the consumption of services provided by these devices and services. One challenge is to model a high-level situation and select the particular device that best meets users' needs, considering their context, location, and disabilities. The paper describes the steps required to create a generic, flexible and modularized model that can be extended to incorporate new domain knowledge regarding the specific requirements of different Ambient Assisted Living Systems.

Keywords: Proactive behavior · Ambient modelling · Assisted living · Ontology

1 Introduction

According to the Department of Economic and Social Affairs of the United Nations [1], life expectancy is augmenting. Such fact indicates that Home Care will receive strong attention, stimulating the development of new products and services in the next few years. It is expected that AAL will enable environments to support people, being sensitive to their needs and capable of predicting behaviors [2]. Systems for AAL, Home Care Systems (HCS), in particular, are emerging. According to Auvinen et al. [3], HCS can be defined as a technology to support the accomplishment of tasks, providing the means to collect, distribute, analyze and manage information related to human care.

Currently, there is a variety of devices to support people's interactions in living environments. To assist users that may be in specific and dangerous situations, we can integrate HCS with these devices. To achieve a good level of efficacy, HCS must be context-aware and present proactive behavior. Therefore, in our approach, we have a

M.A. Jeusfeld and K. Karlapalem (Eds.): ER 2015 Workshops, LNCS 9382, pp. 14–25, 2015.
DOI: 10.1007/978-3-319-25747-1_2

particular interest in turning HCS into proactive systems that consider users' needs. It is important to state that "proactive behavior" means being aware of a situation and learning from it. In particular, to learn from recurrent situations so that the system can predict them and act in advance to eliminate, mitigate or take advantage of previous knowledge when situations of interest emerge.

One of the main challenges to model the proactive behavior is the complexity of the representation of semantic relationships among the things of the real world with a degree of uncertainty. This situation is easily understandable by humans but difficult to be interpreted by automated systems. Therefore, it is necessary to model the environment's semantics. The main challenge is to provide support to HCS at the semantic level so that it can recognize and predict situations of interest and choose the most suitable action to manipulate a specific situation.

In the ontology model developed and presented in this paper, ontology networks are applied to represent the contextual knowledge that is implicit in a situation, creating a classification of context-sensitive concepts and their relationships. One aspect to consider is the identification of the user's situation in different contexts, which helps the adaptation of the system to the features of the individual environment. Our goal is to obtain an ontology to support semantic interoperability between the physical environment and the software environment, allowing the identification of the users' context identifying the most suitable plan of actions. One significant challenge in this model is to represent situations in a more abstract level. This representation must allow the selection of specific device's functionalities to manipulate the situation, while, at the same time, best meet users' needs based on their context, location, and disabilities.

This paper is organized as follows. Section 2 discusses background and related work. Section 3 presents the Systems for Ambient Assisted Living. In Sect. 4 presents the Ontology Network, Sect. 5 presents reasoning over AAL Ontology. Finally, in Sect. 6, we present and discuss our conclusions and future works.

2 Background and Related Work

AAL characterizes an automated domestic ambient in its different user's interactions with physical objects involved in home context (e.g., patient, relatives, nurses, doctors). Thus, before we move on, we need to define 'context', 'situation' and 'proactivity'. Among a large number of existing definitions, we adopt the one of Ye, Dobson, and McKeever [4], in which context is *"the environment in which the system operates"*. Events can be detected in the context, so systems need to verify the current user's contextual state and act upon it or on its changes. According to Etzion and Niblet [5], *"an event is an occurrence within a particular system or domain, it is something that has happened or is contemplated as having happened in that domain"*. Events can change the state of the environment, producing new situations.

Ye, Stevenson, and Dobson [6] define situation as *"the abstraction of the events occurring in the real world that are derived from the context and hypotheses about how the observed context relates to factors of interest"*. Therefore, we consider the current state of the user environment as a situation.

Engel and Etzion [7] describe proactivity as *"the ability to mitigate or eliminate future event of interest, identifying and taking advantage of future opportunities by applying prediction and automated decision-making technologies"*. For that class of systems, the main characteristic is the ability to predict a situation and act in advance; therefore, these systems need to manipulate uncertainty. Probability theory is a natural candidate to represent uncertain phenomena.

Multi-Entity Bayesian Networks (MEBN) can be used to generate expressive models because they combine first-order logic and probability. MEBN is a collection of MEBN fragments (MFrags) organized into MEBN Theories (MTheories). An MFrag represents a conditional probability distribution for instances (ontology instance) of its random resident variables, given their parents in the fragment graph and the context nodes. An MTheory is a set of MFrags that collectively satisfies consistency constraints ensuring the existence of a unique joint probability distribution over instances of the random variables represented in each of the MFrags. In fact, a template can be repeatedly instantiated to form *Situation Specific Bayesian Network* (SSBNs). SSBNs are regular BNs that are formed, usually in response to a query, to address a particular situation of domain knowledge [8].

Researchers [9–11] have modeled these concepts using ontologies to describe existing knowledge, and this facilitates the semi-automation of situations and actions. In this context, the concept of ontology network emerges. Ontology network is based on the integration of existing ontologies favoring modularization, reuse and re-engineering of knowledge resources as well as collaborative and argumentative ontology development [12]. The work of Pernas et al. [13] proposes a semantic modeling of adaptive Web-based learning systems. Díaz et al. [14] describe the role of an ontology network within a Semantic Educational Recommender System. The model proposed in this paper is very similar to the ones of Pernas et al. [13] and Díaz et al. [14] in terms of current situation and reactive actions. However, we added a predictive situation model using aspect of uncertainty and advanced actions. Our model also adds support for proactive behavior, thus being different from other studies.

3 Ontology for Ambient Assisted Living

The proposed AAL Ontology Network is shown in Fig. 1, where different arrows represent different kinds of meta-relationships. In this network, some ontologies are related to other ontologies of their domain. We refer to these as intra-relationships (intra-domain relationships). For instance, in Fig. 1, the dependence (*dependsOn*) among User and Domotic ontologies occurs as users use devices. The Device ontology also *dependsOn* Services and Location ontologies as the devices are contextualized in the physical space according to the services provided by them in specific locations. A proactive action consists of automatic executions of an action in the environment. Actions of type *dependsOn* need a particular situation to be detected or predict; they interact with the environment consuming services offered by devices. Events *dependsOn* services that are consumed by actions, and, when that happens, events are generated and the information about the environment is updated; this update may describe a new situation.

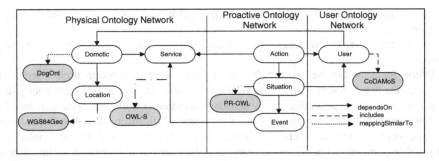

Fig. 1. Ambient assisted living network ontology

The intra-relationship *includes* occurs between different ontologies: (i) *User* and *CoDAMoS* [15], since the last has a set of concepts from the user ontology (i.e., profile, mood, role); (ii) *Domotic* and *DogOnt* [16], as DogOnt describe where a domotic device is located, its capabilities, technology-specific features needed for interfacing with it, and the possible state configurations it can assume; (iii) *Location* and *WGS84*, since the last defines all concepts and relations needed to define the localization of some point [17]; (iv) *Services* and *OWL-S* [18], as OWL-S is a top-level ontology having a set of concepts that are important for the semantic description of Web services; and (v) *Situation* and *PR-OWL2* [17], which provides an upper ontology based on Multi-Entity Bayesian Network (MEBN) [18] theories. The last one allows us to express a probability distribution on interpretations providing support to reasoning over uncertainty using first logic order and probability. Each of these ontology networks has their internal structure, and they do not interfere with the others except by the inter-relationships. Each network is described in the following sections.

3.1 User Ontology Network

In this work, users are the persons who live in an AAL. The context of an environment is represented by a set of entities that surround or interact with the user. Their semantic relations $\{R\}$ that form the context are represented by triples $\langle Es, p, Eo \rangle$. In these triples, the subject Es and the object Eo represent environment entities instances, which could belong or not to the same domain [10]. We also use semantic relations $\{R\}$ to describe the User Ontology. There, a *Person* is categorized into several sub-concepts. Besides, a *Person* has associated *Devices* to interact with the environment. Therefore, the AAL system uses these *Devices* to interact with the user.

<Person, *hasSubClass*, Non_Patient, Patient > ; < Non_Patient, *hasSubClass*, Doctor, Caregiver, Visitor, ... > ;

<Person, *hasPatientStatus*, Patient > ; < Person, *hasDevice*, Device > ;

<Person, *hasDisability*, Disability > ; < Disability, *hasSubClass*,

Visual, Auditive, Motor, Cognitive, ... > ; < Disability, *hasLevel*, Level > ;

<Person, *hasLocation*, Location > ; < Patient, *hasDisease*, Disease > ;

Users' location can be detected by one RFID sensor or through their interaction with a device that is located in a place inside the house. Disability is an incapacity that the person may have, and affects how devices can interact with this person. It has the *datatypeProperty* Level, which indicates the degree of disability. It is subdivided into four categories: (i) visual, where people may have difficulty to understand written text and graphic content; (ii) auditive, meaning that the user has a decreased ability to hear certain or all frequencies levels, which affect the reception of auditory information; (iii) motor: people may have limited use of their hands, or cannot use them, which affects their interaction with a device; (iv) cognitive, which involves a broad range of memory, perception, problem-solving and conceptualization of change and could affect any interaction with the person since information must be repeated more often.

3.2   Physical Environment Ontology Network

The physical environment ontology network is a structure of the domotic domain concepts. This domain includes the *DogOnt* ontology, which comprises device/network independent descriptions of *Building Environment*, *Building Thing*, *Controllable*, *Uncontrollable*, *Functionality*, and *State* [16].

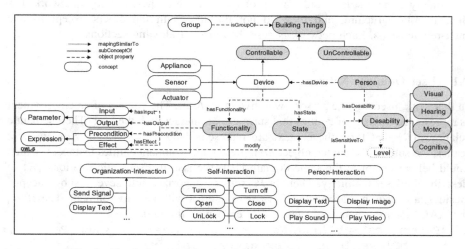

Fig. 2. Physical ontology network (adapted from Silva et al. [20])

In Fig. 2, the *Device* concept has the same characteristics of the *Controllable* concept of DogOnt, hence the existence of the triple < Device, mappingSimi-lartTo, Controllable > . From now on, to facilitate reading, all *Controllable*

Things will be referred as *Devices*. In the proposed model, there is a relationship between *Group* and *Building Thing* (either controllable or not). *Devices* are described in terms of possible configurations (*State*) and capabilities (*Functionality*). *State* refers to the internal configurations that the device can assume in a time instance, and *Functionality* refers to what the device can do to change *State* values. Appliances can be either *dumb* devices that can only be physically controlled by switching them on and off or *smart* devices able to provide complex functionalities. Actuators can control moving objects such as *Doors* and *Windows*, as suitable sensors can detect their state. Sensors also are linked to users, and they can provide variables like health, status, and location.

Based on OWL-S [18], *Functionality* has zero or more *Inputs, Outputs, Precon-ditions,* and *Effects.* According to Silva et al. [20], functionalities can be classified into: (i) *Person-Interaction*, when one wants to use a device to interact with a person; (ii) *Self-Interaction*, when a device needs to perform some action on itself; and (iii) *Organization-Interaction*, when one wants to communicate or ask something to an entity that is outside the house. In our model, *Person-Interaction* is a type of *Func-tionality*, hence it inherits certain relationships (*hasInput, hasOutput, hasPrecondition, hasEffects*). Thus, some characteristics of a given functionality may be previously indicated.

3.3 Proactive Ontology Network

This ontology describes the concepts related to proactivity in HCS (Fig. 3).

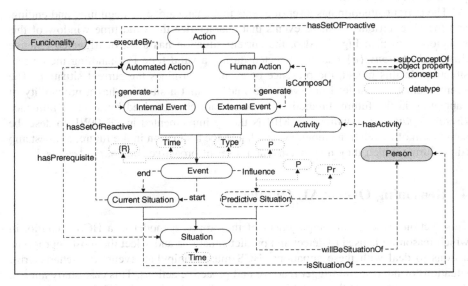

Fig. 3. Model's core (adapted from Machado et al. [10])

An activity represents daily activities that are made up of human actions performed by *Persons* in the home environment, like breakfasting, watching television, taking medicine or doing exercises. An *Action* is understood as something that is done willingly, executes, or entails something in an intentionally, deliberately and effortful way. In our work, *Action* is something that an entity executes, does, or performs, either manually or automated; *Automated Action* is an action that changes the status of one or more entities. It can be further classified as: *Person-focused*, referring to actions that are performed in order to communicate something to a person; *Device-Focused*, referring to actions that modify a device; *Organization-Focused*, referring to actions to inform/call an organization. *Automated Actions* are executed by the *Functionality* of a device.

Thus, when the *Acting* is *Person-Focused*, it will be executed by a *Person-Interaction Functionality*; similarly, *Organization-Focused* and *Device-Focused* will be processed by their corresponding *Functionalities*. Agents (humans or devices) carry out actions to achieve a goal. When an action does or does not achieve its objective, it may generate events, which return the status of an entity. An event has a name and is characterized by an internal or external type, a timestamp and a set of contextual semantic relations {R} (described in Sect. 3.2). Events can be linked to one or more contexts. For instance, a pattern that defines that an event must be detected if a particular sequence of events happens within a given window of time involving the "user" in his/her living room. In this work, events can determine the evidence of the beginning and the ending of a situation. Thus, events change the state of the environment and characterize a new current or predictive situation [10]. To describe health situations, we need the knowledge of experts in the application domain to indicate which events can produce relevant situations.

The current situation has a set of events that characterize its beginning and ending, and the time attribute of these events that characterize the valid time window of this situation, shown in Fig. 3. Also, the current situation has a set of triggered reactive *Automatic Actions* {a} that are detected during a valid time for handling the current situation. In this model, the presence of events determines the current situation. The event evaluation can lead the system to find out that a situation has a probability of happening in the future. Predictive Situations are characterized by a set of influence *Events*, a *pattern* (p), which is a MEBN theory implemented in PR-OWL to describe some form of correlation among events that shape a situation in the future, a timestamp (time during which they may occur), and a set of proactive *Automatic Actions*.

4   Reasoning Over AAL Ontology

This section presents the employment of the proposed model in a HCS scenario, in which reasoning is used to detect and predict situations and select the most appropriate actions to deal with these situations. HCS must manipulate events that characterize situations of interest and trigger reactive and proactive actions. This case study aims to demonstrate the use of the model in scenarios where the necessity of a mechanism that acts in a proactive way is emphasized.

Imagine John, a 78 years old citizen without the need for hospitalization but having diseases such as diabetes, hypertension, and lightweight memory problems. Therefore, John requires continued treatment, and his house was configured as a smart environment with a Home Care System (SIaaS middleware) to manage situations that involve him. Based on this scenario, his doctor identified he is presenting agitation behaviors. This situation causes problems for his health. Thus, there is an embedded infrastructure in John's residence that provides Automated Actions. In this context, a pervasive application, called *appPervAgitation*, was developed, and it manages agitation situations in patients with Alzheimer disease. The application provides the current and predictive situation for the middleware manipulate. The Current Situation is started when the Event (HeartbeatMore101) that represent the Heartbeat Sensor collects values greater than 101 and is ending (HeartbeatLess101) when the value's sensor produces value less than or equals 100.

Current Situation

Event	Type	Rule
Start	External Event HeartbeatMore101	`Patient (John) ∧ SensorHeatbeat (Sensor_Heartbeat1) ∧ hasValue (Sensor_Heartbeat1, CollectValue) ∧ swrlb:greaterThan(CollectValue,101) → isSituationOf (John, Emergency_Situation)`
End	External Event HeartbeatLess101	`Patient (John) ∧ SensorHeatbeat (Sensor_Heartbeat1) ∧ hasValue (Sensor_Heartbeat1, CollectValue) ∧ swrlb:greaterThanOrEqual(CollectValue,50) ∧swrlb:lessThanOrEqual (?CollectValue,100) → isSituationOf (John, Emergency_Situation)`

The application executes a plan with the objective of aiding an agitated patient with Alzheimer disease. The corresponding Automated Actions are: (a1) Notify caregiver; (a2) indicate the use of urgent drugs; (a3) play music; (a4) send message to the caregiver after his appointment; and (a5) request assistance from the health care provider.

These actions generate influence events managed over the time by the HCS application, and their detection generates values to the Local Probability Distribution (LPD) of the model. This knowledge must be provided by a predictive situation model specified by an expert in this particular situation.

The Predictive Situation model was developed in UnBBayes[1], which is a tool for this purpose. A node in an MFrag must have a list of arguments. These arguments are placeholders for entities (instance of ontology) in the domain. For example, argument *us* in the expression *willBeSituationOf (ps, t, us)* is a placeholder for an entity of User while the argument *t* is a placeholder for the time step this instance represents.

Figure 4 shows the MTheory to Predictive Situations. Green nodes at the top of each figure are context nodes; darker nodes are the input nodes, and the yellow ones are

---

[1] http://unbbayes.sourceforge.net/.

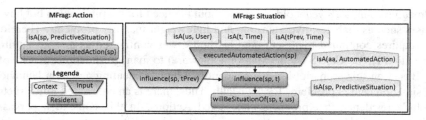

Fig. 4. MEBN theory for Predictive Situation in AAL Systems

resident nodes. The MFrag Action describes the fragment that represents the incidence of Automated Actions performed by the HCS. An MFrag Situation presents the probability of an unwanted situation involving the User in the future, thus the resident node *willBeSituationOf(ps, t, us)* presents the probability of a Predictive Situation "*ps*" at time "*t*" be a situation of the User "*us*". It is a resident node influenced by another resident node called *influence(ps,t)*, which have the input node *executedAutomatedAction(ps)* and its own local probability distribution at an earlier time "tPrev". In the MEBN theory for Predictive Situation of Fig. 4, the TimeStemp entity is an order variable, which represents discrete time (normally used in Bayesian Networks).

Table 1. Local probability distribution to MEBN theory predictive situation

RESIDENT: executedAutomatedAction(sp)
[a1 = 0.6, a2 = 0.1, a3 = 0.2, a4 = 0.05, a5 = 0.05]
 	
RESIDENT:
willBeSituationOf(ps, t, us)
if any ps have (influence = HeartbetLess101) [
  true = 0.01,
  false = 0.99
] else if any ps have (influence =
HeartbetMore101) [
  true = 0.99,
  false = 0.01
]else [true = 0.5, false = 0.5]
	RESIDENT:
	Influence(ps,t)
	if any ps have (executedAutomatedAction = a1) [
	  HeartbetLess101 = 0.70,
	  HeartbetMore101 = 0.30
	] else if any ps have (executedAutomatedAction = a2) [
	  HeartbetLess101 = 0.40,
	  HeartbetMore101 = 0.60
	] else if any ps have (executedAutomatedAction = a3) [
	  HeartbetLess101 = 0.30,
	  HeartbetMore101 = 0.70
	] else if any ps have (executedAutomatedAction = a4) [
	  HeartbetLess101 = 0.05,
	  HeartbetMore101 = 0.95
	] else if any ps have (executedAutomatedAction = a5) [
	  HeartbetLess101 = 0.05,
	  HeartbetMore101 = 0.95
	]else [HeartbetLess101 = 0.5, HeartbetMore101 = 0.5]

Table 1 presents local probability distributions for each resident node of the MTheory for Predictive Situation. This table shows the resident node *executedAutomatedAction(sp)*, which describes the incidence of actions for manipulating the Predictive Situation "*sp*", whereas 60 % of cases were a1 (notify caregiver); 10 % - a2, (urgent administration of drugs), 20 % - a3 (play music), and so on (details in Table 1).

The resident node *influence(ps,t)* means that if an Automated Action "a1" was performed for manipulating some Predictive Situation (*ps*), then the event HeartbeatLess101 happens in 70 % of cases and HertbetMore101 in 30 %, the remaining of the local probability distribution follows the same logic. The resident node *willBeSituationOf(ps, t, us)* means that the agitated situation is 99 % true when the Event HeartbeatMore101 is detected.

The reasoning process in PR-OWL ontology is an automatic generation of SSBN to determine the probabilities of a query. In this case, the query is "What is the probability of an agitated situation involving John happening in time T1?". Using the MTheory for Predictive Situation in AAL systems and the Local Distribution of Table 1, the SSBN of Fig. 4 was generated. To answer the question, it was determined that the current time is "T0" and the HeartbeatMore101 Event was detected in T0. Such evidence determines that John is agitated.

In the Specific Situation Bayesian Network presented in Fig. 5, there is a probability of 58,41 % in *T1* that John will be agitated. Therefore, the execution of a proactive plan of is needed for manipulating an agitated situation that may happen in the future.

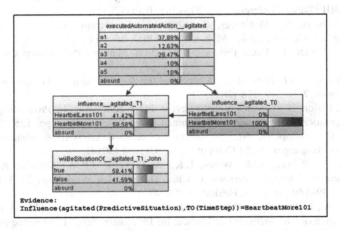

Fig. 5. Specific Situation Bayesian Network to Agitated *willBeSituationOf* John

5 Conclusion

Most of the research efforts in situation awareness are generally directed to implementation with a little preoccupation for the modeling of all the concepts involved. In the domotic application area, mainly in the complex environment of home-care for supporting elderly people with cognitive restrictions, we need models to support semantic interoperability between a smart environment and smart applications, allowing the identification of the current user situation and identifying the most suitable action to be executed. In this paper, we presented current issues in modeling for building Ambient Intelligence Systems for home-care. Our model was developed according to the methodology defined to build ontology networks. An ontology was developed, and it can be reused in several applications to improve interoperability, offering more semantics, allowing the detection of user's current and future situations and identifying the most suitable action to be performed. After developing the network, we conclude that this structure can be easily modified to incorporate new knowledge data, allowing to model concepts from different Ambient Intelligence environments. Our goal is to design models to describe an automated residential environment entirely controlled by a middleware. Currently, we are working on testing the situation detection over a real automated environment.

References

1. World Population Prospects: The 2012 Revision [WWW Document], United Nations, Dep. Econ. Soc. Aff c(2013). http://esa.un.org/wpp/Documentation/pdf/WPP2012_Press_Release.pdf
2. Sadri, F.: Ambient intelligence: a survey. ACM Comput. **43**(4), 1–66 (2011)
3. Auvinen, A., Silen, R., Groop, J., Lillrank, P., Defining service elements in home care. In: Annual SRII Global Conference, pp. 378–383. IEEE (2011)
4. Ye, J., Dobson, S., McKeever, S.: Situation identification techniques in pervasive computing: a review. Pervasive Mob. Comput. **8**(1), 36–66 (2011)
5. Etzion, O., Niblett, P.: Event Processing in Action. Manning Publications Co, Greenwich (2010)
6. Ye, J., Stevenson, G., Dobson, S.: A top-level ontology for smart environments. Pervasive Mob. Comput. **7**(3), 359–378 (2011)
7. Engel, Y., Etzion, O.: Towards proactive event-driven computing. In: Proceedings of the 5th ACM International Conference on Distributed Event-Based System, pp. 125–136 (2011)
8. Howard, C., Stumptner, M.: A survey of directed entity-relation-based first-order probabilistic languages. ACM Comput. Surv. **47**(1), 4 (2014)
9. Machado, A., Pernas, A.M., Wives, L.K., de Oliveira, J.P.M.: Situation-Aware smart environment modeling. In: Parsons, J., Chiu, D. (eds.) ER Workshops 2013. LNCS, vol. 8697, pp. 139–149. Springer, Heidelberg (2014)
10. Machado, A., Lichtnow, D., Pernas, A.M., Wives, L.K., Oliveira, J.P.M.: A reactive and proactive approach for ambient intelligence. In: 16th International Conference on Enterprise Information Systems, Lisbon, pp. 501–512 (2014)
11. Machado, A., Pernas, A.M., Augustin, I., Thom, L. H., Wives, L.K., Oliveira, J.P.M. Situation-awareness as a key for proactive actions in ambient assisted living. In: Proceedings of the 15th International Conference on Enterprise Information, pp. 418–426 (2013)
12. Allocca, C., d'Aquin, M., Motta, E.: Door– towards a formalization of ontology relations. In: International Conference on Knowledge Engineering and Ontology Development, INSTICC Press, Setubal, pp. 13–20 (2009)
13. Pernas, A.M., Yamin, A.C., Lopes, J.L., Oliveira, J.P.M.D.: A semantic approach for learning situation detection. In: IEEE 28th International Conference on Advanced Information Networking and Applications (AINA), pp. 1119–1126. IEEE (2014)
14. Díaz, A., Motz, R., Rohrer, E., Tansini, L.: An ontology network for educational recommender systems. In: Educational Recommender Systems and Technologies: Practices and Challenges: Practices and Challenges, p. 67 (2011)
15. Preuveneers, D., Van den Bergh, J., Wagelaar, D., Georges, A., Rigole, P., Clerckx, T., Berbers, Y., Coninx, K., Jonckers, V., De Bosschere, K.: Towards an extensible context ontology for ambient intelligence. In: Markopoulos, P., Eggen, B., Aarts, E., Crowley, J.L. (eds.) EUSAI 2004. LNCS, vol. 3295, pp. 148–159. Springer, Heidelberg (2004)

16. Bonino, D., Corno, F.: Dogont-ontology modeling for intelligent domotic environments. Springer, Heidelberg (2008)
17. W3C Semantic Web Interest Group: WGS84 geo positioning: an RDF vocabulary (2009). www.w3.org/2003/01/geo/wgs84_pos
18. Martin, D., Paolucci, M., McIlraith, S.A., Burstein, M., McDermott, D., McGuinness, D.L., Parsia, B., Payne, T.R., Sabou, M., Solanki, M., Srinivasan, N., Sycara, K.: Bringing semantics to web services: The OWL-S approach. In: Cardoso, J., Sheth, A.P. (eds.) SWSWPC 2004. LNCS, vol. 3387, pp. 26–42. Springer, Heidelberg (2005)
19. Carvalho, R.N., Laskey, K.B., Costa, P.C.: PR-OWL 2.0– bridging the gap to OWL semantics. In: Bobillo, F., Costa, P.C., d'Amato, C., Fanizzi, N., Laskey, K.B., Laskey, K.J., Lukasiewicz, T., Nickles, M., Pool, M. (eds.) URSW 2008-2010/UniDL 2010. LNCS, vol. 7123, pp. 1–18. Springer, Heidelberg (2013)
20. Kambara, J.S., Medeiros, G.M., Thom, L.H., Wives, L.K.: Business process modeling and instantiation in home care environments. In: International Conference on Enterprise Information Systems, Lisboa, pp. 513–525 (2014)

Understanding Care Work and the Coordination of Care Process Conglomerations

Monica Winge, Erik Perjons[✉], and Benkt Wangler

Department of Computer and Systems Sciences,
Stockholm University, Stockholm, Sweden
{winge,perjons,benkt}@dsv.su.se

Abstract. Health and social care is becoming ever more complex as a consequence of societal trends, including an aging population and increased reliance on care at home. One aspect of the increased complexity is that a single patient may receive care from several care providers, which easily results in situations with potentially incoherent, uncoordinated, and interfering care processes. In order to describe and analyze such situations, the article introduces the notions of patient-centered care process and a conglomeration of such. The latter is defined as a set of patient care processes that all concern the same patient, are overlapping in time, and are all sharing the overall goal of improving or maintaining the health and social well-being of the patient. The processes are based on a PDCA-cycle comprising phases for assessing, planning, performing and following up the care for the patient independently of health and social care organizations.

Keywords: Care process · Processes coordination · Health care · Social care · Home care · Patient-centered care · Collaboration · Coordination

1 Introduction

Health and social care in Sweden and in much of the rest of the world face several challenging trends: (i) The population is ageing and hence more patients, as a consequence of getting older, are suffering from multiple diseases. (ii) More patients, for reasons of preference and cost containment, are treated and taken care of in their homes. (iii) Health care has become much better at treating serious diagnoses, and hence, patients live with their diseases for a long time, requiring more care resources. Therefore, (iv) several care organizations, care professionals, and informal care actors, such as relatives and neighbors, will be involved in caring for these patients. As a consequence, (v) demands for communication and coordination among all these different care providers are increasing. Communication and coordination among care providers is a central theme in this article.

There is, however, a lack of appropriate tools for bringing about communication and coordination among care providers. Therefore, care actors belonging to different organizations and professions, and who are taking part in caring for one and the same patient, are often not well aware of each other's roles or even existence. This may

M.A. Jeusfeld and K.Karlapalem (Eds.): ER 2015 Workshops, LNCS 9382, pp. 26–37, 2015.
DOI: 10.1007/978-3-319-25747-1_3

lower the quality of care, cause inconveniences and put the safety of patients at risk. In such situations there is, hence, a strong demand for coordination of care plans such as to avoid patients being subject to contraindicatory treatments. Another central theme of this paper is therefore Care Planning, i.e. for the individual care process as well as for a set of processes that all concern the same patient.

A third central theme concerns the fact that care should be patient-centered, which in this paper means that the patient, his/her wishes and care needs, must be governing the planning and the carrying through of all care activities. Some of these care activities are health care activities and some of these are social care activities. In this paper we use the term care to include both health care and social care.

The vision and principles of patient-centered care have been difficult to realize in the care practice. One important reason for this is that there is a limited understanding of patient-centered care processes, in particular concerning how to manage coordination among autonomous care providers and to coordinate care processes in cases where one patient is subject to several care processes. This reason is also the problem addressed in this paper.

Some Swedish projects have developed collaborative process and information models. SAMBA [1] was an initiative to coordinate seven Swedish counties for a common health and social care process. Also the Flu-model [2] had the aim to develop a common care process for an improved logistic flu. Yet another initiative was the National information structure, a government commission with the aim to develop a national health care process and an information structure to support collaboration in health care [3].

The main goal of the paper is to propose a process model for managing patient-centered care among autonomous care providers. The process model can be used both to describe existing ways of working and to prescribe ways of working that contribute to patient-centered care, including situations where a patient is involved in several care processes.

1.1 Care Process

A process is a partially ordered set of activities that ultimately aims to produce goods or services of some kind, or in many cases some combination of the two. An instance of a process is the actual execution of the process, resulting in the production of actual goods and services. Each instance of the process has a start and an end. As we try in our mind to imagine the process, i.e. how it works (or should work) in some detail, we build a process model. The model may be illustrated by means of diagrams of various kinds complemented by textual descriptions and perhaps formal rules. In daily talk we usually refer to the combination of diagrams, textual descriptions, rules and perhaps more, as a process model. Process models can be descriptive, i.e. they depict the current workings of the process, or they can be prescriptive, i.e. they prescribe a desired state.

A *care process* is hence an (partially) ordered set of activities aiming to improve a person's health or social situation. Both from the patient's and the care organizations' point of view, the care of a single patient may be described as a chain of investigatory and interventionary activities, all carried out in order to improve the patient's health or social situation.

1.2 Further Definitions

In this section we will clarify our view on some further important terms, see Fig. 1. As far as possible we adhere to the CEN standard CONTSYS and its conceptual model of care concepts [4], but whereas CONTSYS merely addresses health care, we have generalized it to include also social care. For this reason and for clarity, we have changed the names of some concepts and relationships. We take the term *care actor* to mean any person, *care professional*, *patient relative*, or *patient friend* or even the *patient* herself, in charge of performing some particular care action. Whereas CONTSYS uses the term subject of care, we have for reasons of intuition preferred to use the term patient, which also may include e.g. frail elderly not having a particular diagnosis, but simply being in need of social care. A patient may suffer from one or more *health issues*, which in our case includes also "social" issues. A care professional may be a nurse or nurse assistant, a social care actor, a physician, a physiotherapist or any other person with a particular professional role and some care education and training, longer or shorter, for carrying out particular care tasks.

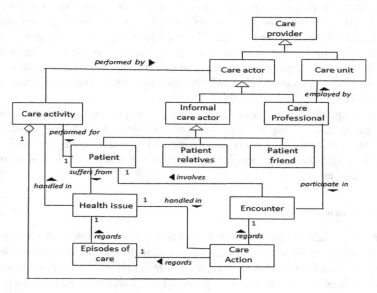

Fig. 1. Some important care concepts. The multiplicity 1 on a relationship indicates that e.g. a care activity is performed for exactly one patient.

We take the term *care unit* to mean an organization or organizational unit responsible to conduct some specific care of the patient, e.g. a primary care center, a hospital clinic, a social service organization. A *care provider* may be a care organization or a care actor. Unlike in CONTSYS we have chosen to regard all care actors, i.e. also *informal care actors*, as care providers.

We use the term *care activity* to refer to any investigatory and interventionary activity conducted for the patient by some health or social care actor. A care activity consists of one or more "atomic" *care actions*. Care activities are sometimes delegated to what in CONTSYS is referred to as informal care actors, i.e. in our case the patient or some relative or friend.

Some new concepts have been introduced, mainly based on results from the SAMS project, which investigated patient-centered collaboration between care parties in health and social care [5]. An *encounter* concerns the situation when a patient and a care professional or simply any passer-by[1] with the proper knowledge meets a patient with the intent to assess and influence the patient's health status and/or social situation. It may be performed according to a plan or not, e.g. it can be conducted on the initiative of the patient. An encounter may encompass several care activities. An *episode of care* concerns one particular health issue and may comprise one or more care activities.

2   Patient-Centered Care Processes

In a previous paper [6], we have suggested the Patient Centered Care Process (PCCP) as a way of viewing care processes. It was inspired by the well-known PDCA method for managing business process improvement [7]. But whereas PDCA runs as a separate process managing the target process, we prefer viewing the CHECK, ACT (here ASSESS), PLAN and DO phases as part of the main (PCCP) process. Furthermore, we let the process start with the ASSESS phase. This is required in patient-centered care, as understanding a patient's current situation is needed as a prelude to taking investigative or interventionary action. We claim, hence, that all sorts of care processes, whether health or social care, can be understood in terms of these phases.

2.1   A Generic Care Process

In its most general form, the care process may be described as in Fig. 2. It is a sort of service process, the phases of which are the ones of Assess, Plan, Do and Check. Starting with Assess and ending with Check, it can be understood as a general service or maintenance and repair process, where the subject of service (maintenance/repair) is the patient.

- *Assess:* In the Assess phase, the service provider investigates the status of the service object and identifies the problems from which it suffers. The Assess phase aims to identify the problems to be addressed and produce other information that can support decisions in the Plan phase.
- *Plan:* In the Plan phase, the service provider decides whether to follow an existing plan, modify an existing plan, or create a new plan. The Plan phase aims to determine the activities to carry out and their order, and confirm or produce

---

[1] The situation with any passer-by refers to e.g. the following situation: One or more persons, with or without care training, happens to be near-by as an accident with injured people occurs. Somebody among these persons understands that some care action needs to be conducted, e.g. stopping bleeding, has some basic knowledge of how to do it, and hence starts doing it. Somebody else calls for an ambulance.

guidance for executing the activities that address the problems of the service object. Goals for the service object should be specified.

- *Do:* In the Do phase, activities are carried out that address the problems of the service object. The activities are guided by the plan from the Plan phase, including the goals specified for the service object. The Do phase aims to improve the status of the service object.
- *Check:* In the Check phase, the service provider investigates to what extent the problem of the service object has been solved or alleviated, and/or the specified goals have been achieved. The Check phase aims to determine whether to end the process or start a new cycle. If the effects of the activities in the Do phase are deemed sufficient, the process stops after this phase; otherwise, the cycle starts anew with an assessment.

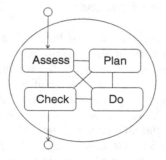

Fig. 2. A generic care process.

The following three sections will outline the utility of the PCCP as a way to understand how health and social care is and should be conducted. It does so in terms of a Basic PCCP, an Action PCCP, and a Coordination PCCP.

2.2   The Basic PCCP

The care process briefly described in Sect. 1.1. would normally be conducted in the order Assess, Plan, Do, Check. We hence call this sequence the basic PCCP or B-PCCP for short. It can be described in the form of a process diagram like in Fig. 3. The activities in each phase deal with things such as those defined in Fig. 1.

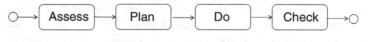

Fig. 3. The B-PCCP.

We claim that: It is always the case that every single care activity, whether investigatory or interventionary, is preceded by some planning activity, i.e. it is conducted according to some plan that may be explicit and exist on paper or in some IT system, or it simply exists in the head of the physician investigating the patient. The planning is done based on some assessment. As all care activities should have been conducted according to plan, there is a follow up to check whether the goals as formulated in the plan have been achieved and/or the stated problems have been addressed.

The B-PCCP appears when a care professional meets a patient without having seen each other previously for that particular reason, which leads to the encounter. For instance, when a patient visits a primary care centre or a hospital, or when she visits/is visited by an assistance assessor from the municipal social care, she will meet a care professional who conducts the following phases:

- *Assess:* An assessment is made of the patient's status or situation, sometimes without explicitly calling it an assessment. The assessment is done based on the information that is at hand, e.g. information in medical records, on information conveyed by the patient, and on information based in observations the care professional makes.
- *Plan:* A plan is worked out for how to deal with the situation, e.g. formulating goals, suggesting one or more care activities to be carried out, perhaps repeatedly, by one or more professionals together. In the simplest case, the plan may not even be referred to as a plan, and only exist in the head of the care professional, but in essence this is what it is.
- *Do:* From the plan follows that one or more activities are carried out by one or more care actors. All activities are carried out by individual care actors on account of the care organization having worked out the plan. They may sometimes be delegated to other care organizations. The care organizations themselves has a communal (in Sweden municipal or county council) mandate to offer care to people in a specific neighborhood. For this mandate it is payed by the municipality or the county council. Note also that activities may be carried out repetitively according to plan.
- *Check:* As the plan has been carried through, which may be a long process of repeated visits to or by the patient, whether at home or in a hospital, a check is made whether the goals of care have been achieved, the stated problems have been addressed, and the patient is satisfied. If so, the process has come to an end. If not, a new assessment is done and a new cycle of the process is started.

To further clarify the B-PCCP, we demonstrate the process with an example, a B-PCCP from the Health Care Domain: A patient arrives at a health center complaining about a "general back pain with some respiratory distress on exertion". He gets first to see a doctor. After a short conversation with the patient and review of anamnesis, i.e. carrying out the assessment phase in the B-PCCP, the doctor decides that she wants to listen to the lungs, examine back injury, measure blood pressure and take blood samples to test for infection. Having decided this she has also made the plan in the B-PCCP.

Upon this follows the Do phase in the B-PCCP, where the doctor delegates the first three activities to herself. She carries out the three individual investigatory care activities. Taking the blood samples is delegated to the health center's lab, and the patient is sent to the lab, where a blood sample is taken.

After the results from the health centre's lab arrive, within an hour or in a couple of days, the B-PCCP continues with the doctor making an overall evaluation of results from examining lungs, back, blood pressure and blood sample, i.e. the Check phase of the B-PCCP. As this has been done, a contact is taken with the patient and a new assessment is made and a plan is worked out for what should be done to the patient, etc.

It should be noted that some of these Assess, Plan, Check phases are done as a routine based on professionality without much thinking about it, but in principle this is what is done.

As can be understood from the above, *a Basic PCCP always concerns one care provider carrying out care for one single patient, sometimes by delegating particular care activities to other care providers.*

2.3   The Action PCCP

The PCCP works as a model also for what happens when someone carries out a planned care activity such as giving an injection or feeding the patient, or e.g. the investigatory activities carried out by the doctor of the example above. One may view it as that the doctor for each of the three activities implicitly makes an Assess phase and a Plan phase in her head, or as that these phases are so trivial that they are omitted, the PCCP collapses to a single Do phase. She then carries out the investigation, i.e. activities in the Do phase, and after each one makes a check of the outcome.

We refer to a PCCP that is planned in a B–PCCP and carried out by a care actor as an Action PCCP, abbreviated A-PCCP. The A-PCCP is the PCCP run as a micro-cycle. One care professional may Do many A-PCCPs in the course of a few minutes. Each A-PCCP can be carried out by the same actor as the one that planned the activities in B-PCCP, such as the three activities carried out by the doctor in the example, or it can be carried out by another care provider to which the activities are delegated, such as the blood sample activity carried out by the health centre's lab in the example.

An A-PCCP has already been allocated resources, since this has been done when working out the plan in a B-PCCP according to which activities are to be performed. The care actor in the A-PCCP may be a doctor, a nurse, a social care professional, a physiotherapist, the patient herself or someone else having been assigned this specific task in the care plan, but in most cases it is a health or social care professional who has the particular competence that is required. The contact may take place in the patient's home as a routine visit as part of a larger care plan, in a primary care centre or in a hospital. All care activities, whether investigatory or interventionary, take place as the result of a care plan (i.e. the plan in the B-PCCP accepted or changed in the Plan phase of A-PCCP, see below). The care activities are conducted by one or more individuals.

An A-PCCP consists of the following phases:

- *Assess:* An initiative to start an A-PCCP comes from a plan as a result from a B-PCCP. First in the A-PCCP, the individual care actor makes an assessment, consciously or unconsciously, of the patient status based on what the care actor sees and reads in the patient EHR or on what the patient tells, or based on some observation that the care actor makes. The patient state may be perfectly normal or something unexpected may have happened such as the patient lying unconscious on the floor as the care actor enters the patient's home.

- *Plan:* Depending on the results of the assessment, the care actor decides to follow the existing plan (as the result of an earlier carried out B-PCCP) for treating the patient, or she decides to change the plan and do something else, e.g. call for an ambulance.
- *Do:* The care actor performs the care activities according to plan, original or new, e.g. gives an injection and possibly other actions, or calls for the ambulance (which would be a new planned activity).
- *Check:* After the activities have been carried out the care actor checks the state of the patient, explicitly or implicitly, and if OK finishes the phase and registers the result. If not OK, a new A-PCCP may be started to deal with the new situation.

After each phase in the A-PCCP or after the A-PCCP has come to an end, the care actor registers the result, i.e.:

- any reassessment (compared to the assessment in the B-PCCP that initiated the A-PCCP),
- any change to plan (compared to the plan from the B-PCCP that initiated the A-PCCP),
- any activities having been carried out or not in the Do phase of the A-PCCP,
- results of the Check phase in the A-PCCP.

In the normal case the care actor simply crosses a box indicating that the A-PCCP has been carried through according to plan and that all went well. Measurements such as blood pressure may be registered. The database must be designed such that the information hangs together and such that it is possible to see who has done what.

2.4   The Coordination PCCP

A single patient may quite so often be involved in several PCCPs at the same time. One reason for this is that one PCCP can be nested within another as a consequence of a care provider requesting another care provider to carry out some activities, as the discussion above about a number of A-PCCP initiated by a B-PCCP. Another reason may be that the patient suffers from and is treated for several diagnoses and hence can be subject to a number of more or less independent PCCPs, each being conducted by a separate care provider.

A set of PCCPs each run by a separate autonomous care organizations and concerning the same patient will form what we refer to as a process conglomeration [6], which includes activities that are potentially incoherent, uncoordinated and interfering. More precisely, we define a *process conglomeration* as a set of PCCPs that all concern the same patient, that are overlapping in time, and that each one has the goal of improving or maintaining the health and social well-being of the patient with respect to the diagnosis that particular organization is responsible for.

For the patient, the resulting conglomeration appears as a cross organizational process in which she meets representatives from a number of organizations, perhaps without knowing precisely who comes from which organization, and without knowing how much or how little they communicate with each other. In addition to the patient feeling confused and unsafe, this situation places the patient at risk e.g. due to different care units offering treatments that are counter indicative. It may also result in waste of resources due to plans being badly coordinated, such that e.g. several care professionals want access to the patient at the same time.

The various PCCPs making up the conglomeration hence need to be coordinated. Today, this is sometimes done by organizing a care planning meeting, e.g. when a patient is handed over to the primary care and the municipal social care after having been treated at the hospital. The aim of such a meeting is to establish a "program of care" (a concept from CONTSYS [4]) for the continuing care of the patient. However, there is a risk that this meeting is not followed up. Furthermore, changes to plan may be done without taking all ongoing PCCPs into account. We propose, therefore, for each conglomeration to establish a coordination process corresponding to a continuously on-going care planning meeting in which representatives of all involved stakeholders participate, and that is not terminated until all involved PCCPs have come to an end. The meeting may be physical or virtual, synchronous or asynchronous. In other words, this corresponds to introducing a coordinating process on top of the care processes going on in parallel. The aim of this process is to instigate and maintain an "integrated program of care" that takes into account and adapts all the individual care plans. We refer to this process as the Coordination PCCP or the C-PCCP for short. In other words, we suggest that this process consists of the same generic phases, i.e. Assess, Plan, Do, Check.

The phases of the C-PCCP are:

- *Assess:* In this phase the care actors involved, i.e. a representative of each involved care unit and the patient herself, a relative or friend, get an overview of all earlier episodes of care for the patient, including specific health problems and diagnoses, earlier operations, general health status, social status, ADL (Activities of Daily Living), and are thus better equipped to make a common assessment of the patient's total care situation.
- *Plan:* In this phase the persons involved should formulate the common goals and objectives, and establish a common plan, to which the individual PCCP plans are adapted. This includes taking all care problems and planned care activities into account as well as earlier results and changes to plans. Dependencies and conflicts should be identified and resolved. We refer to this plan as an integrated program of care.
- *Do:* In this phase care activities are carried out in accordance with the integrated program of care. Information about outcomes of all activities are registered and fed back into the common care planning meeting.
- *Check:* This phase is carried out according to the integrated program of care, either on a pre-planned occasion or as needed due to what happens in the single PCCPs. It involves most importantly checking the outcome of the total care against the common goals and plan. It involves evaluating the total care situation in relation to the care goals, including the patient's own goals.

The C-PCCP, i.e. the common integrated care planning meeting should be started as soon as possible after it has been observed that a conglomeration is at hand. Figure 4 depicts three types of care plans and their relationships to other concepts.

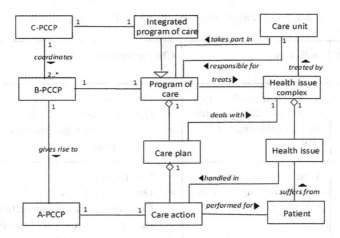

Fig. 4. The care planning model (adapted from CONTSYS [4]).

In CONTSYS [4] *Health Issue Complex* is referred to as a Health Issue Thread. A *Care Plan* is a description of planned and duly personalized care activities to be provided to a patient by one health care professional (see Fig. 1). A *Program of Care* is a description of planned and duly personalized care activities adopted by one care unit addressing one or more health care issues (see Fig. 1). The *Integrated Program of Care* is a program of care which is constructed as the result of adapting a set of programs of care such that they work together and in the best interest of the patient. The Integrated Program of care also needs to be complemented with the result of a common assessment, common overall care goals, and a plan for a common check of the total care.

3   Conclusion

In the previous sections we have explained how we view the Patient Centered Care Process and provided a few examples showing how it should be understood. Table 1 summarizes the characteristics of the three types of PCCPs.

It deserves pointing out also that, due to the generality of the PDCA cycle, the PCCP process could also be used for planning the development of care at higher levels, i.e. at the greater hospital or even at the county council level. This might be referred to as the Care Development PCCP or D-PCCP for short. However, we refrain from discussing this further here.

We claim that, by introducing the PCCP in a more systematic way in the training of all health and social care professionals,

1. they will be taught to clearly and in detail focus on the patient, her needs and wishes by formulating clear care goals and by making explicit follow ups (Check);
2. patients will become more involved and get a better control over the care they are subject to, in other words patient empowerment.

Table 1. Characteristics of A-, B- and C-PCCP respectively.

Type of PCCP	Definition	Characteristics
A-PCCP	A care actor conducting a single care action according to an existing *care plan*	➢ One patient ➢ One care provider ➢ One care action performed according to care plan
B-PCCP	A care provider establishing and carrying through a *program of care* for one patient	➢ One patient ➢ One care unit ➢ Comprising a set of care activities, started as an unprepared meeting between a patient and one or more care actors
C-PCCP	Two or more care providers establishing and carrying through an *integrated program of care* for a conglomeration.	➢ One patient ➢ Many care units ➢ Coordinating process for a conglomeration

Furthermore, by introducing it as a model to steer conglomerations and by coordinating care, actors will get a better overview of the patients care situation, i.e. what has been done to the patient and what is planned, as well as which other units and individuals are involved.

However, a number of things remains to be done. We hence need to:

– refine the PCCP by elaborating the description of the four phases,
– develop tools and e-services that obey and support the PCCP activities and what should be done in each one of them. This may be done within the framework of a coordination hub software, which also interfaces to sources of information such as sensors, EHR systems, and patient society web sites. This idea is further elaborated in [6], and
– clarify responsibilities for the care provider acting as the process owner, and to what degree coordination is one of those responsibilities.

Finally, it should also be noted that many things remain to be done at regional and national levels as concerns general regulation and policies as well as strategies for how to make the ideas put forward in this paper come true.

References

1. SAMBA Consortium: SAMBA, a Swedish national common project for collaboration, concept and information architecture (2003), Carelink, (in Swedish). www.ljungskilerevyn.se/fogare/samba/dokument/samba_2_3.doc. Accessed May 23th 2015
2. Swedish Association of Local Authorities and Regions: The Flu-modell (Flödesmodellen 2009) (in Swedish). http://www.flodesmodellen.se/content/view/9/14/. Accessed May 23 2015
3. Swedish National Board of Health and Welfare (Socialstyrelsen): National Information Structure– the steps before ICT - A foundation for access to appropriate information in health services. Sweden, 2009 (in Swedish). http://www.socialstyrelsen.se/nationellehalsa/nationellinformationsstruktur. Accessed May 23 2015
4. CONTSYS. ISO EN-13940–13941:2007. Health Informatics – systems of concepts to support continuity of care. Part 1: basic concepts
5. Gustafsson M., Winge M.: SAMS Konceptuell Informationsmodell. version 2.0 (in Swedish). http://winge.blogs.dsv.su.se/files/2014/04/Sams-Konceptuell-Informationsmodell4.pdf. Accessed May 24 2015
6. Winge, M., Johanneson, P., Perjons, E., Wangler, B.: The coordination hub: towards patient-centered and collaborative care processes. Health Inf. J., 1460458214528822, First Published on April 29, 2014
7. Walton, M.: The Deming management method. Perigee Books, New York (1988)

A Method to Analyze, Diagnose and Propose Innovations for Complex Ecosystems: The InnoServ Project

Mario Cortes-Cornax[1(✉)], Dominique Rieu[1], Christine Verdier[1],
Agnès Front[1], Fabrice Forest[2], Annabelle Mercier[3],
Anne Marie Benoit[4], and Aurélien Faravelon[5]

[1] LIG, University of Grenoble Alpes, 38000 Grenoble, France
{Mario.Cortes-Cornax,Dominique.Rieu,
Christine.Verdier,Agnes.Front}@imag.fr
[2] SFR INNOVACS, MSH-Alpes, 38040 Grenoble, France
Fabrice.Forest@upmf-grenoble.fr
[3] LCIS, University of Grenoble Alpes, 2600 Valence, France
Annabelle.Mercier@lcis.grenoble-inp.fr
[4] PACTE, CNRS, 38000 Grenoble, France
AnneMarie.Benoit@umrpacte.fr
[5] GIS, ENS, Institut Rhone-Alpin des Systèmes Complexes,
69342 Lyon, France
Aurelien.Faravelon@ens-lyon.fr

Abstract. Understanding and modeling complex ecosystems, where a great number of entities interact in different ways, is a great challenge in the information systems' domain. In this context, the *InnoServ* project aims to understand and support innovations around fragile people considering public, private and volunteering structures. The aim of this paper is to present the *ADInnov method*, which facilitates the analysis, the diagnosis and the proposition of innovations for complex ecosystems. This method has been extracted in an empirically way, from the lessons learned in the *InnoServ* project combining different techniques such as expert interviews, goal modeling and serious games. This method could be used in other areas where it is necessary to analyze complex ecosystems. Drawing out and discussing the results of the *InnoServ* project, we prove the efficiency of our method.

Keywords: Method · Services · Complex ecosystem · Business processes · Organizational innovations

1 Introduction

The western countries deal with a great problem, which is the necessity to avoid the hospitalization of the non serious cases and to favor the home care. A lot of organizations propose housework, but sometimes, a lack of services appears and the fragile people must be hospitalized (even if the situation does not require hospitalization) [1]. A person is considered "fragile" if she permanently settles in a medical and/or social

M.A. Jeusfeld and K. Karlapalem (Eds.): ER 2015 Workshops, LNCS 9382, pp. 38–48, 2015.
DOI: 10.1007/978-3-319-25747-1_4

fragility situation implying dependency (e.g., people receiving care at home for a chronic disease, elderly and/or disabled people that do not require hospital care but a regular support at home or people requiring long-term or temporary medical care) [1].

The *InnoServ* project[1] (Innovation in Services for Fragile People) tries to find organizational and low-tech-based solutions to maintain as long as possible fragile people at home in total autonomy. The project aims to understand and support innovation strategies and services around a fragile person. One of the initial aims of the project was to build a generic process model for fragile people home. Such a model is extremely complex: an intricate ecosystem with a large number of actors playing various and variable functions, diversity of scenarios and special cases, abundance of flows, various interaction kinds, etc. Complex ecosystems, where many entities interact in different ways can be found in many fields such as Physics, Economics, Mathematics or Computer Science [2]. In the context of Information Systems, such ecosystems are found in Virtual Organizations (VO) [3], collaborative business processes (choreographies) [4] or multi-agent systems [5]. Understanding and modeling these kinds of systems is still a great challenge. To overcome this complexity in the *Innoserv* context, the challenge of the project has been repositioned to study and improve the ecosystem around the fragile person: identify blocking points, organizational and technical solutions to meet them, and build the introduction of these solutions.

Starting from the specific domain of the *InnoServ* project, we have generalized the method until proposing the *ADInnov method* (Analysis, Diagnose, Innovation) that could be used in other areas where it is necessary to analyze a complex ecosystem. *The originality of this method relies in the consolidation of the empirical approach that has been used, integrating the lessons learned during the project.* The application of this method lead to several organizational innovations designed to improve efficiency and quality to take care of fragile people. These results prove the efficiency of our method. The innovations are mainly focused on the people and organizations around the fragile person.

The key concepts terminology is explained in Sect. 2. Section 3 describes the method, developing in detail the different phases. We draw out conclusions and future work in Sect. 4.

2 Context of the Study and Key Concepts

Effective solutions adapted to fragile people are yet to come. Technological solutions are only part of them. Organizational innovations, designed to improve care efficiency and quality are necessary. As a consequence, the *InnoServ* project undertakes this task in France. This project is one of seven co-financed projects by the French National Agency of Research (ANR) as part of its *Innovative Societies*[2] program. It is a multidisciplinary project that gathers eleven partners including six laboratories, an innovation research federation, an association, a local authority and two companies.

---

[1] http://bit.ly/1cvUC25.

[2] http://bit.ly/1OxinTq.

Launched in March 2012, it reaches today its fourth and last year. A second part of the project is envisaged to be starting in 2016.

Figure 1 captures the key concepts of the *InnoServ* ecosystem, which are then used to present the method. An *actor* is a type of physical or legal person who operates under its own business. Note that we call « actor » a type of actor. For instance, "nurse", or "physician" are (types of) actors. A *function* corresponds to a skill or responsibility in the ecosystem involved in the realization of a concrete service in the ecosystem. This notion is equivalent to the well known notion of "role" in the business process management domain [6]. However, we decided to use the term "function" which is more adequate in our multidisciplinary domain. Figure 1 also shows that nurse and physician are both health professionals. Health professionals refer to individuals or certified institutions working in physical or mental health with knowledge and specialized expertise to maintain or improve the health care of individuals. We will not go into detail in all the defined functions. More information can be found in [3, 7]. Note that an actor can play several functions and a function can be played by several actors. An example illustrating this case is given in the next section.

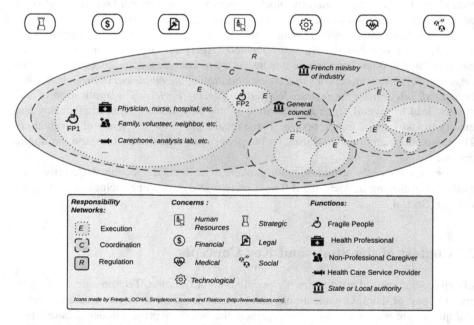

Fig. 1. Illustration of the responsibility networks, concerns, actors and their functions

In order to manage the ecosystem's complexity, a decomposition approach is needed [8]. We propose the concept of *responsibility networks* (RN) to tackle this problem. A responsibility network is a view on the ecosystem determined by the proximity (e.g., national, regional, individual, etc.) between a target (e.g., the fragile person) and its concerns. A *concern* relates to a cross-cutting issue in the responsibility network that determines a point of interest of a provided service (e.g., financial, medical). In Fig. 1 responsibility networks are represented as ellipsis more or less close to the fragile person. In our case, the following responsibility networks are identified: *Regulation* deals with new laws and rules concerning home care of fragile people; *Coordination* deals with home care organization of fragile people; and *Execution* focus on the direct interaction with the fragile person.

In the *InnoServ* ecosystem, seven concerns were identified: *Social, Medical, Human Resources, Technological, Financial, Legal (refers to legislations)*, and *Strategic (refers to plans to achieve a goal)*. In an *Execution RN*, social and medical concerns will be the focus. Concerning *Coordination RN*, human resources and technology concerns will be more important whereas in *Regulation RN*, financial, legal or strategic concerns are essential. Nevertheless, this point does not avoid having for example financial concerns in the *Execution RN*.

A *blocking point* corresponds to a concrete problematic in the context of a responsibility network or a concern. An example of identified blocking point for the *Execution* RN is: *"There are skill problems for the care activity concerning some actors. There are also problems of unavailability as well as lacks of required actors for care giving"*. One or more blocking points can be identified concerning a responsibility network and a concern (in an exclusive way). *Goals* are prescriptive statements about the system, capturing desired states or conditions [9]. Goals are hierarchically organized, starting from high level goals which can be iteratively refined into sub-goals. Goals do not define here the intentional process level, but the objectives to resolve blocking points. One of the goals resolving the aforementioned blocking point is: *"Have available actors in the fragile person's house"*.

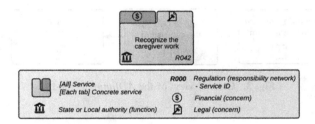

Fig. 2. Illustration of a service divided in concrete services categorized by concerns

A *service* relates to a delivery consisting in the provision of technical and intellectual capacity or the provision of useful work for a beneficiary. A service is attached to a responsibility network and is composed of one or several concrete services treating a concern. A concrete service is performed by one or more functions. In Fig. 2, we illustrate the following service *"Recognize the caregiver work"*. This recognition can be done in a legal way (i.e., recognizing the caregiver status) and in a financial way (i.e., establishing a salary for caregivers).

Note that the concepts presented in this section are generic terms that can be considered independent from the *InnoServ* project. Therefore, they can be easily transposed to other domains.

3 *ADInnov*: The Empirical Method Extracted from the InnoServ Project

This section presents the method extracted from the *InnoServ* project, called *ADInnov*, which stands for Analysis, Diagnose and Innovation. An overview of the method in given in Sect. 3.1. Sections 3.2, 3.3, 3.4 develop each of the three main phases of the method, presenting some important results of each phase. Section 3.5 discusses related work.

3.1 General View of the ADInnov Method

The *ADInnov* method follows a three steps process in order to elicit the innovation needs of the considered ecosystem and formulate innovation strategies (Fig. 3):

- **Analyze the Ecosystem**: the first phase studies the ecosystem and aims to identify responsibility networks, concerns, actors and their functions.
- **Diagnose the Ecosystem**: this phase studies the ecosystem's strengths and weaknesses. It mostly focuses on the goal models' construction relying on the previous identification of blocking points and responsibility networks.
- **Design Innovations**: this phase proposes to use empirical approaches such as serious games in order to reach the goals defined in the previous step, resulting on the proposition of organizational and service innovations. This phase proposes a way to illustrate the innovations via a set of scenarii.

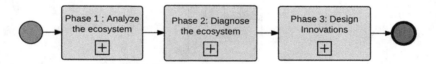

Fig. 3. General view of the *ADInnov* method

Most of the activities of the method are realized by the consortium, which have multidisciplinary representation from the eleven partners (6 research laboratories, an innovation research federation, an association, a local authority and two companies). A consortium's subgroup that gathers people called "animators" performs some activities in order to prepare and animate the consortium activities. Several activities are performed by the actors in the field of the specific domain (such as the physicians, the council administrators or the caregivers in the *InnoServ* project), mainly through interviews. Actors in the field put forward essential information to analyze, diagnose and propose innovations in the specific domain.

The three steps of our methodology are developed in the following sections. The phases are presented in detail and results for each phase are also put forward.

3.2   Phase 1 - Analyze the Ecosystem

Phase 1 analyzes the ecosystem. Figure 4 illustrates the different activities that compose this phase. The aim of these activities is to draw up a map of the studied eco-system.

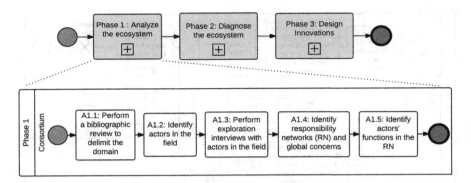

Fig. 4. Phase 1 - analyze the ecosystem

The first step to perform is a bibliographic review in order to gather the domain information (**A1.1**). This step is crucial to identify and describe the target of the studied eco-system (in our case, the fragile person). The next step consists in identifying the actors in the ecosystem (**A1.2**). We contact these actors and perform exploration interviews in order to complete the understanding of the domain (**A1.3**). Then, the ecosystem has to be decomposed in different responsibility networks and global concerns (**A1.4**). As previously explained in Sect. 2.2, we identified three responsibility networks in the *InnoServ* ecosystem: *Execution, Coordination* and *Regulation*. Moreover, seven concerns were identified: *Social, Medical, Human Resources, Technological, Financial, Legal,* and *Strategic*. Relying on responsibility networks, the functions played by actors can be completed (**A1.5**).

Results of the Phase 1: The bibliographical review and the exploration interviews should result in a report that gives a good understanding of the domain. The *InnoServ's* bibliographic report is described in [1]. At the end of this phase, the responsibility networks and concerns in the ecosystem are identified. Actors and their functions are also identified resulting in a model such as the one presented in Fig. 1.

3.3   Phase 2 - Diagnose the Ecosystem

The diagnose of the ecosystem should provide insights about the major blocking points. The different activities concerning this second phase, which is focused on goal modeling, are developed in Fig. 5.

The consortium identifies a first set of blocking points according to the responsibility networks and the concerns identified in the previous phase (**A2.1**). The first blocking points are potentially extended thanks to the interviews (targeting the actors in the field). The interviews take into account the actors' responsibility network in order to

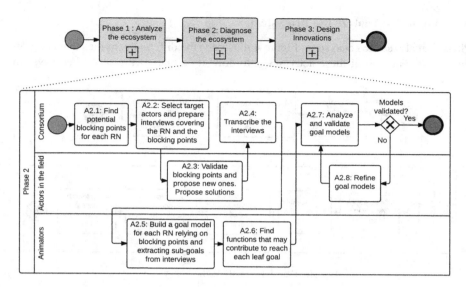

Fig. 5. Phase 2–diagnose the ecosystem

cover all of them (**A2.2**). Interviews may outline possible or partial solutions to the blocking points. Inquiring actors in the field helps validating and proposing new blocking points (**A2.3**). The interviews also provide clues about potential and partial solutions. The interviews have to be transcribed in order to be exploitable (**A2.4**).

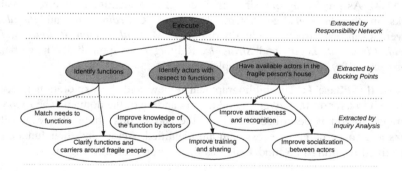

Fig. 6. Excerpt of the execution goal model indicating the origin of the goals

Simple goal models are built relying on responsibility networks and concerns. We suggest to develop a first version of the goal models by a subset of the consortium playing the role of animators (**A2.5**). Figure 6 illustrates an excerpt of the goal model corresponding to the *Execution* responsibility network. The figure shows that the root goal corresponds to the responsibility network. Then, the first sub-goals are extracted from the blocking points identified in the previous phase. Sub-goals are developed by analyzing the interviews, so they will correspond to the resolution of the blocking points. Here, new blocking points could appear. Functions that contribute to reach the goal model have to be identified (**A2.6**). This will help (in the next phase) to propose services resolving the goals performed by the identified functions. The goal models have to be analyzed by the consortium in order to validate them (**A2.7**). Iterations can be considered to refine the goal models until they are validated (**A2.8**).

Results of Phase 2: The main result of phase 2 is the set of goal models such as the one shown in Fig. 6 covering the different responsibility networks. What is interesting here is that the high level goals have been extracted from the blocking points, so the sub-goals focus on resolving these issues. The interviews (which also relied on the blocking points) are used to construct the goal models. The fact of attaching the actors to the leaf-goals will highlight potential lacks that could imply the proposition of new functions. This case is treated in the next section.

3.4 Phase 3 - Design Innovations

Phase 3 aims to propose innovations to achieve goals (and thus resolve blocking points) by playing a serious game (Fig. 7).

First, the animators explain the serious game, which is a Lego game[3] in our case and root goals are chosen. These root goals correspond to the responsibility networks to be treated (**A3.1**). Then, the different members of the consortium play scenarios (**A3.2**). Everyone put on a function hat in order to propose innovation services to resolve the blocking points. To propose the services, the consortium members rely on the sub-goals extracted from the interviews that were identified in the previous phase. In parallel, the consortium members propose innovations. For example new services or new necessary functions can be proposed in order to reach the defined goals (**A3.3**). A consolidation work has to be performed in order to check the coherence and the good alignment between goals and innovation services resulted from the previous phases (**A3.4**). Then, scenarios (i.e., story boards) are defined relying on dependency relations between services (**A3.5**). A scenario is a current language text, that can be illustrated, based on a specific case to exemplify the innovations. A simplified version of the homecoming scenario, which is one of the *InnoServ* case studies, is described as follows: *"Mrs. Dupont is a widow woman in her late 80's. She lives alone in a small village in the mountains. She was taken to the hospital emergency services due to a fall while at home. Since the accident, she had considerable lost autonomy. In addition, she has always faced economic difficulties. Returning home becomes complicated. Her brother wants to help her organizing her necessities".* This case is the starting point of the scenario. The actors in the field will have to validate the evolution scenarios (**A3.6**) before building the animated scenario that serves as demonstrator of the project's innovations (**A3.7**).

Figure 8 shows the scenario where the members of the consortium worked in order to find solutions to the blocking points concerning a responsibility network. The goal model constructed in the previous phase serves as guide to propose organizational and

---

[3] http://www.lego.com/fr-fr/seriousplay/.

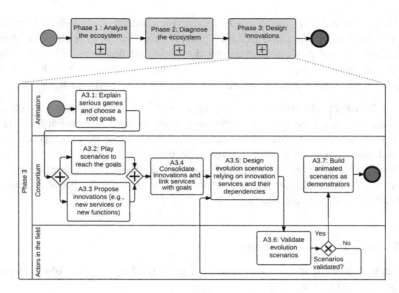

Fig. 7. Phase 3 - design innovations

Fig. 8. Scenario applying a serious game approach to propose innovations

service innovations. The example highlights a function played by a member of the consortium, the *Non Health Care Service Provider (i.e.,* personal home- assistance).

Results of Phase 3: The serious game session can lead to a set of services in order to reach the goals extracted from the blocking points. Each service responds to a specific goal and proposes a set of alterations on the ecosystem. This phase may also result in the formulation of organizational changes. In the case of the *InnoServ* project, a set of services[4] and several organizational changes were induced, such as the introduction of two new functions: the **Orchestrator**, which refers to a function that uses the resources near the fragile person and performs the prescription services for a fragile person and

---

[4] http://bit.ly/1Hvtq0t.

the **Coordinator**, which refers to a function responsible for organizing, coordinating and managing territories. The coordinator assigns the orchestrators and arbitrate their requests. These two functions implies extending the prerogatives of some actors. Nurses, for instance, could become orchestrators. The use of serious games will lead to concrete implementation of the organizational innovations and services. This implementation has to be illustrated graphically in an animation film format, which is used as demonstrator. This animation is now under construction in the case of our project, but we have already built an illustrated storyboard.

3.5 Method Synthesis and Related Works

The method presented in this paper, extracted in an empirically way, combines several techniques to diagnose, analyze and propose innovations in the context of complex ecosystems. For the analysis and diagnose phases, we rely on conceptual modeling as a reliable requirement engineering elicitation technique to "facilitate communication, uncover missing information, organize information gathered from other elicitation techniques, and uncover inconsistencies" [10]. In the diagnose phase, we used a simplified version of the goal models that are used in the KAOS method [9].

Analysis methods in the Information System's community such as Merise [11] or SSADM [12] provide systems' analysis techniques relying on sub-problem decomposition. This decomposition governed by the flow of information between the system and its environment or between different actors in the ecosystem. Michael and Mayr [13] propose a domain specific language in order to model a person's daily activity. The authors focus on a similar but very concrete situation, which allows a process oriented approach. In our case, we tried at first to represent all the flows between actors/functions. This approach allowed us to better understand the ecosystem but it has been proved to be very difficult to be implemented comprehensively. The concepts of *responsibility network* and *concern* (i.e., both representing different point of views of the ecosystem) are the answers to this problem in order to manage the complexity of the ecosystem.

For the innovation propositions, serious games were used. The effectiveness of this technique has already been proven in other methods such as the one proposed by Santorum et al. [14] in the context of business process management (BPM).

4   Conclusion and Future Work

We have presented the *ADInnov* method to analyze, diagnose and propose innovations for complex ecosystems. The "Analyze" phase proposes to explore the domain, identifying actors and their function. It also divides the ecosystem in different views to manage its complexity. The "Diagnose" phase focuses on finding blocking points which are completed and validated by actors in the field. It also develops goal models to project solutions to these blocking points. The "Design Innovation" phase relies on serious games to play scenarios in order to reach the goals defined in the previous phase. Here, innovation services and organizational innovations are proposed. The innovations are animated in order to be illustrated and validated by actors in the field.

The *ADInnov* method is built in an empirical manner, inspired by the different techniques in the *InnoServ* project context, which aims to understand and support innovation strategies and services around a fragile person. By showing up the results of the different phases, we illustrate the application of the method.

We have also presented the terminology used in the method. In future work, we consider developing a domain specific language to capture all the possible organizational innovations resulting from the method. We also consider to apply the method in other domains in order to validate the genericity of the terms and the applicability of all the used techniques.

References

1. InnoServ Consortium, Innovation in Services for frail people: Rapport Year 1. Coordinated by Christine Verdier, ANR Project, Université de Grenoble (2013)
2. Newman, M.E.J.: Complex systems: a survey. Phys. Rep. **79**(I), 10 (2009)
3. Priego-Roche, L.-M., Verdier, C., Front, A., Rieu, D.: A virtual organization modeling approach for home care services. In: Demey, Y.T., Panetto, H. (eds.) OTM 2013 Workshops 2013. LNCS, vol. 8186, pp. 373–377. Springer, Heidelberg (2013)
4. Hasegawa, Y.: Introduction. In: Hasegawa, Y. (ed.) Algebraically Approximate and Noisy Realization of Discrete-Time Systems and Digital Images. LNEE, vol. 50, pp. 3–10. Springer, Heidelberg (2009)
5. Kolp, M., Giorgini, P., Mylopoulos, J.: Multi-agent architectures as organizational structures. Auton. Agent. Multi. Agent. Syst. **13**(1), 3–25 (2006)
6. Russell, N., van der Aalst, W.M., ter Hofstede, A.H., Edmond, D.: Workflow resource patterns: identification, representation and tool support. In: Pastor, Ó., Falcão e Cunha, J. (eds.) CAiSE 2005. LNCS, vol. 3520, pp. 216–232. Springer, Heidelberg (2005)
7. InnoServ Consortium, Innovation in Services for frail people: Rapport Year 2. Coordinated by Christine Verdier, ANR Project, Université de Grenoble (2014)
8. Moody, D.: The 'physics' of notations: toward a scientific basis for constructing visual notations in software engineering. IEEE Trans. Softw. Eng. **35**(6), 756–779 (2009)
9. van Lamsweerde, A.: Goal-oriented requirements engineering: a guided tour. In: Fifth IEEE International Symposium on Requirements Engineering, pp. 249–262 (2001)
10. Hickey, A.M., Davis, A.M.: elicitation technique selection: how do experts do it ? In: 11th IEEE International Requirements Engineering Conference (2003)
11. Nanci, D., Espinasse, B., Cohen, B., Asselborn, J.-C.: Heckenroth Henri, Ingénerie de Systèmes d'Information: Merise Deuxième génération, 4th edn. Vuibert, Paris (2001)
12. Ashworth, C.M.: Structured systems analysis and design method (SSADM). Inf. Softw. Technol. **30**(3), 153–163 (1988)
13. Michael, J., Mayr, H.C.: Conceptual Modeling for Ambient Assistance. In: Ng, W., Storey, V.C., Trujillo, J.C. (eds.) ER 2013. LNCS, vol. 8217, pp. 403–413. Springer, Heidelberg (2013)
14. Santorum, M.: ISEA: une méthode ludique et participative pour la représentation et l'amélioration des processus métier, Thèse de doctorat d'université. Université de Grenoble (2011)

Conceptual Modelling of Services

Preface to the 6th International Workshop on Conceptual Modelling of Services

The 6th International Workshop on Conceptual Modelling of Services (CMS 2015) was co-located with the 34th International Conference on Conceptual Modeling (ER 2015) and organized in Stockholm in October 2015.

The CMS workshop aims to bring together researchers in the areas of services computing, services science, business process modelling, and conceptual modelling. The emphasis of this workshop is on the intersection of the rather new, fast growing services computing and services science paradigms with the well established conceptual modelling area. This workshop was organized 6th time and as before we particularly aimed at a close linkage between the conceptual modelling community and the services computing / services science communities. The 1st and 3rd CMS Workshops were organized in conjunction with ER 2010 and 2012. The 2nd CMS Workshop was co-located with the 1st International Conference on Data and Knowledge Engineering (ICDKE 2011). The 4th and 5th CMS Workshops were co-located with DEXA 2013 and 2014.

This workshop proceeding contains two papers and the summaries of two invited talks on the subject of conceptual modelling of services, which were presented at CMS 2015. In CMS 2015 our invited speakers were Paul Johanesson, who is Professor of the department of Computer and Systems Sciences at Stockholm University and Bernhard Thalheim, who is Professor of Information Systems Engineering at the University of Kiel. Both of them are known among others for conceptual modeling and theoretical foundational contributions. Each scientific paper submitted to CMS 2015 was subject to peer review by at least three members of an international program committee.

In *A Conceptual Model for Services* Bernhard Thalheim and Ajantha Dahanayake focus on the support provided by models to understand how a system works, how it can be used or should not be used, and what would be the benefit of conceptual models in general. In *A Use and Exchange Perspective for Explicating the Notion of Service* Paul Johannesson discusses three mechanisms for clarifying the notion of service based on a use and exchange perspective: rights distribution, abstraction and co-creation. In *Integration and Exchangeability of External Security-Critical Web Services in a Model-Driven Approach* Marian Borek, Kurt Stenzel, Kuzman Katkalov and Wolfgang Reif present the integration and exchangeability of external web services in a model-driven approach called SecureMDD for security-critical applications as well as discuss the verification of the entire application including the communication with external services. Finally the article *Providing Ontology-Based Privacy-Aware Data Access through Web Services* by Sven Hartmann, Hui Ma, Panrawee Vechsamutvaree proposes an ontology-based data access model so that different level of data access can be provided to Web service users with different roles.

Károly Bósa (CDCC, Johannes Kepler University, Austria)
Thomas Ziebermayr (Software Competence Center Hagenberg GmbH, Austria)

Acknowledgements. We would like to thank our invited speakers and authors for their contributions to this workshop proceeding. We are grateful to the reviewers for their detailed reviews. We are thankful to the ER 2015 organizers for the opportunity to organize this workshop.

A Conceptual Model for Services

Bernhard Thalheim[1](✉) and Ajantha Dahanayake[2]

[1] Department of Computer Science, Christian Albrechts University Kiel,
24098 Kiel, Germany
thalheim@is.informatik.uni-kiel.de
[2] Department of Computer Information Science, Prince Sultan University, Riyadh,
Kingdom of Saudi Arabia
adahanayake@pscw.psu.edu.sa

Abstract. Models are a mainstay of every scientific and engineering discipline. Models are typically more accessible to study than the systems. Models are instruments that are effectively functioning within a scenario. The effectiveness is based on an associated set of methods and satisfies requirements of usage of the model. A typical usage of a model is explanation, informed selection, and appropriation of an opportunity. This usage is declared through information and directions for usage or more specifically through an informative model in the case of a service model.

1 Services and the Conception of a Service

Today, the service has gained recognition as the more realistic concept for dealing with complexities of cross-disciplinary systems engineering extending its validity beyond the classical information systems design and development realm [4]. In this respect the service concept combines and integrates the value created in different design contexts such as person-to-person encounters, technology enabled self-service, computational services, multi-channel, multi-device, location-based and context-aware, and smart services [13]. Therefore, the service concept reveals the intrinsic design challenges of the information required to perform a service, and emphasizes the design choices that allocate the responsibility to provide this information between the service provider and service consumer.

1.1 Some Well-Known Service Notions

The service is being defined using different abstraction models with varying applications representing multitude of definitions of the service concept [7]. The increasing interests in services have introduced service concept's abstraction into levels such as; business services, web services, software-as-a-service (SaaS), platform-as-a-services, and infrastructure-as-a-service [2]. Service architectures are proposed as means to methodically structure systems [1,5,16].

There are number of service notations available in the in the literature, and research has looked into the service mainly from two perspectives, (a) from the

© Springer International Publishing Switzerland 2015
M.A. Jeusfeld and K. Karlapalem (Eds.): ER 2015 Workshops, LNCS 9382, pp. 51–61, 2015.
DOI: 10.1007/978-3-319-25747-1_5

low-level technological point of view and (b) from the higher abstract business point of view. These two categories of service descriptions have derived number of service notations. Some of those main stream service notations are:

The *REA (Resource-Event-Agent) ontology* [8,11] uses as core concepts resources, economic event, and agent. The *RSS (Resource-Service-Systems) model* [12] is an adaptation of REA ontology stressing that REA is a conceptual model of economic exchange and uses a Service-Dominant Logic (SDL) [21]. The *model of the three perspectives of services* uses abstraction, restriction, and co-creation. It concentrates on the use and offering of resources [2]. The perspectives addressed by this model are: service as a means for abstraction; service as means for providing restricted access to resources; and service as a means for co-creation of value. The logics behind is the Goods Dominant Logic (GDL) model [22]. *Web service description languages* concentrate on Service-Orientated Architectures (SOAs) for web service domain. Software systems are decomposed into independent collaborating units [14]. Named services interact with one another through message exchanges. The *seven contexts of service design* [6,9,13] combine person-to-person encounters, technology-enhanced encounters, self-service, computational services, multi-channel, multi-device, and location-based and context-aware services description.

1.2 The Explanation, Selection, and Appropriation

Explanation, understanding and informed selection of a tool is one of the main usage scenarios for a software models. People want to solve some problems. Services provide solutions to these problems and require a context, e.g. skills of people, an infrastructure, a specific way of work, a specific background, and a specific kind of collaboration. In order to select the right service, a model of the service is used as an *instrument for explanation and quick shallow understanding* which service might be a good candidate, what are the strengths and weaknesses of the service under consideration, which service meets the needs, and what are the opportunities and risks while deploying such a service.

The best and simplest instrument in such usage scenario is the *instruction leaflet* or more generally as a specification of the information and directions on the basis of the *informative model*. We shall show in the sequel that this model of a service extends the cargo dimension [10] to the general notion of the informative model. Such models of a service enable people in directed, purposeful, rewarding, realistic, and trackable deployment of a service within a given usage scenario, i.e. use according to the qualities of the model [4]. After informed selection of a service, it might be used in the creation of new work order based on the assimilation of the service into the given context, i.e. appropriation of the service.

1.3 Developing a Service Model Based on the W*H Frame

Systems are typically characterised by a combination of large information content with the need of different stakeholders to understand at least some system aspects. People need models to assist them in understanding the context of their own work and the requirements on it. We concentrate in this paper on the support provided by models to understand how a system works, how it can be used or should not be used, and what would be the benefit of such a model. We illustrate this utilisation of models for services.

We develop a novel service model based on the W*H specification frame [4]. The W*H model [4] provides a high-level and conceptual reflection and reflects on the variety of aspects that separates concerns such as service as a product, service as an offer, service request, service delivery, service application, service record, service log or archive and also service exception, which allows and supports a general characterization of services by their ends, their stakeholders, their application domain, their purpose and their context.

2   The Notion of a Model

The theory of models is the body of knowledge that concerns with the fundamental nature, function, development and utilisation of models in science and engineering, e.g. in Computer Science. In its most general sense, a model is a proxy and is used to represent some system for a well-defined purpose. Changes in the structure and behaviour of a model are easier to implement, to isolate, to understand and to communicate to others. In this section we review the notion of the model that has been developed in [18–20].

2.1   Artifacts that Are Models

A model is a well-formed, adequate, and dependable artifact that represents origins. Its criteria of well-formedness, adequacy, and dependability must be commonly accepted by its community of practice within some context and correspond to the functions that a model fulfills in utilisation scenarios.

The model should be well-formed according to some well-formedness criterion. As an instrument or more specifically an artefact a model comes with its *background*, e.g. paradigms, assumptions, postulates, language, thought community, etc. The background its often given only in an implicit form. A model is used in a *context* such as discipline, a time, an infrastructure, and an application.

Models function as an instrument in some usage scenarios and a given usage spectrum. Their function in these scenarios is a combination of functions such as explanation, optimization-variation, validation-verification-testing, reflection-optimization, exploration, hypothetical investigation, documentation-visualisation, and description-prescription functions. The model functions effectively in some of the scenarios and less effectively in others. The function determines the *purpose* and the *objective* (or goal) of the model. Functioning of models is supported by methods. Such methods support tasks such as defining, constructing, exploring, communicating, understanding, replacing, substituting, documenting, negotiating, replacing, optimizing, validating, verifying, testing, reporting, and accounting. A model is *effective* if it can be deployed according to its objectives.

Models have several *essential properties* that qualify an artifact as a model. An well-formed artifact is *adequate* for a collection of origins if it is *analogous* to the origins to be represented according to some analogy criterion, it is more *focused* (e.g. simpler, truncated, more abstract or reduced) than the origins being modelled, and it sufficiently satisfies its *purpose*.

Well-formedness enables an artifact to be *justified* by an *empirical corroboration* according to its objectives, by rational coherence and conformity explicitly stated through formulas, by falsifiability, and by stability and plasticity.

The artifact is *sufficient* by its *quality* characterisation for internal quality, external quality and quality in use or through quality characteristics [17] such as correctness, generality, usefulness, comprehensibility, parsimony, robustness, novelty etc. Sufficiency is typically combined with some assurance evaluation (tolerance, modality, confidence, and restrictions).

A well-formed artifact is called *dependable* if it is sufficient and is justified for some of the justification properties and some of the sufficiency characteristics.

2.2 Artifacts as Instruments in Some Usage Scenario

Models will be used, i.e. there is some usage scenario, some reason for its use, some goal and purpose for its usage and deployment, and finally some function that the model has to play in a given usage scenario. A typical usage scenario is problem solving. We first describe a problem, then specify the requirements for its solutions, focus on a context, describe the community of practices and more specifically the skills needed for the collaborative solution of the problem, and scope on those origins that must be considered. Next we develop a model and use this model as an instrument in the problem solving process. This instrument provides a utility for the solution of the problem. The solution developed within the model setting is then used for derivation of a solution for the given problem in the origin setting.

A similar use of models is given for models of services. Service models might be used for the development of a service system. They might be used for assessment of services, for optimisation and variation of services, for validation-verification-testing, for investigation, and for documentation-visualization. In this paper we concentrate on the *explanation, informed selection, and appropriation* use of a service model. It must provide a high level description of the service itself. This usage is typical for a process of determining whether a service is of high utility in an application. Such usage is based on specific usage pattern or more specifically on a special model that is the *usage model of an instrument as a model*.

2.3 Conceptional Modelling: Modelling Enhanced by Concepts

An information systems model is typically a schematic description of a system, theory, or phenomenon of an origin that accounts for known or inferred properties of the origin and may be used for further study of characteristics of the origin. *Conceptional modelling*[1] aims to create an abstract representation of the situation under investigation, or more precisely, the way users think about it. *Conceptual models* enhance models with concepts that are commonly shared within a community or at least within the community of practice in a given usage scenario. Concepts specify our knowledge what things are there and what properties things have. Their definition can be given in a narrative informal form, in a formal way, by reference to some other definitions, etc. We may use a large variety of semantics [15], e.g., lexical or ontological, logical, or reflective.

2.4 Adequacy and Dependability of Informative Models

Models are used in *explanation, informed selection, and appropriation* scenarios. We call such models *informative models*. Their main aim of is to inform the user according to his/her information demand and according to the profile and portfolio. The instrument steers and directs its users which are typically proactive. It supplies information that is desired or needed. Users may examine and check the content provided. Typical methods of such instruments are communication, orientation, combination, survey, and feedback methods.

Users have to get informed what is the issue that can be solved with the instrument, what are the main ingredients of the instrument and how they are used, what is the main background behind this instrument, and why they should use this instrument. They need a quick shallow understanding how simple, how meaningful, how adequate, how realistic, and how trackable is the instrument (*SMART*). They must be enabled to select the most appropriate instrument, i.e. they should know the strengthes, weaknesses, opportunities, and threats of the given instrument (*SWOT*).

The SWOT and SMART evaluation is the basis for adequateness and dependability of informative models. The informative model must be analogous in structure and function to its origins. It is far simpler than the origin and thus more focussed. Its purpose is to explain the origin in such a way than a user can choose this instrument because of its properties since all demanded properties are satisfied. The selection and appropriation of an instrument by the user depends on the explanatory statement on the profile and the portfolio of the given instrument, on coherence to the typical norms and standards accepted by the community of practice, on a statement on applicability and added value of the instrument, and the relative stability of the description given. The instrument usage becomes then justified. Furthermore, the instrument must suffice the demands of such scenarios. The quality in use depends on understandability and parsimony of description, worthiness and eligibility of presented origins, and the added value

---

[1] The words 'conceptual' and 'conceptional' are often considered to be synonyms. The word 'conceptual' is linked to concepts and conceptions. 'Conceptual' means that a thing - e.g. an instrument or artifact - is characterised by concepts or conceptions. The word 'conceptional' associates a thing as being or of the nature of a notion or concept. Conceptional modelling is modelling with associations to concepts. A conceptual model incorporates concepts into the model.

it has for the given utilisation scenarios. The external quality is mainly based on its required exactness and validation. The internal quality must support these qualities. The quality evaluation and the quality safeguard is an explicit statement of these qualities according to the usage scenarios, to the context, to the origins that are represented, and to community of practice.

2.5   The Cargo of a Model

The cargo of any instrument is typically a very general instrument insert like the package insert in pharmacy or an enclosed label. It describes the instrument, the main functions, the forbidden usages, the specific values of the instrument, and the context for the usage model. Following [10, 20] we describe the cargo by a description of the *mission* of the instrument in the usage scenarios, the *determination* of the instrument, an *abstract declaration of the meaning* of the instrument, and a narrative explanation of the *identity* of the instrument.

The mission of a model consists of functions (and anti-functions or forbidden ones) that the model has in different usage scenarios, the purposes of the usages of the model, and a description of the potential and of the capacity of the model. The determination contains the basic ideas, features, particularities, and the usage model of the given instrument. The meaning contains the main semantic and pragmatic statements about the model and describes the value of the instrument according to its functions in the usage scenarios, and the importance within the given settings. Each instrument has its identity, i.e. the actual or obvious identity, the communicated identity, the identity accepted in the community of practice, the ideal identity as a promise, and the desired identity in the eyes of the users of the instrument.

2.6   The Informative Model

The *informative model* consists of the cargo, the description of its adequacy and dependability, and the SMART and SWOT statements. It informs a potential users through bringing facts to somebody's attention, provides these facts in an appropriate form according their information demand, guides them by steering and directing, and leads them by changing the information stage and level. Based on the informative model, the user selects the origin for usage with full informed consent or refuses to use it. It is similar to an instruction leaflet provided with instruments we use. The informative model is semantically characterized by: objectivity; functional information; official information; explanation; association to something in future; different representational media and presenters; degree of extraction from open to hidden; variety of styles such as short content description, long pertinent explanation, or long event-based description.

In the case of a service model, the informative model must state positively and in an understandable form what is the service, must describe what is the reward of a service, and must allow to reason about the rewards of the service, i.e. put the functions and purposes in a wider context (*PURE*). Informative models of a service are based on a presentation that is easy-to-survey and to understand, that is given in the right formatting and form, that supports elaboration and surveying, that avoids learning efforts for their users, that provides the inner content semantics and its inner associations, that might be based on icons and pictographs, and that presents the annotation and meta-information including also ownership and usability.

We shall now explore in the sequel what are the ingredients of such informative instruments in the case of a service model.

3   Service Specifications

3.1   Scenarios and Functions of Service Specifications

To capture the scenarios and functions of service specification we introduce W^*H *model* in Fig. 1 that is a novel conceptual model for service modelling.

Service	Service Name				
Concept	Ends	*Wherefore?*			
		Purpose	*Why?*		
			Where to?		
			For When?		
			For Which reason?		
Content	Supporting means	*Wherewith?*			
		Application Domain	Application are	*Wherein?*	
			Application case	*Wherefrom?*	
			Problem	*For What*	
			Organizational unit	*Where*	
			Triggering Event	*Whence*	
			IT	*What*	
				How	
Annotation	Source	*Where of?*			
		Party	Supplier	*By whom?*	
			Consumer	*To whom?*	
			Producer	*Whichever?*	
		Activity	Input	*What in?*	
			Output	*What out?*	
Added Value	Surplus Value	*Worthiness?*			
		Context	Systems Context	*Where at?*	
			Story Context	*Where about?*	
			Coexistence Context	*Wither?*	
			Time Context	*When?*	

Fig. 1. The W*H Specification Frame for the Conceptual Model of a Service

The W*H model in Fig. 1 fulfills the conceptual definition of the service concept composing the need to serve the following purposes:

- The composition of the W*H model consisting of *content space, concept space, annotation space,* and *add value space* as orthogonal dimensions that captures the fundamental elements for developing services.
- It reflects number of aspects neglected in other service models, such as the handling of the service as a collection of offering, a proper annotation facility, a model to describe the service concept, and the specification of added value. It handles those requirements at the same time.
- It helps capturing and organizing the discrete functions contained in (business) applications comprised of underlying business process or workflows into interoperable, (standards-based) services.
- The model accommodates the services to be abstracted from implementations representing natural fundamental building blocks that can synchronize the functional requirements and IT implementations perspective.
- It considers by definition that the services to be combined, evolved and/or reused quickly to meet business needs.
- Finally, it represents an abstraction level independent of underlying technology.

In addition, the W*H model in Fig. 1 also serves the following purposes:

- The inquiry through simple and structured questions according to the primary dimension on wherefore, whereof, wherewith, and worthiness further leading to secondary and additional questions along the concept, annotation, content, add value or surplus value space that covers usefulness, usage, and usability requirements in totality.
- The powerful inquiring questions are a product of the conceptual underpinning of W*H grounded within the conceptional modelling tradition in the Concept-Content-Annotation triptych extended with the Added Value dimension and further integration and extension with the inquiry system of Hermagoras of Temnos frames.
- The W*H model is comprise of 24 questions in total that cover the complete spectrum of questions addressing the service description; (W5 + W4 + W10H +W4) and H stands for how.
- The models compactness helps to validate domain knowledge during solution modelling discussions with the stakeholders with high demanding work schedules.
- The comprehensibility of the W*H model became the main contributor to the understanding of the domain's services and requirements.
- The model contributes as the primary input model leading to the IT-service systems projection on solution modelling.
- It contribute as the primary input model leading to the IT-service systems projection on the evaluations criteria of systems functioning on its trustworthiness, flexibility to change, and efficient manageability and maintainability.

3.2   Dimensions of Service Specification

The Content Dimension: Services as a Collection of Offerings. The service defines the what, how, and who on what basis of service innovation, design, and development, and helps mediate between customer or consumer needs and an organizations strategic intent. When extended above the generalized business and technological abstraction levels, the content of the service concept composes the need to serve the following purposes:

- Fundamental elements for developing applications;
- Organizing the discrete functions contained in (business) applications comprised of underlying business process or workflows into inter operable, (standards-based) services;
- Services abstracted from implementations representing natural fundamental building blocks that can synchronize the functional requirements and IT implementations perspective;
- Services to be combined, evolved and/or reused quickly to meet business needs; Represent an abstraction level independent of underlying technology.

The abstraction of the notion of a service system within an organizations strategic intent emphasized by those purposes given above allow us to define the content description of services as a collection of offers that are given by companies, by vendors, by people and by automatic software tools [3]. Thus the content of a service system is a collection of service offerings.

The service offering reflects the supporting means in terms of with what means the service's content is represented in the application domain. It corresponds to identification and specification of the problem within an application area. The problem is a specific application case that resides with an organizational unit. Those problems are subject to events that produce triggers needing attention. Those triggering events have an enormous importance for service descriptions. They couple to the solution at hand that is associated with how and what of a required IT solution.

The Annotation Dimension. According to [14], annotation with respect to arbitrary ontologies implies general purpose reasoning supported by the system. Their reasoning approaches suffer from high computational complexities. As a solution for dealing with high worst-case complexities the solution recommends a small size input data. Unfortunately, it is contradicting the impressibility of ontologies and define content as complex structured macro data. It is therefore, necessary to concentrate on the conceptualisation of content for a given context considering annotations with respect to organizations intentions, motivations, profiles and tasks, thus we need at the same time sophisticated annotation facilities far beyond ontologies. Annotation thus must link the stakeholders or parties involved and activities; the sources to the content and concept.

The Concept Dimension. *Conceptional modelling* aims at creation of an abstract representation of the situation under investigation, or more precisely, the way users think about it. Conceptual models enhance models with concepts that are commonly shared within a community or at least between the stakeholders involved in the modelling process.

According to the general definition of concept as given in [19], *Concepts* specify our knowledge what things are there and what properties things have.

Concepts are used in everyday life as a communication vehicle and as a reasoning chunk. Concept definition can be given in a narrative informal form, in a formal way, by reference to some other definitions etc. We may use a large variety of semantics, e.g., lexical or ontological, logical, or reflective.

Conceptualisation aims at collection of concepts that are assumed to exist in some area of interest and the relationships that hold them together. It is thus an abstract, simplified view or description of the world that we wish to represent. Conceptualisation extends the model by a number of concepts that are the basis for an understanding of the model and for the explanation of the model to the user.

The definition of the ends or purpose of the service is represented by the concept dimension. It is the curial part that governs the service's characterization. The purpose defines in which cases a service has a usefulness, usage, and usability. They define the potential and the capability of the service.

The Added Value Dimension. The added value of a service to a business user or stakeholder is in the definition of surplus value during the service execution. It defines the context in which the service systems exists, the story line associated within the context, which systems must coexist under which context definitions prevailing to time. Surplus value defines the worthiness of the service in terms of time and labor that provide the Return of Investment (ROI).

4   Conclusion

There are many other usage models for services. This paper elaborated the *explanation, informed selection, and appropriation* usage model for a service. Other usage models of an instrument as a model are, for instance, optimization-variation, validation-verification-testing, understanding, extension and evolution, reflection-optimization, exploration, documentation-visualization, integration, hypothetical investigation, and description-prescription usage models. We introduced in this paper a general notion of the model and showed what makes description or specification a service to be become a model of the service.

References

1. Arsanjani, A., Ghosh, S., Allam, A., Abdollah, T., Ganapathy, S., Holley, K.: SOMA: a method for developing service-oriented solutions. IBM Syst. J. **47**(3), 377–396 (2008)
2. Bergholtz, M., Andersson, B., Johannesson, P.: Abstraction, restriction, and co-creation: three perspectives on services. In: Trujillo, J., Dobbie, G., Kangassalo, H., Hartmann, S., Kirchberg, M., Rossi, M., Reinhartz-Berger, I., Zimányi, E., Frasincar, F. (eds.) ER 2010. LNCS, vol. 6413, pp. 107–116. Springer, Heidelberg (2010)
3. Dahanayake, A.: CAME: an environment for flexible information modeling. Ph.D. dissertation, Delft University of Technology, The Netherlands (1997)

4. Dahanayake, A., Thalheim, B.: Co-design of web information systems. In: Thalheim, B., Schewe, K.D., Prinz, A., Buchberger, B. (eds.) Correct Software in Web Applications and Web Services. Texts & Monographs in Symbolic Computation, pp. 145–176. Springer, Wien (2015)
5. Erl, T.: SOA: Principles of Service Design. Prentice-Hall, Englewood Cliffs (2007)
6. Glushko, R.J.: Seven Contexts for Service System Design. In: Maglio, P.P., Kieliszewski, C.A., Spohrer, J.C. (eds.) Handbook of Service Science. Service Science: Research and Innovations in the Service Economy, pp. 219–249. Springer Science+Business Media LLC, New York (2010). doi:10.1007/978-1-4419-1628-0_11
7. Goldstein, S.M., Johnston, R., Duffy, J.A., Rao, J.: The service concept: the missing link in service design research? J. Oper. Manage. **20**, 121–134 (2002)
8. Hurby, P.: Model-Driven Design of Software Applications with Business Patterns. Springer, Heidelberg (2006)
9. Maglio, P., Srinivasan, S., Kreulen, J., Spohrer, J.: Service Systems, Service Scientists, SSME, and Innovation. Commun. ACM **49**(7), 81–85 (2006)
10. Mahr, B.: Zum Verhältnis von Bild und Modell. In: Visuelle Modelle, pp. 17–40. Wilhelm Fink Verlag, Mnchen (2008)
11. McCarthy, W.E.: The REA accounting model: a generalized framework for accounting systems in a shared data environment. Acc. Rev. **57**, 554–578 (1982)
12. Poels, G.: The resource-service-system model for service science. In: Trujillo, J., Dobbie, G., Kangassalo, H., Hartmann, S., Kirchberg, M., Rossi, M., Reinhartz-Berger, I., Zimányi, E., Frasincar, F. (eds.) ER 2010. LNCS, vol. 6413, pp. 117–126. Springer, Heidelberg (2010)
13. Spohrer, J., Maglio, P.P., Bailey, J., Gruhl, D.: Steps towards a science of service systems. IEEE Comput. **40**, 71–77 (2007)
14. Schewe, K.-D., Thalheim, B.: Development of collaboration frameworks for web information systems. In: IJCAI 2007 (20th International Joint Conference on Artificial Intelligence, Section EMC 2007 (Evolutionary models of collaboration)), pp. 27–32, Hyderabad (2007)
15. Schewe, K.-D., Thalheim, B.: Semantics in data and knowledge bases. In: Schewe, K.-D., Thalheim, B. (eds.) SDKB 2008. LNCS, vol. 4925, pp. 1–25. Springer, Heidelberg (2008)
16. Stojanovic, Z., Dahanayake, A.: Service - Oriented Software Systems Engineering: Challenges and Practices. Idea Group Publishing, Hershey (2004)
17. Thalheim, B.: Towards a theory of conceptual modelling. J. Univ. Comput. Sci. **16**(20), 3102–3137 (2010). http://www.jucs.org/jucs_16_20/towards_a_theory_of
18. Thalheim, B.: The conceptual model ≡ an adequate and dependable artifact enhanced by concepts. In: Information Modelling and Knowledge Bases, vol. XXV, Frontiers in Artificial Intelligence and Applications, vol. 260, pp. 241–254. IOS Press (2014)
19. Thalheim, B.: Models, to model, and modelling - towards a theory of conceptual models and modelling - towards a notion of the model. In: Collection of Recent Papers (2014). http://www.is.informatik.uni-kiel.de/~thalheim/indexkollektionen.htm
20. Thalheim, B., Nissen, I. (eds.): Wissenschaft und Kunst der Modellierung. De Gruyter, Ontos Verlag, Berlin (2015)
21. Vargo, S.L., Lusch, R.F.: Evolving to a new dominant logic for marketing. J. Mark. **68**, 1–17 (2004)
22. Vargo, S.L., Maglio, P.P., Akaka, M.A.: On value and value co-creation: a service systems and service logic perspective. Eur. Manage. J. **26**, 145–152 (2008)

A Use and Exchange Perspective for Explicating the Notion of Service

Paul Johannesson[✉]

Department of Computer and Systems Sciences, Stockholm University,
Stockholm, Sweden
pajo@dsv.su.se

The notion of service has proved elusive, in practice as well as in academic research. The lack of a common view of the notion of service makes it difficult to describe, classify and manage services in an efficient and effective way.

One attempt to defining the notion of service has focused on identifying properties (such as intangibility, inseparability, heterogeneity, and perishability) that distinguish services from other kinds of resources. While this approach offers advantages of simplicity and familiarity, it is problematic as the suggested properties are neither necessary nor sufficient. For example, not only services but also many other resources can be intangible, such as information and rights. The same observation holds for perishability and heterogeneity, with examples as fruits and handicraft objects.

Another approach for explicating the notion of service is to shift the attention to the use and exchange context of services. In this view, services are about enabling and regulating resource use and exchange within a community. For this purpose, services can provide convenient and flexible mechanisms that would not be attainable with a goods-oriented view.

The talk discusses three mechanisms for clarifying the notion of service based on a use and exchange perspective: rights distribution, abstraction and co-creation. First, services enable people to provide access to resources without transferring ownership but instead offering more restricted rights on them. Thereby, rights are distributed allowing for flexible arrangements of resource exchange. Secondly, services do not need to be specified in detail, in the sense that a service specification can focus on functionality and not structure. This abstraction allows for flexible arrangements with respect to the production and delivery of resources. Thirdly, services typically involve not only resources provided by the service supplier but also resources from the consumer, thereby allowing for co-creation. The talk also shows how these perspectives can be modelled using the REA ontology and how the approach can be compared to commitment-based views on services.

© Springer International Publishing Switzerland 2015
M.A. Jeusfeld and K. Karlapalem (Eds.): ER 2015 Workshops, LNCS 9382, p. 62, 2015.
DOI: 10.1007/978-3-319-25747-1_6

Integration and Exchangeability of External Security-Critical Web Services in a Model-Driven Approach

Marian Borek[(✉)], Kurt Stenzel, Kuzman Katkalov, and Wolfgang Reif

Department of Software Engineering, University of Augsburg, Augsburg, Germany
{borek,stenzel,katkalov,reif}@informatik.uni-augsburg.de

Abstract. Model-driven approaches facilitate the development of applications by introducing domain-specific abstractions. Our model-driven approach called SecureMDD supports the domain of security-critical applications that use web services. Because many applications use external web services (i.e. services developed and provided by someone else), the integration of such web services is an important task of a model-driven approach. In this paper we present an approach to integrate and exchange external developed web services that use standard or non-standard cryptographic protocols, in security-critical applications. All necessary information is defined in an abstract way in the application model, which means that no manual changes of the generated code are necessary. We also show how security properties for the whole system including external web services can be defined and proved. For demonstration we use a web shop case study that integrates an external payment service.

1 Introduction

The use of external web services is essential for many applications. For example, a web shop needs to communicate with different external services, such as authentication and authorization services, different payment services or supply chain management services. Therefore, a model-driven approach for developing such applications needs to support the integration of external web services. One way to invoke external web services from a modeled application is to extend the generated code manually. However, our model-driven approach generates from a UML application model runnable code as well as a formal specification for verification of security properties for that application. The manual extension of the generated code would introduce a gap between the formal model and the runnable code, so that the verified properties do not hold necessarily for the running code. Another way is to integrate the external web service into the application model and generate everything from that model. Thereby, everything that is application-specific has to be modeled (e.g., message conversion or security mechanism) in order to be considered by formal verification. Furthermore, it is often necessary to be able to exchange those services against cheaper,

© Springer International Publishing Switzerland 2015
M.A. Jeusfeld and K. Karlapalem (Eds.): ER 2015 Workshops, LNCS 9382, pp. 63–73, 2015.
DOI: 10.1007/978-3-319-25747-1_7

more popular or more efficient ones. The challenge is to make the replacement of external services very easy and minimize verification effort.

Another benefit of the integration of external web services in a model-driven approach is the possibility to extend the approach by application-specific functionality without changing the transformations for code and formal specifications. With this approach also libraries and legacy systems can be integrated by being wrapped inside a web service.

This paper focuses on the integration and exchangeability of external web services in a model-driven approach for security-critical applications by considering different cryptographic mechanisms and discusses the verification of the entire application including the communication with external services.

This paper is structured as follows. Section 2 gives an overview of our model-driven approach and Sect. 3 describes the integration and exchangeability of web services. Section 4 considers assurances and the verification of security properties of the entire application and Sect. 5 explains how external services that use cryptography mechanisms can be integrated and exchanged. Section 6 discusses related work and Sect. 7 concludes this paper.

2   The SecureMDD Approach

SecureMDD is a model-driven approach to develop secure applications. From a UML application model using a predefined UML profile and a platform-independent and domain-specific language (MEL [6,15]), runnable code for different platforms as well as formal specifications are generated (see Fig. 1). One formal specification is used for interactive verification with KIV [4] (see [16,17]) and the other to find vulnerabilities with the model-checker platform AVANTSSAR [1] (see [7]). Additionally, platform-specific models are generated for incremental transformations and better documentation. The approach supports smart cards (implemented in Java Card [21]), user devices like secure

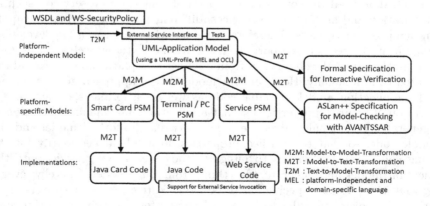

Fig. 1. SecureMDD approach

terminals or home PCs (implemented in Java), web services (also Java) and external web services. The static view of an application is modeled with UML class diagrams and deployment diagrams. The dynamic behavior of system components is modeled in UML activity diagrams with our platform-independent and domain-specific language MEL. Application-specific security properties are expressed with OCL in class diagrams (see [8]) and test cases that generate code for testing the generated application are modeled in UML sequence and activity diagrams (see [12]). The approach is fully tool-supported and all model transformations are implemented. For further information about our approach visit the SecureMDD website[1].

3   Modeling Communication with External Web Services

To communicate with a web service, the client which invokes the service needs to know its public interface. For SOAP web services this interface is defined by a WSDL document, which provides the offered web service functionality, and especially the expected messages in a machine-readable description. Our approach takes a WSDL document and transforms it automatically into an external service interface represented by a UML class diagram that is imported as a module into the UML application model (see Fig. 1). As a result, the external web service and all message data types are included in the application model as classes with operations, attributes and stereotypes. The model abstracts from information like the service address, namespaces and coding algorithm because they are not relevant for modeling an application in a platform-independent way and it is also not relevant for verification of the supported security properties. Because of this abstraction the resulting meta-model for external web services remains simple and it can be used for other web service specification languages like WADL. But the omitted information is available in the generated code as stubs that are generated automatically from the WSDL specification. We use WSDL2Java from Apache Axis2[2] with JiBX[3] as our stubs-generator to bind arbitrary class structures on XML documents. That is important because the data types from external web services differ from the predefined data types in our approach. The transformation from WSDL to UML is done by hyperModel[4] that uses generic XML schema documents as input.

The communication with external web services is mainly described in UML activity diagrams using our platform-independent and domain-specific language called MEL. The external web service is represented by a UML class with the stereotype ≪ExternalService≫ and the external web methods are represented by operations of that class and UML call behavior actions without modeling the behavior. The invocation of a web method is modeled by UML send signal actions and accept event actions that are connected with the UML call behavior actions.

---

[1] www.isse.de/securemdd.
[2] axis.apache.org/axis2.
[3] jibx.sourceforge.net.
[4] xmlmodeling.com/hypermodel/.

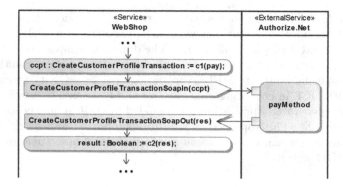

Fig. 2. Invocation of external web service

For conversion of the message data types between the modeled application and the external service, conversion methods have to be defined. This is done by sub activities using MEL. They have to be invoked before sending a message to an external web service and after receiving a message from the external web service.

Figure 2 shows how a modeled web service (*WebShop*) invokes the external service *Authorize.Net* for payment issues. Therefore the conversion methods *c1* and *c2* are used. *c1* converts the data from the modeled application into the required message structure of *Authorize.Net* and *c2* converts the result of *Authorize.Net* back. That means the payload *pay* from type *Pay* and *result* from type *Boolean* belong to the modeled application and *CreateCustomerProfileTransactionSoapIn* and *CreateCustomerProfileTransactionSoapOut* are data types used by *Authorize.Net*.

Figure 3 shows the definition of the conversion method *c1* that converts the *pay* object into *CreateCustomerProfileTransaction*. Some classes can be mapped

Fig. 3. Convert method *c1*

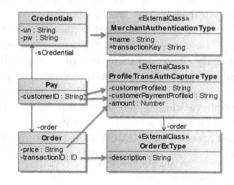

Fig. 4. Converted classes

one-to-one (e.g., *Credentials* and *MerchantAuthenticationType*) other classes consist of merged information from different classes (e.g., *ProfileTransAuthCaptureType* contains attributes from the *Pay* and *Order* classes) and if the output class has more attributes than the input class, the missing information has to emerge from the existing one by duplication or transformation (e.g., *ProfileTransAuthCaptureType* needs a *customerProfileId* and a *customerPaymentProfileId* that can be both extracted from *customerID*) (see Fig. 4). The conversion in Fig. 3 is chosen minimal but the output class *CreateCustomerProfileTransaction* has roughly 100 optional attributes and if all attributes are needed this leads to a very large and error-prone converting method. But because this method must be verified, mistakes that violate specified security properties will be found in contrast to a manually programmed conversion method.

Should the external payment service *Authorize.Net* in Fig. 2 be replaced with a different one, the protocol diagrams have to be changed and the verification of the entire application would need to be redone. To avoid this, the security-critical protocols and the invocation of an external service can be separated. In order to achieve that, we support a proxy pattern. Therefore, a proxy interface that is independent from the external payment service has to be modeled and used in the protocols described by activity diagrams. For each external service a proxy has to be modeled that implements this interface and invokes the external service. Then the external web services can be easily switched by changing the proxy in the class diagram. In our case study the *WebShop* has to invoke a *PayService* proxy interface. To add a concrete payment service like *Authorize.Net*, a new proxy (e.g., *Authorize.NetProxy*) has to be created that inherits from *PayService* and defines the behavior of the *pay* method and the conversion methods.

4   Security Properties and Assurances

For the verification of certain security properties of the entire application, assumptions about the external service are necessary. Those are assured by the service provider. If those assurances are informal, they have to be formalized by the developer. An example for a security property for our web shop is that "only goods that are paid for will be shipped". Obviously, some information about the external payment service method are necessary, e.g., that "if the return value is positive, then the payment was or will be successful". This assumption is specified for the proxy. It represents an abstraction of the external service and manages the conversion between different messages and the invocation of the external service. As a result, the security property is provable independently from the external web service.

Figure 5 shows that a security property uses classes from the client and the proxy and of course the assumptions specified for the proxy. The assurance of the external service uses classes from the external service interface that is generated from the WSDL and the assurance has to be a refinement of the assumption. The security property for the application, the assurance of the external service and the assumption about the proxy are formally defined as OCL constraints

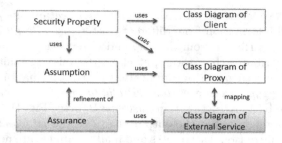

Fig. 5. Relation between security property, assumption and class diagrams

on classes that represent internal states and messages of the application participants. The mapping between messages are handled by the modeled conversion methods that are automatically transformed to executable Java code, and also to formal specifications. The relationship between the internal states is only necessary for verification. Hence, it is not modeled but specified during the verification. Those two mappings make it possible to show the refinement between the external service and the proxy. If the external service is a refinement of the proxy, the security property that holds for the payment method of the proxy holds also for the payment method of the external service. This way, the external services can be exchanged without influence on the security property if the assurances of the new external service are also an refinement of the assumptions of the proxy.

5   Cryptography and External Web Services

There are different ways to secure the communication by cryptography for web services. The simplest and most common way is to use TLS. It is a standard protocol that is independent from any specific web service. But TLS does not fulfill all possible requirements, e.g., end-to-end encryption. WS-SecurityPolicy is a language to describe individual cryptographic protocols for web services. But the design of application-specific security protocols is error-prone and requires verification. Additionally, it is likely that different web services have different WS-SecurityPolicies. This influences the exchangeability of web services. Our approach supports three different ways to secure the modeled functionality using cryptography.

1. The first one is to apply TLS on a connection between two system participants (e.g., web shop and an external payment service). This is modeled using a stereotype that is applied on a UML Communication Path between two UML Nodes in a deployment diagram. Furthermore, the stereotype has two properties to distinguish between mutual authentication and server side authentication. From this model runnable code that uses TLS to secure the communication as well as the key stores and default keys that have to be exchanged during deployment are generated automatically.

2. The second way uses predefined security data types for encryption, signatures, macs, hashes, nonces, keys and predefined operations to create those data types. Because in the past our focus was not exchangeability but ensuring application-specific security properties, there is no strict separation between application logic and cryptography. But for exchangeability this approach is unsuitable.
3. Therefore, the third way to secure the modeled functionality using cryptography in our approach is WS-SecurityPolicy. It applies cryptography directly before sending a message and directly after receiving a message but always independent from application logic. WS-SecurityPolicy is integrated in WSDL so the policies can be automatically extracted from the WSDL and transformed to an abstracted UML representation using stereotypes, classes and attributes. Additionally, it abstracts from WS-SecurityPolicy assertions like *AlgorithmSuite* because it is not used for the formal verification. A WS-SecurityPolicy specification of a web service can contain several alternative policies so the application designer has to choose one that should be used by the client. This is modeled with an attribute of the client or the proxy class. Because reusability makes software more clear, maintainable and reduces errors we mapped WS-SecurityPolicies to the already supported notation that is used for the generation of formal specifications. Therefore, MEL expressions whose behavior is equivalent to the policies are injected inside the modeled activity diagram that invokes the external service. This is done with model-to-model transformations in QVTo [19] and the resulting model is used with our existing generator for formal specifications.

Figures 6 and 7 show a part of a protocol with injected policy behavior. In the original protocol, without the injected policy, the client collects the payment information (first activity node in Fig. 6) and sends it to the service proxy that invokes the pay method (last activity node in Fig. 7), which handles the conversion and invokes the external service. The regarded WS-SecurityPolicy describes a simple security protocol with symmetric binding and body encryption. The symmetric binding uses a X.509 certificate as protection token that is already exchanged and will be addressed in messages by its thumbprint reference. Hence, the injected part in Fig. 6 (second activity node) generates a symmetric key, stores it in the key store to be able to decrypt an optional response, encrypt the symmetric key with the public key from the X.509 certificate that belongs to the external service, creates the SOAP header including the encrypted symmetric key, encrypts the payment information with the symmetric key and puts it in a SOAP body object. The injected part in Fig. 7 (second activity node) decrypts the symmetric key from the header and uses the symmetric key to decrypt the payment information, that is used to invoke the pay method. The send and receive nodes are modified because the original modeled messages were exchanged with SOAP messages by the transformations. This is all done automatically together with the generation of the required classes. Besides the encrypted symmetric key the real SOAP header contains also algorithm information that can be omitted and token references like the thumbprint of the public key that is not necessary if the formal representation of the external service has only one key pair.

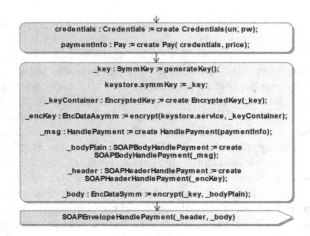

Fig. 6. Send HandlePayment with injected policy behavior

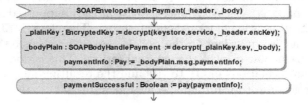

Fig. 7. Receive HandlePayment with injected policy behavior

Because the policy behavior is injected before the pay method (which handle the conversion and invoke the external service) is invoked, replacing external services that both use WS-SecurityPolicy can be done without additional verification if the policy of the replaced external service is a subset of the new one. In this case the new external service ensures the same security properties like the old external service plus some additional ones. This can be checked very fast and automatically during the transformation with QVTo.

6   Related Work

There are many works that consider web services in a model-driven approach. The most related works can be mainly categorized in static web service representation, orchestration and security.

Castro et al. [9] describe web services with a UML meta-model that is very close to the WSDL one. That means that each WSDL element is described by a stereotype with the same name. They also define transformation rules that generate a UML model from a WSDL specification. The advantage of this approach is that the WSDL specification and the generated UML model have the same information content, but the disadvantage is that the resulted UML model has the same complexity like the WSDL specification. But the aim of a UML model is abstraction. [10, 22] describe approaches that transform a WSDL specification in an abstract UML model by predefined rules. This is very close to our WSDL to UML transformation, but because our abstraction level differs from theirs we defined modified abstraction rules that fit better to our approach. They do not describe a model-driven approach that integrates external web services.

Self-Serv [3,5] is a model-driven approach for web service development with focus on orchestration. It uses state machines and generates BPEL based service-skeletons with orchestration logic but without modeling or generating application-specific logic. It does not consider security aspects and it does not integrate existing services. MDD4SOA [13] also illustrates a model-driven approach for web service orchestration. From a UML model code is generated for BPEL, WSDL, Java and the formal language Jolie. Security or the integration of external web services is not considered.

Nakamura et al. [18] enable the model-driven development of WS-Security-Policy specifications. They describe standard security properties with stereotypes that are used to select predefined security patterns from a library and apply them on the model. From that model, configuration documents for IBM Web-Sphere Application Server (WAS) and WS-SecurityPolicy specifications are generated. In contrast we generate an abstract model from the WS-SecurityPolicy of an existing web service that is selected and applied on the client as well as used for formal verification. Menzel et al. [14] also introduce a model-driven approach that uses abstract security patterns to generate XML-based configuration documents for the Apache Rampart-Modul that implements the WS-Security Stack. Jensen et al. [11] is also a model-driven approach that generates WS-BPEL, WSDL and WS-SecurityPolicy specifications from a model. The mentioned works do not integrate external web services and do not transform WS-SecurityPolicies into a formal representation for verification.

Pironti et al. [20] generate verified client-code, which uses an existing TLS-Service but they have to write thousand lines of code for the data conversion manually and without security guarantees. In [2] they explore the verification of systems with external services but they do not generate code, and verifying the security of the application is not part of that work.

We are not aware of a model-driven approach that considers the secure integration and replacement of existing web services in security-critical applications and verifies security properties about the whole application including the external services.

7   Conclusion

The integration and replacement of external security-critical web services in a model-driven approach is a novel and important topic. It enables the model-driven development of realistic applications that use existing code, e.g., services, legacy systems or libraries. In this paper we have shown how to model the communication with external web services and how runnable code is generated automatically from the model without the necessity of manual changes. We have also discussed how security properties for the modeled application that uses external web services can be verified and how web services that use different cryptographic protocols are handled. An important issue was also the replacement of external web services with minimal verification effort. As a result, we were able to develop a simple web shop with our model-driven approach that integrates the real payment service *Authorize.Net*. Additionally, we are now able to extend our approach by application-specific functionality without changing the transformations for code and formal specifications. This can be done by providing the functionality as a web service and specifying the behavior with OCL. In our opinion this work extends model-driven development with verification significantly and makes the development of real applications that use external components feasible.

References

1. Armando, A., Arsac, W., Avanesov, T., Barletta, M., Calvi, A., Cappai, A., Carbone, R., Chevalier, Y., Compagna, L., Cuéllar, J., Erzse, G., Frau, S., Minea, M., Mödersheim, S., von Oheimb, D., Pellegrino, G., Ponta, S.E., Rocchetto, M., Rusinowitch, M., Torabi Dashti, M., Turuani, M., Viganò, L.: The AVANTSSAR platform for the automated validation of trust and security of service-oriented architectures. In: Flanagan, C., König, B. (eds.) TACAS 2012. LNCS, vol. 7214, pp. 267–282. Springer, Heidelberg (2012)
2. Bagheri Hariri, B., Calvanese, D., De Giacomo, G., Deutsch, A., Montali, M.: Verification of relational data-centric dynamic systems with external services. In: Proceedings of the 32nd Symposium on Principles of Database Systems, pp. 163–174. ACM (2013)
3. Baïna, K., Benatallah, B., Casati, F., Toumani, F.: Model-driven web service development. In: Persson, A., Stirna, J. (eds.) CAiSE 2004. LNCS, vol. 3084, pp. 290–306. Springer, Heidelberg (2004)
4. Balser, M., Reif, W., Schellhorn, G., Stenzel, K., Thums, A.: Formal system development with KIV. In: Maibaum, T. (ed.) FASE 2000. LNCS, vol. 1783, p. 363. Springer, Heidelberg (2000)
5. Benatallah, B., Sheng, Q.Z., Dumas, M.: The self-serv environment for web services composition. Internet Comput. IEEE 7(1), 40–48 (2003)
6. Borek, M., Moebius, N., Stenzel, K., Reif, W.: Model-driven development of secure service applications. In: 2012 35th Annual IEEE Software Engineering Workshop (SEW), pp. 62–71. IEEE (2012)
7. Borek, M., Moebius, N., Stenzel, K., Reif, W.: Model checking of security-critical applications in a model-driven approach. In: Hierons, R.M., Merayo, M.G., Bravetti, M. (eds.) SEFM 2013. LNCS, vol. 8137, pp. 76–90. Springer, Heidelberg (2013)
8. Borek, M., Moebius, N., Stenzel, K., Reif, W.: Security requirements formalized with OCL in a model-driven approach. In: Model-Driven Requirements Engineering Workshop (MoDRE), pp. 65–73. IEEE (2013)
9. de Castro, V., Marcos, E., Vela, B.: Representing wsdl with extended uml. Revista Columbiana de Computation, vol. 5 (2004)

10. Gronmo, R., Skogan, D., Solheim, I., Oldevik, J.: Model-driven web services development. In: 2004 IEEE International Conference on e-Technology, e-Commerce and e-Service, EEE 2004, pp. 42–45. IEEE (2004)
11. Jensen, M., Feja, S.: A security modeling approach for web-service-based business processes. In: 16th Annual IEEE International Conference and Workshop on the Engineering of Computer Based Systems, ECBS 2009, pp. 340–347. IEEE (2009)
12. Katkalov, K., Moebius, N., Stenzel, K., Borek, M., Reif, W.: Modeling test cases for security protocols with SecureMDD. Comput. Netw. **58**, 99–111 (2013)
13. Mayer, P.: MDD4SOA: model-driven development for service-oriented architectures. Ph.D. thesis, lmu (2010)
14. Menzel, M.: Model-driven security in service-oriented architectures. Ph.D. thesis, Potsdam University (2011). http://opus.kobv.de/ubp/volltexte/2012/5905/
15. Moebius, N., Stenzel, K., Reif, W.: Modeling security-critical applications with UML in the secureMDD approach. Int. J. Adv. Soft. **1**(1), 59–79 (2008)
16. Moebius, N., Stenzel, K., Reif, W.: Generating formal specifications for security-critical applications - a model-driven approach. In: ICSE 2009 Workshop: International Workshop on Software Engineering for Secure Systems (SESS 2009). IEEE/ACM Digital Libary (2009)
17. Moebius, N., Stenzel, K., Reif, W.: Formal verification of application-specific security properties in a model-driven approach. In: Massacci, F., Wallach, D., Zannone, N. (eds.) ESSoS 2010. LNCS, vol. 5965, pp. 166–181. Springer, Heidelberg (2010)
18. Nakamura, Y., Tatsubori, M., Imamura, T., Ono, K.: Model-driven security based on a web services security architecture. In: IEEE International Conference on Services Computing, pp. 7–15. IEEE Press (2005)
19. Nolte, S.: QVT-Operational Mappings: Modellierung mit der Query Views Transformation. Springer, Heidelberg (2009)
20. Pironti, A., Pozza, D., Sisto, R.: Formally-based semi-automatic implementation of an open security protocol. J. Syst. Softw. **85**(4), 835–849 (2012)
21. Sun Microsystems Inc., Java Card 2.2 Specification (2002). http://java.sun.com/products/javacard/
22. Thöne, S., Depke, R., Engels, G.: Process-oriented, flexible composition of web services with UML. In: Olivé, À., Yoshikawa, M., Yu, E.S.K. (eds.) ER 2003. LNCS, vol. 2784, pp. 390–401. Springer, Heidelberg (2003)

Providing Ontology-Based Privacy-Aware Data Access Through Web Services

Sven Hartmann[1], Hui Ma[2]([✉]), and Panrawee Vechsamutvaree[2]

[1] Clausthal University of Technology, Clausthal-Zellerfeld, Germany
sven.hartmann@tu-clausthal.de
[2] Victoria University of Wellington, Wellington, New Zealand
hui.ma@ecs.vuw.ac.nz, panraweev@gmail.com

Abstract. Web services enable software systems to exchange data over the Internet. Often Web services need to disclose sensible data to service consumers. For data providers, the disclosure of sensitive data is often restrictive only to particular users for some particular purposes. Therefore, preserving privacy is a fundamental requirement in Web services. Hippocratic database has been introduced for privacy protection in relational database systems where the access decisions, allowed or denied, are based on privacy policies and authorization tables. To provide more options of data access, purpose trees are proposed to capture purpose hierarchies so that information can be provided to users according to proposes. Ontology has been used for classification hierarchies, which can be efficiently accessed via ontology query languages. In this paper, we propose an ontology-based data access model so that different level of data access can be provided to Web service users with different roles for different purposes. To do this we will use ontology to capture purpose hierarchies and data generalization hierarchy. We demonstrate our access model with prototypes of finance services, and also provide performance evaluation results.

1 Introduction

Service-oriented computing promises rapid development of software systems by composing many distributed interoperating autonomous services on the Web. Web-based software systems in areas like e-health, e-government, e-science or e-commerce frequently require the exchange of sensitive data among invoked Web services. Examples include electronic health records, contact details, salary statements, payment details, location data, and behavioural data (that allows one to track where customers have been and what they were doing). Privacy preservation (in compliance to legal regulations) is a major economic concern for many organizations and enterprises using such software. Software systems that are used for processing sensitive data of customers are expected to be privacy-aware, that is, to provide suitable mechanisms for protecting sensitive data from disclosure and misuses [1].

The preservation of data privacy for shared data has attracted considerable research interest. Hippocratic databases have been proposed in [2] to define and

© Springer International Publishing Switzerland 2015
M.A. Jeusfeld and K. Karlapalem (Eds.): ER 2015 Workshops, LNCS 9382, pp. 74–85, 2015.
DOI: 10.1007/978-3-319-25747-1_8

enforce privacy rules in database systems by adding purposes to tables. The use of Hippocratic databases for limiting data disclosure has been studied in [3,4]. Note that the access of data in a Hippocratic database is binary, i.e. either allowed or denied. Providing only binary access of data is not flexible. In [5], the Hippocratic database mechanism [2] is extended by supporting hierarchical purposes as well as distributed and minimal sets of authorizations. In [3], Hippocratic databases are enhanced to enforce minimal disclosure of data so that data owners can control who is allowed to see their personal information and under what circumstances. [6] extends the work in [2] by providing different access levels using generalization hierarchies, of which the data elements are generalized and stored in the metadata table in the database. Generalization hierarchies are also used in other work for privacy awareness [7–9]. K-anonymity, which is achieved by generalizing or suppressing values in the specific tuples of the table, is a well-known privacy protection using the generalization technique [10–12]. However, k-anonymity generalization often leads to an information loss [13,14], i.e., the reduction of the utility in the masked data [15]. To minimize information loss, [14] proposes to use ontology concepts for data anonymity and classification hierarchy. In [16], it is proposed to use ontologies for ensuring authorized access of user profiles among third parties. However, it is not discussed how authorized accesses can be ensured.

Role-based access control model (RBAC) and attribute-based access control model (ABAC) using ontology are presented in [17,18]. To achieve a fine-grained access control and maximize the usability of customer data, [19] presents a role-involved purposed-based access control model, where a conditional purpose is defined as the intention of data accesses or usage under certain conditions. The access model is based on purposes that are defined with purpose hierarchies. Access decisions are determined by implied purposes that are computed from the purpose hierarchy. However, there is no performance evaluation of the proposed access model. The computation of the implied purposes can be expensive and therefore affect the overall performance of the data access control.

With the emergence Web services, some works have been done to ensure the privacy of data accessed via Web services. [1] proposes to use Hippocratic databases to provide data for Web services so that related information will be released only to authorized users and for a limited period, based on purpose. In [20], the authors present semantic based privacy framework for Web services. However, there are only three permission level rules that are imposed on a data element for a given service class, Free, Limited and NotGiven. Also, generalization of the data elements was not considered.

Ontologies are explicit formal specifications of the terms in the domain and relations among them [21]. They have been widely used as concept hierarchies [13,22]. Ontologies can be queried with special query languages, e.g. SPARQL. Various tools (e.g., Protégé) are available to develop ontologies. To avoid expensive computation of implied purposes as in [19] and to minimize information loss we will employ ontologies in this paper for constructing purpose hierarchies and data generalization hierarchies.

Table 1. Customer

Firstname	Lastname	DoB	Gender	Salary	Deposit	Illness
Matt	Rovel	1960-08-18	Male	$2400	$8520	Pericarditis

In this paper we propose an ontology-based access model that provides different levels of data access based on roles and purposes of service users. For this we will employ ontologies to capture privacy rules and generalization hierarchy of data. We will evaluate the performance of our access model with experiments and report on prototypes of financial Web services that were implemented as a proof-of-concept.

This paper is organized as follows. Section 2 presents a motivating example to set up a context of our research. Section 3 contributes to defining role purpose ontology hierarchies and data generalization ontology hierarchies. Detailed descriptions of our proposed access control model is presented in Sect. 4. Evaluation of the access model is presented in Sect. 5. Finally, Sect. 6 concludes the paper.

2   A Motivating Example

Assume we have a Web service that provides personal information of customers, e.g., contact details, health information or financial information to users with different roles for different purposes. The customer, who is the owner of the data would only share their personal data with users who have a particular role and want to use it for a particular a purpose. That is, for a customer the privacy policy of data is different for different roles and different purposes. Table 1 shows the micro data of a customer stored in the Customer table.

Assume the privacy policy of using Customer data includes the following usage rules:

1. For a user of a role of system administrator with the purpose of maintaining customers personal data in the system, the customer would allow him/her to view all the information of the customers.
2. For a user of the role of insurance officer who accesses the data with the purpose of providing insurance advices, the customer only wants to provide information about his/her salary range, the birth year and the amount of deposit in the bank. That is, he/she would like to provide generalized information that is enough for the users to accomplish the purpose, i.e., to generalize the value of the salary or deposit to an interval value.
3. For a user of a role of banker with the purpose of providing credit card service, the customer would only provide approximate information of his/her deposit amount at a bank.
4. For a user of a role of banker with the purpose of providing home loan service, the customer is willing to provide the banker the approximate information of his/her salary.

Note that, for the same role with different purposes, the user often would like to provide different data. Similarly, micro data of illness does not have to be revealed for all users. For example, a banker only needs more general information of customer's health than an insurance officer does, i.e., a generalized heart disease. From the above access rules we can see that we need an access model of Web services that provides data according to the role of the users and purposes of accessing the data so that the privacy of data can be preserved.

3   Role, Purpose, and Generalization

The privacy policies are declared in term of usage rules that define which data can be used by whom for which purpose and for how long. In this paper, ontologies are used to manage the privacy policies in term of usage rules and generalization. The usage rules are assigned to each attribute in the database tables. By this, the access of each attribute depends on the user's roles and the purpose of the access.

Purposes of data access often have hierarchical associations among them [19]. In this paper we use ontologies to construct purpose hierarchies. Ontology defines concepts used to describe and represent a knowledge area. In particular, ontology can be used to construct concept hierarchies. Ontologies are constructed by using formal languages, which allow to include reasoning rules that support the processing of that knowledge.

In this section we will present an ontology-based access model for Web services. As mentioned in Sect. 1, using ontologies to capture data access purposes hierarchies we do not need to define the set of all the implied purposes as in [19]. Also, we will use ontologies to define data generalization hierarchies, which can be used to define different levels of data access. The remaining of the section starts with defining role-purpose ontology hierarchies, followed by defining data generalization ontology hierarchies.

3.1   Defining Service Access Roles and Purposes

Roles and purposes are important factors when deciding data shared through Web services. Access decisions are based on roles and purposes. Our access model makes use of an ontology hierarchy to capture roles and purposes of service users together with relationships between roles and purposes. The root of the hierarchy is *role*. Each *role* may have different access purpose. Therefore, we define its access purposes as a subconcept *role_purpose* of *role*.

Consider our example in Sect. 2. We can define *Admin_MaintCustomer* as subconcept of *Admin*, and *Bank_HomeLoan* as a subconcept of *Bank*. Figure 1 shows an example of a role-purpose ontology hierarchy tree.

Using the concept of *role_purpose* hierarchy we can define access rules for each attribute in a database. Therefore usage rules can be represented by a triple: $\langle role\_purpose, attribute, access\_level \rangle$

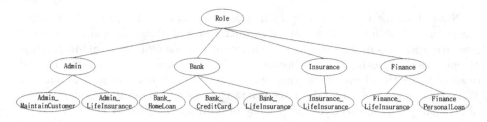

Fig. 1. Roles and purposes hierarchy

3.2   Defining Data Generalization Hierarchies

Generalization can help the organizations provide better services to customers without unnecessary violation to individual privacy. Generalization is a process of replacing a value with a less specific but semantically consistent value [10].

To provide more flexible access to data, generalization has been used to provide different levels of data access without actual data (microdata). In this section we use ontology to define generalization hierarchies for data. Using generalization can avoid unnecessary revealing of sensitive data, e.g., customers' salary, date-of-birth, illness and address [23]. Using ontology has been proved by [24] that it makes the generalization more meaningful.

There are various approaches of generalization in the literature. How to build generalization is not in the scope of this research. In this paper we apply the generalization approach proposed in [25] due to its simplification. Information of attributes of a table is normally divided into two types, *categorical information* and *numeric information*. For the categorical information, such as diseases, generalization for these data elements is typically described by a taxonomy tree. The leaf nodes ($k = 1$) depict all the possible values of data elements. Generalization for numeric data, such as ages, salary and deposit, is done by discretization of its values into a set of disjoint intervals.

For example in Fig. 2(a), the leaf nodes of disease hierarchy are *endocarditis*, *pericarditis*, *myocarditis* and *cardiomyopathy*. These diseases can be grouped into *heart functional malfunctions*, which is the parent level of the leaf nodes. Further, *heart functional malfunction* can be generalized to *heart disease*. Figure 2(b) shows the example of generalization hierarchy of numeric data, deposit and salary.

In the ontology, the generalization level k is defined by using the *isLevel* datatype property. The microdata is defined to be at *isLevel* = 1 and is stored in the database. The ontology stores the data of generalization level $k > 1$. The more generalized the data is, the higher the value of *isLevel* is. Different (*role*, *purpose*) have different data access levels of generalization hierarchies.

3.3   An Example of Access Rules Based on Roles, Purposes

As we see above, data access rules can be defined by assigning an access level to each (*role-purpose*, *attribute*) pair. Accessing data is not only via SELECT operation

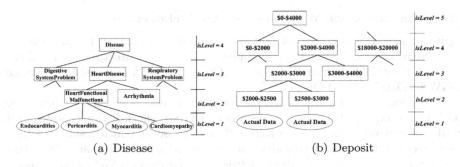

(a) Disease   (b) Deposit

Fig. 2. Example data generalization hierarchies

but can also via other operations, i.e. INSERT, UPDATE and DELETE. Therefore access models should support multiple DML operations. In our access model each attribute of a table is assigned an access level. We will use three access levels in our access model, $canRead$, $isLevel$ and $canWrite$. $canReadBy$: refers to SELECT operation and $canWriteBy$: refers to INSERT, UPDATE and DELETE operations, while $isLevel\_X$, where $X \in \{1, 2, \ldots, n\}$, is the level of generalization. Note that $isLevel\_1$ has an equivalent property as $canReadBy$. Also, an attribute that has the access type $canWrite$ should also have the access type $canReadBy$. Therefore we can model $canReady$ as a subtype of $canWriteBy$.

For example, we can define attribute access levels for all attributes in table Customer in Sect. 2 as shown in Table 2. It shows attribute access levels for the $LifeInsurance$ purpose for different roles.

To ensure usage rules on attribute $illness$ we assign role $Insurance$, purpose $LifeInsurance$ and access level $isLevel\_2$. It means that insurance officers can view generalized data of customer personal_illness. Similarly, on the same attribute we assign role-purpose $Insurance\_LifeInsurance$ and role-purpose $Bank\_LifeInsurance$ we assign access level $isLevel\_3$. Ontologies can be implemented with RDF files and queried by SPARQL.

4   Ontology-Based Web Services Access Model

In this section we first present an architecture of a web-based system that provide data access via Web services to service users. We will then provide a detailed description of an ontology-based access model that is used by the architecture.

Table 2. Assigning access levels to attributes for $LifeInsurance$ purpose

Role	Firstname	Lastname	DoB	Gender	Salary	Deposit	Illness
Admin	$canReadBy$	$canReadBy$	$isLevel\_1$	$canReadBy$	$isLevel\_1$	$isLevel\_1$	$isLevel\_1$
Insurance	$canReadBy$	$canReadBy$	$isLevel\_4$	$canReadBy$	$isLevel\_3$	$isLevel\_3$	$isLevel\_2$
Bank	$canReadBy$	$canReadBy$	$isLevel\_4$	$canReadBy$	$isLevel\_4$	$isLevel\_4$	$isLevel\_3$

4.1   Data Access via Web Services: An Architecture

Figure 3 shows the components and the relationships among the components in the architecture. There are six components in the architecture: Web Client, servlet, Credential Checking Web Service (CCWS), Data Gathering Web Service (DGWS), Database and Ontology.

Web client provides interfaces for users to access data via Web services. CCWS is used to check user's authority. DGWS checks which tables and attributes can be accessed by a role with a purpose at which level. Ontology stores access rules while the database stores microdata of customers. Using this architecture we can provide different levels of data access via Web services based on roles and purposes. CCWS, DGWS and ontology are used for access control of data in the database and are therefore the core of this architecture.

4.2   A Web Service Access Model

The access model used in the architecture above is shown in Fig. 4. The access model can be described with the following steps.

1. A user logs in with *username*, *password*, which are passed to CCWS to check user's credential by using a SPARQL query (Query 1) to query the role-purpose ontology. If the user has access right, the query will return user's role (*role*) and accessible purposes *acc_pur*.
2. The user selects a customer name *cus_name*, and a purpose *acc_pur* for accomplishing his/her task for the customer. Using values of *role* and *acc_pur* DGWS sends a SPARQL query (Query 2) to retrieve accessible attributes *acc_attr* from the ontology.
3. Take input *acc_attr*, DGWS creates a SQL query to retrieve the customer's microdata *microdata* from a table $tables in the database.
4. Take attributes list *acc_attr* as input, DGWS retrieves a set of attributes *gen_attr* that needs to be generalized before displayed to the user. If such attributes *gen_attr* exist, DGWS uses a SPARQL (Query 4) to get the generalization level *gen_level* from the ontology.

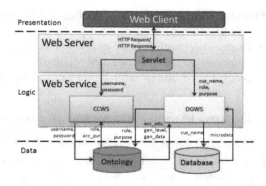

Fig. 3. An ontology-based web service access model

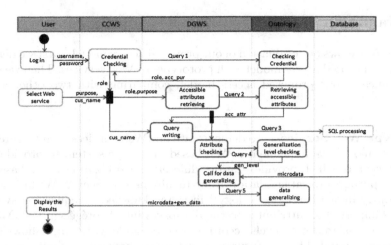

Fig. 4. A web service access model

5. Take input *gen_level*, DGWS sends a SPARQL (Query 5) to get the generalization value *gen_data* for attribute *gen_attr*.
6. The results are displayed in a Web service for the user.

Lets $x and ?y be parameters used in a query, where x is a value that we pass to the Web services and y is a parameter in the query. Due to the page limit, in the following we show two of the SPARQL queries used in the steps above.

Query 1 (login). SPARQL query for credential checking.
    PREFIX Fi: <http://www.owl-ontologies.com/Finance2#>
    PREFIX db: <http://biostorm.stanford.edu/db_table_classes/
              DSN_jdbc.mysql.//localhost.3306/db#>
    PREFIX rdfs: <http://www.w3.org/2000/01/rdf-schema#>
    SELECT ?user ?role ?acc_pur
    WHERE { ?user db:user_account.user_id $username.
              ?user db:user_account.password $password.
              ?user Fi:hasRole ?role.
              ?acc_pur rdfs:subClassOf ?role.}

Query 5 (getGenData). SPARQL query for retrieving generalized data.
    PREFIX rdfs: <http://www.w3.org/2000/01/rdf-schema#>
    PREFIX Fi: <http://www.owl-ontologies.com/Finance2#>
    SELECT ?gen_data
    WHERE { $microdata rdfs:subClassOf ?gen_data.
              ?gen_data Fi:isLevel $gen_level.}

5   Evaluation

This sections shows our evaluation of our proposed access model. First we demonstrate our proposed access model with prototypes of Web services. Then we show performance of our proposed access model, comparing with two other access models.

Prototype Web Services. To demonstrate our Web Services architecture and the access model, we implement a Web-based prototype system to provide web services, each of which provides data of different generalization levels based on roles and purposes to satisfy data privacy requirement in Sect. 2. We first set up our ontology in the Protégé ontology editor and knowledge acquisition system. Then we imported all attributes in the databases into Protégé via DataMaster plug-in, and assign access levels according to our ontology. Figure 5 shows three Web services provided for LifeInsurance purpose to three roles: admin, insurance and bank. Data released by Web services satisfies usage rules in Table 2. We can see that for the same purpose *LifeInsurance* our system provide different Web services to different roles. For example, the Web service for insurance role presents generalized data of salary, deposit and illness. Our prototype system demonstrate that data privacy can be preserved while necessary information is released to users to meet their access purposes.

Performance Evaluation. We evaluated the performance our access model by comparing Web services based on three different access models: Simple WS, None-generalization WS, and Ontology WS that uses our access model. Simple WS simply retrieves all the value of all attributes of Customer table using simple SQL, while None-generalization WS retrieves actual values of only accessible attributes. We evaluated the average response time with different numbers of users that access a database table with 100 records. The results are summarized

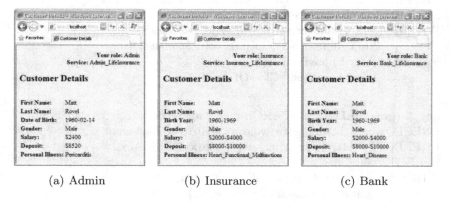

     (a) Admin   (b) Insurance   (c) Bank

Fig. 5. The results accessed with LifeInsurance purpose by different roles

in Fig. 6, on which the x-axis indicates the number of users while the y-axis indicates the average response time in milliseconds.

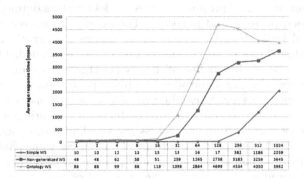

	1	2	4	8	16	32	64	128	256	512	1024
Simple WS	10	10	12	13	13	13	16	17	382	1186	2039
Non-generalized WS	48	48	62	58	51	259	1265	2738	3183	3259	3645
Ontology WS	86	88	99	88	119	1098	2864	4699	4534	4050	3962

Fig. 6. Experimental results.

From Fig. 6, we can see that the average response time of the three WSs when the number of users is 1 to 16 is not significantly different from others. When there are more than 16 users, even though the average response time of Ontology WS is longer than the other two Web Services, but it is still within acceptable range. Further, Ontology WS provides better privacy protection than the Simple WS, and more flexible access of data than None-generalization WS, with which access of data is limited to only allowed and denied.

Discussion. In this paper we have proposed a privacy preservation approach based on roles and purpose of users. Compare with the approach in [2] that make use Hippocratic databases, our approach considers roles and supports data generalization. [19] proposes a role-based purpose-involved access control model to ensure privacy preservation, which needs to compute a set of conditional purposes implied by intended purpose using a propose tree. In our approach, we do not need to compute conditional purposes. In stead, we select suitable purposes by querying role-purpose ontology hierarchies using ontology query languages. Further, our purposed access model can provide a much finer-grained access control using data generalization ontology hierarchies. In [7], the authors present an access control system for Web services that combines trust-based decision policy and ongoing access control policy to create a secure protection system. The limitation of this approach is that the storage overhead increases dramatically when the number of records grows and the number of accessed attributes increases. Our approach has less storage overheard because we use ontology generalization hierarchy and therefore does not need to include all possible generalized data for each level.

6   Conclusion and Future Work

This paper proposes an access model to ensure privacy of data while sharing data via Web services. The proposed access model employs ontologies to define access rules based on roles and purposes. The access model controls the information provided by Web services to users to ensure privacy of customers can be preserved while tasks of service users can be accomplished. Our proposed access model can be used to define Web services that release only information necessary for accomplishing a purpose. A prototype system is implemented to show that different web services can be provided to service users based on their roles and purposes of access. Further, we conducted an experimental evaluation to evaluate the performance of the access model. The results shows that our proposed access model can preserve privacy of customers while sharing data via Web service with reasonable and acceptable performance. Future work can be done to evaluate and analyze the storage overhead of our proposed approach. Also, we will extend our approach to support data owners to customize data accesses for each data user.

References

1. Ghani, N.A., Sidek, Z.M.: Privacy-preserving in web services using hippocratic database. In: International Symposium on Information Technology, vol. 1, pp. 1–5 (2008)
2. Agrawal, R., Kiernan, J., Srikant, R., Xu, Y.: Hippocratic databases. In: 28th International Conference on Very Large Data Bases (VLDB), pp. 143–154 (2002)
3. LeFevre, K., Agrawal, R., Ercegovac, V., Ramakrishnan, R., Xu, Y., DeWitt, D.: Limiting disclosure in hippocratic databases. In: 30th International Conference on Very Large Data Bases (VLDB), pp. 108–119 (2004)
4. Agrawal, R., Kini, A., LeFevre, K., Wang, A., Xu, Y., Zhou, D.: Managing healthcare data hippocratically. In: ACM SIGMOD International Conference on Management of Data, pp. 947–948 (2004)
5. Massacci, F., Mylopoulos, J., Zannone, N.: Hierarchical hippocratic databases with minimal disclosure for virtual organizations. VLDB J. 15(4), 370–387 (2006)
6. Laura-Silva, Y., Aref, W.: Realizing privacy-preserving features in hippocratic databases. In: IEEE 23rd International Conference on Data Engineering Workshop, pp. 198–206 (2007)
7. Li, M., Sun, X., Wang, H., Zhang, Y., Zhang, J.: Privacy-aware access control with trust management in web service. World Wide Web 14(4), 407–430 (2011)
8. Xiao, X., Tao, Y.: Personalized privacy preservation. In: ACM SIGMOD International Conference on Management of Data, pp. 229–240 (2006)
9. Samarati, P., Sweeney, L.: Generalizing data to provide anonymity when disclosing information. In: ACM SIGACT SIGMOD SIGART Symposium on Principles of Database Systems, vol. 17, p. 188 (1998)
10. Sweeney, L.: Achieving k-anonymity privacy protection using generalization and suppression. Int. J. Uncertainty Fuzziness Knowl. Based Syst. 10(05), 571–588 (2002)
11. Miller, J., Campan, A., Truta, T.M.: Constrained k-anonymity: privacy with generalization boundaries. In: Practical Privacy-Preserving Data Mining, p. 30 (2008)

12. Kisilevich, S., Rokach, L., Elovici, Y., Shapira, B.: Efficient multidimensional suppression for k-anonymity. IEEE Trans. Knowl. Data Eng. **22**(3), 334–347 (2010)
13. Omran, E., Bokma, A., Abu-Almaati, S.: A k-anonymity based semantic model for protecting personal information and privacy. In: IEEE International Advance Computing Conference, pp. 1443–1447 (2009)
14. Martínez, S., Sánchez, D., Valls, A., Batet, M.: The role of ontologies in the anonymization of textual variables. In: 13th International Conference of the Catalan Association for Artificial Intelligence, vol. 220, p. 153 (2010)
15. Domingo-Ferrer, J., Torra, V.: Disclosure control methods and information loss for microdata. In: Confidentiality, Disclosure, and Data Access: Theory and Practical Applications for Statistical Agencies, pp. 93–112 (2001)
16. Iqbal, Z., Noll, J., Alam, S., Chowdhury, M.M.: Toward user-centric privacy-aware user profile ontology for future services. In: 3rd International Conference on Communication Theory, Reliability, and Quality of Service, pp. 249–254 (2010)
17. Finin, T., Joshi, A., Kagal, L., Niu, J., Sandhu, R., Winsborough, W., Thuraisingham, B.: R owl bac: representing role based access control in owl. In: 13th ACM Symposium on Access Control Models and Technologies, pp. 73–82 (2008)
18. Cirio, L., Cruz, I.F., Tamassia, R.: A role and attribute based access control system using semantic web technologies. In: Meersman, R., Tari, Z. (eds.) OTM-WS 2007, Part II. LNCS, vol. 4806, pp. 1256–1266. Springer, Heidelberg (2007)
19. Kabir, M.E., Wang, H., Bertino, E.: A role-involved purpose-based access control model. Inf. Syst. Front. **14**(3), 809–822 (2012)
20. Tumer, A., Dogac, A., Toroslu, I.H.: A semantic based privacy framework for web services. In: Proceedings of ESSW (2003)
21. Gruber, T., et al.: A translation approach to portable ontology specifications. Knowl. Acquisition **5**(2), 199–220 (1993)
22. Wang, Y., Liu, W., Bell, D.: A concept hierachy based ontology mapping approach. In: Bi, Y., Williams, M.-A. (eds.) KSEM 2010. LNCS, vol. 6291, pp. 101–113. Springer, Heidelberg (2010)
23. Li, M., Wang, H., Plank, A.: Privacy-aware access control with generalization boundaries. In: 32nd Australasian Conference on Computer Science, pp. 105–112 (2009)
24. Talouki, M., NematBakhsh, M.a., Baraani, A.: K-anonymity privacy protection using ontology. In: 14th International CSI Computer Conference, pp. 682–685 (2009)
25. Iyengar, V.S.: Transforming data to satisfy privacy constraints. In: 8th ACM SIGKDD International Conference on Knowledge Discovery and Data Mining, pp. 279–288 (2002)

Event Modeling and Processing in Business Process Management

Preface to the 2nd International Workshop on Event Modeling and Processing in Business Process Management (EMoV 2015)

Big Data, Sensors, and Cyber-Physical-Systems provide a huge and valuable source of event information for the execution, monitoring, and analysis of business processes. The second international workshop on Event Modeling and Processing in Business Process Management (EMoV 2015) dealt with problem statements, solution proposals, and future development perspectives in the area of conceptual modeling of events in business process models, specifications for event-processing in business processes including event-based process execution, and business intelligence analysis of events in relation to business processes.

The paper *Production Process Monitoring Using Model-Driven Event Processing Networks* by Falko Kötter and Tobias Krause discusses a novel method for production monitoring using event processing networks while separating machine and production processes to increase flexibility and minimize configuration efforts. The contribution *User Study of Different Representations for Visualizing Differences in Process Models* by Manuel Gall, Günter Wallner, Simone Kriglstein and Stefanie Rinderle-Ma focuses on the evaluation of possibilities for visualizing differences between two process models and if available their instances calculated based on a difference graph approach. John Wondoh, Georg Grossmann, Dragan Gasevic, Manfred Reichert, Michael Schrefl, and Markus Stumptner discuss in their paper titled *Bitemporal Support for Business Process Contingency Management* possible relationships between bitemporal properties of events and their impact on business processes, and demonstrate bitemporal event processing to prevent certain undesired effects on the business process. The paper titled *Towards an Extended Metamodel of Event-driven Process Chains to Model Complex Event Patterns* by Julian Krumeich, Nijat Mehdiyev, Dirk Werth and Peter Loos presents an extension of the Event-driven Process Chain (EPC) metamodel to allow complex event pattern modeling within process models.

The second international workshop on Event Modeling and Processing in Business Process Management was held in conjunction with 34th International Conference on Conceptual Modeling (ER 2015) in Stockholm, Sweden, on 22 October 2015. We received eight research paper submissions. The program committee provided 29 reviews. Based on these, we accepted four papers for presentation at the workshop and publication in the proceedings *Advances in Conceptual Modelling – ER 2015 Workshops*.

Nico Herzberg (SAP SE, Germany)
Falko Kötter (Fraunhofer-Institut IAO, Germany)
Stefan Appel (Siemens AG, Germany)
Nenad Stojanovic (FZI Research Center for Information Technologies, Germany)

Acknowledgements. The organizers of the EMoV 2015 workshop would like to thank all authors for their contributions to this workshop. Special thanks to the members of the program committee whose expert input made this workshop possible. Finally, we thank ER 2015 workshop chairs Manfred Jeusfeld and Kamal Karlapalem for their direction, guidance and support.

Production Process Monitoring Using Model-Driven Event Processing Networks

Falko Koetter[(✉)] and Tobias Krause

University of Stuttgart IAT, Nobelstr. 12, 70569 Stuttgart, Germany
{falko.koetter,tobias.krause}@iao.fraunhofer.de

Abstract. Economic realities make flexibility in production processes a necessity. Small batch production necessitates reuse of machines within different production processes. Monitoring in such production environments must adapt to process changes without impacting production machines and software. In this work we propose a novel method for production monitoring using event processing networks, separating machine and production processes, thus increasing flexibility and minimizing configuration efforts.

Keywords: Business process management · Process monitoring · Complex event processing · Event processing networks · Model-driven architecture

1 Introduction

The term *Industry 4.0* describes the increasing use of information technology, networking, smart objects, services and data in manufacturing [20]. Akin to the trend of business process management, production processes become IT-supported. In a production process, products are manufactured according to given orders using production resources and materials [5].

One part of Industry 4.0 is the monitoring and optimization of production processes with respect to cost, quality and time [14]. Production processes are stricter organized in single activities, while business processes provide more degrees of freedom during execution. The reason for this is that machines used in production need to be fine-tuned to work seamlessly together and provide a high throughput and quality, especially in assembly-line production. However, due to trends like just in time production and mass customization, production in smaller batches becomes a necessity and thus, more flexibility in production processes is needed [20, p. 90].

According to [20, p. 93] the majority of manufacturing companies note a lack of accurate and up-to-date process information, which makes manual intervention in production processes necessary. However, 72 % of companies estimate a high or very high potential to avoid these interventions if current process information is available via monitoring.

© Springer International Publishing Switzerland 2015
M.A. Jeusfeld and K. Karlapalem (Eds.): ER 2015 Workshops, LNCS 9382, pp. 89–98, 2015.
DOI: 10.1007/978-3-319-25747-1_9

In this work we describe a novel approach to monitoring of small-batch production processes. Extending an approach for model-driven process monitoring, we present a method to model, deploy and link multiple process monitoring instances in an event processing network (EPN). We apply this method to small-batch production processes, separating the machine, machine process and production process levels to facilitate easy rearrangement of machines for monitoring different batches with batch specific processes, goals and fault tolerances.

The remainder of this work is structured as follows. Section 2 gives an overview of related work. Section 3 describes the example scenario. Section 4 gives an overview of the model-driven process monitoring approach used in this work. Section 5 describes how EPNs can be utilized to monitor and reconfigure production processes. In Sect. 6 the prototype and evaluation are described. Finally, Sect. 7 gives a conclusion and outlines future work.

2   Related Work

In this section we give an overview of relevant work in the fields of production monitoring, distributed process monitoring and EPNs.

Monitoring of production processes measures Key Performance Indicators (KPI) like timeliness, workload, machine productivity, availability, reaction time, inventory and stock levels as well as product and process quality [8, p. 13ff]. When monitoring production processes, existing approaches differ in their scope, purpose and position within the process. To monitor single machines, so-called machine-integrated monitoring systems are used. An example is the monitoring and enforcement of thresholds to prevent damage to parts currently being worked on [23, p. 331ff]. Machine-integrated monitoring systems can use a wide array of sensors to measure mechanical, electrical, thermal, magnetic or chemical parameters [9, p. 387]. If the monitoring tool is integrated in the control, existing values of the controls like position of spindles and speed can be monitored, for example to prevent self-damaging of machines [23, p. 376ff]. On a larger scope, Manufacturing Execution Systems (MES) connect business management and production processes [8, p. 7]. MES provide overarching functionality, e.g. product tracking, monitoring data gathering, analysis and process monitoring [13]. MES are used in assembly line and mass production, but lack the flexibility to be used for small batch production [19, p. 157].

Niche solutions exist for specialized processes. For example, [18] describes a monitoring software for production logistics processes. Maintenance of machines can be costly if it leads to extended downtime, which makes monitoring and proactively detecting maintenance important [22]. Maintaining machines before an outage would occur is called *predictive maintenance* [17, p. 4-6]. Monitoring solutions to predict necessary maintenance can take into account cost and other factors [4]. Overall, the state of the art in production monitoring shows sophisticated solutions at the machine level and for large-scale processes. However, these solutions lack the flexibility needed in small batch production.

Complex Event Processing (CEP) is a technology for processing large amounts of events in near real-time [15]. For example, the CEP Engine Esper uses an event processing language (EPL) to filter, aggregate, change and generate streams of events [1]. An *event processing network* (EPN) consists of multiple so-called *event processing agents* (EPA) processing events in unison, consuming and producing them [15]. Such an EPN can be used for distributed event processing, to handle large amounts of events and to separate concerns and abstraction levels [16]. [16] shows how CEP can be used to monitor production processes. [2] shows a case study of using CEP to control and monitor a modular manufacturing line. However, the rearrangement for different batches or products is not tackled in both approaches. [21] shows an approach to connect a process engine with a CEP engine to monitor and adapt business processes using graphically modeled EPL rules. This approach however is limited to a single process engine and allows reuse only of EPL rules, not EPAs. [6] presents an approach to use event data for process control in a process engine. In comparison to our approach, a high degree of manual implementation is necessary.

3   Motivational Example

Consider a metal-working company producing parts which are used in other products, for example in the IT, automotive and furniture industries. Due to raising demands in flexibility [20, p. 90], most parts are produced in small batches using multiple machines as part of an individualized process for each part. The CNC (Computerized Mechanical Control) machines [12] are programmable to produce the desired part. Programs can be exchanged relatively quickly, but the overall process involving multiple machines is more complex to change. For a simplified process, we introduce three machines.

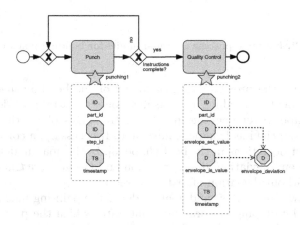

Fig. 1. Example process and goal model for punching machine.

Figure 1 shows the process model of the punching machine. Holes are punched into a metal part until all punching instructions are executed. Afterwards, a machine-integrated quality control step takes place, comparing the shape of the part to a set reference using the envelope method [11]. Attached to the process model is a *goal model* in the ProgoalML notation. Measuring points (e.g. *punching1*) are attached to both activities, indicating that a measurement of monitoring data should take place. Inside the measuring points, the parameters to be measured are given. For example, in *punching2* attached to *Quality Control* the id of the current part, the timestamp of the measurement and the expected (set) and actual (is) value of the metal shape from the envelope method are measured. From both values, a KPI is calculated, indicating the deviation in percent according to the envelope deviation. Note that no concrete goal regarding deviation is given in the machine process. KPIs in ProgoalML are defined using a formula editor, providing mathematical operations, aggregations, etc. [10].

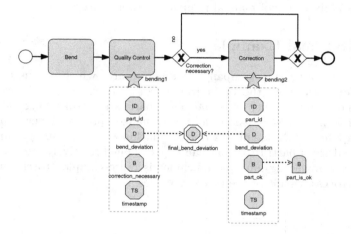

Fig. 2. Example process and goal model for bending machine.

Figure 2 shows the process and goal model of the bending machine. A flat metal part is bent according to specifications to attain a desired three-dimensional shape. After bending quality control takes place, the deviation of the bent part from the ideal shape is measured. If necessary, a correction step is used to fix minor deviations in the bent shape [3]. In the goal model, a KPI measures the final bend deviation after correction and the goal *part_is_ok* is fulfilled if the part is without deviation after the correction step.

Figure 3 shows the process and goal model of the painting machine. A metal part is painted by dipping or spraying paint, after which the part needs to dry before the paint job is considered finished. The goal model only monitors paint level and stipulates that the paint level must be sufficient (i.e. above 5 %).

Using these three machines, a variety of metal parts can be created. Consider for example a metal part of a head gasket in a car. This part needs to be punched and bent precisely, as it is critical to sealing the cylinders. Not considering rust

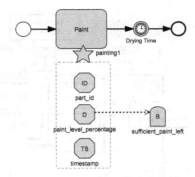

Fig. 3. Example process and goal model for painting machine.

protection, the part does not need to be painted, as it is not visible from the outside. In comparison, consider a metal part that is going to be the faceplate for an electronic device. This faceplate needs to be painted, as it is visible to the customer. The deviation in punching and bending is comparably relaxed. Both parts can be created with the three machines, but the overall processes have different steps and quality criteria.

4 Model-Driven Process Monitoring

In previous work we introduced aPro, a model-driven architecture for business process monitoring [10]. Figure 4 gives an overview of the most important components of the approach.

To monitor a process, first, a process model is graphically modeled and augmented with process goals, metrics and KPIs as shown in the motivational example. The process and monitoring model are stored in a *ProGoalML* file. This file is used as basis for automatic model transformation, which serves to create technical components from the conceptual model. A monitoring container is created, containing a dashboard and CEP engine, both configured with event processing rules detecting process instances from measurement patterns and calculating KPIs and goals as well as a dashboard configuration (*VisML* [7]). This monitoring container receives monitoring data via monitoring web services. To support a wide array of executing systems, ranging from process engines to legacy applications to machines, monitoring stubs are used. Monitoring stubs are integrated with the executing systems and send monitoring data to monitoring web services. To achieve this, events can be sent from the application, triggered to be sent by an application, sent by an external component monitoring the executing systems status etc. Some monitoring stubs can be automatically generated (e.g. shell scripts and Java classes), others need to be manually implemented. Note that monitoring stub integration is the only part of aPro which is not fully automated.

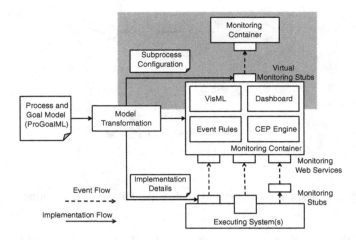

Fig. 4. Overview of model-driven process monitoring (focus of this work highlighted in grey)

During operation, events are generated by the monitoring stubs and sent to the monitoring container. The CEP engine processes these events with rules generated according to the conceptual model, assembling process instances from single events, calculating KPIs and goals and aggregating data. The results are visualized in a dashboard. While this model-driven approach allows to setup a process monitoring infrastructure without component configuration supporting arbitrary systems executing the process, the degree of abstraction is limited. aPro separates the conceptual monitoring model from the implementation in event processing rules. However, all monitoring events are processed and aggregated in the same CEP engine, regardless of their role within the monitored process, making a new model transformation and redeployment of the monitoring container necessary, whenever a change in the monitoring model is made.

5   Event Processing Networks

Considering the motivational example, the three machine processes are subprocesses of the overall production processes. To allow monitoring of these overarching processes, either the machine process monitoring has to be remodeled on the production process level or it has to be reused. While reusing measuring points via copy and paste recreates the behaviour on a model level, the monitoring stubs of the machine processes still need to be adapted during model transformation.

We propose using an EPN to facilitate hierarchical monitoring of machine level subprocesses and production level main processes. To enable the building of model-driven EPNs, a relationship between different monitoring containers acting as event processing agents need to be defined. Expanding on the monitoring stub concept, we propose using a monitoring container itself as a monitoring stub for another, higher-level monitoring container. Thus, a subset of result data can be reused as a complex event in a downstream monitoring container.

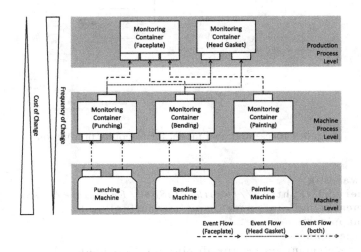

Fig. 5. Event processing network of production process scenario

Figure 5 shows the proposed concept applied to the production process scenario. On the *machine level*, production machines are instrumented with monitoring stubs gathering data as indicated in Sect. 3. On the *machine process level*, for each machine, a monitoring container receives the gathered data and processes it according to the goal model of the respective machine process. These monitoring containers monitor the machine processes, calculating KPIs and goals for each instance. For each process instance, they send a *complex event* to the monitoring container on the *production process level*, which monitors the production process. As indicated in Fig. 5, two configurations of the EPN are possible, depending on which production process is currently running.

Machine process level monitoring containers serve as virtual monitoring stubs for both production processes. Consider the production process for the faceplate in Fig. 6. This process uses all three machines to produce faceplates. Quality criteria specific to the use case have to be met by a part, otherwise it is scrapped before painting. These criteria are determined using data from the machine processes. Also, both completed and scrapped parts per hour are measured.

Three of the four measuring points of the faceplate production process represent the machine processes. In order to measure at these measuring points, the monitoring containers of the machine processes need to act as virtual monitoring stubs. As shown in the highlighted part of Fig. 4, a *subprocess configuration* is used to determine the virtual monitoring stubs. This configuration indicates which virtual monitoring stubs are to be created and maps data of the monitored process instance to the input of the monitoring stubs.

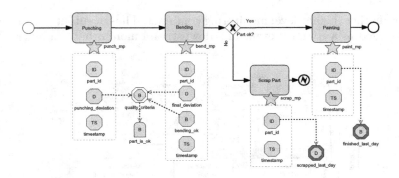

Fig. 6. Process and goal model for faceplate production

```
1    <forwarding>
2      <serverUrl>http://localhost:8080/Faceplate/</serverUrl>
3      <measuringPoint>punch_mp</measuringPoint>
4      <mappings>
5        <mapping>
6          <element>envelope_deviation</element>
7          <parameter>punching_deviation</parameter>
8        </mapping>
9        <mapping>
10         <element>part_id</element>
11         <parameter>part_id</parameter>
12       </mapping>
13     </mappings>
14   </forwarding>
```

An example subprocess configuration is listed above, creating a virtual monitoring stub for the measuring point *punch_mp* withing the punching process. *serverUrl* and *measuringPoint* elements are used to address the monitoring web service. *Mappings* determine which *elements* of the punching process goal model are mapped to which *parameters* of the *punching_mp* measuring point. Note that multiple virtual monitoring stubs can be contained within the configuration.

Using subprocess mappings, the measuring points of the faceplate process can be provided with events. The fourth measuring point, *scrap_mp* corresponds to no machine and needs to be triggered whenever a part is scrapped. This can be done automatically or manually using an automatically generated webform monitoring stub [10].

If instead of faceplates different parts shall be produced, another production process has to be used, for which individual steps, quality criteria, KPIs etc. can be modeled. Using the subprocess mappings, the machine processes and monitoring stubs can be reused without change. Thus, the production process level is flexible while avoiding unnecessary, costly changes on the machine level.

6   Prototype and Evaluation

We implemented subprocess mapping and virtual monitoring stubs within the aPro prototype described in [10]. The prototype provides web-based modeling of process and goal models as well as model transformation and monitoring container deployment. We used the prototype to model all five processes, deploy them and create the EPN between monitoring containers.

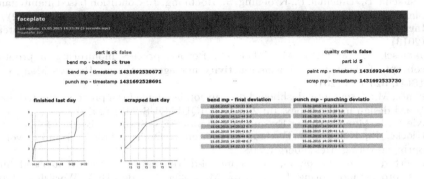

Fig. 7. Live dashboard of faceplate process with synthetic data

Figure 7 shows the generated dashboard of the faceplate production process. We evaluated the EPN using synthetic test data generators posing as monitoring stubs for the machine processes. We found the EPN to work as described, passing data from machine process monitoring containers to production monitoring containers. Switching production processes was achieved by changing the subprocess configuration files. While proving the feasibility of the concept, we have not yet evaluated the prototype within a real production process environment. We are currently searching for industry partners to perform such trials.

7   Conclusion and Outlook

In this work we described a method for production process monitoring using a model-driven monitoring architecture and connecting multiple monitoring containers to form an event processing network. This approach effectively separates sub and main processes and makes reuse and reconfiguration feasible, minimizing the need for change on lower levels when high level processes change. We evaluated this approach with a prototype using the example scenarios.

In future work, we would like to apply the work in a real-life production environment. Additionally, we would like to further investigate the formation of EPNs between different processes, in particular more user-friendly ways to visualize and change an EPN.

References

1. Esper EPL Reference. http://esper.codehaus.org/esper-4.11.0/doc/reference/en-US/html/index.html
2. Ahmad, W.: Formal modelling of complex event processing and its application to a manufacturing line (2012)
3. Boettger, U.: Messtechnik mit kurzem draht zur biegemaschine. Industrieanzeiger. http://www.industrieanzeiger.de/home/-/article/12503/28869833/Messtechnik-mit-kurzem-Draht-zur-Biegemaschine/
4. Denkena, B., Bluemel, P., Kroening, S., Roebbing, J.: Condition based maintenance planning of highly productive machine tools. Prod. Eng. **6**(3), 277–285 (2012)
5. Ingenieure, V.D.: Vdi-richtlinie: Vdi 5600 blatt 1 fertigungsmanagementsysteme (2013)
6. Janiesch, C., Matzner, M., Mller, O.: Beyond process monitoring: a proof-of-concept of event-driven business activity management. Bus. Process Manage. J. **18**(4), 625–643 (2012)
7. Kintz, M.: A semantic dashboard description language for a process-oriented dashboard design methodology. In: 2nd MODIQUITOUS 2012 (2012)
8. Kletti, J.: Manufacturing Execution Systems-MES. Springer, Berlin (2007)
9. Klocke, F., König, W.: Fertigungsverfahren 1: Drehen, Fräsen, Bohren, vol. 1. Springer-Verlag, Heidelberg (2008)
10. Koetter, F., Kochanowski, M.: A model-driven approach for event-based business process monitoring. In: La Rosa, M., Soffer, P. (eds.) BPM Workshops 2012. LNBIP, vol. 132, pp. 378–389. Springer, Heidelberg (2013)
11. Kopka, T., Schwer, A., Faulhaber, W.: Sensoren sichern die stabilitaet im stanzprozess. BLECH InForm **5**, 48–51 (2004)
12. Koren, Y.: Computer Control of Manufacturing Systems. McGraw-Hill, New York (1983)
13. Louis, P.: Manufacturing Execution Systems. Springer, Berlin (2008)
14. Lucke, D.M.: Ad hoc informationsbeschaffung unter einsatz kontextbezogener systeme in der variantenreichen serienfertigung (2014)
15. Luckham, D.C.: The Power of Events: An Introduction to Complex Event Processing in Distributed Enterprise Systems. Addison-Wesley, Boston (2001)
16. Luckham, D.C., Frasca, B.: Complex event processing in distributed systems. Technical report CSL-TR-98-754. Stanford University (1998)
17. Mobley, R.K.: An Introduction to Predictive Maintenance. Butterworth-Heinemann, Boston (2002)
18. Münzberg, B., Schmidt, M., Beck, S., Nyhuis, P.: Model based logistic monitoring for supply and assembly processes. Prod. Eng. **6**(4–5), 449–458 (2012)
19. Pfeifer, T., Schmitt, R.: Autonome Produktionszellen: Komplexe Produktionsprozesse Flexibel Automatisieren. VDI-Buch. Springer, Heidelberg (2006)
20. Spath, D., Ganschar, O., Gerlach, S., Hämmerle, M., Krause, T., Schlund, S.: Produktionsarbeit der Zukunft-Industrie 4.0. Fraunhofer Verlag (2013)
21. Vidačković, K., Weiner, N., Kett, H., Renner, T.: Towards business-oriented monitoring and adaptation of distributed service-based applications from a process owner's viewpoint. In: Dan, A., Gittler, F., Toumani, F. (eds.) ICSOC/ServiceWave 2009. LNCS, vol. 6275, pp. 385–394. Springer, Heidelberg (2010)
22. Weck, M., Brecher, C.: Werkzeugmaschinen: Maschinenarten und Anwendungsbereiche. VDI-Buch. Springer, Heidelberg (2005)
23. Weck, M., Brecher, C.: Prozessüberwachung, prozessregelung, diagnose und instandhaltungsmaßnahmen. Werkzeugmaschinen 3: Mechatronische Systeme, Vorschubantriebe, Prozessdiagnose, pp. 267–404 (2006)

A Study of Different Visualizations for Visualizing Differences in Process Models

Manuel Gall[1]([✉]), Günter Wallner[2], Simone Kriglstein[3],
and Stefanie Rinderle-Ma[1]

[1] Faculty of Computer Science, University of Vienna, Vienna, Austria
{manuel.gall,stefanie.rinderle-ma}@univie.ac.at
[2] Institute Art & Technology, University of Applied Arts Vienna, Vienna, Austria
guenter.wallner@uni-ak.ac.at
[3] Institute for Design & Assessment of Technology,
Technical University of Vienna, Vienna, Austria
simone.kriglstein@tuwien.ac.at

Abstract. Finding differences between two processes can be a complex, time consuming, and expensive task. Our work is based on the difference graph approach which calculates the differences between two process models and – if available – their instances. In this paper we evaluate different possibilities for visualizing these differences. For this purpose we have selected some common visual properties such as color, shape, and size and evaluated these different visualizations with 31 participants through an online survey. Our results show that color coding and symbols were the preferred methods of the participants for depicting differences in a graph visualization.

Keywords: Process differences · Difference graph · Visualization · Process model · Instance flow

1 Introduction

Processes are an indispensable part of today's businesses. Be it for visualizing processes for communication or optimization purposes, companies constantly use processes to gain additional business intelligence. Using process mining algorithms on data collection during process execution allows, for example, detection of bottlenecks, problems, and violations (cf. [2]). Conformance checking [18] is a process mining technique which assesses if an event log of a process deviates from the process model. Unfortunately conformance checking focuses only on detection of deviations between event logs and process models. However, the analysis of differences and commonalities between process models and, optionally, their instance traffic – which shows how the instances have progressed through the model – are also of interest for different use cases in business process management (cf. [3]). This includes finding deviations between two process models which have been generated through process mining techniques. Consider, for example, a company which executes the same task at two different locations. Unfortunately in

© Springer International Publishing Switzerland 2015
M.A. Jeusfeld and K. Karlapalem (Eds.): ER 2015 Workshops, LNCS 9382, pp. 99–108, 2015.
DOI: 10.1007/978-3-319-25747-1_10

one location the execution takes twice as long. Comparing the process models of these locations can reveal why the execution takes longer. When comparing two process models one can also gain additional information if these processes can be merged. Finding deviations allows an analyst to determine where problems may occur. Another example is to assess one process at different points in time, for instance, to evaluate how one process has evolved from one year to the next. In addition to the analysis of process models, Kriglstein et al. [13] point out that the analysis of instances and how they have progressed through the model (i.e., instance traffic) based on execution logs or simulation data can give interesting insights into the distribution of instances between different process models.

In this regard, visualizing data is a very important task to enhance the users understanding of the data. For example, Kriglstein et al. [13] presented a visualization approach to visualize differences and commonalities between process models and their instances by means of color coding. The input models themselves can either be generated through process mining or manually. However, the approach presented by Kriglstein et al. [13] is lacking in regard to the evaluation in order to identify how to best visualize the differences to support an effective interpretation of them. In this paper, we address this issue by investigating which visualizations of differences suit the interpretation of differences in process models and instance traffic best. To answer this question we evaluated nine different visualizations which are based on different visual properties (gathered through a literature review) with company employees and students via an online survey.

The remainder of this paper is structured as follows. Related work is shortly discussed in the next section. Section 3 then gives an overview of the difference graph model and its calculation. This is followed by a short introduction of the investigated visualizations in Sect. 4. The evaluation itself is then covered in Sect. 5. The limitations of the study are discussed in Sect. 6. Section 7 concludes the paper and shortly discusses possible directions for future work.

2   Related Work

To represent differences in a graph, various approaches like difference map (e.g., [6]), animation (e.g., [8]), and small multiples (e.g., [4]) were developed in the last years. With regard to business processes, there exist several approaches that focus on the analysis of differences and similarities between process models (see, e.g., [1,12–14,19,20]). Often changes are directly visualized within the process model via color coding, for example, by coloring new activities in green or activities that were removed in the newer version in red (cf. [13]). However, evaluations about how suitable the suggested approaches for visualizing differences within process models are, are often missing. An example for an evaluation is the user study from Kabicher et al. [12] in which the authors evaluated the visual properties color, brightness, and size for the change operations *add* and *delete* (which correspond to our markings NEW and DELETED) in order to identify which visual property the participants preferred for visualizing changes in process models. In contrast to our study the visual properties were preassigned to the two change operations. For example, they used orange to represent deleted elements and green to highlight added elements. Furthermore, we consider six additional visualizations (e.g., shapes, symbols) and three further markings (UNCHANGED, INCREASED, and DECREASED).

Overloading existing process modeling languages leads to a more complex visualization which, in turn, can lead to an increase in cognitive load. For example, Moody and Hillegersberg [16] investigated the cognitive effectiveness of UML based on five principles. Similarly, Genon et al. [10] investigated the cognitive effectiveness of the visual notation of BPMN 2.0. Both studies showed that the cognitive effectiveness can be improved within those languages and agree that involving the users within the development of these languages is a key aspect.

3 Difference Graph Model

The difference graph concept presented by Kriglstein et al. [13] consists of two parts: difference model and instance traffic. A process model is considered to be a directed connected graph consisting of a set of nodes and a set of edges. Optionally, nodes and edges may have weights assigned which represent the instance traffic. Instance traffic measures how often a specific activity has been executed. As an example, Fig. 1 shows two versions of a process model with their instance traffic. When visually comparing these two variants one can observe that, for example, B has been deleted from the right model. However, with increasing size of the model manually finding the differences and commonalities can become increasingly cumbersome and time-consuming. For this purpose the difference model was introduced by Kriglstein et al. [13]. The difference model is calculated by subtracting two process models, in our example referred to as PM_1 and PM_2. Calculating $PM_2 - PM_1$ results in a difference model with markings associated with its nodes and edges (for an in-depth discussion see [13]). The following list shows the different markings and describes in which case these markings are assigned:

NEW: a node/edge is marked as NEW if the node/edge was added to PM_2.

UNCHANGED: a node/edge is marked as UNCHANGED if it appears in both input models (and has the same weights in case instance traffic is available).

DELETED: a node/edge is marked as DELETED if the node/edge was removed from PM_2.

In case instance traffic is available, two further markings exist:

INCREASED: a node/edge is marked as INCREASED when the weight has increased from PM_1 to PM_2.

DECREASED: a node/edge is marked as DECREASED when the weight has decreased in PM_2.

Figure 2 shows the resulting graph when the left model in Fig. 1 is subtracted from the right model. For example, Node B was deleted from PM_2 and is therefore marked as DELETED while the weight of node C has increased from 2 to 3 and thus C has been marked as INCREASED.

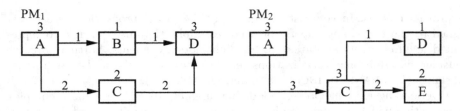

Fig. 1. Two variants of a process model with their instance traffic.

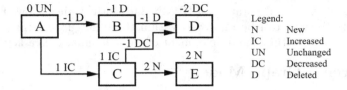

Fig. 2. Calculating the differences between the process models and their instance traffic from Fig. 1 ($PM_2 - PM_1$) leads to this difference graph. Above each node and edge the calculated weights and assigned markings are shown.

4   Visualizations

The main focus of this paper is how to best visualize such a difference graph in order to promote an effective interpretation by users. For this purpose we used different visual properties (see, e.g., [5,7,11,15] to mention but a few) for the visual encoding of the five markings: NEW, UNCHANGED, DELETED, INCREASED, and DECREASED.

In order to identify relevant visual properties which can be used for the different markings we conducted a literature review to analyze different visualizations that were used in the last years to depict differences between process models. In summary 31 papers were found. Collected literature as well as categorization can be found on our website [9]. We analyzed these papers to identify different potential visualizations and their corresponding visual properties. Based on these findings nine different visualizations (summarized in Fig. 3) were created based on different visual properties. Each visualization depicted the markings in a different way, for example, through different colors, shapes, or symbols. For example, the visualization *Color* uses the colors green, blue, black, orange, and red to distinguish between the different markings.

5   Evaluation

The goal of the evaluation was to identify which of the nine visualizations (cf. Fig. 3) – *Brightness, Font Size, Line Width, Edge Pattern, Symbols, Background Color, Color, Edge Ending,* and *Node Shape* – gathered through our literature review suit the interpretation of differences in process models and their instance traffic best.

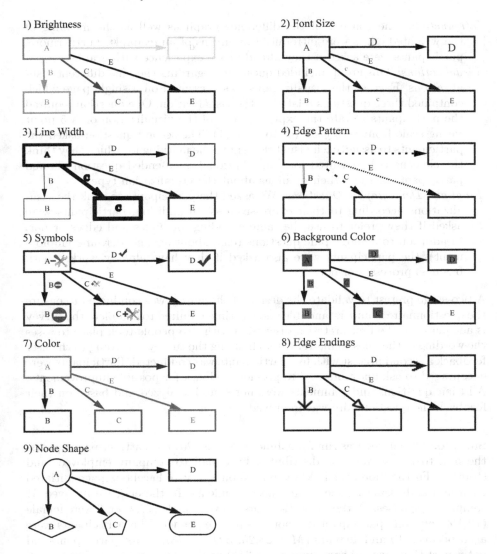

Fig. 3. The nine visualizations to present the difference graph of two process models and their instance traffic. The design of the visualizations is based on the findings from our literature review (Color figure online).

Design. For the evaluation we used an online questionnaire in order to be more flexible and to reach a broader community than it would be possible with face-to-face interviews (e.g., to attract not only local participants). Each question was developed in accordance with the *Ten Commandments* by Porst [17]. The questionnaire was divided into three groups:

Introduction: The concept of the difference graph as well as the meaning of the weighted edges were introduced by means of an example. Furthermore, participants were asked if they already have experience with graphs.

Visualizations: This group included questions regarding the nine different visualizations. Each of the visualizations was presented on a single page which contained three questions related to the visualization. One question required the participants to rate the expressiveness of the visualization on a 5 point rating scale from *very good* (5) to *poor* (1). The second question asked the participants to assign each visual element to the marking for which they think the element is best suited for. An additional open-ended question allowed participants to share their opinions about the visualization type.

Final and Demographic Questions: We asked the participants to rank the visualizations according to their expressiveness. In addition, participants were asked if they prefer to use the same encoding for nodes and edges or not. In addition to demographic questions (e.g., about age, gender, and employment), the participants were also asked if they have already worked with business processes or not.

A two-stage pretest to validate the design of the survey was conducted to ensure the questionnaire is understandable and the time required to complete the survey is adequate. In the first pretest a discussion with two people took place to asses the wording of the questionnaire. After changing the survey according to the user feedback a second pretest with five participants was conducted. Participants were encouraged to ask questions and to provide feedback for possible improvements. All their questions and comments were noted and analyzed and based on their feedback the questionnaire was improved.

Sample. The survey was run from June to August 2014. To attract participants, the link to the survey was distributed by e-mail to company employees and students. Furthermore, the link was posted on a private Facebook page initiated from and addressing business informatics students. In the end, we received 31 complete responses. Of the 31 participants, 24 were male (77.4 %), 6 were female (19.4 %) and one participant did not specify the gender. The participants were aged between 19 and 46 years ($M = 28.25$, $SD = 7.43$). Three participants did not report their age. 19 participants (61.3 %) worked with graphs before and 12 participants (38.7 %) did not. With regard to process modeling, 13 participants (41.9 %) had already worked with process models while 17 (54.8 %) had not. One participant did not answer the question.

5.1   Results and Discussion

Figure 4 shows the average expressiveness rating (5 is best) across all participants for the nine evaluated visualization types. We then assessed if experience with graphs and process models influenced the rating of the expressiveness of the different visualizations using two separate one-way MANOVAs. In the former

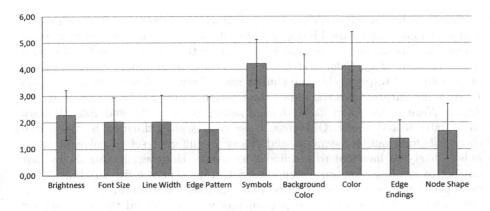

Fig. 4. Average expressiveness rating across all participants for each of the nine visualizations (error bars represent standard deviation).

case, no statistically significant difference in the rating of the visualizations could be observed ($F(9, 21) = 2.224, p = .063$). However, there was a statistically significant difference in the rating of *Font Size* ($F(1, 28) = 10.845, p = .003$) and *Line Width* ($F(1, 28) = 5.449, p = .027$) if prior experience with process models was taken into account. Participants who worked with process models before rated these two visualizations considerably lower than people who did not. Specifically, $M = 1.46, SD = .66$ compared to $M = 2.35, SD = .79$ in case of *Font Size* and $M = 1.54, SD = .66$ compared to $M = 2.35, SD = 1.11$ for the *Line Width* visualization.

After the participants had seen all nine visualizations they had to rank them from best (9) to worst (1). Analysis of the ranking with a Friedman test revealed a rank-ordered preference for the visualizations, $\chi^2(8) = 155.84, p < .001$, with *Color* being the most highly ranked visualization with a mean rank of 7.97, followed by *Symbols* (7.50) and *Background Color* (6.87). *Node Shape*, *Edge Endings*, and *Edge Pattern* where the lowest ranked with a mean rank of 2.65, 2.58, and 2.39 respectively. *Brightness*, *Line Width*, and *Font Size* received moderate mean rankings of 5.77, 4.79, and 4.48. In general this ranking reflects the average expressiveness rating of the individual visualizations. Due to space limitations we will focus on the three top and lowest ranked visualizations in the following. Post hoc analysis with Wilcoxon signed-rank tests and a Bonferroni corrected p-value of 0.0014 between all pairs of visualizations showed no significant differences in the ranking of the *Color* and *Symbols* visualization ($Z = -1.66, p = .098$) as well as between the *Background Color* and *Symbols* visualization ($Z = -1.77, p = .077$). Differences in the ranking of the three lowest ranked visualizations were also statistically insignificant. It is noticeable that visualizations which only depicted changes of either nodes or edges were ranked lowest. This is, however, in line with the participants preference (77.4 %) to use the same visualization of changes for both, nodes and edges.

To assess how much participants agree on which visual element should represent which marking we used Krippendorffs' alpha (α) as a measure of inter-rater agreement. The highest agreement was found for the *Symbols* visualization with $\alpha = .742$ followed by *Color* and *Background Color* with almost identical values of .575 and .57 respectively. The similar result between *Color* and *Background Color* is not surprising as the same colors have been used in both visualizations. Again, *Node Shape* ($\alpha = .095$), *Edge Endings* ($\alpha = .053$), and *Edge Pattern* ($\alpha = .001$) scored lowest. Of course, these results are influenced by the actual choice of, for example, symbols and colors. A different set of colors or symbols is likely to have led to a different outcome. However, it also shows that our set of symbols was quite well chosen to represent the five markings. The poor performance of the latter three visualizations is also in line with the qualitative feedback by some of the participants who considered the edge endings to be *not suitable* or *not very meaningful and hard to discern in large graphs* (2 participants). Similarly, line patterns were also perceived as *not meaningful* (1 participant).

In summary these results suggest that symbolic visualizations of the markings as well as color coding of edges and nodes are best suited to visualize differences in process models. However, further evaluations should assess which encodings should be used and how these visualizations scale with increasing size of the process models. We suspect, that in large process models it might be challenging to relate symbols to their corresponding edges. Figure 5 shows the example from Fig. 2 by using color coding or symbols.

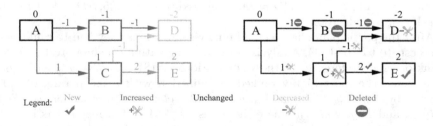

Fig. 5. *Color* and *Symbols* visualization of our example from Fig. 2. Encodings of markings have been chosen according to the participants preference (Color figure online).

6   Limitations

It should be noted that the survey only investigated one specific encoding scheme (e.g., color scheme, set of shapes) for each visualization. The concrete choices of symbols or colors, however, may have an important influence on the result as pointed out above. The results of the survey should thus be rather viewed as an indication of which encodings are promising and which should be investigated in more detail in the future. In addition, the survey mainly assessed the expressiveness and the participants' preferences of the investigated visualizations. Subsequent studies should thus also assess these visualizations in terms of correctness of interpretation. Such studies may also take into account the participant's background in certain business process notations and how these background influences the perception of the utilized difference encodings which has been outside the scope of this study.

7   Conclusion

In this paper we investigated nine different visualizations (based on different visual properties) in order to assess which visualization suits the interpretation of differences in process models best. The findings of our user study show that color coding or symbolic visualizations are very promising for visualizing differences between two process models and their instance traffic. In order to support the users' intuitive understanding we suggest to use a legend describing the encodings. The results presented here have contributed to the implementation of a prototype implementation of the difference graph concept utilizing color coding and symbolic encoding for the ProM framework. An installation guide for the plug-in as well as survey results are available on our website [9].

A possible direction for future work is to conduct further studies to find specific colors and symbols for encoding and to investigate if overloading of nodes and edges is reasonable for different process modeling languages (e.g., overloading *BPMN* with shapes could influence the different semantic meaning). In addition, we were only concerned with visualizing the differences between two models and, optionally, their instance traffic. Therefore another interesting topic for future work would be the visualization of process evolution, for example, to visualize how a process evolves over the period of one year.

Acknowledgments. Simone Kriglstein was supported by CVAST (funded by the Austrian Federal Ministry of Science, Research, and Economy in the exceptional Laura Bassi Centres of Excellence initiative, project nr: 822746).

References

1. van der Aalst, W.M.P.: Business alignment: using process mining as a tool for delta analysis and conformance testing. Requir. Eng. **10**(3), 198–211 (2005)
2. van der Aalst, W.M.P.: Process Mining: Discovery, Conformance and Enhancement of Business Processes. Springer Science & Business Media, Heidelberg (2011)
3. van der Aalst, W.M.P.: A decade of business process management conferences: personal reflections on a developing discipline. In: Barros, A., Gal, A., Kindler, E. (eds.) BPM 2012. LNCS, vol. 7481, pp. 1–16. Springer, Heidelberg (2012)
4. Albrecht, M., Estrella-Balderrama, A., Geyer, M., Gutwenger, C., Klein, K., Kohlbacher, O., Schulz, M.: Visually comparing a set of graphs. In: Graph Drawing with Applications to Bioinformatics and Social Sciences. Dagstuhl Seminar Proceedings, vol. 08191 (2008)

5. Andrienko, N., Andrienko, G.: Exploratory Analysis of Spatial and Temporal Data: A Systematic Approach. Springer, Heidelberg (2005)
6. Archambault, D.: Structural differences between two graphs through hierarchies. In: Proceedings of Graphics Interface, pp. 87–94. Canadian Inf. Processing Society (2009)
7. Bertin, J.: Semiology of Graphics: Diagrams, Networks, Maps/Jacques Bertin; Translated By William J. Berg. University of Wisconsin Press, Madison (1983)
8. Erten, C., Harding, P.J., Kobourov, S.G., Wampler, K., Yee, G.: GraphAEL: graph animations with evolving layouts. In: Liotta, G. (ed.) GD 2003. LNCS, vol. 2912, pp. 98–110. Springer, Heidelberg (2004)
9. Gall, M., Rinderle-Ma, S.: Differencegraph (2015). http://gruppe.wst.univie.ac.at/projects/diffgraph/
10. Genon, N., Heymans, P., Amyot, D.: Analysing the cognitive effectiveness of the BPMN 2.0 Visual notation. In: Malloy, B., Staab, S., van den Brand, M. (eds.) SLE 2010. LNCS, vol. 6563, pp. 377–396. Springer, Heidelberg (2011)
11. Green, M.: Toward a perceptual science of multidimensional data visualization: Bertin and beyond. ERGO/GERO Human Factors Science (1998)
12. Kabicher, S., Kriglstein, S., Rinderle-Ma, S.: Visual change tracking for business process models. In: Jeusfeld, M., Delcambre, L., Ling, T.-W. (eds.) ER 2011. LNCS, vol. 6998, pp. 504–513. Springer, Heidelberg (2011)
13. Kriglstein, S., Wallner, G., Rinderle-Ma, S.: A visualization approach for difference analysis of process models and instance traffic. In: Daniel, F., Wang, J., Weber, B. (eds.) BPM 2013. LNCS, vol. 8094, pp. 219–226. Springer, Heidelberg (2013)
14. Küster, J.M., Gerth, C., Förster, A., Engels, G.: Detecting and resolving process model differences in the absence of a change log. In: Dumas, M., Reichert, M., Shan, M.-C. (eds.) BPM 2008. LNCS, vol. 5240, pp. 244–260. Springer, Heidelberg (2008)
15. Mackinlay, J.: Automating the design of graphical presentations of relational information. ACM Trans. Graph. 5(2), 110–141 (1986)
16. Moody, D., van Hillegersberg, J.: Evaluating the visual syntax of UML: an analysis of the cognitive effectiveness of the UML family of diagrams. In: Gašević, D., Lämmel, R., Van Wyk, E. (eds.) SLE 2008. LNCS, vol. 5452, pp. 16–34. Springer, Heidelberg (2009)
17. Porst, R.: Fragebogen. Ein Arbeitsbuch, 3rd edn. VS Verlag für Sozialwissenschaften, Wiesbaden (2011)
18. Rozinat, A., van der Aalst, W.: Conformance checking of processes based on monitoring real behavior. Inf. Syst. 33(1), 64–95 (2008)
19. Soto, M., Münch, J.: Process model difference analysis for supporting process evolution. In: Richardson, I., Runeson, P., Messnarz, R. (eds.) EuroSPI 2006. LNCS, vol. 4257, pp. 123–134. Springer, Heidelberg (2006)
20. Wang, Z., Wen, L., Wang, J., Wang, S.: TAGER: transition-labeled graph edit distance similarity measure on process models. In: Meersman, R., Panetto, H., Dillon, T., Missikoff, M., Liu, L., Pastor, O., Cuzzocrea, A., Sellis, T. (eds.) OTM 2014. LNCS, vol. 8841, pp. 184–201. Springer, Heidelberg (2014)

Bitemporal Support for Business Process Contingency Management

John Wondoh[1]([email]), Georg Grossmann[1], Dragan Gasevic[2], Manfred Reichert[3], Michael Schrefl[4], and Markus Stumptner[1]

[1] University of South Australia, Adelaide, Australia
john.wondoh@mymail.unisa.edu.au, {georg.grossmann,mst}@cs.unisa.edu.au
[2] University of Edinburgh, Edinburgh, UK
dgasevic@acm.org
[3] Ulm University, Ulm, Germany
manfred.reichert@uni-ulm.de
[4] Johannes Kepler University of Linz, Linz, Austria
schrefl@dke.uni-linz.ac.at

Abstract. Modern organisations are increasingly moving from traditional monolithic business systems to environments where more and more tasks are outsourced to third party providers. Therefore, processes must operate in an open and dynamic environment in which the management of time plays a crucial role. Handling time, however, remains a challenging issue yet to be fully addressed. Traditional processing systems only consider business events in a single time dimension, but are unable to handle bitemporal events: events in two time dimensions. Recently, back-end systems have started to provide increased support for handling bitemporal events, but these enhanced capabilities have not been carried through to business process management systems. In this paper, we consider the possible relationships that exist between bitemporal properties of events and we show how these relationships affect a business process. In addition, we demonstrate how bitemporal events can be handled to prevent certain undesired effects on the business process.

Keywords: Bitemporal events · Business process design · Business rules · Process reconfiguration

1 Introduction

Time is an essential aspect in business process modelling and, therefore, has gained much attention over the years [6,7,9]. Business process management systems (BPMSs) need to reflect what is happening in the real world in a timely manner. The ability to model temporal dimensions of the real world within BPMSs is important to enable business processes to be time-aware, flexible and adaptive. Events and objects are the main parts of a business process captured in temporal databases. In general, a temporal database is a database system that supports time perspectives and, thus, is able to manage time-varying data [8,11].

© Springer International Publishing Switzerland 2015
M.A. Jeusfeld and K. Karlapalem (Eds.): ER 2015 Workshops, LNCS 9382, pp. 109–118, 2015.
DOI: 10.1007/978-3-319-25747-1_11

An event occurs at a specific point in time while an object exists within a time interval. We focus on business events as they can be used to trigger and control the execution of business processes. In addition, events can be used to monitor the progress of business processes.

There are two main time dimensions in temporal databases as discussed in [5,13]: (i) *business time (or valid time)* captures the time a fact becomes true in reality; (ii) *system time (or transaction time)* records the time the fact was captured in a database. A *bitemporal database* captures both business time and system time.

Traditional BPMSs are built to handle ideal situations where it is assumed that there are no system outages nor communication delays that can result in delayed event consumption [2,15]. This results in three main problems with traditional systems:

1. Events are considered in only a single time dimension and are ill-equipped to handle situations that require the analysis of two time dimensions.
2. In a distributed event-based system, the difference between the time an event is sent by an external system and the time the event is received by a local system is not considered.
3. Delays in processing an event after it has been received are not considered.

Consider the scenario where home care is provided by an organisation to some patients discharged from hospitals. Work in such organisations is planned well in advance at a higher level. Typically, workplace legislation requires the schedules for staff to be in place weeks in advance. This is often produced by an automated scheduling tool based on optimisation software that must consider many different factors such as: general skill level of the medical personnel; required level of support for the patient; minimum travel distance of medical personnel to patients residence; and the same set of medical personnel for a given patient to establish a relationship with the patient.

However, once in place, the actual schedules are subject to frequent disruption due to variation in the timing of real world events. For example, a patient scheduled for home care might be discharged from the hospital earlier than expected. The moment this becomes known, the organisation must react to this contingency by making adjustments to its original schedule. Notably, these changes do not require repeating the entire scheduling process as that would be slow to respond and disruptive to long-term planning. Instead, the BPMS should be adaptive and flexible enough to incorporate these changes on the fly.

A concrete scenario is shown in Fig. 1. At system time st_1, a patient is scheduled to be discharged at business time bt_1. Following this, regular home care is scheduled for business times bt_2, bt_3 and bt_4. Further, assume that the patient is discharged from the hospital earlier (at time bt_0) compared to the scheduled time (bt_1). In addition, this fact is updated in the hospital system at st_2, which may not be immediately communicated to the home care organisation. Once the new discharge time is known to the home care organisation, it will have to prepare and provide home care for the patient within a shorter time interval.

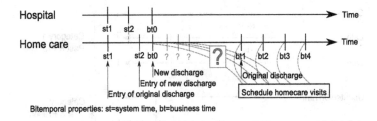

Fig. 1. Bitemporal scenario in hospital–home care process

A lack of support for two time dimensions in business processes may result in delayed reactions to discrepancies, inappropriate actions being taken, and contract and legal issues in inter-organisational processes. Moreover, the external system time and the processing time of an event must be considered during decision making. Considering bitemporal properties of events introduces additional complexity to the execution of business processes, which traditional BPMS are incapable of handling.

This paper addresses the issue of discrepancies between system time and business time by providing bitemporal support for handling two time dimensions within business processes. We first provide a classification of the relationships between system time and business time as well as the external system and processing system time of an event. We proceed to discuss the impact of these relationships to a business process and our approach to handling them.

The remainder of this paper is organised as follows: Sect. 2 discusses bitemporal properties of business events and the permitted relationships that exist between them. Section 3 presents an approach to handling these relationships in BPMSs. Related works are discussed in Sects. 4 and 5 concludes the paper and discusses future work.

2   Bitemporal Properties of Events

This section addresses the relationships permitted between bitemporal properties of events and how these relationships affect business processes. We first consider the possible relationships that exist between the system time and the business time of an event and introduce further considerations.

2.1   Bitemporal Property Categorisation

Different relationships may exist between the system and business time of an event. Each relationship affects the business process in a particular way. We sub-divide these relationships into four main categories based on their time of occurrence as well as when updates are applied to them. These categories, as shown in Fig. 2, illustrate how bitemporal property relationships are different in past and present situations as compared to future ones. In addition, it shows

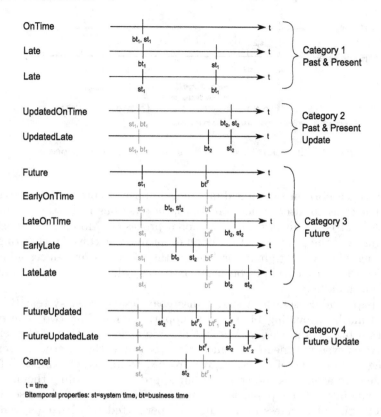

Fig. 2. Relationship between system time and business time

the implications of these events being updated. This will equip business process designers with the knowledge of how to handle each type of relationship.

Category 1 (Past and Present). First, we consider the three basic relationships that exist between business and system time of an event occurring within a business process. Assuming e is a bitemporal event that has occurred with properties st_1 and bt_1, then by comparing the bitemporal properties of the event, two relationships can be derived: $bt_1 = st_1$ and $bt_1 \neq st_1$. The former represents *OnTime*, which indicates that system time is equal to business time, i.e., the event is detected in the real world at the same time it is captured in the database system. A late event, $bt_1 \neq st_1$, may be the result of an event being recorded in a database some time after it has occurred in the real world ($bt_1 < st_1$). It may also result when an event has already been captured within a database before becoming true in the real world ($bt_1 > st_1$). However, for the sake of simplification, we shall only consider the first type of late events for the rest of the discussion. A late event may be a result of delayed detection of the event which may result in delayed processing of the event and, consequently, deadlocks within the process. An event may not be processed at all or may be considered irrelevant if the BPMS has no late event handling capabilities.

Category 2 (Past and Present Update). An event that has already occurred within a business process may be updated when additional information is obtained about the event or when some information needs to be changed. In this category, we consider updates applied to events in Category 1. Once the update has occurred, the original business and system time (bt_1, st_1) will change to their respective new times (bt_2, st_2). We assume that the original event is an OnTime event, even though this may not always be the case. We draw a distinction between *UpdatedOnTime* and *UpdatedLate* as shown in Fig. 2. UpdatedOnTime means the new business and system time are equal, while UpdatedLate has a system time that is later than its business time.

Category 3 (Future). Within business processes, certain events are planned to occur in the future or expected to happen sometime in the future. These events, denoted as future events, have a business time that is in the future. We denote such a time as bt^F such that $bt^F > \text{NOW}$, where NOW is the present wall clock time. Being able to capture future events and changes that can occur to these events during business process execution is essential to managing contingencies within the process. The relationships in this category corresponds to changes in the business time as events occur in the real world.

1. *Future*: A future event is an event that has not yet occurred in the real world.
2. *EarlyOnTime*: A future event occurs at an earlier time w.r.t its planned time. The system time, st_1, is updated with a new timestamp, st_2 and the future business time, bt^F, is replaced by an earlier time, bt_0. The system is notified immediately about the change in the business time, i.e., $(st_2 = bt_0) \wedge (bt_0 < bt^F) \wedge (st_2 > st_1)$. For example, a patient is discharge from the hospital earlier than the expected time and this fact is updated in the home care organisation system immediately.
3. *LateOnTime*: A future event that occurs at a time later than its expected time. Its system time, st_1, is updated to st_2 and the future business time, bt^F, is replaced with bt_2. The system is notified immediately about the change in the business time, i.e., $(st_2 = bt_2) \wedge (bt_2 > bt^F) \wedge (st_2 > st_1)$. For example, a patient is discharge from the hospital later than expected and this fact is updated in the home care organisation system immediately.
4. *EarlyLate*: same as 2 (EarlyOnTime) except that the system is notified late about the change in business time, i.e., $(st_2 > bt_0) \wedge (bt_0 < bt^F) \wedge (st_2 > st_1)$. For example, the patient is discharged at an earlier time than expected but the home care system is updated after fact.
5. *LateLate*: same as 3 (LateOnTime) except that st_2 occurs sometime after bt_2, i.e., $(st_2 > bt_2) \wedge (bt_2 > bt^F) \wedge (st_2 > st_1)$. For example, the patient is discharged at a later time than expected and the home care system is updated after the fact.

Category 4 (Future Update). In business processes, updates can be made to a future event before its occurrence. For example, the home care organisation may receive an update to a home care request event sent by a hospital. This update may notify the home care organisation that the planned discharge day of the patient has been extended or the patient has recovered fully and will no longer need any home care services. If this occurs, the event information is updated and its original system time is updated to a new system time. The future business time may change to an earlier or later future time with respect to the original future time as shown in Category 4 of Fig. 2. There are three relationship types in this category: *FutureUpdated*, *FutureUpdatedLate*, and *Cancel*. For FutureUpdated, the update is made before the future business time bt_1^F, and the system time is updated from st_1 to st_2, i.e., $st_2 < bt_1^F$. A new future business time may be set, which may be earlier, bt_0^F or later, bt_2^F with respect to bt_1^F. FutureUpdatedLate is similar to FutureUpdated, except that the update occurs after bt_1^F, i.e., $st_2 < bt_1^F$. A later business time is set which may be a future time bt_2^F. The future event can also be prevented from happening by cancelling it, in which case bt_1^F becomes irrelevant and st_1 is updated to st_2 (timestamp corresponding to when the cancellation took place).

2.2   Local and External System Time

So far, we have categorised and discussed only the relationships that exist between the business and system time of an event. In a distributed event-based system, however, discrepancies may also exist between the time an event was produced and when it is detected within a BPMS. For instance, home care services requested for a patient by a hospital may be received by the home care organisation hours after it was sent. In addition, an update of the request that may potentially change actions being taken within the process may be received at a later time than it was sent. As discussed earlier, this may result in delayed reactions to discrepancies, inappropriate actions being taken, and contract or legal issues in an inter-organisational process. Therefore, this discrepancy needs to be accounted for. Events in a distributed event-based system consist of two system times, i.e st_e and st_l, where st_e is the system time of the event producer (*external system time*) and st_l is the system time registered locally in the event consumer (*local system time*). When an event is received by a local system at the moment it is sent by an external system, then $st_l = st_e$. On the other hand, $st_l > st_e$ indicates that the event was received late. Since these two system times may differ due to system outages and delayed or disrupted communication, we need to consider them both during the execution of business processes.

2.3   Processing Time

The time at which an event is processed constitutes an important temporal aspect to be considered in a BPMS since events are not always processed immediately upon receiving them. In other words, an event may be processed either immediately when it is received or it may be processed late. Delayed event processing may be either planned or unplanned. Planned delays include event queuing systems and event prioritization, whereas unplanned delays include communication disruption and system outages. Either type of delay, however, requires the consideration of the time at which the event was received during event processing. This is important for ensuring that correct event records are maintained as well as for avoiding violation of temporal requirements.

Let us denote the time at which an event e is processed within a business process by st_p. In turn, st_l is the local system time, which is the time at which the event is received by the system. The permitted relationship between these two times is as follows: $st_p \geq st_l$. That is, an event cannot be processed before it is received. If $st_p = st_l$ then the event is processed immediately, otherwise if $st_p > st_l$ then the event is processed late.

3   Managing Bitemporal Events for Process Control

Information from bitemporal event properties in combination with artifact structure and process execution information such as execution traces, can increase the automation of contingency management. In this section, we present an overview of our proposed architecture for bitemporal event-driven process control. We adopt the approach presented in [3,4] for achieving dynamic service reconfiguration. Figure 3 illustrates the main components of our architecture capable of managing bitemporal events and indicates the information flow between them.

3.1   Business Process Design

At this stage, the business process is designed ensuring that the process specifications and temporal requirements of the process are taken into consideration. A process specification provides a description of how the process should behave by providing the design requirements of the entire process. The entire process model must comply to the specification of the process provided. Temporal requirements of a business process are time constraints put in place by the business process designer. For example, in our home care process, temporal requirements include: begin provision of services to home care patient one day after discharged from hospital, and care workers must not be more than 15 min late to their respected patients. Measures must be put in place to ensure that these requirements are not violated. Business rules are also specified at this stage and they must ensure that the specifications and temporal requirements of the process are not violated.

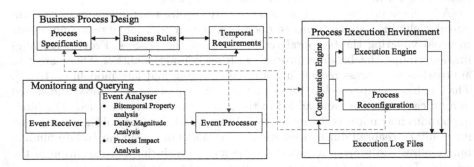

Fig. 3. Dynamic bitemporal event handling architecture

3.2   Monitoring and Querying

The monitoring and querying component is responsible for receiving, analysing and processing events within the business process. The subcomponents determine the relationships between bitemporal properties and temporal requirements of the process. First, bitemporal event information is obtained by the *Event Receiver* and analysed by the *Event Analyser*. The analyser accesses event bitemporal properties and determines the type of relationship that exists between the properties by taking into account the external system time, local system time and business time of the event. When discrepancies exist between the properties, the magnitude of delay is calculated and the extent to which this delay affects the process is determined. The event processor provides the necessary event information needed for triggering business rules specified in the design stage, provided other conditions of the rule are met. Rules specified for preserving temporal requirements by triggering process reconfiguration utilise the bitemporal information of events to determine the type and extent of reconfiguration required.

3.3   Process Execution Environment

The business process execution environment controls the execution of a business process, manages process instances and re-configures the business process. Bitemporal information obtained from the *Monitoring and Querying* component is used to adapt the process to avoid violating its temporal requirements. The input for the process execution are process specifications, business rules, temporal requirements of the process as well as bitemporal event information. This information is used to determine how the process shall proceed during execution. During process execution, all information pertaining to activities within the process is stored in the execution log file system. This includes information about the state of activities, i.e., it keeps a record of whether an activity has been completed, is in progress, or is uninitiated. This information, the business process design and bitemporal information obtained from the monitoring and querying stage serve as the inputs to the configuration engine. The latter is responsible for deciding how the process should proceed.

A business process model or instance may require rearrangement of its components, elimination of existing components, and/or addition of new components to avoid violating the temporal requirements of the process. Process reconfiguration equips the business process with such functionalities. There are two approaches to process reconfiguration: late binding and late modelling [10,12]. The late binding approach requires that process fragments are created and stored in a process repository and added to the process model when needed. The binding options may not necessarily be available at the design time of the process and may only be realised during execution. Late modelling is similar to late binding but requires the process fragments to be modelled during the execution of the process. The modelled fragments are then added to the process model.

4   Related Work

Temporal support for business processes has been of great interest to the community with most research focusing on preventing violations of temporal constraints in business processes or providing contingencies when they occur. Examples of work in this area include [6,7,9,14]. Lanz et al. [6] defines basic modelling elements for designing time-aware business process schemas. They take into consideration the dynamic nature of process instances and temporal constraints of the process. An approach for avoiding deadline violation during business processes execution is provided in [9], where activities within the process are performed in a flexible and time-aware manner in order to proactively avoid violating the set deadline. None of the above approaches take into consideration the two dimensional nature of time and as such, do not take into account discrepancies that may exist between bitemporal properties of business events. In effect, they do not provide support for the relationship types outlined in Sect. 2 in their approaches.

An approach that considers time in two dimension is presented in [1]. It distinguishes between occurrence time and detection time of an event with the aim of handling uncertainties with event occurrences. This considers the situation where the detection time of an event is known but its exact occurrence time is unknown. In this work, we do not deal with uncertainty because we assume that all the bitemporal information of an event is available.

The most closely related work was presented by Furche et al. [2]. This work investigated bitemporal complex event processing of web events. They distinguished between occurrence time and detection time and proposed an event processing language that can be mapped to standard SQL. The main difference to this work is that they did not consider how this applies to business processes. In addition, they did not draw a distinction between external system time, local system time and processing time of an event and assumed these can be represented by a single system time.

5   Conclusions

This paper introduces the concept of bitemporality of events into business process management. We discuss the permitted relationships that exist between bitemporal properties and how they impact business processes. We proceed to propose a contingency approach to handle these relationships during business process execution so as to avoid violation of temporal requirements. Future work includes implementing the architecture on top of a bitemporal database and evaluating the framework. Furthermore, ACID properties of bitemporal events and bitemporal event correlation in the context of business process management will be considered.

Acknowledgment. This research was partially funded by the Data to Decisions Cooperative Research Centre (D2D CRC).

References

1. Artikis, A., Etzion, O., Feldman, Z., Fournier, F.: Event processing under uncertainty. In: Proceedings of DEBS, pp. 32–43. ACM (2012)
2. Furche, T., Grasso, G., Huemer, M., Schallhart, C., Schrefl, M.: Bitemporal complex event processing of web event advertisements. In: Lin, X., Manolopoulos, Y., Srivastava, D., Huang, G. (eds.) WISE 2013, Part II. LNCS, vol. 8181, pp. 333–346. Springer, Heidelberg (2013)
3. Grossmann, G., Schrefl, M., Stumptner, M.: A conceptual modeling approach for web service composition supporting service re-configuration. In: Proceedings of APCCM, pp. 43–52 (2010)
4. Koetter, F., Kochanowski, M., Kintz, M.: Leveraging model-driven monitoring for event-driven business process control. In: Proceedings of EMoV, pp. 21–33 (2014)
5. Kulkarni, K., Michels, J.E.: Temporal features in SQL:2011. SIGMOD Rec. **41**(3), 34–43 (2012)
6. Lanz, A., Posenato, R., Combi, C., Reichert, M.: Controllability of time-aware processes at run time. In: Meersman, R., Panetto, H., Dillon, T., Eder, J., Bellahsene, Z., Ritter, N., De Leenheer, P., Dou, D. (eds.) ODBASE 2013. LNCS, vol. 8185, pp. 39–56. Springer, Heidelberg (2013)
7. Lanz, A., Weber, B., Reichert, M.: Time patterns for process-aware information systems. Requir. Eng. **19**(2), 113–141 (2014)
8. Mareco, C., Bertossi, L.: Specification and implementation of temporal databases in a bitemporal event calculus. In: Chen, P.P., Embley, D.W., Kouloumdjian, J., Liddle, S.W., Roddick, J.F. (eds.) Advances in Conceptual Modeling. LNCS, vol. 1727. Springer, Heidelberg (1999)
9. Pichler, H., Wenger, M., Eder, J.: Composing time-aware web service orchestrations. In: van Eck, P., Gordijn, J., Wieringa, R. (eds.) CAiSE 2009. LNCS, vol. 5565, pp. 349–363. Springer, Heidelberg (2009)
10. Reichert, M., Rinderle-Ma, S., Dadam, P.: Flexibility in process-aware information systems. In: Jensen, K., van der Aalst, W.M.P. (eds.) Transactions on Petri Nets and Other Models of Concurrency II. LNCS, vol. 5460, pp. 115–135. Springer, Heidelberg (2009)
11. Salzberg, B., Tsotras, V.J.: Comparison of access methods for time-evolving data. ACM Comput. Surv. **31**(2), 158–221 (1999)
12. Schonenberg, H., Mans, R., Russell, N., Mulyar, N., van der Aalst, W.: Process flexibility: a survey of contemporary approaches. In: Albani, A., Barjis, J., Dietz, J.L.G. (eds.) CIAO! 2008. LNBIP, vol. 10, pp. 16–30. Springer, Heidelberg (2008)
13. Snodgrass, R.: Temporal databases. In: Frank, A.U., Campari, I., Formentini, U. (eds.) Theories and Methods of Spatio-Temporal Reasoning in Geographic Space. LNCS, vol. 639, pp. 22–64. Springer, Hiedleberg (1992)
14. Sun, H., Yang, J., Zhao, W., Su, J.: TiCoBTx-Net: a model to manage temporal consistency of service-oriented business collaboration. Serv. Comput. **5**(2), 207–219 (2012)
15. Wieringa, R.J.: Design methods for reactive systems: Yourdon, Statemate, and the UML. Elsevier, San Francisco (2003)

Towards an Extended Metamodel
of Event-Driven Process Chains to Model
Complex Event Patterns

Julian Krumeich$^{(\boxtimes)}$, Nijat Mehdiyev, Dirk Werth, and Peter Loos

Institute for Information Systems (IWi) at the German Research Center
for Artificial Intelligence (DFKI GmbH), Saarbrücken, Germany
{julian.krumeich,nijat.mehdiyev,
dirk.werth,peter.loos}@dfki.de

Abstract. This paper proposes an extension of the Event-driven Process Chain (EPC) metamodel in order to provide means to model complex event patterns within process models. There are some first attempts aiming to graphically depict such patterns; however, none of them focus EPC as a widely-used modeling language, especially in a business-related context. Thus, the paper first of all derives and defines typical complex event patterns and analyzes whether they are representable using standard EPC models. On this basis, a metamodel extension is conceived and additional modeling notations proposed. Finally, the notation is applied on two application examples.

Keywords: Complex event processing · Business process management · Event-driven business process management · Event-driven process chain · Metamodel

1 Introduction

Today, enterprises compete in a globalized world characterized by its constantly changing economic conditions. To be successful in this highly-competitive environment, enterprises are forced to react on threats and opportunities in a timely manner. In this regard, it is a mandatory task to continuously monitor and control business processes towards current business situations. With advancements in system integration and new technologies like the Internet of Things (IoT), real-time information availability, especially in manufacturing operations, has reached a new dimension [1]. This allows for in-depth insights into intra-organizational as well as cross-company business processes. Consequently, myriads of internal and external business events become visible forming increasingly big data [2].

To turn this enormous quantity of low level events (such as single sensor signals) into business value (like a discovery of machinery failures or breakdowns), it is crucial to filter and analyze event streams to detect meaningful patterns that indicate important situations with a decisive impact on the control and efficiency of business processes [3]. With Complex Event Processing (CEP) the required technology to detect such complex event patterns in real-time is already available. In this regard, CEP is considered to be an important driver to further advance the domain of business process management

© Springer International Publishing Switzerland 2015
M.A. Jeusfeld and K. Karlapalem (Eds.): ER 2015 Workshops, LNCS 9382, pp. 119–130, 2015.
DOI: 10.1007/978-3-319-25747-1_12

(BPM) [4]. In the last years, this has motivated numerous research efforts coining the term Event-Driven Business Process Management (ED-BPM) [5].

However, considering existing research, it is still an obstacle to express complex event patterns within business process models in order to transparently illustrate their relation in terms of an event-driven business process control, i.e. describing reactions to complex event occurrences in business processes [6]. Thus, domain experts are struggling to communicate event patterns, which are crucial for business operations, with technical CEP experts and vice versa [6]. Thus, latest research dedicatedly call for integrated event modeling methods, i.e. to specify event patterns and their relations within process models [5]. Conventional, business process modeling languages like Business Process Modeling Notation (BPMN), Event-driven Process Chains (EPC) or Unified Modeling Language (UML) Activity Diagrams cannot express complex event patters such as sequential, temporal or spatial relations between single events [7]. Whereas a few first extensions exist for the BPMN, there is a particular lack regarding a dedicated support in EPC. EPC are a typical starting point for non-technical domain experts to model their associated business processes and are widely used in industry and research [8]. Since complex event patterns originate commonly from business scenarios for which non-technical experts are responsible for [6], EPC represent also a promising means for depicting these patterns in relation to business processes.

To address this research gap, the paper at hand first of all derives and examines characteristic event patterns considered in corresponding literature. Furthermore, the feasibility to model them in standard EPC models is evaluated and last but not least an extended EPC metamodel (incl. a modeling notation) proposed that allows for a comprehensive graphical depiction of the derived event pattern. This should eventually support business and domain experts to express event patterns in process models that can be later on transformed into executable rules consumed by CEP engines.

Hence, this paper applies a design-oriented research approach following the design science research guidelines proposed by [9]. In this regard, the EPC metamodel extension proposed in Sect. 4 represents the underlying design science artifact (*Guideline 1*). The relevance for constructing the underlying artifact and the relating research gap is pointed out in the introductory section as well as by analyzing complex event patterns and their support in EPC (cf. Sect. 3) (*Guideline 2*). To comply with *Guideline 3*, the paper exemplifies the application of the artefact by modeling two complex event patterns based on the extended metamodel in Sect. 5. Following the principle of design as an iterative process (*Guideline 6*), the metamodel extension in general builds upon previously proposed model constructs (cf. Sect. 4). *Guideline 5* was accomplished by outlining the applied research methodology in Sect. 1. Last but not least, the submission of this paper aims at fulfilling *Guideline 7*, the dissemination of research results.

2   Theoretical Foundation and Related Work

Complex Event Processing (CEP) has emerged as a novel event processing technology in addition to alternative approaches such as simple event processing and event stream processing. CEP systems enable to determine potential threats and recognize opportunities in real-time. Alongside being researched intensively as a specific research domain, successful industry applications of CEP can be observed in various fields such as manufacturing, logistic and supply chain processes, financial investment, military, traffic tracking, social sensing and so forth [10]. Integrating CEP with other technologies, namely Business Process Management (BPM), is a challenging task requiring domain knowledge in both areas. The primary purpose of such an integration lays in the potential usage of real-time information gained from distributed systems, services and sensor networks for monitoring, controlling and eventually optimizing business processes. In this regard, CEP enables to initiate new process instances, to stop running ones and to influence their behavior based on recognized event correlations stemming from massive streams of (sensor) data [5].

Event patterns represent templates which specify certain event combinations. They can be classified into various categories such as temporal, spatial, spatial-temporal, trend, modal and basic patterns where each category has various subcategories [11]. These patterns can be provided by experts or being automatically derived using machine learning algorithms. The actual detection of event patterns within continuously streaming data is realized through special predetermined queries. They are enabled by query processing techniques that are more evolved and differ from approaches applied to classical database analysis. To technically describe event patterns and rules dedicated Event Pattern Languages (EPL) are used. Yet there is no language standard, which results in diverse competing approaches [5], such as datastream-oriented languages building upon the Structured Query Language (SQL), production rules or rule-based languages applying Event-Condition-Action (ECA) principles originating from the Business Rule Management (BRM) as well as imperative script languages.

In the business process management domain, several process modeling languages have been proposed in the last two decades [12], such as BPMN, UML Activity Diagrams, EPC and many more. Their common goal is to graphically represent business processes in order to bridge the gap between business and IT perspectives. By providing a transparent view on business processes, process models can be used for optimization purposes and to have a blueprint for their technical implementation. As it is for example expressed by the name of the EPC, incorporating events within the flow of business processes is one key characteristic. However, despite of strong modelling abilities in terms of representing business processes, these languages commonly fall short in depicting complex event patterns as they are considered in the field of CEP [7].

This shortcoming again creates barriers between business and IT perspectives in terms of involving business users and process owners in CEP implementations [6]. Thus, as already pointed out in Sect. 1, methods to achieve an integrated event modeling within business process modeling are required. This could be a starting point for CEP experts to transform complex event patters from a conceptual level into precise and technical CEP specifications, which is more helpful than having them written down in a textual form [6]. Thus, representing complex event patterns in process modeling notations, is a crucial step to take to progress ED-BPM, which has already motivated some research activities in recent years. However, in most cases these contributions propose an extension to BPMN for modeling goals, key performance indicators, high-level events or even whole business situations [13–17]. One recently presented concept copes with the integration of dedicated event stream processing units within the BPMN representation of the overall business process [18]. In contrast, some first approaches explicitly seek a graphical solution for the specification of CEP event patterns [14–16]. Other concepts researched possible integration possibilities of business events [19] or even whole BAM artifacts [20] with e.g. process and/or information models [21].

3   Complex Event Patterns and Their Support in EPC

The paper at hand proposes a metamodel extension of EPC, which is a widely-used process modeling notation both in research and industry. Neither the standard EPC modeling notation [7], nor proposed extension [6], are able to depict event patterns that can be considered as complex ones. Even though simple event relations and hierarchies can for example be described with so-called event-diagrams, in which a complex event (such as "order checked") is decomposed into detailed events (such as "customer data checked" and "product data checked") [22], these aggregations should not be confused

Table 1. Complex event patterns and their support in standard EPC models

	Patterns	Definition	EPC support
Logical Patterns	L1: Event Conjunction	Two or more events have to have taken place in order to trigger complex event L1.	+
	L2: Event Disjunction	Alternative events have to have taken place. In a special case, the occurrence of events needs to be mutually exclusive.	+
	L3: Event Cardinality	One or more events have to have taken place a specified number of times. The number can be fixed, variable or defined by a range.	–
	L4: Event Sequence	Two or more events have to have occurred according to a specified sequence. *EPC support only by modelling them into a sequential flow, however this would contradict to EPC conventions (alternation of events and functions)*	–*
	L5: Event Exclusion	This event pattern is triggered, if one or more events have taken place while one or others have been absence. In this regard, both the occurring and the inhibiting events can be represented through a complex composition. *EPC support only textual via event labeling.*	o*

(Continued)

Table 1. (*Continued*)

Temporal Patterns	T1: Event Time Relation	One or more events have to have occurred within or outside a given time window. Windows can be defined as fixed intervals (e.g. Mon 8am – Fr 5 pm) or event intervals (starting event – [ending event OR expiration time offset = 1 day]).	–
	T2: Absolute Time Relation	One or more events have to have occurred before or after an absolute point in time.	–
Spatial Patterns	S1: Fixed Location	One or more events have to have occurred at a fixed location.	–
	S2: Entity Distance Location	One or more events have to have occurred within a range around a certain location.	–
	S3: Event Distance Location	One or more events have to have occurred at or within a range around a certain event happing.	–
Trend	TP: Trend Pattern	Two or more events have to have occurred that satisfy a (non-)increasing, (non-)decreasing or stable pattern.	–
Data	DP: Data Dependency Pattern	One or more events have to have occurred whose data properties match certain data dependencies. ** EPC support only textual via event labeling.*	o*

Key:	+ is fully supported	o is partly supported	– is not supported

with what is understand with complex event patterns. Although EPC models provide several modeling elements to link events and activities, including logical operators, there is e.g. no means to express temporal or spatial related correlations [23].

Thus, the first step towards an extended EPC metamodel, which is capable to depict complex event patterns, is to identify characteristic event patterns from literature. These patterns of common event correlation are depicted in Table 1. The patterns are mainly derived from [23] which already synthesized a survey on complex events of possible business scenarios as well as a survey on common features of EPL languages. In addition, patterns considered by [11, 12] are added resulting in twelve patterns that also partly contain sub patterns.

Patterns specifically dealing with technical characteristics of CEP engines, such as subscription and consumption time, are omitted from this combination as they will not be of interest to domain experts (cf. Sect. 5 on limitations).

4 EPC Metamodel Extension and Modeling Notation Proposal

In order to provide a possibility to model the event patterns illustrated in Table 1, the standard EPC metamodel has been extended. As a foundation, the standard EPC metamodel proposed by [24] was chosen, which is represented using a UML Class Diagram (cf. Fig. 1, grey elements). Their metamodel is one of the frequently quoted ones and includes all required rudimentary elements [8]. To reduce complexity, elements detailing the element "Function" are omitted as the conceived extension deals with a dedicated "Event" specification; "Functions" are not the focus of interest. In general, EPC models contain at least one "Function" and two "Events", which are reusable in other EPC models. In doing so, each function has one successor and one predecessor "Event" element. Thus, in contrast to "Events", "Functions" are connected with exactly two "Control Flow Connectors", which again can be connected with "Logical Operators".

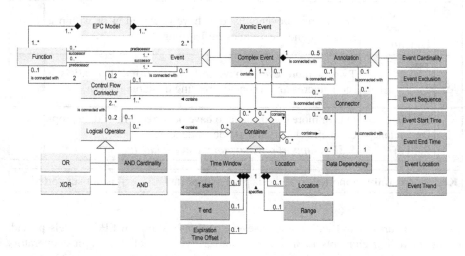

Fig. 1. Extended metamodel of EPC to represent complex events (based on [24])

As pointed out in Table 1—with few exceptions (L1 and L2)—none of the derived event patterns can be represented in standard EPC models. Thus, additional types of modeling element are required (cf. Fig. 1, blue elements). First of all, the generic element "Event" is split into atomic events and complex ones. The latter can be connected with several "Annotations" that will be detailed introduced in Table 2. Furthermore, the metamodel comprises an "AND Cardinality" operator to define certain cardinality restrictions to complex event patterns. Moreover, to express additional constraints in relation to event data, dedicated "Data Dependencies" can be mapped via undirected "Connectors" to "Annotations", "Logical Operators" as well as "Complex Events". In order to specifically represent temporal as well as spatial relations of

Table 2. Description of metamodel extension and proposal of modeling notation

	Relation to Metamodel	**Modeling Notation**
L3: Event Card.	To express event cardinalities in EPC models, "Events" are connected with "Event Cardinality" annotations. These "Annotations" are labeled with the number respectively range of cardinality in square brackets. In case, a complex event pattern needs to have occurred a certain amount of time, the "AND Cardinality" operator is to be used.	
L4: Event Sequence	A specific sequential occurrence of "Events" can be expressed by "Event Sequence" annotations whose order is directly connected to the respective events.	
L5: Event Exclusion	To indicate the necessity of absence of specific events, these events can be connected with "Event Exclusion" annotations.	
T1 & T2: Temporal Patterns	To express temporal relations between "Events" they are combined into "Time Windows" acting as a container. To indicate time intervals, the container is specified by a start time "T start" and an associated end time "T end" (T1). To represent event intervals (T2), an "Event" is allocated as a start event, regarding the time window, and another one as the end event. Optionally, an "Expiration Time Offset" can be added. To visually differentiate between "Time Windows" and "Location" containers, the first one is illustrated with vertical lines as a background pattern symbolizing the temporal process flow in accordance to standard modeling conventions. Furthermore, the detailing property area is modeled on the left side of the container.	

(Continued)

Table 2. (*Continued*)

S1 – S3: Spatial Patterns	In accordance with temporal relations, spatial ones are also expressed by mapping the respective events in a "Location" container. To specify the location at which the event pattern has to have occurred, the container is detailed with a "Location" property (cf. pattern S1). In order to indicate a location range, the container is additionally specified by a "Range" property (cf. pattern S2). To satisfy pattern S3, an event can be allocated by an "Event Location" event in contrast to specify a certain location a priori.	
TP1: Trend Pattern	To define relations between events in terms of a trend pattern, the concerning event whose trend value is under consideration is annotated by "Event Trend" symbols: >> ≙ increasing; << ≙ decreasing; ¬ >> ≙ non-increasing; ¬ << ≙ non-decreasing. Generally, specifying trend patterns is only reasonable if combined with a temporal relation.	

complex events, a dedicated "Container" element is established, which comprises several complex events as well as other concepts. Furthermore, a "Container" itself can be a part of another one and is further specified by "Time Windows" or "Locations" as well as their linked properties.

As an inherent characteristic of "Complex Events", the proposed model elements can be jointly combined in multiple, complex ways (cf. Sect. 5 for examples).

Table 2 explains, how the identified event patterns introduced in Table 1 can be represented using the extended EPC metamodel (excluding L1 and L2 as they are already supported in EPCs) and proposes a corresponding modeling notation.

5   Application Example, Discussion and Limitations

This section illustrates how the previously introduced event patterns can be combined in order to graphically represent complex event patterns that are defined by textual descriptions.

The first example stems from fraud detection, which is a typical application scenario for CEP. As conventional business process engines typically only consider individual events, i.e. "it is checked on a per-message basis if a message matches a registered subscription and only one message is consumed in a *receive* or *onMessage* activity", CEP engines dedicatedly consider event rules, i.e. patterns of events that have to be matched and which may stem from different process instances across time [12]. In this regard, the fraud pattern defines four different conditions that need to be fulfilled in order to assume a case of fraud (cf. Table 3a). To represent this event pattern using the extended EPC metamodel, the event "Incorrectly entered PIN" is connected with cardinality restrictions—in terms of the same cardID as a "Data Dependency" annotated to the event annotation and as a combination of several of these complex events via an "AND Cardinality" operator—and embedded into a combined "Time Window" and "Location" container. In doing so, spatial and temporal relations are represented in an overlapping container, which is also visually represented by a grid pattern for the background of this container (cf. Table 2 regarding background patterns).

Table 3. Examples of complex event patterns and their representation in extended EPC models

Example	a) ATM Fraud Detection	b) Production Line Malfunction
Pattern Description	• at least wrongly entered PIN twice • event occurred more than five times • within a range of 5 km • within 1 hour	• sensor temperature above threshold • increasing trend • for more than 8 sensors • within 5 minutes • at plant 4711
Modeling Example		

As the second example, continuously occurring events from temperature sensors attached to a production line are examined to detect a specified malfunction pattern (cf. Table 3b). In this regard, the event "Sensor temperature above threshold" is connected with an "Event Trend" annotation that is further specified by a "Data Dependency" expressing a trend in increased temperature values. Whereas this event annotation focuses a specific sensor instance defined by a sensorID, the constraint of having more than eight sensors matching this pattern is expressed by an "AND Cardinality" operator connected with a corresponding "Data Dependency". Moreover, this complex event is embedded into an overlapping "Time Window" and "Location" container.

At this point, it should be explicitly pointed out that the proposed metamodel extension is not as expressive as existing CEP languages (cf. Sect. 2). Especially technical issues in terms of CEP implementations are omitted. Nevertheless, there is no claim to have a graphical modeling representation on the same level of detail as technical implementations, neither for business process representations and thus nor for complex event pattern representations in process models. Further, the metamodel does not differentiate the specific type of events (e.g. message, timeout or exception as in BPMN); yet, this can still be expressed in textual way using an associated labeling.

6   Conclusion and Future Work

This paper proposed an extension of the EPC metamodel in order to provide a means to model complex event patterns within process models. In literature, there are some first attempts aiming to graphically depict such patterns; however, none of them focus EPC as a widely-used modeling language, especially in a business-related context. To do so, the paper first of all derived and defined typical complex event patterns and analyzed whether they are representable using standard EPC models. On this basis, a metamodel extension is conceived and additional modeling notations proposed. Finally, the notation is applied on two application examples.

In future work, a set-theoretic definition [8] of the extended metamodel will be conceived to achieve a formal definition of complex event patterns within EPC models. Furthermore, in ongoing research activities, the representation of real-world complex event patterns in the context of the German research project iPRODICT is expedited in order to proof the feasibility of the proposed extension beyond the two application scenarios outlined in Sect. 5 (cf. [25] for more details on the research project). In this regard, the involvement of domain and technical experts in the modeling and usage of extended EPC models will also be evaluated regarding its actual usefulness and understandability. Since EPC models get more expressive through the extension, two views could be provided in a tooling context. One expressive view that visualize complex events in full detail and another one of reduced complexity through graphically differentiating between the model elements "Atomic Event" and "Complex Event". The Complex Event then encapsulates all dedicated extensions such as annotations or containers. In this regard, we are also currently investigating how to integrate the metamodel extension into the ARIS Business Process Analysis Platform.

Another interesting research question will be how to induce complex event patterns out of event stream instances and how to visualize them either using the metamodel proposed in the paper at hand or in others proposed in literature (cf. Sect. 2). Future work will also deal with the transformation of extended EPC models respectively modeled event patterns into templates usable within executable Event Processing Languages (EPL). In this context, we are currently investigating how to build transformation algorithms for the Apama Complex Event Processing Engine. Since the patterns specified in EPC model cannot and should not be as expressive as common EPLs, the respective transformation will result in a first blueprint that has to be detailed and complemented by CEP experts. Yet the main goal of modeling complex events in

EPC is warranted as domain knowledge by business experts can be depicted in process models that can then be reused by CEP experts.

Acknowledgements. This research was funded in part by the German Federal Ministry of Education and Research under grant numbers 01IS12050 (project IDENTIFY) and 01IS14004A (project iPRODICT).

References

1. Bruns, R., Dunkel, J.: Event-Driven Architecture: Softwarearchitektur für ereignisgesteuerte Geschäftsprozesse. Springer, Berlin (2010)
2. Dhar, V., Jarke, M., Laartz, J.: Big data. Bus. Inf. Syst. Eng. **6**, 257–259 (2014)
3. Luckham, D.: Event Processing for Business. John Wiley & Sons, Hoboken (2012)
4. Dixon, J., Jones, T.: Hype Cycle for Business Process Management. https://www.gartner.com/doc/1751119
5. Krumeich, J., Weis, B., Werth, D., Loos, P.: Event-driven business process management: where are we now? Bus. Process Manag. J. **20**, 615–633 (2014)
6. Schimmelpfennig, J., Mayer, D., Walter, P., Seel, C.: Involving business users in the design of complex event processing systems. In: BTW 2011. LNI, vol. 180, pp. 606–615 (2011)
7. Vidackovic, K.: A method for the development of dynamic business processes based on event processing (PhD thesis). Fraunhofer IAO, Stuttgart (2014)
8. Houy, C., Fettke, P., Loos, P.: Zur Evolution der Ereignisgesteuerten Prozesskette. In: Multikonferenz Wirtschaftsinformatik 2014, pp. 1020–1033 (2014)
9. Hevner, A.R., March, S.T., Park, J., Ram, S.: Design science in information systems reesearch. MIS Q. **28**, 75–105 (2004)
10. Aggarwal, C.: An introduction to sensor data analytics. In: Aggarwal, C. (ed.) Managing and Mining Sensor Data, pp. 1–8. Springer, Berlin (2013)
11. Etzion, O., Niblett, P.: Event Processing in Action. Manning Publications, Greenwich (2011)
12. Barros, A., Decker, G., Grosskopf, A.: Complex events in business processes. In: Abramowicz, W. (ed.) BIS 2007. LNCS, vol. 4439, pp. 29–40. Springer, Heidelberg (2007)
13. Baumgrass, A., Herzberg, N., Meyer, A., Weske, M.: BPMN extension for business process monitoring. In: EMISA 2014. LNI, vol. 234, pp. 85–98 (2014)
14. Decker, G., Grosskopf, A., Barros, A.: A graphical notation for modeling complex events in business processes. In: 11th IEEE International Enterprise Distributed Object Computing Conference, pp. 27–36. IEEE Press, New York (2007)
15. Estruch, A., Heredia Álvaro, J.A.: Event-driven manufacturing process management approach. In: Barros, A., Gal, A., Kindler, E. (eds.) BPM 2012. LNCS, vol. 7481, pp. 120–133. Springer, Heidelberg (2012)
16. Kunz, S., Fickinger, T., Prescher, J., Spengler, K.: Managing complex event processes with business process modeling notation. In: Mendling, J., Weidlich, M., Weske, M. (eds.) BPMN 2010. LNBIP, vol. 67, pp. 78–90. Springer, Heidelberg (2010)
17. Koetter, F., Kochanowski, M.: A model-driven approach for event-based business process monitoring. In: La Rosa, M., Soffer, P. (eds.) BPM Workshops 2012. LNBIP, vol. 132, pp. 378–389. Springer, Heidelberg (2013)
18. Appel, S., Frischbier, S., Freudenreich, T., Buchmann, A.: Event stream processing units in business processes. In: Daniel, F., Wang, J., Weber, B. (eds.) BPM 2013. LNCS, vol. 8094, pp. 187–202. Springer, Heidelberg (2013)

19. Döhring, M., Karg, L., Godehardt, E., Zimmermann, B.: The convergence of workflows, business rules and complex events. In: 12th International Conference on Enterprise Information Systems, pp. 338–343 (2010)
20. Friedenstab, J.P., Janiesch, C., Matzner, M., Müller, O.: Extending BPMN for business activity monitoring. In: Proceedings of the 45th Hawaii International Conference on System Sciences, pp. 4158–4167. IEEE Computer Society, Washington D.C. (2011)
21. Mulo, E., Zdun, U., Dustdar, S.: Domain-specific language for event-based compliance monitoring in process-driven SOAs. SOCA **7**, 59–73 (2013)
22. Loos, P., Allweyer, T.: Process orientation and object-orientation. In: Publications of the Institute for Information Systems, Paper 144. Saarland University, Saarbrücken (1998)
23. Kim, H., Oussena, S.: A case study on modeling of complex event processing in enterprise architecture. In: 14th International Conference on Enterprise Information Systems, pp. 173–180 (2012)
24. Korherr, B., List, B.: A UML 2 profile for event-driven process chains. In: Tjoa, A.M., Xu, L., Chaudhry, S.S. (eds.) Research and Practical Issues of Enterprise Information Systems 2006. IFIP, vol. 205, pp. 161–172. Springer, Heidelberg (2006)
25. Krumeich, J., Werth, D., Loos, P., Schimmelpfennig, J., Jacobi, S.: Advanced planning and control of manufacturing processes in steel industry through big data analytics: case study and architecture proposal. In: IEEE International Conference on Big Data, pp. 16–24 (2014)

Modeling and Management of Big Data

Preface of the Fourth International Workshop on Modeling and Management of Big Data (MoBiD 2015)

Due to enormous amounts of data present and growing in the Web and other data sources such as sensors and social networks, there has been an increasing interest in incorporating these huge amounts of external and unstructured data, normally referred to as Big Data, into traditional applications. This necessity has made that traditional database systems and processing need to evolve and accommodate them to this new situation. We view that several key themes with the Big Data trend include (i) developing an architecture for a big data environment to conceptualize goals, tasks, and problem-solving methods to apply to domains; (ii) exploring problem-solving methods for big data;(iii) managing big data projects to discover business values; (iv) using a cloud for managing large-scale external and internal data; and (v) providing an easy-to-use but powerful services to access/manage/analyze the big data in the cloud.

This new era of Big Data and cloud environment requires conceptualization and methods to effectively manage big data and accomplish intended business goals. Thus, the objective of MoBiD'15 is to be an international forum for exchanging ideas on the latest and best proposals for modeling and managing big data in this new data-drive paradigm. Papers focusing on novel applications and using conceptual modeling approaches for any aspects of Big Data such as MapReduce, Hadoop and its ecosystems, Big Data Analytics, social networking, security and privacy, data science approaches, etc. are highly encouraged. The workshop is a forum for researchers and practitioners who are interested in the different facets related to the use of the conceptual modeling approaches for the development of next generation applications based on Big Data.

The workshop has been announced in the main announcement venues and attracted papers from nine different countries distributed all over the world: Italy, Spain, Sweden, Russia, France, Cube, Germany, Switzerland and Netherlands. We have finally received 11 papers and the Program Committee has selected 5 papers, making an acceptance rate of 45%. The workshop also includes a keynote by Paolo Atzeni.

We would like to express our gratitude to the Program Committee members for their hard work in reviewing papers, the authors for submitting their papers, and the ER 2015 organizing committee for supporting our workshop. MoBiD'15 was organized within the framework of the following project GEODAS-BI (TIN2012-37493-C03-03) from the Ministry of Economy and Competitiveness (MINECO)

July 2015

Il-Yeol Song
Juan Trujillo
David Gil
Alejandro Maté
Program Co-Chairs
MoBiD'15

Models for NoSQL Databases: A Contradiction?

Paolo Atzeni[✉]

Università Roma Tre, Rome, Italy
atzeni@dia.uniroma3.it

NoSQL systems have gained their popularity for many reasons, including the flexibility they provide with modeling, which tries to relax the rigidity provided by the relational model and by the other structured models. The talk will discuss how traditional notions related to modeling can be useful in this context as well, both in the search for standardization and uniform access (as the variety of systems and models can create difficulties in developers and in their organizations) and in the support to generic approaches to logical and physical design (with the idea that there are some principles that apply to most systems, despite the significant heterogeneity).

The talk will be based on two recent papers coauthored by the speaker, the first on a metamodeling approach to a common interface to non relational systems [1] and the other on a design methodology for NoSQL systems, based on a system-independent ("logical") representation of the application data [2].

References

1. Atzeni, P., Bugiotti, F., Rossi, L.: Uniform access to NoSQL systems. Inf. Syst. **43**, 117–133 (2014)
2. Bugiotti, F., Cabibbo, L., Atzeni, P., Torlone, R.: Database design for NoSQL systems. In: ER 2014, pp. 223–231 (2014)

© Springer International Publishing Switzerland 2015
M.A. Jeusfeld and K. Karlapalem (Eds.): ER 2015 Workshops, LNCS 9382, p. 133, 2015.
DOI: 10.1007/978-3-319-25747-1_13

A Food Recommendation System Based on Semantic Annotations and Reference Prescriptions

Devis Bianchini[✉], Valeria De Antonellis, and Michele Melchiori

Department of Information Engineering, University of Brescia,
Via Branze, 38, 25123 Brescia, Italy
{devis.bianchini,valeria.deantonellis,michele.melchiori}@unibs.it

Abstract. Food recommendation, as well as searching for health-related information, presents particular characteristics unlike conventional recommender systems, since it often has educational purposes, to improve behavioural habits of users. In this paper, we present a menu generation system that uses a recipe dataset and annotations to recommend menus according to user's preferences. Moreover, reference prescription schemes are defined to guide our system for suggesting suitable choices. Firstly, relevant recipes are selected by content-based retrieval, based on comparisons among features used to annotate both users' profiles and recipes. Then, menus are generated using the selected recipes and are ranked taking into account also prescription schemes.

1 Introduction

Recommendation systems find information of interests, properly customized according to the users' own preferences [1]. This is valid also for specific application domains, such as health and nutrition, where any choice made upon automatically provided recommendations might have an impact on users' health and wellness. Existing approaches for recommending food and health-related information consider four main aspects, namely personal and cultural preferences, health and religion constraints [2] to implement a food recommendation approach. Nevertheless, to the best of our knowledge educational purposes have not been taken into account yet. Personalized Health Information System (PHIRS) [3] is a recommendation system for health information that matches the user's profile against the retrieved health information, without considering culture and religion in the profile. CarePlan [4] is a semantic representation framework for healthcare plans that mixes the patients' health conditions, personal preferences, the medical knowledge and clinical pathways, but ignores other aspects, such as personalization coming from educational health information, user's culture and religion, that impact on the food choice. Same limitations affect the system described in [5]. Other systems do not address personalization at all, such as the HealthFinland project [6], a smart semantic portal that helps the users to find relevant health information using simple keywords instead of

© Springer International Publishing Switzerland 2015
M.A. Jeusfeld and K. Karlapalem (Eds.): ER 2015 Workshops, LNCS 9382, pp. 134–143, 2015.
DOI: 10.1007/978-3-319-25747-1_14

medical vocabularies. This variety of approaches demonstrates that users' profiling, in particular for sectors and domains such as the food and health recommendation, is mainly addressed in an ad-hoc manner, without aiming at providing some educational effect on the users.

In this paper, we present a menu generation system that uses a recipe dataset and annotations to recommend menus. Given the specific characteristics of food recommendation systems, reference prescription schemes are used to guide our system for suggesting suitable choices. Firstly, relevant recipes are selected by content-based retrieval, based on comparisons among features used to annotate both users' profiles and recipes. Then, candidate menus are generated, using the selected recipes, and are ranked also taking into account reference prescription schemes. The system is being developed and tested within a food recommendation regional project funded in Lombardy region, Italy[1]. Therefore, the contribution of this paper mainly relies on the innovative recommendation method, that is *education-oriented*, aiming at satisfying both user's preferences and reference prescriptions.

The paper is organized as follows: Sect. 2 provides detailed definitions about the recommendation model; in Sect. 3 we describe the menu generation procedure; Sect. 4 discusses preliminary experimental results; finally, in Sect. 5 we sketch conclusions and future work.

2 Recommendation Model

Let's consider, for example, Jasmine, who is looking for recipe suggestions to have lunch during her working hours. Jasmine is registered within a food recommender system, where she has an associated profile. Jasmine declared a preference for having meat during lunches. She suffers from long-term diseases, such as diabetes and high-blood-pressure, therefore white meat is more advisable. She belongs to the Islamic religion, so recommendations about any food that contains alcohol or pork are not acceptable, since this food is prohibited to Muslims. Other characteristics emerge if she is looking for recipes to cook at home, for which ingredients and cooking procedures assume a specific relevance. Each factor may be represented through a feature, that in turn might assume different values. Features can be used both to characterize the recommended items (e.g., recipes, dishes) and to represent users' profiles. Moreover, feature matching can be based either on the feature values contained in a request for suggestions by the user (short-term feature matching), or on the frequency of feature values contained within the history of past choices made by the user (long-term feature matching, aiming at considering long-term user's preferences). Existing food recommendation web sites[2] and approaches do not consider some important aspects that could be exploited for recommendation purposes. Firstly, recipes can be combined into different menus, but not all aggregations are suitable. Specific combinations of recipes might be due to particular menu configurations (e.g.,

---

[1] The Smart BREAK project, http://www.smartbreakproject.it.

[2] See for example http://www.food.com/, http://allrecipes.com.

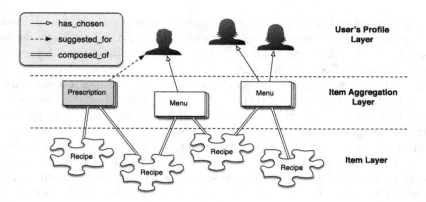

Fig. 1. The multi-layered framework adopted for food recommendation.

appetizer, first course, second course, dessert). Secondly, new challenges raise within application domains (food recommendation, healthcare, wellness), that present the particular features highlighted above. For instance, some Jasmine's preferences (e.g., having meat during lunches, all the days throughout the week) may contrast with best habits, according to up-to-date medical prescriptions. Therefore, recommendations of recipes also might be suggested in accordance with recent medical prescriptions, that recommend variety and balancing of different ingredients and nutrients, which recipes are composed of. This means that reference prescriptions might be used as first class citizens in recommending recipes to users who present particular profiles. Nevertheless, prescriptions cannot be totally imposed to users, disregarding their own preferences. Lifestyle improvements should gradually guide users towards better choices.

To this aim, the recommendation model we propose in this paper is based on the multi-layered framework shown in Fig. 1 and detailed in the following. Each layer is focused on specific elements, namely items to be recommended (i.e., recipes), item aggregations (menus, prescriptions) and users, further described with proper features and relationships with elements of the other layers.

The Item Layer. In this layer, recipes represent the most fine-grained items to be recommended. According to our general model, a recipe is described as $r_i = \langle ID_i, n_i, C_i, T_i \rangle$, where: ID_i ($\forall i = 1, \ldots N$) is the unique identifier of the recipe (we denote with $\mathcal{R}$ the overall set of N recipes available within the dataset); n_i is the name of the recipe; C_i and T_i are sets of features used to characterize the recipe. We distinguish among: (i) categories (C_i), that classify the recipe and are taken from top-down domain-specific ontologies; (ii) semantic tags, that is, bottom-up keywords assigned to the recipes by users to annotate them and semantically disambiguated using a general-purpose lexical system or thesaurus, to face polisemy (that is, the same tag refers to different concepts) and synonymy problems (i.e., the same concept is pointed out using different tags), that traditional tagging may present. For semantic definition of categories, we extended the `food.owl` ontology[3]. For example, in our approach each recipe is classified through categories directly related to food, such as the `RecipeType` (e.g., appetizer, first course, second course, fruits, dessert), the `CookingStyle` (e.g., Asian cuisine), the ingredients used in the recipe (e.g., chicken, beef, rice), and other categories such as the `Religion` (e.g., Islamic) for which the recipe is meant, or the `Pathology` (e.g., diabetes, high-blood pressure), for which the recipe is advised. In Fig. 2 eight different recipes are depicted, with categories extracted from the ontology partially shown on the left. In our approach, semantic tagging is supported using the semantic disambiguation system extensively described in [7], where a semantic tag $t \in \mathcal{T}_i$ is a triplet, composed of: (i) the tag itself extracted from WordNet; (ii) the set of all the terms in the synset; (iii) the human readable definition associated with the synset.

The Item Aggregation Layer. In this layer, recipes are aggregated to be proposed in a combined way. In the context of our food recommendation approach, we distinguish two kinds of aggregations: (a) available *menus*, that is, combinations of recipes chosen in the past by the users of the system (these menus are used to extract the preferences of the users, exploiting them during the recommendation phase, see next section for details); (b) *prescriptions*, that is, proper combinations of recipes that are advisable for specific kinds of users. Formally, we define an aggregation (either a menu or a prescription) $a_j \in \mathcal{A}$ as $a_j = \langle n_{a_j}, \mathcal{R}[a_j], \tau_{a_j} \rangle$, where: $\mathcal{A}$ denotes the overall set of aggregations; n_{a_j} is the name of the aggregation; $\mathcal{R}[a_j] \subseteq \mathcal{R}$ is the set of recipes aggregated in a_j; τ_{a_j} is the template of the aggregation, expressed in terms of specific categories. In our approach, given an aggregation a_j, τ_{a_j} is identified considering the `RecipeType` category. Examples of templates may be [appetizer, first course, second course, dessert] or [first course, fruit]. Templates will play an important role for the formulation of the request for suggestions and to speed up the generation of the recommendation output (see Sect. 3). The way prescriptions are associated with users depends on the features used to describe users' profiles. In our food recommendation approach, Food Frequency Questionnaires (FFQ) are issued to collect users' habits and BMI (Body Mass Index), in order to automatically classify users within specific phenotypes [8], for which prescriptions have been inserted within the system. This task is supervised by medical doctors, who participate to the Smart BREAK project (see Sect. 4). The point here is that prescriptions are given and will be used, as shown in the next section.

The User's Profile Layer. In this layer, users are profiled according to their preferences and past menu choices, that are collected to represent the history of recipe and menu selections made by the user. Formally, we define the profile $p(u)$ of a user $u \in \mathcal{U}$ as $p(u) = \langle ID_u, \mathcal{C}[u], \mathcal{T}[u], \mathcal{M}[u], \mathcal{P}[u] \rangle$, where: $\mathcal{U}$ denotes the overall set of users; ID_u is used to identify the user u; $\mathcal{C}[u]$ and $\mathcal{T}[u]$ are the sets of features (namely, categories and tags) used to denote the preferences of u; $\mathcal{M}[u]$ is the set of menus chosen by the user in the past, that in turn may

---

[3] http://krono.act.uji.es/Links/ontologies/food.owl/view.

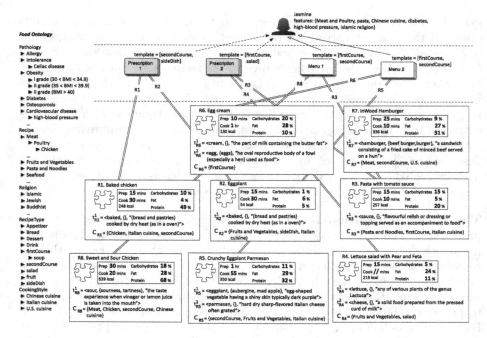

Fig. 2. Items to recommend (recipes) and aggregations (menus and prescriptions) of the running example.

represent the preferences of the user u about recipes to be recommended; $\mathcal{P}[u]$ is the set of prescriptions assigned to the user in the system. To characterize user's profiles, we rely on the classification features (i.e., categories and tags), whose values represent long-term preferences of the user, that might be collected and updated using traditional techniques from the literature [1].

3 Menu Recommendation System

When Jasmine is looking for menu suggestions, she generates a request $r_r(u)$ formulated as $r_r(u) = \langle \mathcal{C}_r, \mathcal{T}_r, \tau_r \rangle$, where: $\mathcal{C}_r$ is a set of categories that represent immediate, short-term preferences of Jasmine; similarly, $\mathcal{T}_r$ is a set of (semantic) tags, specified by issuing the request; τ_r is the menu template Jasmine is searching for. The recommender system takes into account the profile of the user u (Jasmine), that is, $p(u)$ whom the request comes from. To this aim, the request $r_r(u)$ is expanded with the categories and semantic tags that are present within the Jasmine's profile $p(u)$. We denote with $\widehat{r}_r(u)$ the expanded version of the request, where $\widehat{r}_r(u) = \langle \widehat{\mathcal{C}}_r, \widehat{\mathcal{T}}_r, \tau_r \rangle$. The set $\widehat{\mathcal{C}}_r$ contains both the categories specified in $\mathcal{C}_r$ and the categories within $p(u)$. The set $\mathcal{C}_r$ might also be empty, thus denoting that the system should exclusively rely on the preferences contained within $p(u)$. Each category $c_r \in \widehat{\mathcal{C}}_r$ is weighted by means of a coefficient $\omega_r \in [0, 1]$ such that: (a) $\omega_r = 1$ if $c_r \in C_r$, (b) $\omega_r = freq(c_r) \in [0, 1]$ otherwise. The value of ω_r means that a category explicitly specified in the request will be considered the most for identifying candidate recipes. The term $freq(c_r)$ computes the frequency of category c_r among all the categories that annotate the recipes contained in the profile $p(u)$. Less frequent categories will be considered as less important for identifying candidate recipes. If a category c_r is present both in C_r and in the profile, then $\omega_r = 1$. The same applies for (semantic) tags. If u is a new user, without a history of past choices, then $\widehat{r}_r(u) = r_r(u)$ (no expansion). In this case, prescriptions are used to differentiate the user's choices, based on the user's phenotypes, as explained in the following. Frequencies are computed on a menu basis, since recipes are recommended only within menus. For instance, let's consider the recipes and Jasmine's profile shown in Fig. 2, and the following request, issued to search for menus and recipes containing **baked poultry**, according to [**firstCourse, secondCourse**] template: $r_r(u) = \langle \{\texttt{poultry}\}, \{\texttt{baked}\}, [\texttt{firstCourse, secondCourse}] \rangle$. The following expanded version of the request is generated (frequency values are specified among parenthesis):

$\widehat{C}_r = \{\texttt{poultry}(1.0), \texttt{meat}(0.5), \texttt{chicken}(0.5), \texttt{secondCourse}(1.0), \texttt{Chinesecuisine}(0.5),$
$\quad \texttt{PastaandNoodles}(0.5), \texttt{firstCourse}(0.5), \texttt{Italiancuisine}(1.0), \texttt{FruitsandVegetables}(0.5)\}$
$\widehat{T}_r = \{\texttt{baked}(1.0), \texttt{sour}(0.5), \texttt{cream}(0.5), \texttt{egg}(0.5), \texttt{eggplant}(0.5), \texttt{parmesan}(0.5)\}$

Feature-Based Recipe Filtering. The input of this step is the set $\mathcal{R}$ of all the available recipes and the request $\widehat{r}_r(u)$. First, τ_r element specified in the request is considered. Those recipes such that their **RecipeType** is not included within τ_r will not pass the feature-based filtering step. In the example above, only the R1, R3, R5, R6, R7 and R8 recipes will be further considered, that is, only recipes that are either first courses or second courses. Not all features can be exploited in the same way to filter out not relevant recipes. For instance, let's consider some constraints imposed by the Islamic religion or by some allergies. Recipes that do not respect these constraints must be excluded before any other kind of comparison. These constraints, to keep our model as more general as possible, are defined within the domain ontology and are expressed in terms of other features. For example, the Islamic religion within the Jasmine's profile excludes all recipes that are annotated with **pork** or **alcohol** as contained ingredients. Modeling of such constraints must be accurate; this explains why we inserted them within the domain ontology, that is developed in a controlled way. After τ_r and ontological constraints have been used to pre-select recipes, the filtering based on remaining features is applied, according to the following similarity metrics.

Category-Based Relevance. The relevance of a recipe $r_i = \langle ID_i, n_i, C_i, T_i \rangle$ with respect to the request $\widehat{r}_r(u) = \langle \widehat{C}_r, \widehat{T}_r, \tau_r \rangle$ taking into account categories in C_i and $\widehat{C}_r$, denoted with $Sim_{cat}(\widehat{r}_r, r_i) \in [0, 1]$, is computed as:

$$Sim_{cat}(\widehat{r}_r, r_i) = \frac{2 \cdot \sum_{c_r, c_i} \omega_r \cdot CatSim(c_r, c_i)}{|C_i|} \in [0, 1] \quad (1)$$

where c_r ranges over the set $\widehat{\mathcal{C}}_r$, c_i ranges over the set $\mathcal{C}_i$, $|\mathcal{C}_i|$ denotes the number of categories in the set $\mathcal{C}_i$, ω_r denotes the weight of category $c_r \in \widehat{\mathcal{C}}_r$, assigned as shown above. $CatSim(c_r, c_i)$ represents the *category similarity* between c_r and c_i. We consider the two categories c_r and c_i as more similar as the number of items (i.e., recipes) that have been annotated with both the categories increases with respect to the overall number of items annotated with c_r and with c_i. The domain ontology is considered in this case: in fact, given two categories c_i and c_j such that $c_i \sqsubseteq c_j$ (c_i is subclassOf c_j), due to the semantics of the subclassOf relationship, all recipes annotated with c_i are considered as annotated with c_j as well. For example, $|\text{Chicken}| = |\{\text{R1}, \text{R8}\}| = 2$, $|\text{Poultry}| = |\{\text{R1}, \text{R8}\}| = 2$, $|\text{Chicken} \cap \text{Poultry}| = |\{\text{R1}, \text{R8}\}| = 2$, therefore $CatSim(\text{chicken}, \text{Poultry}) = 1.0$, since Chicken $\sqsubseteq$ Poultry. Pairs of categories to be considered in the $Sim_{cat}(\widehat{r}_r, r_i)$ computation are selected according to a maximization function, that relies on the assignment in bipartite graphs and ensures that each category in $\mathcal{C}_i$ participates in at most one pair with one of the categories in $\widehat{\mathcal{C}}_r$ and the pairs are selected in order to maximize the overall $Sim_{cat}(\widehat{r}_r, r_i)$. In the running example, for computing $Sim_{cat}(\widehat{r}_r, \text{R1})$, the pair $\langle \text{Poultry}, \text{Chicken} \rangle$ ($\omega_r = 1.0$) is considered instead of $\langle \text{Chicken}, \text{Chicken} \rangle$ ($\omega_r = 0.5$) in order to maximize the final result, therefore $Sim_{cat}(\widehat{r}_r, \text{R1}) = (1.0 + 1.0 + 1.0)/3 = 1.0$.

Tag-Based Relevance. The relevance of a recipe $r_i = \langle ID_i, n_i, \mathcal{C}_i, \mathcal{T}_i \rangle$ with respect to the request $\widehat{r}_r(u) = \langle \widehat{\mathcal{C}}_r, \widehat{\mathcal{T}}_r, \tau_r \rangle$ taking into account (semantic) tags in $\widehat{\mathcal{T}}_r$ and $\mathcal{T}_i$, denoted with $Sim_{tag}(\widehat{r}_r, r_i) \in [0, 1]$, is computed by evaluating the terminological affinity between pairs of tags, one from the first set ($\widehat{\mathcal{T}}_r$) and one from the second set ($\mathcal{T}_i$), and by combining them through the following formula, that is:

$$Sim_{tag}(\widehat{r}_r, r_i) = \frac{2 \cdot \sum_{t_1 \in \widehat{\mathcal{T}}_r, t_2 \in \mathcal{T}_i} TermAff(t_1, t_2)}{|\mathcal{T}_i|} \in [0, 1] \tag{2}$$

where t_1 and t_2 are tags, $|\mathcal{T}_i|$ denotes the number of items in $\mathcal{T}_i$. The rationale behind Eq. (2) is the same behind $Sim_{cat}()$ computation. The point here is how to compute $TermAff(t_1, t_2) \in [0, 1]$, since t_1 and t_2 might be both semantic and traditional tags. Let's consider t_1 and t_2 as tags semantically disambiguated using WordNet: in this case, the term affinity between t_1 and t_2 is computed as extensively described in [7], where WordNet-based techniques from the literature have been adopted. In all cases where either t_1 and t_2 do not have a disambiguation based on WordNet, we compare the names of terminological items using the normalized Levenshtein distance (thus obtaining a measure $StringSim(\cdot) \in [0, 1]$). In particular, if both t_1 and t_2 have not been disambiguated, then $TermAff(t_1, t_2) = StringSim(t_1, t_2)$. Otherwise, if t_1 has not been disambiguated, while t_2 presents a sense disambiguation (or viceversa), let's denote with $\mathcal{S}_2$ the set of synonyms of t_2, then $TermAff(t_1, t_2) = max_{t_2^i \in \mathcal{S}_2}\{StringSim(t_1, t_2^i)\}$.

The overall feature-based relevance of a recipe r_i with respect to the request $\widehat{r}_r(u)$ is computed as $Sim(\widehat{r}_r, r_i) = \omega_c \cdot Sim_{cat}(\widehat{r}_r, r_i) + \omega_t \cdot Sim_{tag}(\widehat{r}_r, r_i) \in [0, 1]$, where ω_c and $\omega_t \in [0, 1]$ and their sum equals 1.0. The weights ω_c and ω_t are used to balance the two kinds of relevance. In our experiments we considered $\omega_c = 0.5$ and $\omega_t = 0.5$, thus giving the same importance to both the metrics. The recipes included in the set $\mathcal{R}' \subseteq \mathcal{R}$, as output of the *feature-based recipe filtering*, are those whose overall relevance with respect to the request $\hat{r}_r(u)$ is equal or greater than a threshold $\gamma \in [0, 1]$ set by the user.

Menu Generation and Ranking. Recipes are aggregated into menus that must be compliant with the template τ_r specified in the request $\hat{r}_r(u)$. This significantly reduces the number of menu configurations to be generated: in fact, a candidate menu can not contain two recipes r_i and r_j annotated with the same `RecipeType`. Generated menus are ranked according to their similarity with: (i) past menu choices made by the user u who is issuing the request for suggestions, represented by the set $\mathcal{M}[u]$; (ii) prescriptions prepared for the user u according to his/her profile, represented by the set $\mathcal{P}[u]$. Since both menus and prescriptions are formally defined as sets of recipes, the building block in this step is the similarity measure between items aggregations (*item aggregation similarity*), that is computed as follows:

$$Sim_{agg}(a_i, a_j) = \frac{2 \cdot \sum_{r_i, r_j} Sim(r_i, r_j)}{|a_i| + |a_j|} \in [0, 1] \tag{3}$$

where a_i and a_j represent the two compared aggregations, r_i (resp., r_j) is an item (i.e., a recipe) included within a_i (resp., within a_j), $|a_i|$ (resp., $|a_j|$) denotes the number of recipes included within a_i (resp., within a_j). Therefore, we consider two aggregations as more similar as the number of similar items in the two aggregations increases.

The final ranking of a generated menu $a_k \in A^*$, recommended to the user u who issued a request for suggestions, is performed through a ranking function $\rho : A^* \mapsto [0, 1]$, computed as follows:

$$\rho(a_i) = \omega_m \cdot \frac{\sum_{a[u] \in \mathcal{M}[u]} Sim_{agg}(a_i, a[u])}{|\mathcal{M}[u]|} + \omega_s \cdot \frac{\sum_{\hat{a}[u] \in \mathcal{P}[u]} Sim_{agg}(a_i, \hat{a}[u])}{|\mathcal{P}[u]|} \tag{4}$$

where $\omega_m, \omega_p \in [0, 1]$, $\omega_m + \omega_p = 1.0$, are weights used to balance the impact of past menu choices and prescriptions on the ranking of recommended menus. We have chosen $\omega_m < \omega_p$ (i.e., $\omega_m \cong 0.4$ and $\omega_p \cong 0.6$) in order to stimulate users on improving their food and nutrition habits, without recommending menus and recipes that are too much distant from users' preferences. This is the most innovative aspect of the approach presented here, compared to recent food recommendation literature.

4   Implementation and Experimental Issues

We implemented the food recommendation approach as a web application called PREFer (**P**rescriptions for **RE**commending **F**ood). The *PREFer Web Interface* guides the user through the registration process, the menu recommendation, the publication of new recipes, also supporting semantic disambiguation of tags (through a WordNet-based *Sense Disambiguation module*), both during the publication of new recipes and the formulation of a request for suggestions, using a wizard similar to the one described in [7]. Registration is performed by answering a food frequency survey (FFQ), that is used to collect information about the users in order to compute their BMI and identify their phenotypes [8], to prepare suggested prescriptions. FFQ is composed of a set of questions (whose structure is shown in table below), aiming at identifying the frequency and quantity of assumption for 145 different types of snacks, meat, fish, pasta, soups, products derived from milk, vegetables and fruits, desserts, drinks.

Food category - Snacks, meat, fish, pasta, soups, products derived from milk, vegetables and fruits, desserts, drinks		
Food type	Frequency of assumption	Quantity
(e.g., hamburger)	*(never), (once per month),*	*(small portion)*
	(2–3 times per month), (once per week),	*(medium portion)*
	(twice per week), (3–4 times per week),	*(big portion)*
	(5–6 times per week), (once per day),	
	(2 or more times per day)	

Phenotype identification is executed by medical doctors, who participate to the regional project where PREFer is being developed. The description of this task is out of the scope of this paper. To just give an idea, medical doctors are supported in the identification of phenotypes and have a simple web interface at their disposal to prepare and insert prescriptions as sets of recipes, depending on the result of phenotype identification. Prescriptions preparation for a given phenotype is manually performed offline, but prescriptions are automatically assigned to all users classified in the phenotype.

Experiments on our food recommendation approach are being carried to demonstrate the performances of the approach, in terms of average precision of the recommendations, and to verify the impact of the approach in improving the users' habits concerning food and nutrition. Performance tests are being performed on a dataset obtained by extending an existing one[4], containing about 220 k recipes, randomly aggregated into about 100 k menus, where the PREFer system is presenting comparable average precision with respect to recent approaches. To verify the impact of the approach in improving the users' habits, further experiments are being performed on a population of about two hundreds students, equally distributed among males and females, with an age included between 18 and 24. The compliance of users' choices with reference prescriptions, in order to quantify how much the system is able to improve their behaviour, is quantified through the average aggregation similarity between users' choices and reference prescriptions, starting from Eq. (3). Experiments will be carried

---

[4] http://mslab.csie.ntu.edu.tw/~tim/recipe.zip.

on until September 2015. Monthly, statistics are generated that, with respect to users' profiles, show the percentage of requests and menu choices that are compliant or closer to reference prescriptions. Experiments carried on the first months showed a satisfying increment of closeness between past preferences and reference prescriptions (around 24 % on average, but reaching about 43 % if we consider only users with preferences that are far from the advisable ones, that is, average closeness that is lower than 0.5).

5   Conclusions

In this paper, we presented a menu generation system that uses a recipe dataset and annotations to discover similarity between kinds of food and user's preferences. The system is being developed and tested within a food recommendation regional project, Smart BREAK. This paper has been meant as a complementary approach to recent food recommendation efforts, in order to take into account reference prescriptions schemes for food recommendation that aim at improving users' nutritional habits. In this sense, our approach can be considered as a step forward compared to existing food recommendation proposals, that could be integrated with our system as well. Experimentation is being performed on the approach, but further experiments will be carried on till the end of the Smart BREAK project, in order to check how much the proposed approach is able to effectively improve nutritional habits and lifestyles.

References

1. Gauch, S., Speretta, M., Chandramouli, A., Micarelli, A.: User profiles for personalized information access. In: Brusilovsky, P., Kobsa, A., Nejdl, W. (eds.) Adaptive Web 2007. LNCS, vol. 4321, pp. 54–89. Springer, Heidelberg (2007)
2. Al Nazer, A., Helmy, T., Al Mulhem, M.: User's profile ontology-based semantic framework for personalized food and nutrition recommendation. Procedia Comput. Sci. **32**, 101–108 (2014)
3. Wang, Y., Liu, Z.: Personalized health information retrieval system. In: AMIA Annual Symposium Proceedings, p. 1149 (2005)
4. Abidi, S., Chen, H.: Adaptable personalized care planning via a semantic web framework. In: 20th International Conference of the European Federation for Medical Informatics (2006)
5. Dominguez, D., Grasso, F., Miller, T., Serafin, R.: PIPS: an integrated environment for health care delivery and healthy lifestyle support. In: 4th Workshop on Agent applied in Healhcare ECAI2006 (2006)
6. Suominen, O., Hyvonen, E., Viljanen, K., Hukka, E.: HealthFinland - a national semantic publishing network and portal for health information. Web Semant. Sci. Serv. Agents World Wide Web **7**(4), 287–297 (2009)
7. Bianchini, D., De Antonellis, V., Melchiori, M.: A multi-perspective framework for web API search in enterprise mashup design. In: Salinesi, C., Norrie, M.C., Pastor, Ó. (eds.) CAiSE 2013. LNCS, vol. 7908, pp. 353–368. Springer, Heidelberg (2013)
8. Rankinen, T., Bouchard, C.: Genetics of food intake and eating behavior phenotypes in humans. Ann. Rev. Nutr. **26**, 413–434 (2006)

Obtaining Key Performance Indicators
by Using Data Mining Techniques

Roberto Tardío and Jesús Peral[(✉)]

Lucentia Research Group, Department of Software and Computing Systems,
University of Alicante, Alicante, Spain
{rtardio,jperal}@dlsi.ua.es

Abstract. Currently dashboards are the preferred tool across organizations to monitor business performance. Dashboards are often composed by different data visualization techniques, amongst which Key Performance Indicators (KPIs) play a crucial role in facilitating quick and precise information by comparing current performance against a target required to fulfill business objectives. It is however the case that not always KPIs are well known, and sometimes it is difficult to find an adequate KPI to associate with each business objective. On the other hand, data mining techniques are often used for forecasting trends and visualizing data correlations. In this paper, we present a novel approach to combine these two aspects in order to drive data mining techniques into obtaining specific KPIs for business objectives in a semi-automatic way. The main benefit of our approach, is that organizations do not need to rely on existing KPI lists, such as APQC, nor test KPIs on a cycle, as they can analyze their behaviour using existing data. In order to show the applicability of our approach, we apply our proposal to the novel field of MOOC courses in order to identify additional KPIs to the ones being currently used.

Keywords: KPI's · Data mining · Big data · Decision trees · Artificial neural network

1 Introduction

Dashboards and Scorecards [11] enable decision makers to quickly assess the status of an organization by visualizing aggregated data through different kinds of visualizations. This capability makes Dashboards the preferred tool across organizations to monitor business performance. Amongst the different visualizations included within Dashboards, Key Performance Indicators (KPIs) [16] play a crucial role, since they facilitate quick and precise information by comparing current performance against a target required to fulfill business objectives.

It is however the case that KPIs are not always well known, and sometimes it is difficult to find an adequate KPI to associate with each business objective [3]. In these cases, it is common to resort to existing lists of KPIs, such as APQC [1], in order to test candidates during short periods of time until a suitable one is

© Springer International Publishing Switzerland 2015
M.A. Jeusfeld and K. Karlapalem (Eds.): ER 2015 Workshops, LNCS 9382, pp. 144–153, 2015.
DOI: 10.1007/978-3-319-25747-1_15

found. What happens, however, when an organization performs an innovative activity or explores a new data source such as Social Media? The absence of lists of KPIs forces managers to rely on their intuition in order to elicit potential KPI candidates. This has several undesired consequences. First of all, KPIs may be redundant [18], misdirecting the effort and resources of the organization. Second, people responsible for (wrong) KPIs develop a resistance to change once they have found how to maximize their value [16]. Third, there is a tendency to focus on results themselves [3,16] (e.g. Sales) rather than on the actual indicators that can be worked on (e.g. Successful deliveries/Total deliveries) and lead to the results obtained.

Therefore, currently there is a need for techniques and methods that improve the KPI elicitation process, providing decision makers with information about relationships between KPIs and their characteristics. This information can be highly valuable for KPI selection, not only on traditional datasets, but also for Big Data, where the implications of the data for the company are unknown, and, thus, eliciting their relationships with internal KPIs can make these data actionable, adding value to them.

Big Data concern huge volume, complex, growing data sets with multiple and heterogeneous sources. With the fast development of networking, data storage, and the data collection capacity, Big Data are now rapidly expanding in all domains and scenarios. In [19] it is presented a HACE theorem that characterizes the features of the Big Data revolution, and proposes a Big Data processing model, from the data mining perspective. The authors analyze the challenging issues in the data-driven model and also in the Big Data revolution.

In many human-computer interaction scenarios, the principle of What You See Is What You Get is followed. Only when the analytical results are friendly displayed, it may be effectively utilized by users. Reports, histograms, pie charts, and regression curves, etc., are frequently used to visualize results of data analysis. These statements lead to see the visualization topic as one of the main challenges to mining big data [4].

In this paper, we present a novel approach to combine these two aspects in order to drive data mining techniques into obtaining specific KPIs for business objectives in a semi-automatic way. The main benefit of our approach, is that organizations do not need to rely on existing KPI lists, such as APQC, nor test KPIs on a cycle, as they can analyze their behaviour using existing data. In order to show the applicability of our approach, we apply our proposal to the novel field of MOOC (Massive Open Online Course) courses in order to identify additional KPIs to the ones being currently used.

The remaining of this paper is structured as follows. Section 2 discusses the related work. Section 3 describes our proposal for KPI elicitation. Section 4 presents our case study, based on a MOOC being run at the University of Alicante. Finally, Sect. 5 draws the conclusions and sketches future works.

2   Related Work

In [11] the authors propose the Balanced Scorecard, a tool that consists on a balanced list of KPIs associated with objectives covering different business perspectives. The usefulness of the Balanced Scorecard has facilitated its quick adoption by companies all around the world. However, while the structure of the Balanced Scorecard is clear, its contents are not. Given that many companies struggle to succeed with their KPIs, in [10] the authors propose the use of Strategy Maps. Strategy Maps link describe the way that the organization intends to achieve its objectives, by capturing the relationships between them in an informal way. Recently, the concepts included within Scorecards and Strategy Maps have been further formalized in the shape of business strategy models. Business strategy models [9] combine KPIs, objectives, and their relationships all together in a single formal view. Despite these efforts, it is still unclear whether the KPIs included in these objective models are adequate, or even if the relationships between objectives perceived by decision makers are indeed reflected between the KPIs selected to measure their degree of achievement.

Therefore, in [16], the author focuses on the design and implementation of KPIs within Dashboards. The author differentiates between Key Result Indicators (KRIs) and KPIs, in order to differentiate between results and actual performance and highlight the importance of relationships between indicators, and discusses the characteristics and target public that each KPI should have. However, there is no discussion regarding how KPIs or their relationships could be elicited from data. On the other hand, in [18], the authors propose the QRPMS method to select KPIs and elicit relationships between them. The method starts from a pre-existing set of candidate KPIs, and performs a series of analysis steps using data mining techniques, such as Principal Component Analysis (PCA), alternated with human intervention in order to identify potential KPIs relationships and help decision makers select those KPIs that seem most relevant for the business.

Big Data is a new and nowadays common term used to identify datasets that we can not manage with current methodologies or data mining software tools principally due to their huge size and complexity. Big Data mining is the capability of extracting useful information from these large datasets or streams of data. New mining techniques are necessary due to the volume, variability, and velocity, of such data. The Big Data challenge is becoming one of the most exciting opportunities for the years to come. [6] is as good reference point as it presents in this issue, a broad overview of the topic, its current status, controversy, and a forecast to the future. They introduce four articles, written by influential scientists in the field, covering the most interesting and state-of-the-art topics on Big Data mining. There are many tools for big data mining and analysis, including professional and amateur software, expensive commercial software, and open source software. In [4] it is described a briefly review of the top five most widely used software, according to a survey of "What Analytics, Data mining, Big Data software that you used in the past 12 months for a real project?" of 798 professionals made by KDNuggets in 2012.

There is no clear consensus on what is Big Data. In fact, there have been many controversial statements about Big Data, such as "Size is the only thing that matters." In [12] the authors try to explore the controversies and debunk the myths surrounding Big Data.

In [20] it is discussed the major differences between statistics and data mining and then speaks to the uniqueness of data mining in the biomedical and health-care fields. A brief summarization of various data mining algorithms used for classification, clustering, and association as well as their respective advantages and drawbacks is also presented.

Summarizing, there are a number of works focused on monitoring perfor-mance by means of KPIs, however, most of the works that tackle the problem of KPI selection require a pre-existing set of KPIs. Obtaining this set of KPIs can be a tough task in already established organizations [3], and becomes a challenge when the business activity is developed in an innovative environment.

3   Methodology Proposed

The steps comprising the methodology are shown in Fig. 1. First of all, we start by focusing on modeling the business strategy and known KPIs (if any) to guide the process. In many organizations, some of these goals and KPIs are already listed in the Balanced Scorecard [11]. However, the business strategy model includes more information. Specifically, it includes the relationships between the different business objectives to be achieved and (optionally) the processes that support them. If a more thorough analysis it is required, it is possible to consider

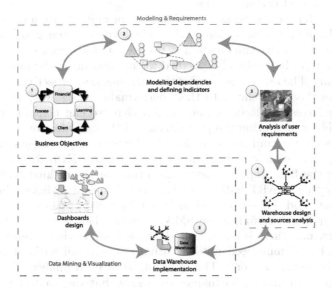

Fig. 1. Generic strategic map. In the steps 5 and 6 data mining is applied to provide visualization and KPI's.

including SWOT analysis (Strengths, Weaknesses, Opportunities and Threats) [8] within the business strategy. This analysis identifies those elements not only external but also internal to the company that affect one or more of the objectives set as priorities. Therefore, SWOT analysis allow to identify quickly the possible causes of indicators deviation and then to make decisions accordingly. A result similar to the concept of Strategy Maps [10] will be obtained after finishing this first step. Once we have modeled the business strategy view, we list and prioritize those objectives that do not have any KPI associated to measure them. Each of these objectives is related to one or more business processes that supports them.

Our first step to tackle the analytical challenges of UniMOOC at the University of Alicante was to carry out several interviews with the organizers of this course. This provided us some abstract and high level information to about the goals and objectives of course managers, thus being able to derive a first set of indicators and create an initial version of the multidimensional model for analysis. The indicators obtained in a generic way, which may be applicable to other online courses are: increment in number of students, dropout ratio, recovery ratio of students, % Of active students, % Of students who fail the course, % Of students passing the exams without seeing the corresponding lessons, % Of students taking the course on a continuous or sequential pattern.

According to these indicators, we created a multidimensional model to support their calculus and provide additional analysis capacities. The model allows the mapping from the indicators to DW elements making possible to generate the DW schema automatically. Our multidimensional model is composed of two analysis cubes: Enrollment and Activity. The first one, Enrollment, allows us to analyze if the characteristics of the students, such as country, interests and expectations present certain patterns.

Each of the business processes listed has one or more decision makers responsible for analyzing the information produced by its daily activity. By interviewing these decision makers we can create new user requirement views or review existing ones that have been already specified for implementing the data warehouse of the company. The aim of this step is to relate business objectives with entities and measures that are related to their performance. This way, we move from abstract objectives to pieces of information that we can combine in order to propose KPIs for measuring the performance of the organization.

Using the entities and measures identified during requirements analysis, we elaborate together with stakeholders a set of candidate KPIs for each objective listed during the first step. To ensure the utility of the defined KPI, everyone should follow the SMART indications [14], being Specific, Measurable, Achievable, Relevant, and Timely available. If a target either has no an associated indicator or it does not follow the SMART rules, then it can not be properly tracked. Therefore, there is a risk that the target will deviate from its expected evolution and it is unnoticed until eventually it will fail without been possible to take corrective actions. The following step is to analyze the candidate KPIs through data mining techniques to ensure that they reflect the relationships identified during business strategy modeling. Finally, we define or update the analysis views for different roles, materialized in dashboards that will allow decision makers to access and monitor the new KPIs.

4   Case Study

In recent years, the effect of the globalization along with the proliferation of open online courses has radically changed the traditional sectors of education. New technologies symbolise a big opportunity, although it is also required to face significant challenges to take full advantages of them [2].

More recently, a new kind of online course has appeared: the Massive Open Online Course (MOOC). A MOOC is an online course with the objective of inter- acting and promoting participation and open access via the web. Apart from the traditional resources such as slides, MOOCs provide video lectures, both off-line and on-line, and user forums that help to build an expert/professional commu- nity for the students and instructors. These advantages have made that MOOCs quickly gain popularity, and thus they have been increasing their number of students exponentially during the last years.

In particular, we present the process followed to elicit and model the critical information from the MOOC named UniMOOC[1], as well as the results of such procedure. UniMOOC is a MOOC that currently has over unique 20,000 students registered and focuses on entrepreneurship. The course includes several units and modules as well as links to social networks for students to interchange opinions. Some of the UniMOOC course objectives are defined in the Fig. 2 according to the methodology proposed in the previous section.

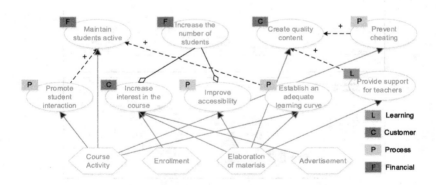

Fig. 2. Diagram for the MOOC course objectives.

This multidimensional model was created by using the conceptual modeling proposal described in [13], where the information is organized according to Facts (center of analysis) and Dimensions (context of analysis) as shown in Fig. 3.

---

[1] UniMOOC can be accessed at http://unimooc.com/landing/.

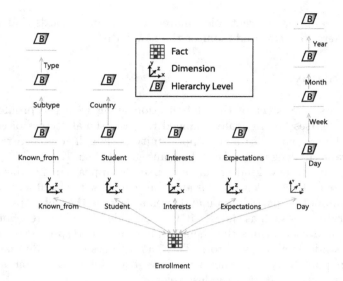

Fig. 3. MOOC Multidimensional modeling for the enrollment analysis.

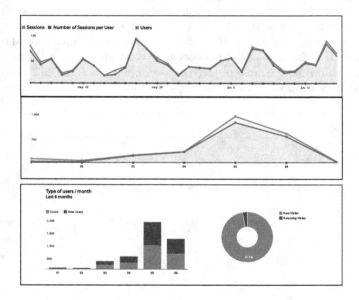

Fig. 4. Visualizations of sessions and type of users.

We have started by applying the classical data mining techniques to the database of the course. However, due to the big amount of data of this course, these techniques are not very suitable because they are difficult to interpret. For instance, they produce a lot of rules in association rules and decision trees; they

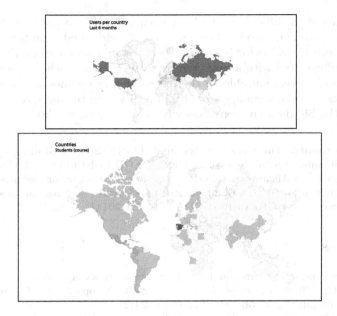

Fig. 5. Visualizations of users per countries.

also produce many hidden neural connections in the artificial neural networks, etc. The best way to analyse these data is by using visualization methods. In addition the visualization techniques allow to see how the graphical grow dynamically. In particular, we use Google Analytics (GA) since it offers a free tool for measuring and analysing several useful statistics [5,7,15,17].

Figure 4 shows the number of sessions per user along the course. We can appreciate different days with higher. In addition it also shows the users and new users per month. This is important to find out the days where there is more traffic and to make a more efficient way with the resources. Figure 5 shows the users per countries; this is very useful to promote these courses in the areas in which there are no students.

5   Discussion

Dashboards are the preferred tool across organizations to monitor business performance. They are often composed by different data visualization techniques, amongst which Key Performance Indicators (KPIs) play a crucial role in facilitating quick and precise information by comparing current performance against a target required to fulfill business objectives.

Dashboards and the Key Performance Indicators (KPIs) in the context of the crucial role they perform in facilitating a quick and precise information. This is carried out by comparing current performance against a target required to fulfill business objectives.

Very often it is difficult to find an adequate KPI to associate with each business objective and here is where the paper is addressed. The main objective is to obtain specific KPIs for business objectives in a semi-automatic way. This approach is illustrated with a case study, a MOOC course, which is a very novel area and therefore very suitable for their purpose. Future lines are to detail more the explanation of the techniques to obtain KPI's from the data, to continue the research of the big data environments with visualization methods.

Acknowledgments. This work has been funded by the Spanish Ministry of Economy and Competitiveness under the project Grant GEODAS-BI (TIN2012-37493-C03-03) and the University of Alicante, within the program of support for official master studies and research initiation (BOUA of 30/07/2013) and within the program of support for research, under project GRE14-10 (BOUA of 03/06/2014).

References

1. American productivity and quality center. https://www.apqc.org/
2. Allison, C., Miller, A., Oliver, I., Michaelson, R., Tiropanis, T.: The web in education. Comput. Netw. **56**(18), 3811–3824 (2012)
3. Angoss. Key performance indicators, six sigma, and data mining. white paper (2011)
4. Chen, M., Mao, S., Liu, Y.: Big data: a survey. Mob. Netw. Appl. **19**(2), 171–209 (2014)
5. Clifton, B.: Advanced Web Metrics with Google Analytics. John Wiley & Sons, Indianapolis (2012)
6. Fan, W., Bifet, A.: Mining big data: current status, and forecast to the future. ACM SIGKDD Explor. Newslett. **14**(2), 1–5 (2013)
7. Fang, W.: Using google analytics for improving library website content and design: a case study. Libr. Philos. Pract. **9**(2), 22 (2007)
8. Hill, T., Westbrook, R.: Swot analysis: it's time for a product recall. Long Range Plann. **30**(1), 46–52 (1997)
9. Horkoff, J., Barone, D., Jiang, L., Eric, Y., Amyot, D., Borgida, A., Mylopoulos, J.: Strategic business modeling: representation and reasoning. Softw. Syst. Model. **13**(3), 1015–1041 (2014)
10. Kaplan, R.S., et al.: Strategy Maps: Converting Intangible Assets into Tangible Outcomes. Harvard Business Press, Boston (2004)
11. Kaplan, R.S., Norton, D.P., Horváth, P.: The Balanced Scorecard, vol. 6. Harvard Business School Press, Boston (1996)
12. Labrinidis, A., Jagadish, H.V.: Challenges and opportunities with big data. Proc. VLDB Endow. **5**(12), 2032–2033 (2012)
13. Lujan-Mora, S., Trujillo, J., Song, I.-Y.: A uml profile for multidimensional modeling in data warehouses. Data Knowl. Eng. **59**(3), 725–769 (2006)
14. Meyer, P.J.: Attitude is Everything: If You Want to Succeed Above and Beyond. The Meyer Resource Group, Waco (2003)
15. Pakkala, H., Presser, K., Christensen, T.: Using google analytics to measure visitor statistics: the case of food composition websites. Int. J. Inf. Manag. **32**(6), 504–512 (2012)

16. Parmenter, D.: Key Performance Indicators: Developing, Implementing, and Using Winning KPIs. John Wiley & Sons, Hoboken (2015)
17. Plaza, B.: Google analytics for measuring website performance. Tourism Manag. **32**(3), 477–481 (2011)
18. Rodriguez, R.R., Saiz, J.J.A., Bas, A.O.: Quantitative relationships between key performance indicators for supporting decision-making processes. Comput. Ind. **60**(2), 104–113 (2009)
19. Xindong, W., Zhu, X., Gong-Qing, W., Ding, W.: Data mining with big data. IEEE Trans. Knowl. Data Eng. **26**(1), 97–107 (2014)
20. Yoo, I., Alafaireet, P., Marinov, M., Pena-Hernandez, K., Gopidi, R., Chang, J.-F., Hua, L.: Data mining in healthcare and biomedicine: a survey of the literature. J. Med. Syst. **36**(4), 2431–2448 (2012)

Big Data Normalization for Massively Parallel Processing Databases

Nikolay Golov[1] and Lars Rönnbäck[2]([⊠])

[1] Avito, Higher School of Economics, Moscow, Russia
ngolov@avito.ru
http://www.avito.ru
[2] Department of Computer Science, Stocholm University, Stockholm, Sweden
lars.ronnback@anchormodeling.com
http://www.anchormodeling.com

Abstract. High performance querying and ad-hoc querying are commonly viewed as mutually exclusive goals in massively parallel processing databases. In the one extreme, a database can be set up to provide the results of a single known query so that the use of available of resources are maximized and response time minimized, but at the cost of all other queries being suboptimally executed. In the other extreme, when no query is known in advance, the database must provide the information without such optimization, normally resulting in inefficient execution of all queries. This paper introduces a novel technique, highly normalized Big Data using Anchor modeling, that provides a very efficient way to store information and utilize resources, thereby providing ad-hoc querying with high performance for the first time in massively parallel processing databases. A case study of how this approach is used for a Data Warehouse at Avito over two years time, with estimates for and results of real data experiments carried out in HP Vertica, an MPP RDBMS, are also presented.

Keywords: Big data · MPP · Database · Normalization · Analytics · Ad-hoc · Querying · Modeling · Performance

1 Background

Big Data analytics is rapidly becoming a commonplace task for many companies. For example, banks, telecommunication companies, and big web companies, such as Google, Facebook, and Twitter produce large amounts of data. Nowadays business users also know how to monetize such data. For example, various predictive marketing techniques can transform data about customer behavior into great monetary worth. The main issue, however, remains to be implementations and platforms fast enough to execute ad-hoc analytical queries over Big Data [2]. Until now, Hadoop has been considered a universal solution, but it has its own drawbacks, especially in its ability to process difficult queries, such as analyzing and combining heterogeneous data, and performing fast ad-hoc analysis [5].

© Springer International Publishing Switzerland 2015
M.A. Jeusfeld and K. Karlapalem (Eds.): ER 2015 Workshops, LNCS 9382, pp. 154–163, 2015.
DOI: 10.1007/978-3-319-25747-1_16

This paper introduces a new processing approach, using Anchor modeling in massively parallel processing (MPP) databases. The approach significantly increases the volume of data that can be analyzed within a given time frame. It has been implemented in HP Vertica [6], a column-oriented MPP RDBMS, and is used on a daily basis for fast ad-hoc query processing at Avito, a popular Russian web site for classified ads [10]. The approach gives their data scientists an ability to execute complex queries that process terabytes of data in minutes. The approach is generic and should apply equally well to other MPP databases, such as Pivotal Greenplum, Actian Matrix, and Amazon Redshift. The paper starts by describing the case for normalized Big Data at Avito, with subsections on Anchor modeling, benefits, theoretical estimates, and practical verification of the approach. The paper ends with the drawn conclusions.

2 The Avito Case for Normalized Big Data

Big Data is commonly defined using the "3Vs": *Volume* (large amounts of data), *Variety* (various forms and evolving structure), and *Velocity* (rapid generation, capturing, and consumption) [2]. Log files are common sources of structured Big Data. Web servers record logs of detailed user actions, click rates, visits, and other property records of web users. The sequence of pages visited by within a particular website is known as the *clickstream* of the user. Clickstreams are analyzed to understand traffic, the number of unique visitors, sessions, and page views. Clickstreams of groups of users often follow distinct patterns, the knowledge of which may help in providing customized content [1]. They may, however, also be generated by a non-human activity. Fake identities and Sybil accounts are responsible for a growing number of threats, including fake product reviews, malware, and spam on social networks. Similar clickstreams can be grouped into behavioral clusters to detect and eliminate non-human accounts [9]. Identification and elimination of a non-human activity is important in all analytical tasks, such as proper traffic estimation and pattern detection. It may also have significant reputational, ethical, and even legal effects if left unattended.

Clickstream analysis was one of the main defined objectives for the Data Warehouse at Avito. Based in Moscow, Avito is Russia's fastest growing e-commerce site and portal, "Russia's Craiglist". It grows ≈ 50 % a year and now second only to Craiglist and Chinese site 58 in the rating of classified sites [10]. In terms of 3Vs, Avito clickstream data have over 600 million user actions a day (Volume), a business model that is constantly evolving, where new features are constantly added (Variety), and users perform up to 1 million actions per minute. User profiles, which help to reject non-humans and generate personalized content, have to be recalculated in near real-time (Velocity).

The BI team at Avito was challenged to develop a scalable Data Warehouse, that could grow in volume and complexity together with their business model, while being able to support analytical workloads, such as clustering analysis, correlation analysis, A/B testing (two-sample hypothesis testing), and Data Mining Algorithms. Hadoop and other NoSQL approaches were rejected in the process, and instead an MPP relational database, HP Vertica [6], and highly normalized data model, Anchor Modeling [7], were selected.

2.1 Anchor Modeling

Anchor modeling [7] is a database modeling technique resulting in implementations where tables are in 6NF, the sixth normal form. Entities and relationships in Anchor modeling are highly decomposed. In 6NF tables have no non-trivial join dependencies [3], making tables *narrow* with few columns in comparison to, for example, the *wide* tables of 3NF. The traditional concept of an entity is thereby spread out over many tables, referred to as an *ensemble* [4]. Massively parallel processing databases generally have shared-nothing scale-out architectures, such that each node holds some subset of the database and enjoy a high degree of autonomy with respect to executing parallelized parts of queries. In order to maximize utilization, each node should perform as much of its assigned work as possible without the involvement of other nodes. The following four constructs are used in Anchor modeling, all having a predefined distribution.

Anchor, table holding surrogate identifiers for instances of an ensemble. Each instance in the modeled domain has its own unique surrogate identifier and they are stored in anchors. Surrogate identifiers are immutable and assumed as the only part of an instance that cannot change over time. Anchors are distributed across the nodes by a modulo operation on a hash of the surrogate identifier, such that no duplication exists.

Attribute, table holding named property values for an ensemble, that cannot be described as ensembles in their own right. An attribute table holds the surrogate identifier of the instance and the property value, with an optional history of changes to those values. Attributes share the same distribution scheme as anchors, which keeps an instance of an ensemble with its history together on the same node.

Tie, table holding a relationship between ensembles, distinguished by the roles those ensembles play. Tie tables have one column for each involved role, holding a reference to a surrogate identifier. Ties are distributed across the nodes for each role, duplicating subsets of the tie such that all relationships that an instance takes part in can be resolved without the involvement of other nodes.

Knot, table holding a set of enumerated values. If the possible values of an attribute fall within a, usually small, finite set of values, or a tie represents a relationship which has or may change categories, such values are best represented through knots. Knots hold surrogate identifiers for every value and the value itself, where values should be unique, mutually exclusive and exhaustive. Knots are fully duplicated on every node.

Attributes and ties may be *static* or *historized* depending on if they keep a record of changes over time. Historized tables contain an additional column indicating since when a value or relationship is in effect. Attributes and ties may also be *knotted* in which case they contain a reference to a value in a knot table, rather than an actual value. All tables may also contain technical columns, such as a reference to custom metadata.

2.2 The Evolution of the Avito Data Warehouse

The first version of the Data Warehouse (DW) at Avito was built in 2013 using Anchor modeling, contained 10TB of data, and ran on an HP Vertica cluster of 3 nodes. It loaded data from two data sources; the back office system at Avito and clickstream web logs. Since then, the DW has grown, and the current size of the Avito data warehouse has been limited to 51Tb for licensing reasons. It now contains years of consistent historical data from 14 data sources (back office, Google DFP/AdSense, MDM system, CRM system, RTB systems, among others), and a rolling half year of detailed clickstream data. The cluster has been increased from 3 to 12 nodes in order to scale up performance.

Clickstream data are loaded every 15 min. At the beginning of 2014 each such batch contained 5 million rows ($\approx$1.5 GB) and 15 million ($\approx$5 Gb) one year later. Avito has evolved their data model over the years. The clickstream records originally had less than 30 attributes, while now containing more than 70. Clickstream data has grown many times, both in terms of velocity (number of rows per minute), volume (size), and variety (number of attributes). The growth was successfully handled through scaling up the cluster by the addition of nodes.

ETL processes are implemented using Python. Data sources are loaded using different approaches: clickstream is loaded using FluentD with MongoDB as intermediate cash, back office data are loaded using intermediate CSV files, and data from Google DFP and CRM system are loaded through web services. The current version of the Avito DW contains $\approx$ 200 anchors, $\approx$ 600 attributes, and $\approx$ 300 ties, loaded from the data sources. Some ties and attributes are historized, some are not. There are two distinctive modes of ETL processes:

- Increment from operational database. Characterized by a small number of rows from a large number of source tables and source columns, with most ties and attributes historized. Data is loaded every 4 hours, taking 30 min, from 79 source tables to 45 anchors, 83 ties, and 238 attributes. The largest source delta contains $\approx$1 million rows.
- Increment from clickstream. Characterized by a large number of rows from a small number of source tables and source columns, with most ties and attributes static. Data is loaded every 15 min, taking 15 min, from 16 source tables to 16 anchors, 39 ties, and 43 attributes. The largest source delta contains $\approx$10–15 million rows.

2.3 Beneficial Effects of Normalization

An important effect of Anchor modeling is the ease of which new attributes, ties, and anchors can be added to the model, only resulting in new tables. The creation of such are close to instantaneous and populating them with data causes no locks for existing operations and ETL processes. Applications remain unaffected, since the existing schema is non-destructively extended [7], and can be dealt with to incorporate new features when time permits.

When data is sparse, arising though the addition of new attributes or when an attribute does not apply to all instances, normalization provides another

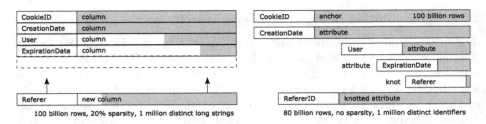

Fig. 1. Extending a less normalized model (left side) and a corresponding Anchor model (right side).

benefit. Only actual values are stored and "nulls" are represented by the absence of rows. For example, when less than half of the cookies have a known user, as in Fig. 1, the attribute contains fewer rows. Furthermore, when the number of distinct values is relatively low compared to the total number of values, knotted attributes can be used. Rather than repeating the relatively few long strings representing referers (URLs), these are stored as unique values of a knot. The knotted attribute instead contains identifier references, much smaller than the strings they represent. A query with a condition on the referer, such as containing a particular substring (UTM mark detection), can then be computed much more efficiently. The licensing cost of Vertica depends on "raw data size", the size of comma-separated lists of values in tables. In the less normalized model, referer strings are repeated 80 billion times, but only 1 million times in the Anchor model. By using Anchor modeling, Avito were able to store substantially more data without affecting its licensing cost.

2.4   Reporting and Ad-hoc Analysis

Using Anchor modeling with a Vertica cluster has proven beneficial at Avito for data modeling, data loading, and data maintenance. Though, from their experience, it has required some additional efforts to implement reporting and ad-hoc analysis. Reporting is considered as frequently spreading information, based on the same queries, to many recipients. Execution time of those queries cannot be longer than a few seconds. Ad-hoc querying is to test hypotheses, train models, or explore data to find suitable reports, using new queries. While shorter execution times are preferable, it is acceptable that these queries run for minutes or even hours in some cases.

Reporting can be implemented by creating dedicated denormalized data marts and using specialized BI software. Such data marts are implemented as regular views or materialized views. For reporting, the experience of Avito is that it is impossible to avoid data marts. The Anchor model stores fully historized versions of instances, which business users are not used to. There may also be the need to impose business logic or aggregate data in the marts. The development of efficient such views, as well as ad-hoc analysis, is based on the creation of high performance queries. While the optimizer in Vertica generally does a good

WebEvent
WebEventID *(pk)*
EventType
EventDate
CookieID *(fk)*

Cookie
CookieID *(pk)*
User
CreationDate
ExpirationDate

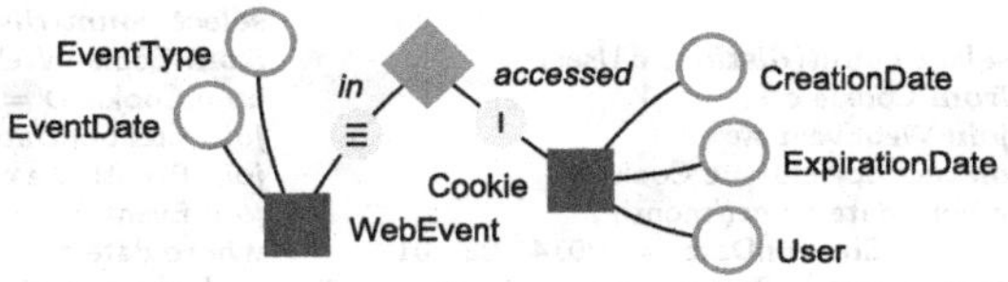

Fig. 2. An example 3NF model (left tables) and corresponding Anchor model (right diagram) of click stream data.

job, when data is big, starting from ≈100 million rows, it may produce poor execution plans.

The BI team at Avito performs ad-hoc queries accessing hundreds of billions of rows in a Anchor model on a daily basis. Because of this, a query modification approach was designed. The approach aims to optimize the query execution plan according to the highly normalized data model. The following sections will describe a sample task illustrating the approach. Its benefits in comparison to the execution plan in a denormalized data model are presented.

2.5 Theoretical Estimates and Practical Verification

The largest data set available at Avito for testing purposes is the clickstream data set. It will be compared using an Anchor model and a 3NF model, seen in Fig. 2, having exactly the same information content. In the models WebEventID is the surrogate identifier of a clickstream record, EventDate is the date and time of an event, EventType is its type, such as 'search', 'message', or 'purchase', CookieID is a surrogate identifier of a cookie, User is the user bound to the cookie, CreationDate is when it was created, and ExpirationDate is when it expires. These models are simple, and only represent a small subset of the actual model used at Avito, but sufficient in order to verify the expected benefits.

Experiments were made in the column-oriented massively parallel processing relational database HP Vertica v.7.1.0.3, with cluster sizes of 5, 10, and 12 nodes, where each node is an HP ProLiant DL380p Gen8 server with double Intel Xeon E5-2680 v2 CPUs, 256 GB RAM, 25 * 300 GB SAS 15 k SFF 2.5" HDDs connected through a RAID card with 2 GB cache, and an HP 530SFP+ Ethernet 10Gbit 2-port LAN-adapter for communication. Since the experiments were carried out in a production environment, daily operations, such as ETL and reporting, may have affected the results. In order to minimize such effects, experiments were repeated several times and averages calculated. The two models in Fig. 2 were populated with data, consisting of approximately 50 billion actual web events accessing 3.4 billion cookies.

2.6 Scenario, Query Optimization, and Results

The chosen ad-hoc query is to calculate the number of unique users who triggered page view events (condition on EventType) during February 2014 (condition on

```
select count(distinct c.User)
from Cookie c
join WebEvent we
on we.CookieId = c.CookieId
where date_trunc('month',
    c.CreationDate) = '2014−02−01'
and c.CreationDate = we.EventDate
and we.EventType in (42, 43)
```

```
select count(distinct u.User)
from Cookie_WebEvent tie join User u
on u.CookieID = tie.CookieID
join CreationDate cd on cd.CookieID = tie.CookieID
join EventDate ed on ed.WebEventID = tie.WebEventID
join EventType et on et.WebEventID = tie.WebEventID
where date_trunc('month', cd.CreationDate) = '2014−02−01'
and cd.CreationDate = ed.EventDate
and et.EventType in (42, 43)
```

Fig. 3. Corresponding queries in the 3NF model (left) and the Anchor model (right).

EventDate), and have new cookies (CreationDate of the cookie is the same date as the EventDate). The query was selected for estimation, because it is typical, it is simple for reading, and it requires great amount of system resources to operate. The SQL code for the queries, as they would look in the 3NF model and the Anchor model, can be seen in Fig. 3.

The execution plan in the 3NF model is the one selected by the Vertica query optimizer. Many modern query optimizers can make use of column statistics, holding information about the distribution of values, to determine the optimal join order. The most selective conditions in a query are applied first, yielding successive intermediate result sets between joins that have as few rows as possible. Since a non-optimal plan was chosen by the optimizer, the execution plan in the Anchor model was forced by producing intermediate steps by hand. The hand made plan demonstrates that efficient query execution plans for complex analytic queries in an Anchor model exists. Based on such, the BI team at Avito implemented a framework for semi-automatic generation of efficient plans for Big Data. Future generations of Vertica optimizers can be complemented with similar logic. The statistics of the sample set is as follows.

- R, row count of Cookie anchor table ≈ 3.4 billion.
- S, attribute value selectivity expressed as selection of "one out of S".
  Condition on CreationDate reduces data to $1/S_1 \approx 1/3.01$.
  Condition on EventType reduces data to $1/S_2 \approx 1/3.20$.
  Condition on EventDate = CreationDate reduces data to $1/S_3 \approx 1/3.17$.
- M, average number of events per cookie. $M \approx 50/3.4 \approx 15$.
- A, average size of each column = 8 bytes.
- P, size of disk page = 4000 bytes.

For **3NF**, according to [8], the optimizer will choose an early materialization strategy for the smaller, inner side, of the join. The experiments confirmed this, with the following execution plan.

1. Read CookieId, User, CreationDate columns from disk to RAM, according to EM-pipeline strategy [8]. Data is filtered by the condition on CreationDate.
2. Read disk pages to match remaining CookieId keys in the WebEvent table. A hash join is used, as well as a resegmentation of the key between nodes.
3. Load EventDate and EventType for the matched WebEvent rows. Data is filtered by the condtition on EventType.

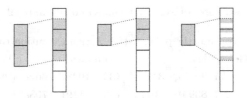

Fig. 4. When a part of a join is reduced, from the two disk pages (left) to one page (center, right), the number of pages needed to be read in order to produce the join depend on whether the joined keys are concentrated (center) or spread out (right). For an arbitrary join, the number of pages to read is normally significantly reduced.

4. Filter loaded data by the condition on EventDate and CreationDate, calculating the number of unique User values.

RAM usage can be estimated as $\frac{3*R*A}{S_1} + \frac{M*R*A}{S_1} + \frac{R*A*M}{S_1*S_2} \approx 190\,Gb$. While servers may have more than 190 GB of RAM, this is but one of many possible ad-hoc queries. A Big Data installation is likely to support multiple concurrent processes (ETL, maintenance, reporting), all competing for resources. It is therefore impossible to guarantee that each type of ad-hoc query will obtain enough RAM at the moment of execution. The plan described above is then no longer possible, forcing the query optimizer to spill the join operation onto disk. A *join spill* (the term may differ between vendors) means that some part of an execution plan requires too much RAM, and data have to be separated into N chunks[1], small enough to fit into available RAM, and that can be processed sequentially with their results assembled afterwards.

Join spill reduces maximum RAM utilization, but increases disk I/O, a slower resource. Figure 4 illustrates, why a condition reducing a table on one side of the join may not reduce the number of disk operations for the table on the other side of the join. Therefore, disk I/O operations can be estimated according to *optimistic* (concentrated keys) or *pessimistic* (spread out keys) scenarios. In the optimistic one, the number of operations is the same as in a RAM join, whereas in the pessimistic one the whole table may need to be scanned for each chunk.

- Disk page ops, optimistic: $\frac{R*A*(4*M+3)}{S_1*P}$
- Disk page ops, pessimistic, RAM join: $\frac{R*A*(4*M*S_1+3)}{S_1*P}$
- Disk page ops, pessimistic, join spill: $\frac{R*A*(4*N*M*S_1+3)}{S_1*P}$
- Logical ops: $\frac{R*M}{S_1} + \frac{R*M}{S_1*S_2} + \frac{R*M}{S_1*S_2*S_3}(log(\frac{R*M}{N*S_1*S_2*S_3})+1)$

For an **Anchor model** the hand-made execution plan aims to maximize merge join utilization. Hash join can be almost as fast as merge, but it requires a lot of RAM. If limited, the join must again be spilled during execution. The following execution plan can either be implemented by hints or by a set of subsequent temporary tables.

---

[1] $N = \langle$pessimistic RAM estimation$\rangle/\langle$available RAM$\rangle$, rounded up.

Table 1. Theoretical estimates of execution times and actual results from experiments.

Plan type	(optimistic–pessimistic), actual execution time		
	5 nodes	10 nodes	12 nodes
3NF RAM join	(671–2075), 3133s[a]	(335–1038), 662s	(280–865), 491s
3NF spilled join	(687–8399), 3017s	(344–4119), 1703s	(287–3423), 1172s
Anchor modeling	(1185–4515), 2643s	(849–2514), 1174s	(719–2074), 959s

[a] This join required $> 38\,\mathrm{Gb}$ of RAM on each node and it also spilled to disk.

1. Read CookieId, CreationDate columns from disk to RAM, according to EM-pipeline strategy [8]. Data is filtered by the condition on CreationDate.
2. Load WebEventID from WebEvent–Cookie tie table via merge join.
3. Streaming sort, resegmentation and storing of WebEventId into temp table.
4. Filtered loading of EventType attribute table, joined with the temp table from step 3, reducing the count of WebEventID keys.
5. Load EventDate and CookieId from EventDate attribute table and triple merge join the WebEvent–Cookie tie and temp table from step 4 inside RAM.
6. Merge join of temp tables from step 1 and step 5, streaming filtering according to the condition CreationDate = EventDate.
7. Loading of User values from User attribute table inside RAM via merge join with temp table from step 6, calculating the number of unique User values.

The CPU in each server is expected to perform 10^9 FLOPS and the I/O able to push $150\,\mathrm{MB/s}$, both considered to be conservative estimates. Using these metrics the estimated execution time was determined together with the presented formulas for 3NF and Anchor modeling, with the results seen in Table 1.

– Disk page read ops, optimistic: $\dfrac{R*A*(2*S_2*S_3+6*S_2*S_3*M+6*S_3*M+2*S_3+2*M)}{S_1*S_2*S_3*P}$

– Disk page read ops, pessimistic: $\dfrac{R*A*(4*S_2+2*M*S_2+8*S_1*S_2*M+2*S_1*S_2+2*M)}{S_1*S_2*P}$

– Disk page write ops: $\dfrac{2*R*A*(1+M)}{S_1*P}$, RAM usage (max): $\dfrac{R*A*M}{S_1*S_2}$

– Logical ops:
$$\frac{R}{S_1}*log(\frac{R}{S_1}) + \frac{M*R}{S_1}*log(\frac{M*R}{S_1}) + \frac{M*R}{S_1*S_2}*log(\frac{M*R}{S_1*S_2}) + \frac{M*R}{S_1*S_2*S_3}*log(\frac{M*R}{S_1*S_2*S_3})$$

Anchor modeling is not able to reach the speed of the RAM joined 3NF query, but it does comparatively well and is faster than the spilled join, which is the more likely of the two. Considering that no work have to put into creating dedicated indexes in Anchor modeling, whereas the problem grows exponentially with the number of columns in a 3NF table, it proves itself very suitable for ad-hoc querying. It also scales similarly to the others when the number of nodes is raised. In 3NF, where non-trivial join dependencies exist, data may also need to be fetched from other nodes. Tables less normalized than 6NF are therefore, with respect to the autonomy of the nodes, suboptimal for MPP.

3   Conclusions

While much have been said about Big Data with respect to information that have little structure, such as media in different forms, there has been little research into structured Big Data outside of NoSQL solutions. Systems that produce logs, sensors that give information, and other high transaction environments, such as banking, stock trading, and retail to name a few, all yield large volumes of structured data and should all benefit from the approach described in the paper. The experiments carried out showed that the approach works well in the simplified case of two linked entities. Real-world business cases sometimes require three, four or even a dozen linked entities in a single ad-hoc query. Such cases multiply the risk of join spill occurring in some step, and amplify its negative effects. When the number of joins, tables, and filtering conditions increase, the accuracy of the estimated RAM requirement decreases. The query optimizer may significantly overestimate RAM requirements and cause unnecessary join spills. Until rectified, forcing plans is necessary in order to achieve maximum performance. The given approach has been in use at Avito for over a year, for ad-hoc and regular reporting, and even for near-real time KPIs. It has demonstrated stability in terms of execution time and resource consumption, flexibility with respect to schema evolution, and low maintenance with respect to total cost of ownership.

References

1. Banerjee, A., Ghosh, J.: Clickstream clustering using weighted longest common subsequences. In: Proceedings of the Web Mining Workshop at the 1st SIAM Conference on Data Mining
2. Chen, M., Mao, S., Liu, Y.: Big data: a survey. Mob. Netw. Appl. **19**(2), 171–209 (2014)
3. Date, C.E., Darwen, H., Lorentzos, N.A.: Temporal Data and the Relational Model. Elsevier Science, San Francisco (2003)
4. Hultgren, H.: Modeling the Agile Data Warehouse with Data Vault, vol. 1. Brighton Hamilton, Brighton (2012)
5. Kalavri, V., Vlassov, V.: MapReduce: Limitations, Optimizations and Open Issues, TrustCom/ISPA/IUCC, pp. 1031–1038. IEEE (2013)
6. Lamb, A., Fuller, M., et al.: The vertica analytic database: C-store 7 years later. Proc. VLDB Endow. **5**(12), 1790–1801 (2012)
7. Rönnbäck, L., Regardt, O., Bergholtz, M., Johannesson, P., Wohed, P.: Anchor modeling - agile information modeling in evolving data environments. Data Knowl. Eng. **69**(12), 1229–1253 (2010)
8. Shrinivas, L., Bodagala, S., et al.: Materialization strategies in the vertica analytic database: lessons learned. In: Christian, S.J., Jermaine, C.M., Zhou, X. (eds.) ICDE. IEEE Computer Society, pp. 1196–1207 (2013)
9. Wang, G., Konolige, T., et al.: You are how you click: clickstream analysis for sybil detection, pp. 241–256. USENIX Security, August 2013
10. Russias Avito Becomes Worlds 3rd Biggest Classifieds Site After $570M Deal With Naspers. http://techcrunch.com/2013/03/11/russias-avito-becomes-worlds-3rd-biggest-classifieds-site-after-naspers-deal/

I8K|DQ-BigData: I8K Architecture Extension for Data Quality in Big Data

Bibiano Rivas, Jorge Merino, Manuel Serrano[(✉)], Ismael Caballero, and Mario Piattini

Instituto de Tecnologías y Sistemas de Información,
Universidad de Castilla–La Mancha,
Camino de Moledores S/N, 13071 Ciudad Real, Spain
{Bibiano.Rivas,Jorge.Merino,Manuel.Serrano,
Ismael.Caballero,Mario.Piattini}@uclm.es

Abstract. During the execution of business processes involving various organizations, Master Data is usually shared and exchanged. It is necessary to keep appropriate levels of quality in these Master Data, in order to prevent defects and failures in the business processes. A way to support the decision about the usage of data in business processes is to include information about the level of quality alongside the Master Data. ISO/TS 8000 parts 100 to 140, may support the provision of this kind of information in a usable manner. Specifically I8K, a reference implementation from academic sources of the aforementioned standard parts (ISO/TS 8000:100-140), may be used for this objective. Regrettably, I8K is not aimed to support the assessment of large Master Data volumes and does not reach the required efficiency in Big Data surroundings. This paper describe an extension of I8K to resolve those problems of efficiency in Big Data projects.

Keywords: Big data · Data quality · I8K · Master data

1 Introduction

Every day more and more data is digitalized, automated and processed in unthinkable large volumes decades ago. This data are habitually stored and exchanged between organizations [1]. Data is one of the most important assets for organizations. To be able to obtain the greatest benefit from data, it is needed to have an adequate level of data quality for the task where data will be used. Otherwise, the operations and processes to support the business decisions might fail or not reach their objectives [2]. In this sense, organizations may benefit from some extra information about the level of data quality attached to the exchanged data. If present, this extra information may be used when including certain data in the intended operations, or even it is possible to demand a level of quality as a threshold for the exchanged data. Thus, Loshin defines Master Data as *"those essential objects for the business used in the different applications of an organization, alongside the related metadata, attributes, definitions, roles, connections and taxonomies"* [3].

ISO/TS 8000 parts 100 to 140 [4–8] describe requirements that must be satisfied to assure the level of data quality when exchanging Master Data [9]. These requirements

© Springer International Publishing Switzerland 2015
M.A. Jeusfeld and K. Karlapalem (Eds.): ER 2015 Workshops, LNCS 9382, pp. 164–172, 2015.
DOI: 10.1007/978-3-319-25747-1_17

are implemented in a service architecture called I8K, developed in [10]. Alongside I8K, ICS-API is included, an application programming interface that allow developers to make use of the I8K services, when it is necessary to assess the quality of the exchanged data.

Albeit, the tests realized using I8K in large data volumes reveal efficiency issues, due to the used technology that, in this circumstances, overcomes the performance limits when processing data sets of around dozens of megabytes of size. In this sense, it might be understood that the problems can be faced from the perspective of new technologies like Big Data.

Gartner defines Big Data as *"high-volume, high-velocity and high-variety information assets that demand cost-effective, innovative forms of information processing for enhanced insight and decision making"* [11]. Therefore, the assessment of large volumes of Master Data can be understood as a Big Data project. Not only that, but also the fact that the exchanged data comes from different sources that may affect the variety of data, depending on the owning organization. This aspects require the use of particular Big Data technologies within the I8K core.

Specifically, and as the main contribution of this paper, a way to extend the I8K architecture to support the assessment of the quality of large volumes of data using a Big Data environment will be explained, leading to a new architecture called I8K-BiDa. Additionally, this paper depicts a rewriting of the algorithms for assessing Data Quality dimensions as Accuracy and Completeness proposed by ISO/TS 8000 parts 130 and 140 respectively, using Hadoop [12] and the programming paradigm called Map-Reduce [13].

The structure of the rest of the paper is described below. Section 2, briefly reviews the existing literature, in particular, the reference development of I8K. In Sect. 3, a Big Data architecture is proposed with the goal of including the Big Data concepts in I8K. In Sect. 4, a working example is carried out. Section 4, exposes the conclusions and future work.

2 Related Work

In [14], Master Data is defined as those concepts that determine the basic knowledge of the business domain in which one an organization develops its business activity. Thus, the organizations that need to exchange Master Data for the execution of some of their business processes, should refer to equivalent concepts represented by coherent versions of Master Data. Moreover, it is important to properly manage the quality values of the exchanged Master Data.

ISO/TS 8000 parts 100 to 140, describe a set of requirements that allows to manage the quality of the data when exchanging Master Data between organizations. [15] proposes a service oriented architecture for I8K as an implementation of ISO/TS 8000 parts 100 to 140 for the Master Data exchange between organizations. Additionally, I8K was conceived as an authorized agent to certify the Data Quality levels. The I8K architecture for regular data is shown in Fig. 1.

I8K architecture is composed by the following services:

- **I8KManager:** Manage the requests done to the I8K architecture, delegating to the corresponding services.

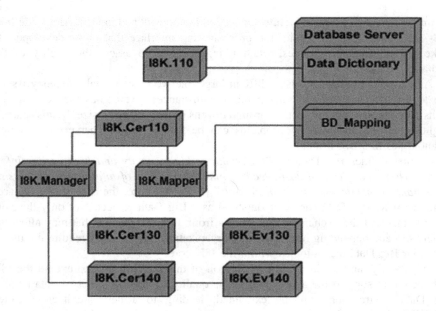

Fig. 1. I8K architecture

- **I8K.Ev130:** Evaluates the Accuracy of the Master Data Message.
- **I8K.Cer130:** Aggregates certifying information to the Accuracy of Master Data Message.
- **I8K.Ev140:** Evaluates the Completeness of the Master Data Message.
- **I8K.Cer140:** Aggregates certifying information to the Completeness of Master Data Message.

To ease the communication between the applications that exchange data using I8K, the authors developed an application programming interface (API) called ICS-API. The way to use I8K alongside ICS-API is shown in Fig. 2.

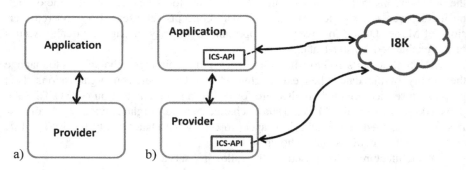

Fig. 2. (a) Interaction of applications without I8K; (b) Interaction of applications' using I8K services

I8K the requirements from ISO/TS 8000-1x0 through SOA Web services. In order to support the I8K operational processes, a set of exchangeable Master Data Messages have been identified. The message sequence regulated by the communication protocol is shown in Fig. 3. In Table 1, the types of messages that are exchanged between applications with I8K are listed, and in Table 2, the messages that are sent between applications that exchange Master Data without I8K are listed.

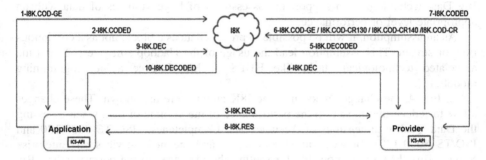

Fig. 3. Communication protocol

Table 1. Types of master data messages exchanged between I8k and applications

Type	Description
I8K.COD-GE	An application needs to encrypt Master Data to make a request to a service.
I8K.CODED	I8K has codified a Master Data Message and the content is returned to the requiring application.
I8K.DEC	An application needs to decrypt a received Master Data Message in order to understand the content.
I8K.DECODED	I8K has decrypted a Master Data Message and the content is returned to the requiring application.
I8K.COD-CR130	An application needs to encrypt a message, assess and certify the *Accuracy* of data.
I8K.COD-CR140	An application needs to encrypt a message, assess and certify the *Completeness* of data.
I8K.COD-CR	An application needs to encrypt a message, assess and certify the Master Data Messages according to the Data Quality levels of *Accuracy* and *Completeness*.

Table 2. Types of master data messages exchanged between applications

Type	Description
I8K.REQ	An application sends a request message of data to a data provider.
I8K.RES	A data provider sends an answer message with the data requested by an application.

3 Proposal

I8K architecture has been thoroughly tested when assessing relational data [15]. Nevertheless, the performance decreases drastically when applying it to large volumes of data. We propose to use Big Data to solve that performance problems, as these solutions are considered a good way to process and analyse large volumes of data.

The main contribution of this paper the extension of the I8K architecture [10], using Big Data technologies, to support the assessment of large volumes of data with an appropriate level of performance.

As an assumption, it will be possible to process data as a block, not as a continuous flow or stream. This assumption lead the usage of the Hadoop software [12] and the associated technological stack, like HDFS or Map-Reduce as a programming model [13].

In Fig. 4, the changes made into the I8K architecture are shown. These changes allow to reduce the impact on the performance of the volume of data when assessing the Data Quality dimensions of Accuracy and Completeness (ISO/TS 8000-130 and ISO/TS 8000-140). Between the I8KManager and the new services an Enterprise Service Bus (ESB) is responsible for routing the messages to the corresponding Big Data services according to the type of the message. The new services (I8K. Cer1x0-BiDa and I8K.Ev1x0-BiDa) work equivalently to the existing ones, but aggregating the ability of assessing large volumes of data using Big Data solutions.

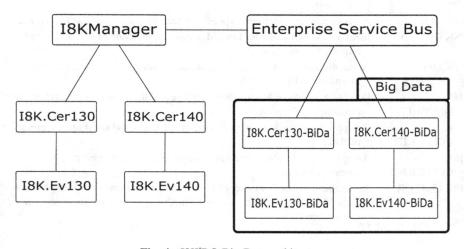

Fig. 4. I8K|DQ-Big Data architecture

Our proposal does not remove the ability of assessing relational data of the architecture. Instead, it adds the ability of assessing large volumes of data using Big Data technologies. Even that this fact is trivial, it includes a small difficulty, when using the I8K architecture. The set of messages shown in Tables 1 and 2, do not allow the I8KManager to know about the type of data assets that are included in the Master Data

Message, and therefore, the I8KManager will not know where to send data for its assessment (i.e. send to I8K.Ev-1x0 or to I8K.ev-1x0-BiDa). To guarantee an appropriate operation of the architecture, it is necessary to add, to the set of message shown in Tables 1 and 2, some new message that allow to tell the I8KManager to use the Big Data services rather than the classic web services used in the context of regular data volumes. Whilst these new messages, the communication protocol is not altered, but it is only needed to include those messages for the services to understand them. The new messages are shown in Table 3.

Table 3. New messages for big data assessment services

Type	Description
I8K.CR-BiDa	An application needs to encrypt the message, assess and certify the Master Data Message, according to the Quality levels of Accuracy and Completeness for large volumes of data (using Big Data technologies).
I8K. CR130-BiDa	An application needs to encrypt the message, assess and certify the Master Data Message, according to the Quality levels of Accuracy for large volumes of data (using Big Data technologies).
I8K. CR140-BiDa	An application needs to encrypt the message, assess and certify the Master Data Message, according to the Quality levels of Completeness for large volumes of data (using Big Data technologies).

The concept of "encrypting" a message corresponds to a map between the definition of the Master Data provided by an organization, and the standard definition of Master Data provided by the I8K data dictionary vocabulary. The operation of the I8K| Big Data Architecture is reproduced below in order to support the comprehension of the process.

1. Application A request to I8K the encryption of a message to make a petition of data to a Data Provider P (I8K.COD-GE).
2. I8K encrypts the message from A (I8K.CODED).
3. A sends the encrypted message requesting data to P (I8K.REQ).
4. P request to I8K to decode the message (I8K.DEC).
5. I8K decodes the message for P (I8K.DECODED).
6. P processes the message and:

   a. If there is a large volume of data, P sends a message to I8K to assess Data Quality using Big Data (I8K.CR-BiDa).
   i. I8KManager sends the data to the ESB.
   ii. ESB route the data to an evaluator or other in function the type of the message.
   b. Otherwise, P sends a message to I8K to assess Data Quality using the regular processing (I8K.COD-CR).

7. I8K assesses and certifies the Data Quality levels and returns the results to P.
8. P sends the data to A with the Data Quality information attached (I8K.RES).

4 Working Example

The I8K|BiDa has been tested with a Master Data message of the financial sector that contains 1056321 records of data to be assessed. The requirements from ISO/TC 130 and 140 defined over the data also must be included into the Master Data message. For this working example the procedure for assessing Completeness (ISO/TC 8000-140), is illustrated bellow (Notice that these two activities correspond to the activities 6 and 7 of the procedure).

1. The company *"Bancancha"* requests the certification of the Completeness of Master Data it needs to exchange. For this purpose and as the exchanged data comes in a large volume, it sends the Master Data Message to the I8KManager of the I8K. CR140-BiDa type (see Table 3).

    a. The I8KManager receives the message from *"Bancancha"* (the Data Provider) and sends the message to the ESB.
    b. The ESB route the data to the I8K.Cer140-BiDa service to certify the level of Completeness of the data included in the Master Data Message.

2. The I8K.Cer140-BiDa module request the assessment services to the 140 evaluator. As the request is for assessing using Big Data technologies, it will send the message to the service I8K.Ev140-BiDa.

    a. The service I8K.Ev140-BiDa receives the Master Data Message and assesses the Completeness of the data included in the message. First the I8K.Ev140-BiDa service stores the included data (the 1056321 records of data) in the HDFS from the Hadoop deployment [16]. To perform the assessment, the I8K.Ev140-BiDa module invokes the web service that encapsulates the Python program, implemented with the Map-Reduce programming model, that is in charge of processing the data to obtain the Data Quality levels of the Completeness dimension, in Big Data surroundings.

To reckon of the Completeness the following variables are managed:

- *Minimum quality*: Minimum Quality level of Completeness required by the organization. This threshold is reached just in the case all the rules (defined in requirements from ISO/TC 8000-140 over data) are met. Variable called *"minlvl"*.
- *Terms without rule*: total number of terms that are not defined in the requirements, but are present in the message. Variable called *"not_rules"*.
- *Not Empty terms without rule*: total number of terms that are not defined in the rules and are not empty but take part in the message. Variable called *"not_empty"*.
- Remaining percentage: The percentage of Completeness that remains after subtracting the *minimum quality* to the total (100 %). Variable called *"r_percentage"*.

To reckon the Completeness level (lvl140) we propose the following function:
lvl140 = minlvl + ((r_percentage*not_empty)/not_rules)
In less than a minute, the partial and final results are obtained after processing more than a million of Master Data. The I8K in normal conditions without the Big Data technologies last 25–30 min to perform the same processing in similar conditions.

Once that the results are obtained, they are sent to the I8K.Cer140 module that prepares a file with the certification of the Data Quality and with the Completeness levels. This file is sent to the I8KManager.

5 Conclusions and Future Work

It is irrefutable that we live in a time in which one data has an essential value. Organizations exchange data to support the execution of their business processes. It is necessary that exchanged data has appropriate levels of quality for those business processes to be executed successfully. This success may be assured if data is filtered by its Data Quality level, and these Data Quality levels should be attached to the exchanged data.

ISO/TS 8000 parts 100 to 140, support this goal. I8K is a service oriented architecture that implement the requirements of the aforementioned ISO/TS 8000 parts. This implementation does not provide enough performance when processing large volumes of data, albeit. To palliate this lack, new parts has been added to the architecture, using Big Data technologies under some initial assumptions.

This paper describes the extension of the I8K architecture in Big Data surroundings, and the procedure to properly use the extended architecture called I8K|BiDa. The new parts provide the ability of assessing the Accuracy and the Completeness of large volumes of data with an appropriate performance.

The resultant foundations have been applied in a working example to test the effectiveness of the changes in the I8K architecture with positive results in the efficiency (from 25–30 min to less than a minute).

As future work, we propose the extension of this architecture with new evaluators to assess more Data Quality dimensions. Also the improvement of the I8K|Big Data architecture with real-time technologies as Apache Storm.

Furthermore, it is important to test the applicability of the architecture in real companies, in order to check whether the I8K|Big Data Architecture is useful not only in the academic world, but also in the real business world.

Acknowledgements. This work has been partially funded by GEODAS-BC project (Ministerio de Economía y Competitividad y Fondo Europeo de Desarrollo Regional FEDER, TIN2012-37493-C03-01); SERENIDAD project (Consejería de Educación, Ciencia y Cultura de la Junta de Comunidades de Castilla La Mancha, y Fondo Europeo de Desarrollo Regional FEDER, PEII-2014-045-P); VILMA project (Consejería de Educación, Ciencia y Cultura de la Junta de Comunidades de Castilla La Mancha, y Fondo Europeo de Desarrollo Regional FEDER, PEII-2014-048-P); GLOBALIA project (Consejería de Educación, Ciencia y Cultura de la Junta de Comunidades de Castilla La Mancha, de la Junta de Comunidades de Castilla La Mancha, y Fondo Europeo de Desarrollo Regional FEDER, PEII-2014-038-P) and CGT – DESARROLLO GLOBAL DEL SOFTWARE (12 FEB 2014).

References

1. Mohanty, S., Jagadeesh, M., Srivatsa, H.: Big Data Imperatives. Apress, New York (2013)
2. Redman, T.C., Blanton, A.: Data Quality for the Information Age. Artech House Inc., London (1997)
3. Loshin, D.: Master Data Management. Morgan Kaufmann, San Francisco (2010)
4. ISO/TS: ISO 8000-100: Data Quality - Part 100: Master data: Exchange of charateristic data: Overview, ed. (2009)
5. ISO/TS: ISO 8000-110, Data quality - Part 110: Master data: Exchange of characteristic data: Syntax, semantic encoding, and conformance to data specification., ed. (2009)
6. ISO/TS: ISO/TS 8000-120, Data quality - Part 120: Master data: Exchange of characteristic data: Provenance, ed. (2009)
7. ISO/TS: ISO/TS 8000-130, Data quality — Part 130: Master data: Exchange of characteristic data: Accuracy, ed. (2009)
8. ISO/TS: ISO/TS 8000-140, Data quality — Part 140: Master data: Exchange of characteristic data: Completeness, ed. (2009)
9. Caballero, I., Bermejo, I., Parody, L., López, M.T.G., Gasca, R.M., Piattini, M.: SLA4DQ-I8K: Acuerdos a Nivel de Servicio para Calidad de Datos en Intercambios de Datos Maestros regulados por ISO 8000-1x0, JCIS (2014)
10. Caballero, I., Bermejo, I., López, M.T.G., Gasca, R.M., Piattini, M.: I8K: An Implementation Of ISO 8000-1X0. In: 17th International Conference on Information Quality (ICIQ) (2013)
11. Chen, C.P., Zhang, C.-Y.: Data-intensive applications, challenges, techniques and technologies: a survey on big data. Inf. Sci. **275**, 314–347 (2014)
12. The Apache Software Foundation, Apache Hadoop, 04 May 2015. https://hadoop.apache.org
13. The Apache Software Foundation, Map Reduce (2015). https://hadoop.apache.org/docs/current/hadoop-mapreduce-client/hadoop-mapreduce-client-core/MapReduceTutorial.html
14. Borek, A., Parlikad, A.K., Webb, J., Woodall, P.: Total Information Risk Management: Maximizing The Value Of Data And Information Assets. Newnes, Oxford (2013)
15. Bermejo, I.: Bachellor dissertation thesis I8K: Arquitectura de Servicios para la Gestión de la Calidad de los Datos: Una implementación de ISO 8000:2009-100 (2013)
16. The Apache Software Foundation, HDFS, 11 March 2015. http://hadoop.apache.org/docs/r1.2.1/hdfs_design.html

Research on Big Data

Characterizing the Field and Its Dimensions

Jacky Akoka[1,2](✉), Isabelle Comyn-Wattiau[1,3], and Nabil Laoufi[1]

[1] CEDRIC-CNAM, Paris, France
{akoka,wattiau}@cnam.fr, laouf_na@auditeur.cnam.fr
[2] TEM-Institut Mines Telecom, Evry, France
[3] ESSEC Business School, Cergy-Pontoise, France

Abstract. Big Data has emerged as a significant area of study for both practitioners and researchers. Big Data is a term for massive data sets with large
structure. In 2012, Big Data passed the top of the Gartner Hype Cycle, attesting
the maturity level of this technology and its applications. The aim of this paper
is to examine whether the Big Data research community reached the same level
of maturity. For this purpose, we provide a framework identifying existing and
emerging research areas of Big Data. This framework is based on five dimensions, including the SMACIT perspective. Current and past research in Big Data
are analyzed using a bibliometric study of publications based on more than a
decade of related academic publications. The results have shown that even if
significant contributions have been made by the research community, attested by
a continuous increase in the number of scientific publications that address Big
Data, it lags behind entreprises' expectations.

Keywords: Big data · Bibliometric study · Framework · Artefact · Usage ·
Analytics

1 Introduction

Nowadays, organizations and individuals generate large amounts of data at a very high
rate. With an impressing amount of data arriving at an exabyte scale, new insights can
be obtained from their contents. The latter will help organizations to gain richer insights
and improve their competitive position. Moreover, it is generally accepted that relevant
information obtained using Big Data technologies will enhance enterprises efficiency
and competitiveness.

International Data Corporation (IDC) found that the created and copied data volume in the world was 1.8 zettabites (ZB). It is estimated that this figure will double
every other two years in the near future [1]. [2] asserts that Big Data can improve the
potential value of the US medical industry estimated at USD 300 billion. It considers
that retailers that fully utilize Big Data may increase their profit by more than 60 %.
Finally, according to McKinsey, Big Data may also be utilized to improve the efficiency of government operations. Let us remind that 5 exabytes (EB) of data were
created by human until 2003. Today this amount of information is created in two days.
In 2012, digital world was expanded to 2.72 ZB. It is predicted to double every two

© Springer International Publishing Switzerland 2015
M.A. Jeusfeld and K. Karlapalem (Eds.): ER 2015 Workshops, LNCS 9382, pp. 173–183, 2015.
DOI: 10.1007/978-3-319-25747-1_18

years, reaching about 8 ZB by 2015 [3]. IBM indicates that every day 2.5 EB of data are created. CISCO predicts that, by 2020, 50 billion devices will be connected to networks and to the Internet. The investment in spending on Information Technology (IT) infrastructure of the digital universe and telecommunications will grow by 40 % between 2012 and 2020[1]. Big Data will account for 40 %. Moreover IDC expects that 23 % of the information in the digital universe (or 643 EB) would be useful for Big Data. It includes data originated from surveillance footage, embedded and medical devices, entertainment, social media, as well as consumer images.

Companies are learning to take advantage of Big Data. They use real-time information from sensors, radio frequency identification to understand their business environments, and to create new products and services. Organizations capitalize on Big Data in three ways: (i) they pay attention to data flows, (ii) they rely on data scientists, (iii) they are moving analytics away from the IT function [4]. Huge investments are being made by companies with great expectations for the gains to be made. Big Data is considered to be the new engine to sustain the high growth of the information industry. Enterprises' competitiveness is increasingly determined by their abilities to leverage the technologies associated with Big Data. However, several questions remain to be answered. What does the future hold? Will the changes be transformative? What domains are likely to benefit the most? Even though it is difficult to bring answers to these questions, companies had great expectations as attested by Gartner. In 2012, Big Data passed the top of the Gartner Hype Cycle. In 2014, Big Data moved to Trough Disillusionment phase, attesting a maturity level of companies which invested in this technology. Successful applications of Big Data in industry are reported in many publications. Thus, it seems that industry is ahead of academia [5].

In order to characterize the emergence of Big Data as a research topic, this paper looks at it from five different perspectives: the timeline, the context, the objectives, the artefacts created, and the applications (usages). We explore the term Big Data using the peer reviewed literature. Our research question may be defined as follows: how do researchers grasp the big data concept? The rest of the paper is worded as follows. Section 2 presents a synthetic literature review on Big Data and associated technologies, structured along the SMACIT perspectives. In Sect. 3, we define our framework as a multidimensional model where SMACIT is one dimension. Section 4 presents our approach to evaluate the evolution of Big Data in terms of contributions by the research community. To this end, we position Big Data in the framework. Section 5 concludes the work.

2   Big Data: A Literature Review

Big Data has been a buzzword in the last decade. The term, coined by Roger Magoulas[2], refers to large data sets almost impossible to manage and process using traditional data management tools. It refers to various forms of large information sets requiring complex computational platforms in order to be analyzed.

---

[1] http://www.emc.com/leadership/digital-universe/2014iview/index.htm.

[2] http://strata.oreilly.com/2010/01/roger-magoulas-on-big-data.html.

There have been some discussions on the definition of Big Data [6, 7]. [8] defined it using the 3Vs model (Volume, Velocity, and Variety). [1] defined Big Data as "a new generation of technologies and architectures, designed to economically extract value from very large volumes of a wide variety of data, by enabling the high-velocity capture, discovery, and/or analysis". [9] presents an extensive review of Big Data research issues. [10] focus on Business analytics resulting from Big Data. [11] introduce the general background of Big Data and review related technologies such as Cloud computing, Internet of Things (IoT), and Hadoop. They also emphasize the four phases of the value chain of Big Data, i.e., data generation, data acquisition, data storage, and data analysis. They examine applications of Big Data, namely enterprise management, IoT, social networks, medical applications, collective intelligence, and smart grids.

Emerging Big Data opportunities can be classified into several topic areas. Jeanne Ross (MIT) proposed the five key areas of Social media, Mobile systems, Analytics, Cloud, and IoT (SMACIT) as significant drivers for enterprise digital transformation. Such a classification aims to emphasize the relations of these technologies with Big Data characteristics. IoT, Mobile and Social network are major sources of Big Data.

Social media is deeply entrenched in our lives [12]. It is considered to reach 82 % of the world's Internet population. It represents the largest portion of individuals' Internet usage, accounting for nearly 1 of every 5 min spent online globally [13]. It has become the new communications paradigm for company-to-consumer message delivery [14]. [15] estimates that US companies spent $5.1 billion on advertising in social media in 2013. By 2018, that number is projected to grow to nearly $15 billion. [16] present a comprehensive overview of the current social networking services. [17] present analyze existing social platforms (social network sites, social media, social games, social bookmarking, and social knowledge). They present more specific instances of computation tasks and techniques (social network analysis, link modeling and mining, ranking, sentiment analysis, etc.) used on these social platforms.

Many organizations are focusing on the mobile market and "are increasingly turning to mobile devices as new sources of data derived from continuously monitoring a wide range of processes and situations" [18]. [19] present an overview of the Mobile Data Challenge (MDC), a research initiative aiming at generating innovations around smartphone-based research. [20] analyzed individual human mobility patterns from a proprietary dataset. Finally [21] present a survey on mobile social networking platforms.

[22] present a literature survey on Big Data analytics. The specificity of analytics involving Big Data is due to the hard deadlines, and to data quality. Methods need to be scaled. The challenges range from building storage systems to collecting data from distributed sources in order to run a diverse set of computations on data. [23] present a description of Big Data focusing on the analytic methods used specifically for Big Data. They emphasize analytics related to unstructured data, which constitute 95 % of Big Data. There is a multi-step pipeline required to extract value from data: heterogeneity, incompleteness, scale, timeliness, privacy, and process complexity [24]. Big Data analytics has been proposed as an advanced technology, which typically includes large-scale and complex programs under specific analytical methods. Some potential

applications from different fields are: evolution of commercial applications, and evolution of scientific applications [23].

There are many solutions for Big Data related to cloud computing. Depending on the level of volume, variety, velocity, it is important to choose appropriate Big Data tools. Thanks to the cloud, we move to Big Data as a Service or Analytics as a Service. [26]. Thus, customer and provider's staff are much more involved in the loop.

[27] describes different visions of IoT paradigm as well as the associated enabling technologies. They group into the following domains potential applications of IoT: (i) Transportation and logistics, (ii) Healthcare, (iii) Smart environment (home, office, plant), and (iv) Personal and social. [28] present a survey serving as a guideline and a conceptual framework for context-aware product development and research in the IoT paradigm. They also provide a systematic exploration of existing IoT products and highlight a number of potentially significant research directions and trends. Although the current IoT data is not the dominant part of Big Data, by 2030, the quantity of sensors will reach one trillion. Then the IoT data will be the most important part of Big Data [29]. Big Data in IoT has three features that conform to the Big Data paradigm: (i) abundant terminals generating masses of data; (ii) data generated by IoT is usually semi-structured or unstructured; (iii) data of IoT is useful only when analyzed.

Finally, [10] mentioned the following applications: e-commerce, e-government, science and technology, smart health, security and public safety. One example is sales planning allowing organizations to optimize their commodity prices. They can also improve their operation efficiency and optimize the labor force, and use Big Data to conduct inventory and logistic optimization. Big Data enables enterprises to predict the consumer behavior. In e-commerce numerous transactions can be conducted and recorded every day.

Despite the success of Big Data applications, some obstacles and challenges in the development of Big Data applications remain. Among them let us mention: data representation, redundancy reduction and data compression, data life cycle management, analytical mechanism, data confidentiality, energy management, expendability and scalability, and cooperation [24, 30].

3   A Framework for Analyzing Big Data Research

The literature review on Big Data revealed many dimensions for analysing contributions. In order to enrich this state-of-the-art, we compiled the most significant dimensions found in the literature and enriched them, resulting in a new framework described as a multidimensional model (Fig. 1). Then we have conducted a bibliometric study to assess some aspects of Big Data research. A chronological study has been conducted to position the research on Big Data according to the different dimensions.

First, *the Context dimension* is linked to the SMACIT perspective. The latter is not often referenced in academic publications. However it deserved much attention from companies as a way to structure their digital transformation. Thus, we propose to analyze how Big Data and each of the SMACIT components, i.e. Social media, Mobility, Analytics, Cloud, and Internet of Things are correlated in academic publications. Each of these components is itself a hot topic in computer science research. Studying the overlapping between them and Big Data is what we call the context.

The state-of-the-art on Big Data (Sect. 2) illustrated the new challenges linked to volume, velocity, and variety. Hence research in Big Data aims to produce concepts, methods, and tools to build high quality IT solutions. Thus, we propose *the Objective dimension* to analyze which are the main targets of researchers in Big Data. Using mainly ISO software quality criteria, we propose to study the correlation of Big Data research with the following quality objectives: integrity, confidentiality, privacy, traceability, reliability, scalability, performance, usability, quality, security. We particularly detailed the security criterion (e.g. integrity, confidentiality, privacy, traceability) since it is a main issue mentioned in Big Data research.

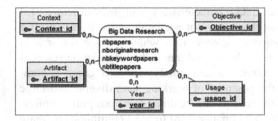

Nb of papers	with chain in AKT	descri- bing original research	with search chain in K	with search chain in T
Dimensions				
SMACIT	264	241	103	49
Artifact	277	263	37	27
Usage	72	56	14	6
Objective	249	237	32	22
Total	486	415	254	187

Fig. 1. Multidimensional framework   **Fig. 2.** Examples of measures

Big Data research aims at providing professionals with models, methods, and tools to deal with Big Data applications. Thus we propose *a third dimension called Artifact*, allowing us to analyze which are the main contributions of Big Data research. In order to obtain a detailed viewpoint of the artifacts proposed in academic publications, we used the typology of artefacts proposed in [31]. Following [33] proposing four categories of artifacts, i.e. constructs, models, methods, and instantiations, [31] refines the categories, distinguishing between language (construct), metamodel, system design, ontology, taxonomy, framework, architecture, metric (models), methodology, guideline, algorithm (methods), and prototype (instantiation). Even if research on Big Data is very dynamic, not all artifacts are actually produced. This analysis will provide researchers with future research avenues.

The maturity of research is also linked to the validation of contributions through real life applications. Thus we also listed the main application domains and analyzed how academics address these domains. We built the list of domains by screening literature and eliciting the main fields where Big Data could bring new solutions for companies. The resulting list constitutes *the Usage dimension* with the following values: healthcare, education, government, finance, marketing, and tourism. Finally, the last dimension considered is time (*Year dimension*). For several dimensions (Artifact and Objective notably), we could have refined them as multilevel dimensions. However, as a first approach, we preferred flat dimension.

The following section will describe the results of our bibliometric study along these five dimensions. Screening the abstract (A), keywords (K), and title (T) of the papers, we defined four measures are respectively the number of papers published with the topic contained in A, K or T, the number of original research papers (as defined by ScienceDirect), the number of papers with the topic mentioned in K, and finally the number of papers with the topic in T.

4 Big Data: An Emerging Research Field

[33] define Big Data aiming at the characteristics of the generated data, containing both the amount and structure of the data. [34] enrich the data characteristics by additional attributes, such as the scope, target, and structure of the data. [35] focus on the amount of data and includes the aspect of method. [10] include the aspect of methods and IT infrastructure topics. [36] incorporate data characteristics and infrastructure. [2] incorporate the method aspect. [37] sees three types of academic units discussing Big Data research. The first one is the hard core science units which include research in astronomy, climate science, and genomics. The second one is the information sciences units contributing to the Big Data paradigm but moderately. The last group is composed of "all units that have realized the potential of working with diverse and large datasets." such as units related to health care, public health, education, public policy, government studies, marketing and retail, and finance. [38] found a continuous increase in the number of publications that address Big Data in scientific databases, such as Scopus. During their literature review, the authors noted that no common understanding of the notion of Big Data exists [36]. [39] review the current literature on Big Data and reveal a focus on the technical perspective.

Based on these definitions, our objective is to consider the term Big Data and to characterize the ways in which the research community used it in the research literature. This effort to understand and characterize the current state of Big Data related research was performed in six steps, all of them being based on the Science Direct corpus. The latter enables different aggregated views of the results based on year, abstract, title, keywords, and specific search chains related to the context of the research, its objectives, the artefacts produced, as well as its usages. In addition to the overall characteristics of the publications on Big Data, a thematic contextual analysis of the abstracts, the titles, and the keywords, was performed leading to an evaluation of measures (an aggregation on all years is provided at Fig. 2):

- Step 1 consists in finding the number of research articles using the term Big Data in the abstract, and/or in the title, and/or in the keywords starting from 1987 (year of the first appearance of the term) to 2015 (2nd column of Fig. 2).
- Step 2 is related to the number of research articles corresponding to a focus level. We defined four focus levels. The first one corresponds to the number of articles using the term Big Data in the abstract, and/or in the title, and/or in the keywords. The second focus level is related to the subset of those papers being considered by Science Direct as "original research articles" (3rd column of Fig. 2). The third level corresponds to research articles containing the term Big Data in the keywords field

(4th column of Fig. 2). The last focus level concerns research articles with the term Big Data in the title (5th column of Fig. 2).

- Step 3 takes into account the context of the research by considering articles which include both the term Big Data and one term of SMACIT.
- Step 4 considers the objectives of the research. We searched for the term Big Data and each objective corresponding to the terms: security, quality, performance, privacy, confidentiality, integrity, traceability, reliability, scalability, and usability.
- Step 5 takes into account one of the artifacts produced by the research, namely: language, metamodel, system design, ontology, taxonomy, framework, architecture, methodology, guideline, algorithm, method fragment, metric, and prototype.
- Step 6 considers usages of the research. We searched for the number of articles containing the term Big Data and one of terms characterizing the usage, namely: healthcare or public health, education, public sector or government, banking or finance, tourism or hospitality, and marketing or retail.

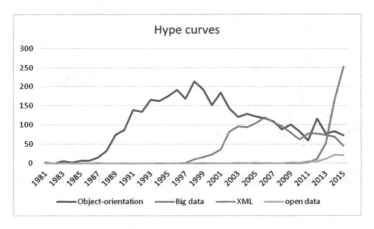

Fig. 3. Frequency of Big Data term in research publications

The main results obtained are summarized below. There is a significant growth of research articles about Big Data from 2011[3] to the present (Fig. 3). This can be explained by the fact that the topic gained much attention over the last few years especially since 2014. Overall, Big Data has a large coverage but a short history. For example, the Big Data related publications numbered 486 (the term appeared once in 1987), whereas publications combining Big Data and SMACIT numbered only 264 and started to appear in 2011. Another interesting finding is related to the focus level. It decreases from 486 to 187[4] publications. In other words, the existence of the term Big

---

[3] One paper published in 1987 mentions big data in its abstract. However it is not linked to the modern understanding of the concept.

[4] 187 publications referenced in ScienceDirect contain the term Big Data in their titles.

Data in an abstract does not imply that the main subject of the research is on Big Data. This is not the case when the term is present in the title meaning that Big Data is the core of the paper. The association of the term Big Data with Analytics or Cloud is much stronger than with the other terms of SMACIT (Fig. 4). As a consequence, it seems that researchers are not yet fully involved in research combining Big Data and IoT or mobility or social media. As for quality objectives, the dominant topic area is performance (Fig. 5). Although the security issues of Big Data are lagging behind, it remains a subject of interest for researchers. Surprisingly, this is not the case for issues such as reliability or usability. In terms of artefacts produced by research on Big Data, two topics emerge: framework and algorithm (Fig. 6). This seems to indicate that researchers on Big Data provide more frameworks and algorithms than taxonomies or ontologies or other artifacts. Usages of Big Data do not yet attract researchers (Fig. 7). However, two domain applications seem to be an area of research: Marketing and retail, and Healthcare.

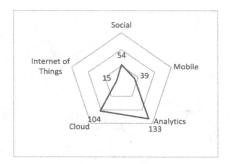

Fig. 4. Big Data and SMACIT

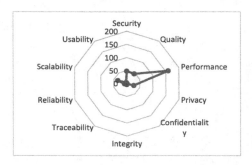

Fig. 5. Big Data and quality objectives

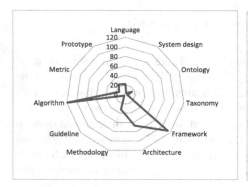

Fig. 6. Big Data and IT artefacts

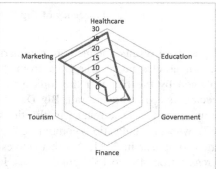

Fig. 7. Big Data and usages

Finally, a comparison of the Gartner's Hype Curve in terms of organizations expectations and the research publications curve on Big Data indicates that the research community is lagging behind (Fig. 3). This research is an invitation to change this trend. Finally, we added at Fig. 3 the results of the same study related to three other past or current buzzwords (object-oriented, open data, XML). The curves of object-orientation and XML confirm that these concepts focused the attention of researchers for many years but this interest finally declined. It might appear that Big Data impacts research more intensively than object-orientation, but this comparison holds only for absolute values. It is also much more important than XML or open data. However, we don't know if this trend will continue.

5   Conclusion and Future Research

Research on Big Data has seen an explosion of publications since 2014. In order to characterize the emergence of Big Data as a research topic, this paper looks at this topic from five different perspectives: the timeline, the context, the objectives, the artefacts created, and the applications (usages). We explore the term Big Data using the peer reviewed literature defining four focus levels. This study was conducted using Science Direct corpus. The numbers presented in this article reflect the indexed publications of Science Direct in June 2015. The main results obtained are: (i) There is a significant growth of research articles about Big Data since 2011. (ii) Big Data has the highest peak compared to topic areas such as object-oriented, or XML or open data. (iii) There is a diversity of interest by researchers on issues such as the objectives, the artefacts produced, the quality criteria used, and the usages and applications of Big Data. It is a multiple viewpoint for practitioners who want to understand what Big Data research produces. Each aspect is also a guideline for researchers in the field helping in the elicitation of correct dimensions (e.g. which application domain should be developed). Finally we show that the research community is lagging behind companies expectations.One limitation of this research is related to the database searched. A similar search on other databases might result in different findings. Future research includes a systematic literature review including a deep content analysis of the complete articles.

References

1. Gantz, J., Reinsel, D.: Extracting value from chaos. IDC iView, pp 1–12 (2011)
2. Manyika, J., Chui, M., Brown, B., Bughin, J., Dobbs, R., et al.: Big Data: the next frontier for innovation, competition, and productivity. McKinsey Global Institute (2011)
3. Intel IT Center: Planning Guide: Getting Started with Hadoop, Steps IT Managers Can Take to Move Forward with Big Data Analytics (2012)
4. Davenport, T., Barth, P.: Bean: R: How Big Data is different. MIT Sloan Mgt Rev. 54(1), 43–46 (2012)
5. Jin, X., Wah, B.W., Cheng, X., Wang, Y.: Significance and challenges of Big Data research. J. Big Data Res. 2(2), 59–64 (2015)

6. Team, O.R.: Big Data Now: Current Perspectives from O'Reilly Radar. O'Reilly Media, Sebastopol (2011)
7. Grobelnik, M.: Big Data Tutorial. http://videolectures.net/eswc2012_grobelnik_big_data/
8. Laney D.: 3-D data management: controlling data volume, velocity and variety. META Group Research Note (2001)
9. Sagiroglu, S., Sinanc, D.: Big data: a review. In: IEEE International Conference on CTS (2013)
10. Chen, H., Chiang, R.H.L., Storey, V.C.: Business intelligence and analytics: from Big Data to big impact. MIS Q. 36(4), 1165–1188 (2012)
11. Chen, M., Mao, S., Liu, Y.: Big data: a survey. Mob. Netw Appl 19, 171–209 (2014)
12. Zhu, Y.Q., Chen, H.G.: Social media and human need satisfaction: Implications for social media marketing. Bus. Horiz. 58, 335–345 (2015)
13. ComScore. It's a social world: Top 10 need-to-knows about social networking and where it's headed. http://www.comscore.com/. Accessed 10 May 2013
14. Mangold, W.G., Faulds, D.J.: Social media: the new hybrid element of the promotion mix. Bus. Horiz. 52(4), 357–365 (2009)
15. Gallup: The myth of social media. http://online.wsj.com/public/resources/documents/sac_report_11_socialmedia_061114.pdf. Accessed 3 July 2014
16. Irfan, R., Bickler, G., Khan, S.U., Kolodziej, J., Li, H., Chen, D., Wang, L., Hayat, K., Madani, S.A., Nazir, B., Khan, I.A., Ranjan, R.: Survey on social networking services. IET Netw. 2(4), 224–234 (2013)
17. King, I., Li, J., Chan, K.T.: A Brief Survey of Computational Approaches in Social Computing. In: Proceedings of International Joint Conference Neural Networks, Atlanta, Georgia, USA (2009)
18. O'Leary, D.: Exploiting Big Data from mobile device sensor-based apps: challenges and benefits. MIS Q. Executive 12(4), 179 (2014)
19. Laurila, J.K., Gatica-Perez, D., Aad, I., Blom, J., Bornet, O.: Pervasive and Mobile Computing, vol. 9, pp. 752–777 (2013)
20. Gonzalez, M.C., Hidalgo, C.A., Barabasi, A.L.: Understanding individual human mobility patterns. Nat. 4, 53–779 (2008)
21. Bellavista, P., Montanari, R., Das, S.K.: Mobile social networking middleware: a survey. Pervasive Mob. Comput. 9, 437–453 (2013)
22. Kambatla, K., Kollias, G., Kumar, V., Grama, A.: Trends in Big Data analytics. J. Parallel Distrib. Comput. 74, 2561–2573 (2014)
23. Gandomi, A., Haider, M.: Beyond the hype: Big Data concepts, methods, and analytics. Int. J. Inf. Manage. 35, 137–144 (2015)
24. Labrinidis, A., Jagadish, H.V.: Challenges and opportunities with Big Data. Proc VLDB Endowment 5(12), 2032–2033 (2012)
25. Polash, F., Abuhussein, A., Shiva, S.: A Survey of Cloud Computing Taxonomies: Rationale and Overview. In: 9th International Conference on Internet Technology and Secured Transactions (2014)
26. Assunçao, M.D., Calheiros, R.N., Bianchi, S., Netto, M.A.S., Buyya, R.: Big Data computing and clouds: Trends and future directions. J. Parallel Distrib. Comput. 79–80, 3–15 (2015)
27. Atzori, L., Iera, A., Morabito, G.: The internet of things: a survey. Comput. Netw. 54, 2787–2805 (2010)
28. Perera, C., Liu, C.H., Jayawardena, S., Chen, M.: A survey on internet of things from industrial market perspective. IEEE Access 2, 1660–1679 (2015)
29. Chen, M., Mao, S., Zhang, Y., Leung, V.C.M.: Big Data : Related Technologies. Challenges and Future Prospects. SpringerBriefs in Computer Science. Springer, Cambridge (2014)

30. Agrawal D, Bernstein P, Bertino E, Davidson S, Dayal U, Franklin M, Gehrke J, Haas L, Halevy A, Han J et al.: Challenges and opportunities with Big Data. A community white paper developed by researches across the United States (2012)
31. Prat, N., Comyn-Wattiau, I., Akoka, J.: Artifact evaluation in information systems design science research – a holistic view. In: PACIS 2014 Proceedings, Paper 23 (2014)
32. March, S.T., Smith, G.F.: Design and natural science research on information technology. Decis. Support Syst. **15**(4), 251–266 (1995)
33. Cuzzocrea, A., Song, I.Y., Davis, K.: Analytics over large-scale multidimensional data: the Big Data revolution. In: Proceedings of the ACM 14th International Workshop on Data Warehousing and OLAP, pp. 101–103. ACM, New York, USA (2011)
34. Bizer, C., Boncz, P., Brodie, M.L., Erling, O.: The meaningful use of Big Data: four perspectives. SIGMOD **40**(4), 56–60 (2011)
35. Jacobs, A.: The pathologies of Big Data. Commun. ACM **52**(8), 36 (2009)
36. Madden, S.: From databases to Big Data. IEEE Comput. **16**(3), 4–6 (2012)
37. Goes, P.B.: Big Data and IS research methods. MIS Q. **38**(3), 3–8 (2014)
38. Hansmann, T., Niemeyer, P.: Big Data - characterizing an emerging research field using topic models. In: IEEE/WIC/ACM International Joint Conferences on Web Intelligence (WI) and Intelligent Agent Technologies (IAT) (2014)
39. Pospiech, M., Felden, C.: Big Data: a state-of-the-art. In: Americas Conference on Information Systems (2012)

Modeling and Reasoning for Business Intelligence

Preface to the 3rd International Workshop on Modeling and Reasoning for Business Intelligence (MORE-BI 2015)

The series of International Workshops on Modeling and Reasoning for Business Intelligence (MORE-BI) aims at advancing the engineering of Business Intelligence (BI) systems. The third edition of the workshop was collocated with the 34th International Conference on Conceptual Modeling (ER 2015), held in Stockholm, Sweden, in October 2015.

BI systems gather, store, and process data to turn it into information relevant for decision-making. Successful engineering, use, and evolution of BI systems require a deep understanding of the requirements of decision-making processes in organizations, of the kinds of information used and produced in these processes, of the ways in which information can be obtained through acquisition and reasoning on data, of the transformations and analyses of that information, of how the necessary data can be acquired, stored, and cleaned, of how its quality can be improved, and of how heterogeneous data can be used together. The third edition of MORE-BI focused on three topics: the use of Key Performance Indicator (KPI) for the development of a model-based RE method for data warehouses, the definition of queries allowing to search the most relevant k-cubes among a set of data cubes, and the fundamentals of ontology-driven RDF analytics.

We thank all authors who have submitted their research to MORE-BI 2015. We are grateful to our colleagues in the steering committee for helping us define the topics and scope of the workshop, our colleagues in the program committee for the time invested in carefully reviewing the submissions under a very tight schedule, the participants who have helped make this a relevant event, and the local organizers and workshop chairs of ER 2015.

We hope that you find the workshop program of interest to research and practice of business intelligence, and that the workshop has allowed you to meet colleagues and practitioners focusing on modeling and reasoning for business intelligence. We look forward to receive your submissions and meet you at the next edition of the workshop.

Accepted Papers

- Rahma Djiroun, Sandro Bimonte and Kamel Boukhalfa. *A First Framework for Top-K Cubes Queries*
- Azadeh Nasiri, Robert Wrembel and Esteban Zimanyi. *Model-based Requirements Engineering for Data Warehouses: From Multidimensional Modelling to KPI Monitoring*

– Joshua Madden, Zirun Qi, Veda Storey, Richard Baskerville, Ephraim McLean and Mark Lyle. *A Method to Model and Compare Unstructured Text in Data Mining*

Keynote

The Business Intelligence Model Foundations, Experiences, and Ongoing Work

Dr. Jennifer Horkoff, City University London, UK
horkoff@city.ac.uk

Business intelligence (BI) offers tremendous potential for business organizations to gain insights into their day-to-day operations, as well as longer term opportunities and threats. However, most of todays BI tools are based on models that are too data-oriented from the point of view of business decision makers, difficult to understand in terms of business objectives and strategies. We have proposed to use conceptual modeling in order to bridge this gap between business-level understanding and representations in data-bases and data warehouses Ð making BI data meaningful. This talk summarizes past, current and future work on the Business Intelligence Model (BIM) conceptual modeling framework. BIM offers concepts familiar to business decision making such as goals, strategies, processes, situations, influences, and indicators. Unlike many enterprise models which are meant to be used to derive, manage, or align with IT system implementations, BIM aims to help business users organize and make sense of the vast amounts of data about the enterprise and its external environment. This talk covers core BIM concepts, focusing especially on reasoning with BIM. BIM includes both qualitative and quantitative reasoning about situations, goals and influences, using data from indicators. Formal reasoning techniques are available using a translation to a subset of the OWL Description Logic (DL). Such reasoning supports strategic analysis of business objectives in light of current enterprise data, allowing analysts to explore scenarios and find alternative strategies. BIM has been expanded to consider tactical refinement (TBIM), and to include the Five Forces Model, to better support strategic decision making. The framework has been applied to several large cases, including a large Canadian Hospital and a leisure cruise business. A prototype implementation has allowed for BIM and TBIM to be taught as part of a graduate course in Information Systems. Ongoing work has focused in several directions, including multidimensional views, comparison of strategic alternatives, and analyzing indicators to find new model relationships or more adequate measures.

Ivan J. Jureta
Corentin Burnay
Stéphane Faulkner
Sarah Bouraga
Program Co-Chairs
MORE-BI'15

A First Framework for Top-K Cubes Queries

Rahma Djiroun[1](✉), Sandro Bimonte[2], and Kamel Boukhalfa[1]

[1] LSI, USTHB, BP 32 El Alia, 16111 Bab Ezzouar, Algeria
{rdjiroun,kboukhalfa}@usthb.dz
[2] IRSTEA, UR TSCF, 9 Avenue Blaise Pascal, 63178 Aubiere, France
sandro.bimonte@irstea.fr

Abstract. Data Warehouse (DW) and OLAP systems are effective solutions for the online analysis of large volumes of data structured as *cubes*. Usually organizations and enterprises require several cubes for their activities. In this context, we define a new kind of queries: "Top-k Cubes queries". Top-K cubes queries allow searching the most relevant k-cubes among a collection of cubes. Then, in this paper we propose a first framework for Top-K cubes queries where queries are expressed in natural language to meet the easiness need of unskilled IT decision-makers. An implementation in a ROLAP architecture is also provided.

Keywords: OLAP · Data Warehouse · Top-K queries

1 Introduction

Data Warehouse (DW) systems are an effective solution for multidimensional online computing and analysis of statistical indicators from large volumes of data [11]. Warehoused data is structured according to the multidimensional model that defines dimensions (such as time, product, etc.) and facts subjects (e.g. the turnover) to define a cube (i.e. multidimensional schema). Warehoused data forms a data cube (i.e. instance of a cube– multidimensional schema instance). OLAP systems allow exploring data cubes, using a set of operators (e.g. Slice, Roll-Up, etc.), to discover unexpected results or trends, and to validate decision assumptions. As for statistical indicators (open data, tabular online data), we assist to a proliferation of available data cubes, such as statistical agro-environmental open-data cubes developed by FAO [12]. Moreover, usually companies or organizations have several activities that require the use of different data cubes. Decentralization of enterprises and organizations on several geographical different locations becomes more and more a reality thanks to tools like wiki, etc. that support collaborative work. In this context, on one hand decision-makers have access to a lot of BI tools and consequently a lot of information, but on the other hand DW experts, designers and managers are not always able to describe warehoused data and/or DW meta-data is not exploitable (for several reasons: meta-data does not exists, meta-data is too much detailed and focused on a particular domain, DW managers leave the company, etc.).

Therefore, in the same way as for tabular statistical indicators, decision-makers need a system allowing them for looking for needed cubes in a simple and user-friendly

© Springer International Publishing Switzerland 2015
M.A. Jeusfeld and K. Karlapalem (Eds.): ER 2015 Workshops, LNCS 9382, pp. 187–197, 2015.
DOI: 10.1007/978-3-319-25747-1_19

way. For example in an agricultural context, a farm manager can ask a question like this: "What are most available relevant cubes concerning milking production at the farm scale among FAO cubes?" to compare and evaluate his/her dairy data to external one. Therefore, in this paper we investigate a new kind of queries: "Top-K cubes queries". We define Top-K cubes queries as queries that allow searching the most relevant k-cubes among a set of cubes. Indeed, although different authors studied recommendation of OLAP queries, and top-k OLAP queries to help decision-makers to explore data [5], to the best of our knowledge, no work has been proposed to explore a set of cubes. Motivated by this lack, in this paper, we propose a first framework for Top-K cubes queries where queries are expressed in natural language to meet the easiness need of unskilled IT decision-makers [1].

2   Motivation

In this section, we present a case study that will be used in the rest of the paper to illustrate our approach. It is adapted from the French project EDEN that aims at the multidimensional analysis of energy consumption of farms. We present in Table 1 a subset of existing cubes. For each cube, we present the following multidimensional concepts: Fact, Measures with their Aggregation function and Dimensions with their Levels. Two types of decision makers use these cubes: farmers and economic managers. Let us suppose that the farmers want to study the milk production. Since they are unskilled IT users, they would find the most relevant dairy cube by a simple natural language query such as "What is the most relevant cube concerning the milk production?". Then, without any additional efforts related to data and metadata exploration, and DW experts consulting, a Top-K cubes queries system should return the cube C_4 among existing cubes (cube C_4 is the top k=1 cube). Therefore, Top-K cubes queries system has to support the following requirements: (i) Using natural language queries, and (ii) ranking returned cubes.

Table 1. EDEN cubes.

Cube	Fact	Measures [Aggregates]	Dimensions[levels]
Sales Cube (C_1)	Sales	Quantity sold [total, avg]; Quantity ordered [avg, total].	Customer; Time [week, month, year]; Production ; localization; command.
Agricultural Production Cube (C_2)	Crop pro-duction	Input quantity [total avg]; Output quantity [total, average]; Pesticide concentration [%].	Technical operations, cultures; pesticides; production; Time [day, month, agricultural companion]; parcel, products;
Energy Consumpt-ion Cube (C_3)	ergy Con-sump	Area [total], consumed fuel quantity [avg, total, rate],	Time [Hour, day, month, year], equipment, fuel, parcels [parcel], culture.
Dairy Produc-tion Cube (C_4)	Milk Produc-tion	Milk quantity produced [total, avg]; Input quantity [total]; Output quantity [total, avg].	Time [day, month, year]; Animal husbandry; ; products; Production; Operators

3 Preliminaries

In this section, we present some preliminaries definitions.

Definition 1. (*Cube*): A cube C_j is represented by: a Fact, a set of Measure [aggregate], a set of Dimensions that are composed of a set of Levels.

Example 1. The cube C_4 of Table 1 is composed of the *"Time"*, *"Animal husbandry"*, *"Products"*, *"Equipment"*, *"Operators"* and *"Production"* Dimensions, *"Milk quantity produced"*, *"Input quantity"*, *"Output quantity"* Measures, etc. (see Table 1).

Definition 2. (*Structural Component* (SC)): We name *structural component* a Fact, or a Measure [aggregate], or Dimension, or a Level.

Let a cube C_i, we define $SC_D(C_i)$, $SC_F(C_i)$, $SC_L(C_i)$, $SC_M(C_i)$, $SC_A(C_i)$ the set of all instances of SC "Dimension" "Fact", "Level", "Measure" and "Aggregate" of C_j respectively. The set of all SC of a cube Ci (named $SC(C_i)$) is defined as: $SC(C_i)=$ $SC_D(C_i) \cup SC_F(C_i) \cup SC_L(C_i) \cup SC_M(C_i) \cup SC_A(C_i)$.

Example 2. $SC_D(C_4)$ = {*Time, Animal husbandry, product, Equipment, Operators, Production*}.

Definition 3. (*Catalog*): We define Catalog, the set of instances of all SC in the set of cubes C. Let C= $\{C_1...C_n\}$ the set of available cubes, the Catalog SC(C) is defined as $\{SC(C_1) \cup ... \cup SC(C_n)\}$.

Definition 4. (Query (Q)): The query is expressed using n terms $(t_1,...,t_n)$ in natural language separated by logic operators. In this work, we consider OR and AND operators such as: $Q(t_1\ OP_1\ t_2\ OP_2\ t_3\ OP_3...\ OP_{n-1}\ t_n)$ where $OP_i \in \{AND, OR\}$.

Example 3. A query can be for example Q1(*Milk product OR producton OR products OR quantity of input product*).

Definition 5. (Cardinality Card(Q,SCx(C_i)): Cardinality is the number of instances of structural component SCx $\in\{A, F, D, M, L\}$ in the cube Ci referenced in the query Q.

Example 4. For the cube C_4, two terms correspond to measure with aggregate {*Total milk quantity produced, Total input quantity*} then, Card(Q1, $SC_M(C_4)$) = 2.

Definition 6. (Relevant cubes RC(Q,C_j)): Relevant Cubes are the cubes as deemed relevant by our approach and will be subsequently returned to the user. A Cube C_j is relevant if the logical expression generated from Q where each term t_i is substituted by the result of the function Exist(t_i,C_j) is true. This function is defines as: Exist(t_i,C_j)=true if $t_i \in SC(C_j)$, false otherwise. More formally, Let $Q(t_1\ OP_1\ t_2\ OP_2\ t_3\ OP_3...OP_{n-1},t_n)$ a query, we define RC(Q,C_j) ={$C_j \in C$/ (Exist(t_1, C_j) OP_1 Exist(t_2, C_j) OP_3 ... OP_{n-1} Exist $(T_n$, C_j))=True}.

Example 5. For the query Q1, the relevant cubes RC={C_1, C_2, C_4}.

4 Top-K Cubes Approach

In this section, we present the different steps of our approach. The main idea is to allow the decision-makers to formulate their query using the natural language. Then, the query is parsed and rewritten using the elements of the cubes by means of some string similarity methods (Sect. 4.1). Once the query terms retrieved, an algorithm returns the top-k cubes (Sect. 4.2) (Algorithm Top-K Cubes query – Fig. 1).

Algorithm Top-K cubes query

Input: Q (Query), C (set of cubes), k (integer), Boolean Similar (string, string), String[] GetSynonym(string)

Output: An ordered list of k cubes

Begin

  1.   Q=QueryAnalyzer(Q,Similarity, GetSynonym); //analyze the terms of the query Q

  2.   Return Top-KCubes(C, Q, k); //ranked relevant cubes

End

Fig. 1. Top-K cubes query Algorithm

4.1 Query Analyzer

In this section, we present our method for expressing the top-k cube query using the natural language. The main idea is to let the decision-makers use natural language terms, then parse these terms, and finally propose them a set of similar SC instances (Fig. 2). This string similarity is achieved via the *Similar* function such as: Cosine similarity, JaroWinkler Distance, Levenshtein Distance, etc. In our approach, we performed a comparison between the results of these measures. We opted for the Levenshtein distance (best results relative to provided terms). However, as it considers only the syntactic aspect, it is not effective when the entered term is not similar to any term in the set of cubes. Indeed, a term may have semantically similar terms in the set of cubes and the analyzer does not detect them. To deal with this problem, we use the ontology of

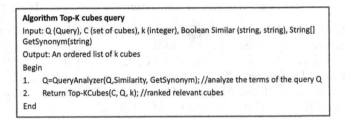

```
QueryAnalyzer
Input: Q (Query), C, Boolean Similar (string, string) a string matching function, String[] GetSynonym(string)
Output: Q (Query)
Begin
  1.   For each ti of Q {
  2.         If Similar(ti, sci) where sci ∈ {sc1...Scn} ⊆ SC(C){
  3.               let user choice sc ∈ {sc1...Scn}
  4.               ti=sc of SC(C)
  5.         }
  6.         else {
  7.               W=GetSynonym (ti) where W={w1...wn} ⊆ Wordnet
  8.               For each wi ∈ W {
  9.                     If Similar (wi, sci) where sci ∈ {sc1...Scn} ⊆ SC(C){
  10.                          let user choice sc ∈ {sc1...Scn}
  11.                          ti=sc of SC(C) go to 1;
  12.                    } else ignore ti, go to 1;
  13.               }
  14.         }
  15. }
  Return Q
End
```

Fig. 2. Query analyzer algorithm

synonyms *WordNet* to conduct an analysis of semantic similarity and replace a term with *WordNet* synonyms.

Example 6. For the first term *"Milk product"* of the query Q1 of example 3, the query analyzer provides the following similar instances of SC: *Milk production, Milk quantity produced, product* and *production*. The user can select the instance of SC *"Milk quantity produced"*. For the term *"yield"*, the query analyzer finds no similar term in the catalog, then the algorithm queries WordNet to find all synonyms of the term *"yield"*. Then, the query analyzer provides to the user the following similar instances of SC: *"output quantity"*, *"production"*, *"product"*. Thereafter, the user can selects the term *"production"*. The resulting reformulated query Q1' is (*Total Milk quantity produced* OR *production* OR *product* OR *total input quantity*).

4.2 Searching Process

In this section, we present the algorithms for searching and ranking cubes. In our approach, the degree of relevance is related to the type of SC referenced by the query terms. These cubes are then returned to the user without any predetermined order. To propose to the user the cubes that best meet his needs, we propose a score function that ranks cubes according to their relevance.

The score function (*Top-K Cubes* function) is based on the following idea: the most relevant cube contains query terms that cover the finest SC of a cube. Then, we have classified the SC of a cube according to the information expressed to identify a fact instance, since OLAP queries aim to retrieve and aggregate fact instances. Therefore, a level of a dimension provides more information than only a dimension (e.g. the level "farm" is more expressive than the dimension "location" for an OLAP dairy analysis), and a measure (with the aggregation) better identify an analysis need (e.g. the measure "milk quantity" is more expressive than the "production" fact). Then, supported by our several years' experience in real OLAP projects, we state that decision-makers define his analysis queries using "facts and measures" as multidimensional elements of first category importance instead of dimensions. This idea leads us the definition of the following order of importance of the SC:

$$Fact \rightarrow Measure[Aggregate] \rightarrow Measure \rightarrow Level \rightarrow Dimension \qquad (1)$$

Therefore, we propose a set of relevance classes. *The Top-1 class* represents the set of cubes, where the query terms cover all SCs of the a subset of cubes. *The Top-1 class* cubes better respond to the user's need. We define 22 relevance classes using the importance of the covered SCs previously defined (1) and we associate each cube to a class according to the terms of the query with the *Global score function*. Global Score is a function defined by: GlobalScore(Query Q, Cube C_j) -> Integer. We note that $1<=$ GlobalScore(Query Q', Cube C_j)$<=22$ (Fig. 3a).

Example 7. The global scores for the cubes C_1, C_2 and C_4 for the query Q are respectively: 1, 9 and 9.

Per contra, since each class can contain one or several cubes and the global score function assigns the same score to all the cubes in the same class (for example C2 and C4), then we propose the *local score* function that allows to establish an order among the cubes of the same class. It returns a partial order for cubes having the same global score. In order to sort cubes inside each class, we use the cardinality of SC in each cube (see Definition 5). We define LocalScore function as: LocalScore (Query Q, Cube C_j) -> integer. We note that for all C_j in RC, $1<=LocalScore(Q, C_j)<=|CGS(GlobalScore(Q,C_j)|$ (Fig. 3b).

Finally, we propose a numerical function that taking as input a Query Q, a set of cubes C, and k, associates a unique numerical score to each cube, using the GlobalScore and the LocalScore functions previously defined (Fig. 4).

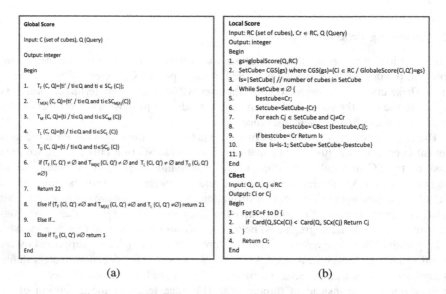

(a)   (b)

Fig. 3. (a) Global Score function, (b) Local Score function

Example 7. Recall that RC= {C_1, C_2, C_4}, $|RC|=3$, GlobalScore of C_1, C_2, C_4 are respectively: 1, 9 and 9. The Final Score for these cubes is calculated respectively: **4** (3*1+1), **28** (3*9+1) and **29** (3*9+2). The final rank is C_4, C_2, C_1. The parameter k determines the top-k cubes returned to the user. For example, if k=2, the only C_4 and C2 are returned to the user.

5 Implementation and Experimentation

We present in this section, the tool we have developed to implement our approach, and some experiments to validate it. Experiments have been done on a Dell PC with the following characteristics: Intel processor I5.2520 M, 2.5 Ghz CPU and 4 GB RAM.

```
Algorithm Top-K Cubes
Input: C (set of cubes), Q (Query), k (integer)
Output: an ordered list of k cubes
Begin
1.      Clist is a list <C, integer>
2.      Clist = ∅
3.      RC= relevant cubes (C, Q)
4.      For each Ci of RC
5.      Begin
6.          Final_score=|RC|*GlobalScore(Ci,Q)+LocalScore(Ci,Q)
7.          Add <Ci, Final_score> to Clist
8.      End For
9.      Ascending order Clist according to the Final_score
10.     Return K First Cubes in Clist
End
```

Fig. 4. Top-K Cubes function

5.1 Implementation

We developed a toll called *Top-K OLAP Cubes* to implement our approach. It is based on a multi-tier architecture as shown on Fig. 5a. The *Data tier* aims to store multidimensional data, and it is implemented using Relational DBMSs (e.g. Postgres, Oracle, etc.). The *Olap tier* is implemented using the OLAP server Mondrian, where the cubes are defined. The *Catalog tier* aims to implement our top-k search algorithm (Sect. 4.2), and improving time performance using the C-index described in Sect. 5.3. The *Explorator tier* is composed of: the *Cube exploratory tool*, which allows the decision-makers to visualize the set of k relevant cubes (Fig. 5C); *Jubik,* which is an OLAP client allows decision-makers to visualize data of a particular cube.

The *Query* tier is responsible for the Query analysis (Sect. 4.1). The Query Analyzer allows the decision-makers to define his needs in natural language (Fig. 5b).

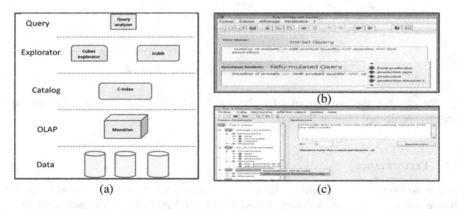

(a)   (b)   (c)

Fig. 5. Top-K RC: (a) architecture, (b) Cube exploratory, (c) Query Analyzer

5.2 Relevance

In this section, we evaluate the quality of proposed k cubes by our approach. To evaluate our approach, we consider two parameters, recall (R) and precision (P). *Recall* is: "How many relevant cubes are selected?" (2); *Precision* is: "How many selected cubes are relevant?" (3).

$$Recall = \frac{\text{the number of relevant cubes returned by the system}}{\text{the number of relevant cubes given by the expert}} \qquad (2)$$

$$Precision = \frac{\text{the number of relevant cubes returned by the system}}{\text{number of cubes returned by the system.}} \qquad (3)$$

We consider a set of 50 cubes downloaded from the FAO [12], and we consider three categories of queries: (1) *AND-Query:* query composed of several terms separated by AND for example: *"total amount of water used for irrigation AND watershed AND for each season"*); (2) *OR-Query:* query composed by several terms separated by OR; (3) *AND-OR-Query:* query composed by several terms separated by *AND* and *OR* operators. For each category, we have defined 36 queries, 4 queries per number of used terms: from 2 to 10 terms. Each set of queries is tested using k from 1 to 4.

Figure 6 shows precision for *AND-OR-Queries*. Figure 6 shows the average precision value and the standard deviation values for each k for the 4 queries. We note that the system provides good precision since the average precision value is mostly 1 and the standard deviation is 0. Our experiments show that the system also provides good recall since the average recall value is mostly 1 and the standard deviation is 0.

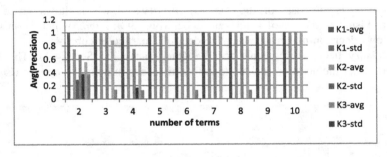

Fig. 6. Average precision for *AND-OR-Queries*

We observe the same results for the *AND* and *OR* categories, but due to space reasons we do not present these results.

5.3 Performance

In this section, we test evaluate the time response performance. To improve performance we have defined an index, called *CIndex*. *CIndex* stores for each term of the catalog the cube containing it. An entry of CIndex is: $<t_i, C_j> \rightarrow SC_i$, where is a term that appears as instance of the structural component SC_i of the cube C_j. An example is shown on Table 2. As for the relevance, we provide experiments of the three type of categories. For each category, we have defined 120 queries, 4 queries per number of used terms: from 2 to 30 terms. Each set of queries is tested using k from 1 to 5.

Table 2. Example of CIndex

Terms of the catalog	C_1	C_2	C_3	C_4
Milk produced quantity	M	/	/	F
Products	D	D	/	M
Years	L	D	/	/

Figure 7 shows worst time for OR queries. We observe for the *AND-OR-Queries* and *AND* categories the same results, but due to space reasons we do not present these results. We present the worst time for each 4 queries group of queries. We test these queries on a simulated set of 5000 cubes created from the real 50 FAO cubes. Figure 7 shows that the usage of the *CIndex* improves of 4 s the top-k cubes queries. It also shows that response time is acceptable for an online and interactive usage of the system. Moreover, it is important note that although response time without the *CIndex* is efficient for one query, usually the searching cubes process is an iterative process where the decision-makers can iteratively and incrementally refine their query terms. Therefore, the 4 s gain repeated several times (for example 15-20 times) can really improve response time on an analysis session.

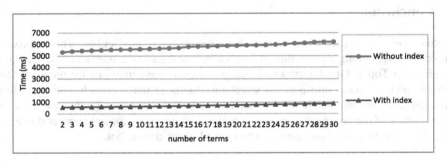

Fig. 7. Max time for *OR-Queries*

6   Related Work

In this section, we present related work. To best of our knowledge, no work proposes a system for searching the best relevant cubes. However, OLAP query recommendation and top-k query work are related to our proposal. OLAP query recommendation is a methodology to propose a query to the decision-makers similar to previously calculated queries [1–6]. Top-k queries aim to find the best k results of an OLAP query [7–10]. Due to reason space, we summarize these works in Table 3.

We compare these work according to some criteria: Input data (how the query is defined and what data is needed by the approach), Output (what is the result of the approach), and Goal (what is the goal of the proposal). From Table 3 we can note the our approach is the only one allowing for retrieving the best k cubes among a collection of cubes, and using the natural language to formulate the initial query.

Table 3. Related work

Research work			Queries Recommendation						Top-K Queries				Our App.
			[2]	[4]	[3]	[1]	[6]	[5]	[8]	[9]	[7]	[10]	
Input	Query type	MDX	X	X	X		X		X	X	X		
		Natural language				X							X
		SQL						X					
	Log file		X	X	X		X						
	User profile			X	X		X	X					
	Cube								X	X	X	X	
	Collection of cubes												X
Output	Query		X	X	X	X	X	X					
	(Aggregated) measures								X	X	X	X	
	Cube(s)												X
Goal	Performance			X			X		X	X	X	X	X
	Relevance			X			X						X

7 Conclusion

In this work, we presented an approach to search the Top-K cubes. This approach allows finding, among a collection, the cubes that best meet the user's needs. We have developed a Top-K OLAP cubes tool that provides an easy interface for the user. Our current work is taking into account warehoused data in the approach, and providing advanced usability studies. If the user needs is scattered over several cubes we work on an extension of the approach consisting to merge these cubes for better meet this need [13]. We plan to extend our proposal to Linked Open data cubes.

References

1. Kuchmann-Beauger, N., Aufaure, M.-A.: A natural language interface for data warehouse question answering. In: Muñoz, R., Montoyo, A., Métais, E. (eds.) NLDB 2011. LNCS, vol. 6716, pp. 201–208. Springer, Heidelberg (2011)
2. Giacometti, A., Marcel, P., Negre, E.: A framework for recommending OLAP queries. In: 11th International Workshop on Data Warehousing and OLAP, DOLAP 2008, pp. 73–80. Proceedings of the ACM, New York (2008)
3. Golfarelli, M., Rizzi, S., Biondi, P.: myOLAP: An approach to express and evaluate OLAP preferences. IEEE Trans. Knowl. Data Eng. 23(7), 1050–1064 (2011)
4. Jerbi, H., Ravat, F., Teste, O., Zurfluh, G.: Preference-based recommendations for OLAP analysis. In: Pedersen, T.B., Mohania, M.K., Tjoa, A.M. (eds.) DaWaK 2009. LNCS, vol. 5691, pp. 467–478. Springer, Heidelberg (2009)
5. Kozmina, N.: Adding recommendations to OLAP reporting tool. In: 5th International Conference on Enterprise Information Systems, vol. 1, pp. 169–176. ICEIS, France (2013)

6. Khemiri, R., Bentayeb, F.: FIMIOQR: Frequent itemsets mining for interactive OLAP query recommendation. In: The Fifth International Conference on Advances in Databases, Knowledge, and Data Applications (DBKDA), pp. 9–14. DBKDA, Seville, Spain (2013)

7. Xin, D., Han, J., Cheng, H., Li, X.: Answering Top-k queries with multi-dimensional selections: The ranking cube approach. In: 32nd International Conference on Very Large Data Bases, pp. 463–474. Korea (2006)

8. Luo, Z.W., Ling, T.-W., Ang, C.-H., Lee, S.-Y., Cui, B.: Range top/bottom k queries in OLAP sparse data cubes. In: Mayr, H.C., Lazanský, J., Quirchmayr, G., Vogel, P. (eds.) DEXA 2001. LNCS, vol. 2113, p. 678. Springer, Heidelberg (2001)

9. Loh, Z.X., Ling, T.-W., Ang, C.-H., Lee, S.-Y.: Adaptive method for range top-k queries in OLAP data cubes. In: Hameurlain, A., Cicchetti, R., Traunmüller, R. (eds.) DEXA 2002. LNCS, vol. 2453, p. 648. Springer, Heidelberg (2002)

10. Ding, B., Zhao, B., Lin, C.X., Han, J., Zhai, C.: Topcells: keyword-based search of Top-k aggregated documents in text cube. In: IEEE International Conference Data Eng. (ICDE), pp. 381–384 (2010)

11. Sagayaraj Francis, F., Xavier, P.P.: An effective method to answer OLAP queries using R*-Trees in distributed environment. Int. J. Comput. Appl. IJCA **107** (2014)

12. Bimonte, S., Pradel, M., Boffety, D., Tailleur, A., André, G., Bzikha, R., Chanet, J.-P.: A New sensor-based spatial OLAP architecture centered on an agricultural farm energy-use diagnosis tool. IJDSST **5**(4), 1–20 (2013)

13. Abelló, A., Darmont, J., Etcheverry, L., Golfarelli, M., Mazón López, J.N., Naumann, F., Vossen, G.: Fusion cubes: towards self-service business intelligence. Int. J. Data Warehousing Min. IJDWM **9**(2), 66–88. USA (2013)

Model-Based Requirements Engineering for Data Warehouses: From Multidimensional Modelling to KPI Monitoring

Azadeh Nasiri[1,2]([✉]), Robert Wrembel[1], and Esteban Zimányi[2]

[1] Institute of Computing Science, Poznan University of Technology, Poznan, Poland
{azadeh.nasiri,robert.wrembel}@cs.put.poznan.pl, nazadeh@ulb.ac.be
[2] Department of Computer and Decision Engineering,
Université Libre de Bruxelles, Brussels, Belgium
ezimanyi@ulb.ac.be

Abstract. A Data Warehouse (DW) is one of the main components of every BI system. It has been convincingly argued that the success of BI projects can be strongly affected by the Requirements Engineering (RE) phase, when the requirements of a DW are captured. Multiple RE methods for DWs have been proposed which have goal models in the core of their approach. Existing methods cover RE up to the static part of a DW, where the Multidimensional (MD) model is obtained. However, the RE for the dynamic part of the DW, where the requirements of operations on the DW are captured, has been neglected in the literature. In this paper, we propose a RE method, covering both the static and the dynamic part of a DW in an integrated manner. Our approach is to use the concept of a Key Performance Indicator (KPI). We initially use KPIs as the main driver to obtain the MD model and then discuss how decision-makers analyse them in order to measure the success of an organisation. In our method, the goal model from the i* framework was extended with UML use case diagrams.

Keywords: Data warehouse · Requirements Engineering · Key performance indicators

1 Introduction

One of the main components of BI systems is a DW, which integrates data from different data sources and structures them to be used in analytical systems. DW systems are sometimes developed based on an incomplete and inconsistent set of requirements, causing many BI projects to fail [13, 16]. This means that the success of BI projects can be strongly affected by the Requirements Engineering (RE) phase. In general, RE is defined as the process of discovering the needs of involved stakeholders and supporting those needs by modelling and documenting them in a form that is analysable and communicable. In order to support RE for DWs, multiple methods have been proposed in the literature, which are based mainly on the Goal-Oriented Requirements Engineering (GORE) approach

© Springer International Publishing Switzerland 2015
M.A. Jeusfeld and K. Karlapalem (Eds.): ER 2015 Workshops, LNCS 9382, pp. 198–209, 2015.
DOI: 10.1007/978-3-319-25747-1_20

[4, 6, 10–12]. This approach uses goals for eliciting, modelling, analysing, negotiating, and modifying requirements.

Most of the RE methods for DWs use GORE frameworks like i*, URN, and KAOS to capture strategic goals of an organisation, alternative decisions to achieve such goals, and required information to support the analysis needed for decision making. Eventually, information requirements are structured into facts (the focus of analysis) and dimensions (the context of analysis), which are the elements of the multidimensional (MD) model. Current research works cover RE up to obtaining the MD model of a DW [2–8, 11, 15]. The MD model refers to the static part of a DW. RE for the static part has received much attention while RE for the dynamic part, defined as the operations conducted on a DW, has been neglected in the literature.

To the best of our knowledge, there is no RE method in the literature that covers both the static part and the dynamic part of a DW. The goal of this paper is to develop a RE method for DWs covering both the static part of DWs, from where the MD model is obtained, as well as the dynamic part of the DW, where the requirements of operations on the DW are captured in a coherent and integrated manner. This integrated approach helps to align the data required to be stored in the DW with the analytics conducted over the data.

Our approach uses the concept of KPIs. KPIs are complex measurements used to monitor the performance of business processes and strategies in an organisation. KPIs are usually included in dashboards, providing a detailed view of each specific area of the organisation [14]. Based on how KPIs are calculated, they are called atomic or composite [1]. Atomic KPIs are those whose values are obtained from data sources. Composite KPIs are those whose values are obtained from other KPIs (called component KPIs). In the RE context, we use the concept of the composite KPI to evaluate the degree of fulfillment of a strategic goal, and the concept of the component KPI to evaluate the performance of various business processes.

Our method uses KPIs as the main driver to obtain the MD model and then discuss how decision-makers analyse KPIs in order to measure the success of an organisation. Our method has the following key features:

- We offer a model-based RE method for DWs, where models provide the basis of requirements artefacts.
- We apply the GORE approach to develop our RE method. The GORE approach is useful to represent how an intended BI system meets organisational goals [4]. Among the existing GORE frameworks, we chose goal modelling techniques of the i* framework to cover the RE for the static part of a DW.
- We extend goal models with modelling techniques of the object-oriented approach like UML, when the RE for the dynamic part of a DW is captured.

2   Running Example

We illustrate the proposed method with a concrete example from the health care sector. In the pharmaceutical industry, Adverse Events (AEs) are crucial for pharmaceutical companies needing the assessment of drugs. An AE is an unexpected and harmful reaction resulting from the use of a prescribed medication. Pharmaceutical companies typically need to collect AE data and carry out analytics over AE data to make well-informed decisions in order to avoid AEs. In this regard, we aim to analyse requirements of a BI system which enables a company to follow up its strategic goals relevant to AEs, to observe the current status regarding goals, and to find the factors influencing them. The company decided to track the AE-related KPIs to meet the aforementioned requirements. To this end, we need to store AEs data in a DW repository and analyse them in a dashboard where KPIs are monitored.

3   Static Part of a DW

RE for the static part of a DW discusses what data and in which form is of particular interest for decision makers to be stored in a DW. Our approach to derive the information requirements is to bring together strategic goals, business processes, and KPIs under the structure of a goal model adapted from the i* framework (the i* framework offers two models to represent organisational context: the Strategic Dependency (SD) model and the Strategic Rationale (SR) model). Eventually, we derive the information requirements from KPIs.

3.1   Strategic Dependency Model

To adapt the SD model in the DW domain, our approach is to incorporate a DW and a dashboard as actors in the i* model, since the organisation depends on a DW to obtain the proper information and depends on a dashboard to analyse the achievement of its strategic goals. The following guidelines are provided to adapt the SD model in the DW domain (see Fig. 1).

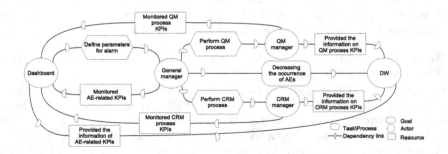

Fig. 1. The SD model adapted in the DW domain

Guideline 1: Business actors are decision makers (e.g. managers, top executives) and process owners. We also represent a DW and a dashboard under development as actors in the SD model.

Guideline 2: Strategic goals of the organisation are determined by decision makers. DWs provides decision makers with the capability of access and analysis of data to evaluate the status of strategic goals. Therefore, we represent strategic goals using a goal between a decision-maker and a DW. For example, "General manager" depends on the "DW" in order to analyse the status of the goal "Decreasing the occurrence of AEs".

Guideline 3: Strategic goals are achieved through performing some business processes. We represent the processes involved by means of a task between decision makers and process owners. For example, "General manager" depends on "QM manager" and "CRM manager" performing "QM process" and "CRM process", respectively, to accomplish "Decreasing the occurrence of AEs".

Guideline 4: Process owners use KPIs to evaluate the performance of their business processes. We represent the information required for KPIs by process owners as a resource dependency between process owners and the DW, since this information is provided by DWs. For example, the "QM manager" depends on the DW for the resource "Provided the information on QM process KPIs".

Guideline 5: Decision makers depend on dashboards to monitor the status of strategic goals. We represent this dependency using a resource between a decision maker and a dashboard, since this monitoring is provided by dashboards. For example, "Monitored AE-related KPIs" is the resource that relates "General manager" to "AE dashboard".

Guideline 6: Dashboards provide process owners with the capability of monitoring KPIs, representing the status of a process. We represent this dependency using a resource between a process owner and a dashboard. For example, "QM manager" depends on "AE Dashboard" for the resource "Monitored QM KPIs".

Guideline 7: Dashboards depend on decision makers to define certain parameters for generating alarms when KPIs are monitored. We represent this dependency using a task between dashboards and decision makers. For example, "AE dashboard" depends on "General manager" to perform "Define parameters for alarm".

Guideline 8: Dashboards depend on DWs to provide the required information to monitor KPIs. We represent this dependency by a resource between a dashboard and a DW. In the example, "AE dashboard" is connected to "DW" through the resource dependency "Provided information of AE-related KPIs".

3.2   Strategic Rational Model

We provide the following guidelines to develop the SR model for the DW actor, where KPIs are used to derive information requirements. Figure 2 illustrates the application of the guidelines to the running example.

Guideline 10: For each strategic goal defined according to Guideline 2, the information on the identified KPI, representing the goal fulfillment, needs to be

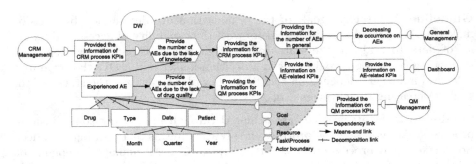

Fig. 2. The SR model for the DW actor

provided by a DW. Typically such KPI is a composite KPI as it measures a high-level goal in the organisation. We represent a goal to provide such information. For example, for "Decreasing the occurrence of AEs", the goal of the DW is "Providing the information on the number of AEs in general".

Guideline 11: For each goal defined according to Guideline 10, the information of corresponding process KPIs needs to be provided in order to achieve the goal. We represent a task, connected with a means-end link, to provide such information. For example, "Providing the information on AE-related KPIs" explains how "Providing the information on the number of AEs in general" is achieved.

Guideline 12: For each task defined according to Guideline 11, providing the KPI information of each process related to the strategic goals is an objective for the DW actor. This information are represented once via a resource dependencies in Guideline 4. We represent a sub-goal for each resource dependency, representing the information on relevant KPIs for each process involved. For example, "Providing the information on CRM process KPIs" and "Providing the information on QM process KPIs" are both sub-goals obtained from "Provide the information on AE-related KPIs".

Guideline 13: For each sub-goal defined according to Guideline 12, the value of each component KPI needs to be aggregated by the DW actor to achieve the sub-goal. We represent a task for each component KPI and connect it to the corresponding sub-goal via a means-end link. For example, "Provide the number of AEs due to the lack of drug quality" explains how "Providing information for the QM process" is achieved.

Guideline 14: For each task defined according to Guideline 13, an analysis needs to be conducted, because each task represents a KPI which is a measure employed to show the status of a process or a strategic goal. The analysis is conducted over some data considered as resources. We illustrate the focus of the analysis as a resource connected to the task with a means-end link. For example, the task "Provide the number of AEs due to the lack of drug quality" defines a measure that requires the resource of "AEs experience" as the focus of the analysis.

Guideline 15: For each resource defined according to Guideline 14, there are contexts that analysis of each measure occurred within them. We represent the concept of a context for the analysis as a resource and we connect them to the focus of analysis by a decomposition link. For example, "Provide the number of AEs due to the lack of knowledge" reveals that AEs can be analysed based on two variables: the AE type, and the patients who are experiencing AEs. For the other KPI it is necessary to analyse AEs in the context of drugs. Both KPIs are evaluated monthly as it has been mentioned in Sect. 2, so that the dates of AE occurrences can be another context to analyse AEs.

Guideline 16: For some of the resources defined according to Guideline 15, which represent a context of the analysis, there are several aggregation levels. We represent these levels of aggregation as resources connected via a decomposition link to the corresponding resource representing a context of the analysis. For example, "Date" as a context for the analysis of AEs can include "Month", "Quarter", and "Year".

3.3   Deriving the MD Model from a Goal Model

In this section, we provide guidelines to derive the MD model from the goal model for the DW actor. The MD schema for the running example is illustrated in Fig. 3.

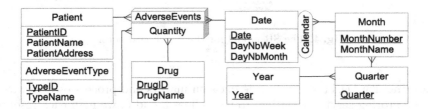

Fig. 3. The MD model derived from the goal model

Guideline 17: Resources representing the focus of the analysis defined according to Guideline 14, are represented as facts in the DW schema. Resources representing the context of the analysis defined according to Guideline 15 are dimensions in the MD model. Resources representing the levels of aggregation defined according to Guideline 16 are represented as hierarchies of dimensions in the DW schema.

4   Dynamic Part of a DW

In this section, we focus on the analytics of data collected in a DW. We narrowed down the scope to KPIs included in a dashboard. We first develop a strategic dependency model for a dashboard. Then, we discuss how to derive a use case diagram, representing the interaction of the business users with the DW, from the SR model.

4.1 SR Model for the Dynamic Part

In this part we provide some guidelines to develop the SR model for a dashboard. A dashboards that monitors KPIs typically provides decision makers and process owners with Performance Level (PL) of KPIs. The PL defined as the current value of a KPI compared against a set of parameters: a target value, a threshold value and a minimum value (refer to [9] for more details). Figure 4 illustrates the SR model of a dashboard actor for the running example.

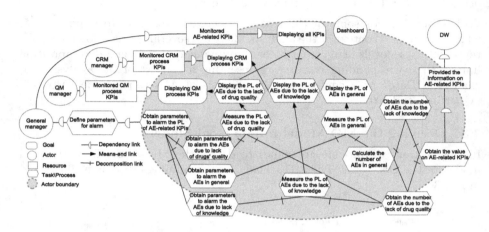

Fig. 4. The SR model for the dashboard actor

Guideline 18: Dashboards provide decision makers and process owners with a KPI monitoring service according to Guidelines 5 and 6; we map each resource defined in the SD model for this purpose to a goal for the dashboard actor. For example, the objective of "AE dashboard" is: (1) "Displaying AE-related KPIs" to "General manager" and (2) "Displaying QM process KPIs" to "QM manager".

Guideline 19: Goals defined according to Guideline 18 are achieved if a dashboard is able to represent the Performance Level (PL) of relevant KPIs for the corresponding decision-maker and business owner actors. We define a task for each KPI to be displayed by a dashboard and connect them with a means-end link. For example, "AE dashboard" performs task "Display the PL of AEs due to lack of drug quality", which explains how goal "Displaying QM process KPIs" is achieved. Thus, a means-end link is created between them.

Guideline 20: Tasks defined according to Guideline 21 are performed if a dashboard is able to measure the PL of KPIs. We represent a task for each KPI to be measured and connect it to the corresponding task defined in Guideline 21 by a means-end link, since it explains how the PL of a KPI is displayed. For example, "Measure the PL of the AEs due to lack of knowledge" is defined and connected by a means-end link to "Display the PL of the number of AEs due to lack of knowledge".

Guideline 21: DWs provide dashboards with the information of atomic KPIs according to Guideline 8; we map the resource defined in the SD model for this purpose to a task for the dashboard actor. Dashboards need this information to measure the PL of KPIs. We represent a task to obtain this information. For example, "Obtaining the value of AE-related KPIs" is defined as a task for "AE dashboard".

Guideline 22: The task defined according to Guideline 21 is decomposed into sub-tasks, each representing the information of an individual atomic KPI. For example, "Obtain the value of AE-related KPIs" is decomposed into "Obtain the value of the number of AEs due to lack of knowledge" and "Obtain the value of AEs due to lack of drug quality".

Guideline 23: Decision makers provide dashboards with parameters according to Guideline 7 in order to measure the PL of KPIs; we map the task defined in the SD model for this purpose to a task for the dashboard actor to obtain these parameters. For example, "Obtain the parameters to alarm the PL of AE-related KPIs" is defined as a task for the "AE dashboard".

Guideline 24: Tasks defined according to Guideline 23 are decomposed into sub-tasks, each representing the parameters required to measure the performance level of a KPI. For example, "Obtain the parameters of AE-related KPIs" is decomposed into "Obtain parameters to alarm the PL of AEs due to lack of knowledge", "Obtain parameters to alarm AEs due to lack of drugs quality", and "Obtain parameters to alarm the AEs in general".

Guideline 25: Tasks defined according to Guideline 20 measure the PL of a KPI. To do that, the dashboard actor needs the current value of the given KPI, as well as parameters defined by decision makers. Depend on what a task represents (an atomic or a composite KPI), we take the following actions:

– For an atomic KPIs, we connect the task defined in Guideline 20 with relevant tasks, defined according to Guidelines 24 and 26, via decomposition links. For example, "Measure the PL of AEs due to the lack of knowledge" is decomposed to "Obtain parameters to alarm the AEs due to the lack of knowledge" and "Obtain the number of AEs due to the lack of knowledge".

– For a composite KPI, we initially define a new task for the dashboard actor to calculate the value of a composite KPI. To calculate this, the dashboard actor needs the value of its component KPIs (obtained from the DW). Thus, we connect the new task with corresponding tasks defined in Guideline 22. Then, we connect each task defined for a composite KPI in Guideline 20, with the new task and corresponding tasks defined in Guideline 24, via decomposition links. For example, a new task is defined to "Calculate the number of AEs in general". This task is decomposed to "Obtain the number of AEs due to the lack of knowledge" and "Obtain the number of AEs due to the lack of drug quality". Also, the task which "Measure the PL of AEs in general" is decomposed into "Calculate the number of AEs in general" and ""Obtain parameters to alarm the number of AEs in general".

4.2   Deriving the Use Case Diagram from the Goal Model

As we continue the development process, we need to focus on how users interact with the system. For this purpose, we initially adapt the use case. A use case contains steps that define interactions between an actor and a system, to achieve a goal. Figure 5 illustrates how the following guidelines are applied to map from a goal model to a use case diagram in the running example (to avoid, complexity we only show some examples mapped, using dashed-arrows).

Guideline 26: Actors of the SD model, which are connected to the dashboard with a dependency link, are candidates for being a use case actor. The boundary of the system is the dashboard, presenting the dynamic part of the DW. Decision makers, process owners, and DWs are actors in a use case diagram.

Guideline 27: For each task and resource dependency with decision makers in the SD model, a task and a goal is defined for the dashboard according to

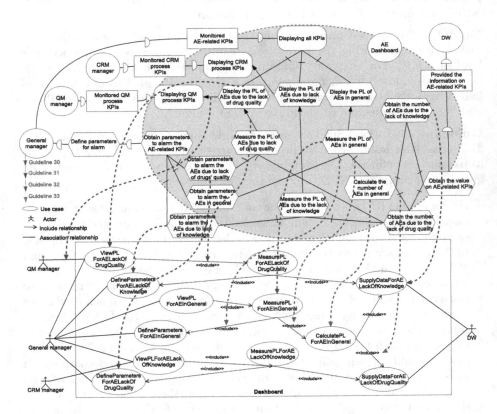

Fig. 5. Use case diagram for the dashboard

Guidelines 18 and 23, respectively. The SR model helps to investigate if there are decomposition links for the defined task and the defined goal. The lowest level tasks are candidates for being a use case as the modelling principle to develop a use case diagram is to ensure that each use case represents a single user goal. Each use case is connected with a corresponding decision-maker actors via an association link.

Guideline 28: For each resource dependency with the DW in the SD model, a task is defined for a dashboard according to Guideline 21. The SR model helps to investigate, if there are decomposition links for the defined task. The lowest level tasks are candidates for being a use case.

Guideline 29: For each resource dependency with process owners in the SD model, a goal is defined for the dashboard according to Guideline 21. In the SR model, these goals are connected with some tasks via means-end-links. The tasks are already candidates according to Guideline 30. We translate means-ends links of the SR model to the association links of a use case diagram, connecting use cases with relevant process owners.

Guideline 30: For each low-level task in the SR model, which is not directly derived from a dependency link of the SD model, we represent a use case. It is important to notice that we can not draw a direct association links between these newly defined use cases and actors. We need to connect them with already existing use cases using an include link (an include link is used to insert the behaviour of a use case to the behaviour of another one called base use case). To define a proper connection, we investigate the discussed tasks in the SR model in terms of links exiting from them as follows: (1) If it is a means-end link, we draw an include link between the newly defined use case and the use case which represents the task in the end side of the means-end link of the SR model (the latter use case is the base use case); (2) If it is a decomposition link, we draw an include link between the newly defined use case and the use case which represents the decomposed task of the SR model (the newly defined use case is the base use case).

5   Conclusion

In this paper, we have addressed the RE regarding the dynamic and the static part of a DW. In our approach models provide the basis Modelling is the core of our approach for requirements artefacts. For the static part, we adapted the goal model from the i* framework to derive a MD schema. We found that, goal models alone are not adequate to deal with the RE of the dynamic part of a DW. Therefore, we extended the goal model with the use case diagram to illustrate how users can interact with a DW through a KPI monitoring dashboard. We initially use KPIs as the main drivers to obtain our MD model and then discuss how decision-makers analyse KPIs in order to measure the success of an organisation. This approach aligns data required to be stored in a DW with the analytics conducted over the data, since both use the concept of KPI to derive the requirements. As future work, our method will be completed with use case scenarios and other behavior and interaction diagrams of UML in order to visualize all aspects of the dynamic part of a DW.

References

1. Barone, D., Jiang, L., Amyot, D., Mylopoulos, J.: Composite Indicators for Business Intelligence. In: Jeusfeld, M., Delcambre, L., Ling, T.-W. (eds.) ER 2011. LNCS, vol. 6998, pp. 448–458. Springer, Heidelberg (2011)
2. Bonifati, A., Cattaneo, F., Ceri, S., Fuggetta, A., Paraboschi, S.: Designing data marts for data warehouses. ACM Trans. Softw. Eng. Methodol. **10**(4), 452–483 (2001)
3. Gallardo, J., Giacaman, G., Meneses, C., Marbán, Ó.: Framework for decisional business modeling and requirements modeling in data mining projects. In: Corchado, E., Yin, H. (eds.) IDEAL 2009. LNCS, vol. 5788, pp. 268–275. Springer, Heidelberg (2009)
4. Ghezzi, C., Jazayeri, M., Mandrioli, D.: GRAnD: a goal-oriented approach to requirement analysis in data warehouses. Decis. Support Syst. **45**(1), 4–21 (2008)
5. Malinowski, E., Zimányi, E.: Requirements specification and conceptual modeling for spatial data warehouses. In: Meersman, R., Tari, Z., Herrero, P. (eds.) OTM 2006 Workshops. LNCS, vol. 4278, pp. 1616–1625. Springer, Heidelberg (2006)
6. Mazón, J.-N., Pardillo, J., Trujillo, J.: A model-driven goal-oriented requirement engineering approach for data warehouses. In: Hainaut, J.-L., et al. (eds.) ER Workshops 2007. LNCS, vol. 4802, pp. 255–264. Springer, Heidelberg (2007)
7. Mazón, J., Trujillo, J., Lechtenbörger, J.: Reconciling requirement-driven data warehouses with data sources via multidimensional normal forms. Data Knowl. Eng. **63**(3), 725–751 (2007)
8. Mazon, J., Trujillo, J., Serrano, M., Piattini, M.: Designing data warehouses: from business requirement analysis to multidimensional modeling. In: Proceedings of International Conference on Requirements Engineering for Business Need and IT Alignment, pp. 44–53 (2005)
9. Nasiri, A., Zimányi, E., Wrembel, R.: Requirements engineering for data warehouses. In: Proceedings of Conference on Journées Francophones Sur Les Entrepôts de Données et l'Analyse en ligne (2015)
10. Prakash, N., Bhardwaj, H.: Early information requirements engineering for target driven data warehouse development. In: Sandkuhl, K., Seigerroth, U., Stirna, J. (eds.) The Practice of Enterprise Modeling. LNBIP, vol. 134, pp. 188–202. Springer, Heidelberg (2012)
11. Silva, V., Mazón, J., Garrigós, I., Trujillo, J., Mylopoulos, J.: Monitoring strategic goals in data warehouses with awareness requirements. In: ACM Symposium on Applied Computing, pp. 1075–1082. ACM (2012)
12. Singh, Y., Gosain, A., Kumar, M.: From early requirements to late requirements modeling for a data warehouse. In: Proceedings of IEEE International Joint Conference on INC, IMS and IDC, pp. 798–804 (2009)
13. Stroh, D., Winter, R., Wortmann, F.: Method support of information requirements analysis for analytical information systems. Bus. Inf. Syst. Eng. **3**(1), 33–43 (2011)
14. Vaisman, I., Zimányi, E.: Data Warehouse Systems: Design and Implementation. Springer, Heidelberg (2014)

15. Winter, R., Strauch, B.: A method for demand-driven information requirements analysis in data warehousing projects. In: Proceedings of IEEE International Conference on System Sciences, pp. 9–18 (2003)
16. Winter, R., Strauch, B.: Information requirements engineering for data warehouse systems. In: ACM Symposium on Applied, Computing, pp. 1359–1365 (2004)

Towards Ontology-Driven RDF Analytics

Bernd Neumayr[(✉)], Christoph G. Schuetz, and Michael Schrefl

Johannes Kepler University Linz, Linz, Austria
{neumayr,schuetz,schrefl}@dke.uni-linz.ac.at

Abstract. The RDF data model lends itself to the organization of graph-structured data. The analysis of such data requires specific tools and techniques broadly summarized as RDF analytics. In particular, traditional approaches to the aggregation of multidimensional data do not apply directly to RDF data due to the lack of information regarding the granularity level of the data and unclear semantics of aggregation. Ontologies, however, may provide the additional information required for RDF data aggregation. Using a vocabulary for ontology-based RDF analytics in conjunction with existing domain ontologies, modelers may declaratively specify aggregated views over RDF data. In this paper we describe the fundamentals of ontology-driven RDF analytics based on RDF, RDF Schema, and SPARQL. We present a proof-of-concept implementation of the basic approach that uses open-source technology, thereby demonstrating feasibility. We further discuss possible future extensions to the basic approach.

Keywords: Business intelligence · Semantic web · SPARQL

1 Introduction

The RDF data model organizes data in triples that consist of subject, predicate, and object. The thus represented information may be thought of as graph. In such a graph, nodes represent subjects and objects of RDF triples, directed edges represent predicates. Social networks are a typical example of graph-structured data conveniently represented as RDF triples. In this case, the individual persons in a social network become the subjects and objects of RDF triples, the relationships between individuals become predicates. For example, Mary, Jane, and Bill may be individual persons, knows and loves relationships between individual persons. The triple Mary knows Jane may then indicate an acquaintance of Mary's to Jane, Bill loves Mary may indicate Bill's fondness of Mary, even though the inverse may not necessarily be the case. Furthermore, RDF triples such as Mary a Woman and Mary age 22 may also indicate class membership and represent attributes of individual persons, respectively.

Analysts may leverage the information represented in RDF models for decision support. In this case, aggregate views over large RDF models may reduce complexity for the analyst. In these aggregate views, single entities at coarser levels of granularity may replace groups of entities; relationships and attributes

© Springer International Publishing Switzerland 2015
M.A. Jeusfeld and K. Karlapalem (Eds.): ER 2015 Workshops, LNCS 9382, pp. 210–219, 2015.
DOI: 10.1007/978-3-319-25747-1_21

are then summarized. For example, an aggregate RDF view may contain relationships between classes of persons, for example, Woman and Man, thus summarizing relationships between individual persons within these classes. The summarized relationships may be attributed with the count of actual relationships between individual persons. Furthermore, attributes such as age that captures an individual person's age may be summarized by aggregate attributes such as avgAge for the average age of individual persons within a class; a count of class members may replace the indication of class membership for individual persons in the aggregated RDF view.

Traditional OLAP employs multidimensional models in order to allow for the aggregation of measures at different levels of granularity. The individual dimensions contain hierarchically-ordered levels that support analysts with data aggregation. In this context, the roll-up operator takes as parameters a set of levels as well as an aggregation function and returns as result a table that contains aggregated measure values. For the analysis of RDF data, however, the definition of granularity levels as well as the semantics of aggregation are less clear and analysts are typically left without guidance.

In ontology-based RDF analytics, in order to obtain an aggregate RDF view, analysts specify an aggregation ontology over the domain ontology that describes the base RDF data. The roll-up operator takes as parameter the aggregation ontology and returns an aggregated RDF view as result. An aggregated RDF view consists of grouped resources, that is, resources that represent sets of resources, and grouped statements, that is, statements that represent sets of statements. The presented approach builds on previous work that employs domain ontologies as dimensions in data warehouses [1]. RDF reification allows for the representation of aggregated data about grouped statements, for example, the number of statements represented by the grouped statement. In a sense, ontology-based RDF analytics specifies a mechanism for performing abstraction on ontology-valued measures as proposed in previous work on the use of business model ontologies as measures in OLAP cubes [7].

The remainder of this paper is organized as follows. In Sect. 2 we introduce a basic approach for ontology-based RDF analytics. In Sect. 3 we present a proof-of-concept implementation based on SPARQL. In Sect. 4 we discuss future extensions. In Sect. 5 we review related work. Section 6 concludes the paper.

2   The Basics of Ontology-Driven RDF Analytics

In this section we introduce the kinds of base RDF data and ontologies involved in ontology-driven RDF analytics. We illustrate these kinds of data and ontologies using the example in Fig. 1. In order to foster a basic intuition of the presented approach, we disregard some of the technicalities of RDF, for example, by using simple names instead of URIs.

The base RDF data may be raw data retrieved from the web of data. The base data may also be the result of prior data integration from various sources as well as data cleansing. The data may even represent an *analytical schema*

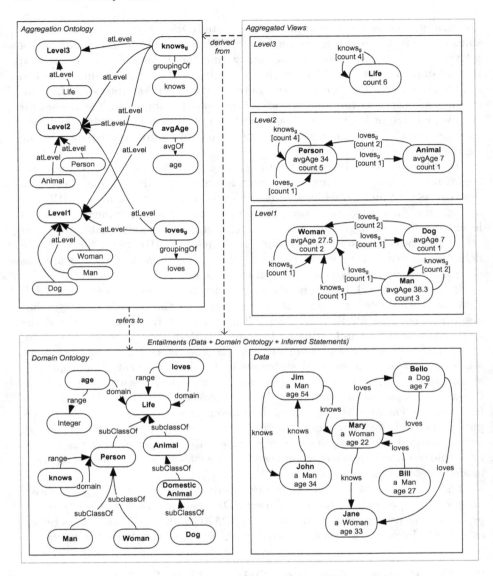

Fig. 1. Example RDF base data (bottom-right compartment), the corresponding domain ontology (bottom-left), as well as an aggregation ontology (top-left) and the derived aggregated RDF views (top-right)

instance [2]. The compartment labeled *Data* in the lower half of Fig. 1 illustrates base data of a social network. We employ a custom notation for RDF data where rounded boxes represent resources, data properties of resources are inside the respective boxes, and edges represent object properties.

We restrict data in such a manner that it can be regarded as assertional knowledge of an OWL 2 DL ontology[1], thus allowing for efficient reasoning. Individuals, for example, Mary, are described by assertions, that is, RDF statements/triples, which come in three basic kinds. First, a class assertion relates an individual to a class, for example, Mary a Woman, meaning that the individual is member of the class. Second, an object property assertion relates an individual to another individual, for example, Mary knows Jane. Third, a data property assertion relates an individual to a literal data value, for example, Mary age 22. In order to exemplify the exact meaning of the custom graphical notation (Fig. 1), Listing 1.1 shows the description of individual Mary in RDF Turtle syntax[2].

A domain ontology describes the meaning of the base data. The compartment labeled *Domain Ontology* in the lower half of Fig. 1 illustrates a domain ontology for the data of a social network. The domain ontology describes the classes, for example, Person, object properties, for example, knows, and data properties, for example, age, which are employed in the base data. Classes are organized in subsumption hierarchies where a subclass axiom, for example, Woman subClassOf Person, connects a subclass to a superclass, meaning that all members of the subclass are also members of the superclass. Properties are described by their domain and range, for example, knows domain Person, meaning that every individual that is the source or target, respectively, of an assertion for that property is member of this domain or range, respectively. Data properties have a primitive type as range, for example, age range Integer. Reasoners may conduct various types of reasoning such as calculating entailment and performing instance checking. The basic setting as discussed in this section considers only derived class membership. Classes (or concepts) in an OWL domain ontology may come with complex definitions and the data may be incomplete, leading to complex reasoning. The basic approach abstracts from the reasoning process, which is delegated to an OWL reasoner, and assumes that individuals are classified to one or more most specific classes, for example, Jane a Woman. From class assertions and the subclass relationships between the corresponding classes, the reasoner may infer additional class memberships of individuals. For example, since Jane is a Woman, she is also a Person and also a Life individual.

Analysts define an aggregation ontology based on a domain ontology. The aggregation ontology specifies a number of abstraction levels, which characterize aggregated views, over the base RDF graph. Based on this aggregation ontology, the OLAP system generates aggregated views, which are again RDF graphs. The top-left compartment in Fig. 1 illustrates an aggregation ontology, the top-right compartment the resulting aggregated RDF views. Notice the entities in the RDF graphs associated with a particular granularity level getting coarser when moving up the level hierarchy, following the subClassOf relationships from the domain ontology. Further notice the different applicability of summarized relationships at different levels being explicitly represented in the aggregation

---

[1] http://www.w3.org/TR/owl2-primer/.
[2] http://www.w3.org/TR/turtle/.

Listing 1.1. Individual Mary of Fig. 1 in RDF Turtle notation

```
1  @prefix rdf:
       <http://www.w3.org/1999/02/22-rdf-syntax-ns#> .
2  @prefix : <http://example.org/> .
3  :mary rdf:type :woman;
4        :knows :jane; :loves :bello; :age 22.
```

Listing 1.2. Representing a statement group using RDF reification

```
1  :animal :loves_g :person .
2  [ rdf:subject :animal; rdf:object :person;
3    rdf:property :loves_g; ra:count 2 ] .
```

ontology. For example, the $avgAge_g$ relationship applies to Levels 1 and 2 but not Level 3.

As with semantic dimensions in previous work [1], the definition of aggregation ontologies involves the reuse of classes from a domain ontology as groups of individuals, allowing for the aggregation of individuals into these groups. In order to avoid higher-order semantics possibly associated with the dual use of entities both as class and as individual, classes from the domain ontology become individuals in the aggregation ontology, thus logically treating the class and the individual as two distinct entities, an approach also referred to as punning [4]. For example, individual Person at Level 2 (Fig. 1, *Aggregation Ontology*) represents the group of members of class Person. The description Person count 5 (*Aggregated Views*) derives from the aggregation of individuals in the Person class by applying the COUNT operator. The subtle difference between a class and the individual that represents the group of the class's members is important when working with OWL DL and its strict distinction between schema and instance level.

Groups of individuals at the different abstraction levels are described by aggregated data property assertions, for example, Person avgAge 34, and are connected by grouped property assertions, for example, Person $loves_g$ Animal. Grouped property assertions are reified to indicate the number of object property assertions in the base data. For example, Listing 1.2 illustrates, using reification, the grouped property $loves_g$ from Animal to Person, indicating that there are two loves relationships from individual animals to individual persons. Aggregated data properties are specified in the aggregation ontology by relating them to a data property in the domain ontology using a property that indicates a specific aggregation operation, for example, avgAge avgOf age. Grouped properties are specified by relating them to an object property in the domain ontology, for example, $knows_g$ groupingOf knows.

Note that the different boxes in the *Aggregated Views* compartment of Fig. 1 represent named RDF graphs. The names of these graphs – in this example, Level1, Level2, and Level3 – are used as resources in the aggregation ontology in order to define the classes and properties that go into each of these graphs. Each graph represents an aggregated RDF view at a particular level of granularity.

3   Proof-of-Concept Implementation

In this section we present a proof-of-concept implementation of the basic approach using standard semantic web technologies, namely RDF and RDF Schema as well as SPARQL Query Language and Update. We rely on the open-source Jena framework and its native graph store Jena TDB. In this first demonstration, we disregard performance considerations. Future work may switch from Jena TDB to industry-scale persistence components, such as 'Oracle Spatial and Graph' or 'AllegroGraph', as well as cloud-based storage and processing [3].

The SPARQL-based implementation takes as input an RDF dataset containing in the data graph the RDF data that is to be analyzed, in the domainOntology graph the domain ontology, and in the aggregationOntology graph the aggregation ontology. The derivation of aggregated RDF views then consists of the following two basic steps:

1. Performing RDFS reasoning over data and domain ontology, writing the entailed graph, which contains base data as well as additional classifications and subsumption relationships, into named graph entailments.
2. Calculating aggregated RDF views as defined by the aggregation ontology by executing generic SPARQL updates (Listings 1.3–1.5) that implement the semantics of the vocabulary used in the aggregation ontology.

The resulting aggregated RDF views are again RDF graphs which may be further processed using standard semantic web technologies.

Listing 1.3 inserts into the aggregated views the count of individuals from the base data that are in a particular class. The update request inserts the count into a graph ?g that corresponds to the level represented by that same resource. For example, the resources Level1, Level2, and Level3 become the bindings for ?g when calculating aggregated views from the aggregation ontology in Fig. 1. The update request calculates the count of individuals for each granularity level and the respective classes that apply to this granularity level.

Listing 1.3. Aggregation of individuals to classes

```
1  PREFIX rdf :
      <http://www.w3.org/1999/02/22-rdf-syntax-ns#>
      PREFIX ra :
2  <http://www.dke.jku.at/rdfanalytics/> PREFIX :
      <http://example.org/>
3  INSERT { GRAPH ?g { ?c ra:count ?cnt } } WHERE {
4    SELECT ?g ?c (COUNT(?x) AS ?cnt)
5    WHERE {
6      GRAPH :entailments { ?x rdf:type ?c. }
7      GRAPH :aggregationOntology { ?c ra:atLevel ?g. }
8    }
9    GROUP BY ?g ?c
10 };
```

Listing 1.4. Aggregation of statements to groups of statements

```
11   INSERT { GRAPH ?g
12     { ?c ?gp ?d.
13       [] rdf:subject ?c; rdf:object ?d;
14          rdf:property ?gp; ra:count ?cnt. }
15   } WHERE {
16     SELECT ?g ?c ?gp ?d (COUNT(*) AS ?cnt)
17     WHERE {
18       GRAPH :entailments {
19         ?x ?p ?y.
20         ?x rdf:type ?c.
21         ?y rdf:type ?d.
22       }
23       GRAPH :aggregationOntology {
24         ?gp ra:atLevel ?g;
25             ra:groupingOf ?p.
26         ?c  ra:atLevel ?g.
27         ?d  ra:atLevel ?g.
28       }
29     }
30     GROUP BY ?g ?c ?gp ?d
31   };
```

Listing 1.4 performs an aggregation of statements to groups of statements, inserting into the graph of each granularity level reified statements for triples from the entailments graph, with subject and object from the base data being replaced by their class, the predicate being replaced by the grouping property. The reified statement contains the count of individual statements that go into the grouped statement. For example, the update request summarizes triples Jim knows John and John knows Jim in the *Data* compartment of Fig. 1 with a reified statement in the Level1 graph with subject and object being Man, the property being knows$_g$, and the blank node having a data property count with a value of 2. Similarly, the update request summarizes triples Bello loves Mary and Bello loves Jane with a reified statement in the Level2 graph with the subject being Animal, the object being Woman, the property being loves$_g$, and the blank node having a data property count with a value of 2.

Listing 1.5 shows the implementation of the avgOf aggregation property. For each data property that is the source of an avgOf property in the aggregation ontology, the update request inserts into the graph for the aggregated view at the respective level a triple with the average property as predicate, the average value as object, and the subject being a class of resources from the base data. For example, the ages of individuals Jim, John, and Bill in the *Data* compartment of Fig. 1 are replaced in the Level1 graph by the data property avgAge of Man. Similarly, the ages of individuals Jim, John, Mary, Jane and Bill are replaced in the Level2 graph by the data property avgAge of Person.

Listing 1.5. Calculation of aggregation property avgOf

```
32  INSERT { GRAPH ?g { ?c ?ap ?av } }
33  WHERE {
34    SELECT ?g ?c ?ap (AVG(?v) AS ?av)
35    WHERE {
36      GRAPH :entailments {
37        ?x ?p ?v.
38        ?x rdf:type ?c.
39      }
40      GRAPH :aggregationOntology {
41        ?ap ra:atLevel ?g;
42            ra:avgOf ?p.
43        ?c  ra:atLevel ?g.
44      }
45    }
46    GROUP BY ?g ?c ?ap
47  }
```

4   Extensions of Basic Approach

In this section we discuss future extensions of the basic approach for ontology-based RDF analytics as described in the previous sections.

Multiple Grouping Hierarchies. The basic approach organizes classes in one subsumption hierarchy at different *global* levels. In a more advanced approach, one may have multiple subsumption hierarchies rooted in distinct classes of one or multiple ontologies. The analyst may then define different sets of levels for the different hierarchies. The combination of these different level hierarchies leads to a lattice of granularities as known from multidimensional modeling and OLAP.

Property Hierarchies in Aggregation Ontologies. OWL and RDFS ontologies typically organize properties in property hierarchies. The basic approach considers these hierarchies only in the RDFS reasoning step.

Groups of Groups and Multistep Aggregation. Aggregation ontologies may specify groups of groups, the group of a group being a different entity than the underlying groups. For example, a GroupOfProducts group and a GroupOfProduct-GroupsAtCategoryLevel group are different entities. Groups are described by first-level measures (such as totalSales). Groups of groups are described by second-level measures (such as avgTotalSales).

More Expressive Ontologies. The proof-of-concept prototype considers only RDF Schema reasoning, with the core reasoning tasks being subsumption checking and instance checking. In the basic approach, these reasoning tasks constitute the first step, and inferencing during data analysis is not necessary. Future work may thus easily replace the RDFS reasoner with, for example, an OWL reasoner.

Reasoning Over Aggregation Ontologies. Reasoning tasks over aggregation ontologies include summarizability checking for levels and pairs of levels. A reasoner should check whether all the classes at one level are pairwise disjoint, whether the classes at one level are complete with respect to some base class, and whether one level rolls up to another level.

Post-coordinated Concepts. The basic approach assumes a fixed set of classes mandated by the domain ontology, these classes being referred to as *pre-coordinated* concepts. Analysts, however, may wish to define ad-hoc classes for consideration in analytical queries, these classes being referred to as *post-coordinated* concepts. The introduction of post-coordinated concepts possibly raises the need for dynamic reasoning during the actual analysis.

Alternative Reification Mechanism. The basic approach to ontology-based RDF analytics uses standard RDF reification vocabulary[3], which has been criticized for its verbosity. Singleton properties [6] provide a more compact form of reified statements and could be used in aggregated views.

Reification of Graph Patterns. The basic approach groups individuals into classes, which are used as groups, and statements into groups of statements that connect groups of individuals. Analysts, however, may wish to select graph patterns in the base data and aggregate the instances of these graph patterns. As in related work on RDF analytics [2], this selection and aggregation may be done as a preliminary step, by reification of the matched instances of the graph pattern as individuals or, in simpler cases, by a derived statement connecting two individuals.

Aggregation along Multidimensional Structures. In previous work [7], we propose business model ontologies for the representation of *ontology-valued measures* in OLAP cubes. Rather than having a single RDF graph with base data, an OLAP cube with ontology-valued measures consists of multiple RDF graphs, each representing knowledge that applies to a particular context. Merge operations allow for the combination of knowledge from different contexts. The combined knowledge may be subject to further analysis. Aggregation ontologies might facilitate the analysis of aggregated ontology-valued measures.

5   Related Work

The Semantic Cockpit [5] employs ontologies in a traditional data warehouse setting in order to facilitate the interpretation of analysis results and the sharing of knowledge among analysts. Existing domain ontologies may become semantic dimensions [1]. Ontology-based RDF analytics employs subsumption hierarchies in domain ontologies as semantic dimensions for the roll-up of RDF data.

Related work on RDF analytics [2] employs analytical schemas over RDF data that produce analytical schema instances which are RDF graphs. These

---

[3] http://www.w3.org/TR/rdf-schema/#ch_reificationvocab.

analytical schema instances may be used as base data for ontology-based RDF analytics. Whereas analytical querying of analytical schema instances produces tabular results, ontology-based RDF analytics produces aggregated RDF graphs representing higher abstraction levels. Ontology-based RDF analytics introduces a declarative mechanism, namely aggregation ontologies, for the specification of aggregated RDF views.

Graph OLAP [8] associates weighted graphs with dimension attributes. Informational and topological roll-up are the basic kinds of operations, with topological roll-up being similar to the derivation of aggregated views in ontology-based RDF analytics. Graph OLAP, however, does not aim at the representation of complex knowledge, rather being another means for structuring numeric measures. Ontology-based RDF analytics deals with potentially more expressive, complex, and heterogeneous graphs than the simple graphs analyzed in Graph OLAP.

6 Conclusion

Traditional approaches to data analysis fail in the context of RDF analytics. Unclear semantics of roll-up relationships and aggregation complicate the analysis task. Ontology-based RDF analytics employs domain ontologies and aggregation ontologies for the specification of aggregated RDF views that reduce complexity for the analyst. Aggregation ontologies allow analysts to declaratively specify the desired semantics of the roll-up operation for each analysis case.

References

1. Anderlik, S., Neumayr, B., Schrefl, M.: Using domain ontologies as semantic dimensions in data warehouses. In: Atzeni, P., Cheung, D., Ram, S. (eds.) ER 2012 Main Conference 2012. LNCS, vol. 7532, pp. 88–101. Springer, Heidelberg (2012)
2. Colazzo, D., Goasdoué, F., Manolescu, I., Roatis, A.: RDF analytics: lenses over semantic graphs. In: Proceedings of the 23rd International World Wide Web Conference, WWW 2014, pp. 467–478 (2014)
3. Kaoudi, Z., Manolescu, I.: RDF in the clouds: a survey. VLDB J. **24**(1), 67–91 (2015)
4. Motik, B.: On the properties of metamodeling in OWL. J. Logic Comput. **17**(4), 617–637 (2007)
5. Neuböck, T., Neumayr, B., Schrefl, M., Schütz, C.: Ontology-driven business intelligence for comparative data analysis. In: Zimányi, E. (ed.) eBISS 2013. LNBIP, vol. 172, pp. 77–120. Springer, Heidelberg (2014)
6. Nguyen, V., Bodenreider, O., Sheth, A.P.: Don't like RDF reification?: making statements about statements using singleton property. In: Proceedings of the 23rd International World Wide Web Conference, WWW 2014, pp. 759–770 (2014)
7. Schütz, C., Neumayr, B., Schrefl, M.: Business model ontologies in OLAP cubes. In: Salinesi, C., Norrie, M.C., Pastor, Ó. (eds.) CAiSE 2013. LNCS, vol. 7908, pp. 514–529. Springer, Heidelberg (2013)
8. Zhao, P., Li, X., Xin, D., Han, J.: Graph cube: on warehousing and OLAP multidimensional networks. In: Proceedings of the ACM SIGMOD International Conference on Management of Data, SIGMOD 2011, pp. 853–864 (2011)

Conceptual Modeling in Requirements and Business Analysis

Preface to the 2nd International Workshop on Conceptual Modeling in Requirements and Business Analysis (MReBA 2015)

Requirements Engineering (RE) aims to capture intended system functionality and qualities. In practice, requirements activities often fall under the heading of Business Analysis (BA), determining how a business can make use of technology in order to improve its operations, meet targets, and thrive in a competitive economy. Use of models in RE and BA allows for a shared perception of requirements and an explicit consideration of business strategy. Models can ease the transformation towards design, specification, and code, operationalizing strategies through socio-technical systems.

The second MReBA (Modelling in Requirements and Business Analysis) workshop aims to provide a forum for discussing the interplay between requirements engineering, business analysis and conceptual modeling. Of course, more than ever, we investigate how goal approaches help in conceptualizing purposeful systems. But also, we are interested in all conceptual modelling issues in RE and BA contexts. What are the unresolved open questions? What lessons are there to be learnt from industrial experiences? What empirical data are there to support the cost-benefit analysis when modelling requirements? Are there applications domains or types of project settings for which conceptual modelling is particularly suitable or not suitable? What degree of formalization, automation or interactivity is feasible and appropriate for what types of participants during requirements engineering and business analysis?

MReBA builds on the success of the first workshop with the International Conference on Conceptual Modeling (ER14) in Atlanta and is an evolution of the previous RIGiM (Requirements Intentions and Goals in Conceptual Modeling) Workshop (2007-9, 12-13). While RIGiM was specifically dedicated to goal modelling and the use of intentional concepts in RE, MReBa handles any kind of modelling notation or activity in the context of RE or BA.

This year, MReBA includes a keynote by Prof. Janis Stirna on Facilitation and Management of Modeling Projects: Experiences and Outlook. In addition four high-quality full papers are presented. Each of the ten submitted papers went through a thorough review process with at least three reviews from our program committee. We thank authors and reviewers for their valuable contributions.

Jennifer Horkoff, City University London, UK
Renata Guizzardi, Universidade Federal do Espírito Santo (UFES), Brazil
Jelena Zdravkovic, Stockholm University, Stockholm

Acknowledgements. The organizers of the MReBA 2015 workshop would like to thank all authors for their contributions to this workshop. We also owe thanks to the members of the Program Committee for providing valuable reviews for the submitted papers. Special thanks go to ER 2015 workshop chairs Manfred Jeusfeld and Kamal Karlapalem for their support.

Invited Keynote: Facilitation and Management of Modeling Projects: Experiences and Outlook

Janis Stirna[✉]

Department of Computer and Systems Sciences,
Stockholm University, Forum 100, 16440 Kista, Sweden
js@dsv.su.se

Abstract. Enterprise Modeling (EM) has proved to be a practicable approach that supports congruent organization and information system (IS) development by creating an integrated and commonly shared model describing different aspects of an enterprise (e.g. goals, business process, concepts, rules, etc.) EM is used for the purposes of (1) developing the business, (2) ensuring the quality of business operations, and (3) using EM as a problem solving tool. EM usually is organized in the form of a project or it is a part of a larger, e.g. organizational or information system development, project.

Much of the success of projects using EM depends more on the quality of the process of modeling than on the modeling language used. A key part of this is stakeholder involvement.

Stakeholders or domain experts provide knowledge about different aspects of organization in its current or perceived future state. They are responsible for the correctness and relevance of the knowledge included in the models. Most EM projects also have a project or problem "owner" – someone who is in charge of the problem domain, allocates resources, and has the authority to implement the decisions and designs developed by the project.

Creation of the Enterprise Models using a participatory approach needs to be supported by a modeling practitioner. The professional EM practitioner may take on a number of sub-roles, e.g. EM project leader, facilitator of a modeling session, and tool expert. As project leader, the modeling practitioner negotiates the goals for the modeling project and plans the modeling process together with the project or problem owner. A facilitator moderates each modeling session. In a session there can be more than one facilitator and also a tool expert. A larger modeling project will typically have several facilitators and tool experts forming a modeling practitioner team, which is headed by project leader.

The main responsibility of the modeling practitioner is that (1) the models produced have good enough quality to accomplish the project goals; (2) that the chosen EM method is suitable for modeling the problem at hand and that (3) the method is effectively used to accomplish the project goals. This means not only using the method's notation in a reasonable way but also constructing and to runing a modeling process to make the best of available resources, e.g. the knowledge and availability of domain experts. The modeling practitioner is responsible for making sure that the project resources are used in a way that enables the modeling project to be completed on time and in such a way that the goals are achieved.

M.A. Jeusfeld and K. Karlapalem (Eds.): ER 2015 Workshops, LNCS 9382, pp. 223–224, 2015.
DOI: 10.1007/978-3-319-25747-1_22

This talk presets author's experiences in the area of facilitating and managing modeling projects in terms of the following competence areas related to EM process: defining scope and objectives of the modeling project, planning for project activities and resources, planning for modeling session, gathering and analyzing background information, interviewing modeling participants, preparing modeling sessions, conduct modeling sessions, writing meeting minutes, analyzing and refining models, as well as resenting the results to stakeholders.

The following competencies will be discussed:

1) *Competencies related to modeling*
   - ability to model, including assessing and improving model quality according to the EM purpose and
   - ability to facilitate participatory modeling sessions.
2) *Competencies related to facilitating modeling sessions*
   - ability to drive the modeling session towards its objectives
   - ability to deal with different stakeholder types and behaviors
   - ability to listen what is said and sense what is left unsaid, e.g. by observing body language
   - ability to identify and address issues arising from factors such as differences in organizational culture, management style, and decision-making structure.
3) *Competencies related to setting up and managing EM projects*
   - ability to select an appropriate EM approach and tailor it in order to fit the situation at hand
   - ability to interview involved domain experts
   - ability to define a relevant problem
   - ability to define requirements on the results
   - ability to establish a modeling project
   - to adjust a presentation of project results and issues related to them to various stakeholders
   - ability to navigate between the wishes of various stakeholders while upholding the EM project goal
   - ability to assess the impact of the modeling result and the modeling process in the organization

Much of the above competences are built on experience. Hence, in practice there are at least two competency profiles for the EM practitioner – the beginner and the expert EM practitioner. These profiles determine the kind of roles they can take on, both in the actual modeling and in the management of EM projects. The definition of these two profiles is needed to construct effective training, both at university level as well as in-practice training/mentoring. One argument for this is that it is difficult to know which competency should be developed at which stage of maturity in the EM expert. E.g., confusing the novice with issues that only a more experienced EM practitioner can understand is ineffective. Looking at EM education and training, particularly in universities, it is mostly focused on modeling languages and on the ability to model. Often it is assumed that with the modeling ability comes, implicitly, the ability to facilitate modeling sessions and to manage EM projects, which is clearly not the case.

Towards a Socio-Institutional Ontology
for Conceptual Modelling
of Information Systems

Maria Bergholtz[1(✉)] and Owen Eriksson[2]

[1] Department of Computer and Systems Sciences,
Stockholm University, Stockholm, Sweden
`maria@dsv.su.se`
[2] Department of Informatics and Media,
Uppsala University, Uppsala, Sweden
`owen.eriksson@im.uu.se`

Abstract. Most work on ontologies for conceptual modelling is based on the assumption that conceptual models represent a pre-existing reality, which they should faithfully reflect. This paper suggests an ontology for conceptual modelling of institutional domains taking into account also the prescriptive role of conceptual models, thereby supporting the design of information systems. The paper draws on the current ontological discourse in information systems engineering; descriptive vs prescriptive conceptual modelling; socio-materiality in terms of clarifying the relationships between physical and social domains; and ontological differences between (physical) properties and rights. The results of the paper can be used to support conceptual modelling in business analysis, in particular requirements elicitation of regulative aspects.

1 Introduction

A fundamental question in conceptual modelling and business analysis is the one stated by Wand and Weber (2002), "How can we model the world to better facilitate our developing, implementing, using, and maintaining more valuable information systems?" This question has been addressed in the research literature using a variety of approaches and research methods. The idea behind the use of ontology as a foundation for conceptual modelling has been that ontology can help us better model the real-world that is under consideration [Wand and Weber 2002; Wand et al. 1999; Gruber 1995]. The most widespread ontology in Management Information Systems conceptual modelling research, the Bunge-Wand-Weber (BWW) ontology (Wand et al. 1999, p. 497), states that "the world is made of things that possess properties". Although "things" refer to substantial (physical) individuals (e.g., a Human being called John), constructions such as "bank account" is also a considered to be a thing because it is a concrete thing in someone's mind. However, as pointed out by March and Allen (2014), work on ontology for conceptual modelling has so far only provided limited guidance, including requirements elicitation.

© Springer International Publishing Switzerland 2015
M.A. Jeusfeld and K.Karlapalem (Eds.): ER 2015 Workshops, LNCS 9382, pp. 225–235, 2015.
DOI: 10.1007/978-3-319-25747-1_23

Most work on ontologies for conceptual modelling is based on the assumption that conceptual models represent pre-existing or potential state of affairs i.e. the general status of things in reality, which they should faithfully reflect. This assumption entails that conceptual modelling is primarily a descriptive activity, in which modellers investigate some reality in order to understand it so well, that they can form an accurate model of it. This assumption is often valid when modelling material worlds, but it easily breaks down for the modelling of social worlds. In the latter case, a conceptual model typically does not only represent state of affairs. Instead, it can also work prescriptively as a blueprint that people can use to construct the social world, including their social relationships. The conceptual model provides a language and rules, which are normative and constitutive, and not just descriptive that people can apply to create and regulate their relationships.

The purpose of this paper is to propose an ontology for institutional domains. The ontology is intended to be used for supporting conceptual modeling in business analysis. In particular, it can help to elicit and structure requirements related to rules and regulations in a business used for creating institutional facts, and by that also supports the identification and constitution of entities in a business domain.

The proposed ontology is an extension of Bergholtz et al. 2013, which uses a socio-material perspective (Orlikowski 2008) as starting point. A key notion in socio-materiality is that of performativity, which has its roots in Searle's and Habermas's work, (Searle 1969, Habermas 1976), on performative utterances (speech acts), where social relationships are created in discourses, thereby constituting and regulating the social world.

The paper is organized as follows. Section 2 presents the research settings and introduces a case study to illustrate the ontology. Section 3 presents the ontology. Section 4 illustrates conceptual problems that we have found in the case study. Section 5 shows how the conceptual problems found in the case could be resolved, thereby outlining how the ontology could be used for conceptual modelling as well as comparing the solutions to other ontological approaches.

2   Research Setting

2.1   Research Approach

The socio-institutional ontology is based on primary data from a rich dataset of longitudinal case studies that we have been performed from 1997 until now. Examples include a sell support system used by car dealers at Volvo (Ågerfalk and Eriksson 2004); an e-infrastructure used at the Swedish National Road Administration in Sweden for providing the RDS-TMC service, a student registry used at all the universities in Sweden (Eriksson and Ågerfalk 2010). The secondary data set we have used is typical modelling patterns and problems depicted in the mainstream metamodelling and modelling literature (e.g. Wand et al. 1999; Guizzardi 2005; Henderson-Sellers and Gonzalez-Perez 2010).

2.2   Case Study

One of the case studies that we use to exemplify the ontology has been a longitudinal action design project in the social welfare sector. An elaborate description of the study can be found in Eriksson and Goldkuhl (2013).

A municipality of Sweden is obliged to provide income support if a person cannot support himself and his family by own means. A person could apply for income support to the social welfare department in a municipality. What claims could be made in the application and what duties the applicants must follow is regulated and pre-scribed in Chapter 4 of the Social Service Act (SoL14), the National Standard for expenditure (NSoE) and the prescriptions made by Socialstyrelsen (the national governing body). The first step made by a social welfare officer is to open or re-open a case that already exists, and register the application in the case handling system. The second step is to create or identify an already existing household, because this is the entity that could be granted income support. The third step is to investigate the social situation of the household, i.e. to scrutinize the information about employment situation, income, costs and assets that have been described in the application. To check this, the social welfare officer has to interact with a number of state agencies, e.g. The Board for Study Support (BSS), The Public Employment Service (PES), The Federation of Unemployment Insurance Funds (FUIF) and The Pensions Agency (PA). The fourth step is to deduce the costs of the household from the income and assets of the household and to decide whether the household could be granted income support, as well as the amount granted. The information exchange between the municipalities and state agencies is prescribed by statute (SFS 2008:975). However, the interaction with the state agencies is difficult due to conceptual problems in the case handling systems. We will elaborate on these problems in more detail in Sect. 4.

3   The Socio-Institutional Ontology

3.1   Institutions

Humans regularly interact and, thereby, become socially related with each other. Thus, social interaction forms communities that may become more or less stable over time. For complex communities, the relationships among their participants are governed by rights and rules that express what people are allowed, or obliged, to do. Such rights are always relational, in the sense that they express that someone has a right in relationship to someone else. For example, a municipality (juridical person) of Sweden is obliged by the Social Services Act to provide income support if a client (person) cannot support himself and his family (the household). This also implies that a person could make a claim for such a support from the municipality. In order to describe the interactions, the notion of institution is helpful. An institution consists of a language and a set of rules expressed in that language, which are upheld through collective intentionality. Institutions are able to work thanks to the collective intentionality of a community, i.e. the intentionality shared by its members, including their shared beliefs and emotions (Searle 2011), in particular this means that "Language does not just describe a pre-existing institutional reality but is partly constitutive of that reality." (ibid.).

3.2   Institutional Entities and Rights

In order to capture the idea that some objects e.g. (a person, juridical person, money) are related to rights, the notion of institutional entity is introduced. An *institutional entity* (see Fig. 1 central part) is an instance of a general institutional concept consti- tuted by the use of language within some institution, which has rights or can bestow rights on other institutional entities.

The notion of right can be clarified using the work of W. N. Hohfeld, (Hohfeld 1978). Hohfeld suggested a classification, in which four kinds of rights (deontic powers) are distinguished. An institutional entity has a *claim* on another institutional entity if the second entity is required to act in a certain way for the benefit of the first one, typically by carrying out some action. An institutional entity has a *duty* to another institutional entity if the second entity has a claim on the first one. An institutional entity has a *privilege* on an action if she is free to carry out that action in accordance with the rules of an institution. A *power* is the ability of an institutional entity to create or modify claims, duties, privileges or powers.

As there exists a large variety of institutional entities, it is helpful to identify and structure various kinds of institutional entities into a taxonomy. We distinguish between physical and institutional grounding. Sometimes institutional entities have to correspond to one physical human being, e.g. in the case of a client to come into existence. This is called *physical grounding*. However sometimes there is no such need e.g. a juridical person does not have to have such a correspondence relationship. Thus it could come into existence without there being a physical thing or human being which becomes the juridical person (Searle 2005, p. 16). The only requirement is that there is a media trace of it. *Institutional grounding* means that an institutional entity must be associated to another institutional entity in order to come into existence. For example a client could come to existence because there already exists an instance of a Swedish citizen that the client could be associated to. For all types of rights, a distinction can be drawn between legal and non-legal rights. A *legal right* is a right that is acknowledged by a state and could be a basis for official sanctions from the state. A *non-legal right* is a right that is acknowledged by a state or some other institution but could not be a basis for official sanctions from a state. At a top level (see Fig. 1, middle part), three kinds of institutional entities can be identified: **institutional subject, institutional thing**, and **institutional contract**.

An *institutional subject* is an institutional entity that can have duties, and there are four types institutional subjects: person, social group, social subject and juridical person: A *person* is an institutional subject, physically grounded in a single human being or socially grounded in another person. A person can have legal and non-legal rights. A *social group* is an institutional subject physically grounded in one or more human beings or socially grounded in one or more persons. In contrast to a person, a social group can only have non-legal rights. A *juridical person* is an institutional subject that, in contrast to a person and social group, is not physically grounded in a human being and who can only have legal rights. A *social subject* is an institutional subject which, like a juridical person, is not physically grounded in a human being and can only have non-legal rights.

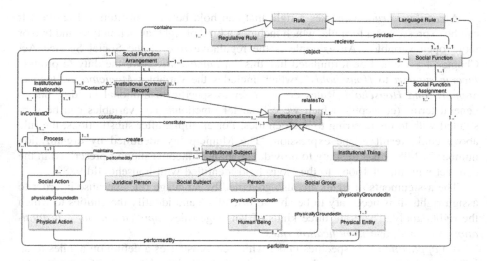

Fig. 1. The Socio-Institutional ontology (due to space restrictions all associations will not be discussed in the text, association-role cardinality assumed 0..* if not otherwise stated)

An *institutional thing* is an institutional entity that cannot have duties, and is physically grounded in a physical entity or socially grounded in another institutional thing.

An *institutional contract* is an institutional entity that cannot have rights but only bestow (mediate) rights between institutional subjects and things (we will explain this in more detail in Sect. 3.4).

This could be exemplified in the social service case like this. Institutional subjects: a client is a *person* which has both legal and non-legal rights and is physically grounded in a human being; a household is a *social group*, which has non-legal rights and is socially grounded in one or several *clients*; a social service office is a *social subject*, which has the power to grant income support to a household, however, not legally responsible for the decisions made; a municipality is a *juridical person* that is legally responsible for the decisions made. Institutional thing; a realisable asset e.g. a vehicle that could be sold in order to provide an income to the household. Institutional contract: a granted income support is a contract between the social service office, the household and the clients who are the members of the household.

3.3   Rules and Social Functions

Institutions precede institutional entities, in the sense that institutional entities can only be created and regulated if there exist institutions with a language and rules so that they can create, maintain, relate and refer to institutional entities. These rules fall into two main categories, *regulative rules* that express what rights that can hold between institutional entities and *language rules* (see Fig. 1 top right part).

A *regulative rule* expresses a right that can hold between institutional entities. It can be expressed as a formula, which includes a kind of right, an action type and two or more open variables. An example is the regulative rule of the Social Service Act Chapter 4 § 1 could be formulated like this. *"Municipalities* have the duty to provide *Income support* to *Households"*, which includes the variables *Municipality, Income Support, and Household*. Rules do not refer to specific institutional entities, but to general terms (concepts), which we call social functions. The variables can be substituted with terms referring to such entities. For example, after substitutions, the rule above could result in the expression "The Municipality identified by organization number 212-0829 has the duty to provide the granted income support prescribed in the contract with the id 16661 to the Household identified with householdId 9882".

The assignments of rights are also governed by language rules because in order to assign rights, it is necessary to be able to instantiate and identify the entities to which the rights apply. There are three kinds of language rules: *application rules, instantiation rules* and, and *identification rules*.

An *application rule* specifies under which circumstances a definition applies to an institutional entity. An example of an application rule is a definition of a household: "A household is a unity for the sustainment of a number of household members which could be adults and children that live together and try to make a living together." Additionally the household member must be understood as clients of the social service, and this applies only to persons who could be identified as Swedish, EU- or EES citizens. Thus only persons that fulfil this definition could count as household members. Hence, a *social function* is a concept that specifies a number of regulative and application rules that could be applied to some institutional entity.

An *instantiation rule* defines how institutional entities are created and assigned social functions. An example is that something becomes a household when it has been registered as such and acknowledged as such by a social welfare officer in the case handling process at the social service department. Thus, the social welfare officer must also know the application rule, i.e. the definition of the household type and its role in this context in order to be able to correctly instantiate an entity of such a type.

An *identification rule* specifies how an institutional entity is to be identified. For example, typing in the household identifier in the case handling system at the social service department, and checking other credentials that is important for the identification of the household. In order to identify an object it must exist, i.e. it must first be instantiated (see above).

Social functions do not appear in isolation but always in groups, or arrangements, of two or more social functions. To represent these arrangements, the notion of *social function arrangement* is introduced. A *social function arrangement* is a set of social functions that are related to each other through a number of rules.

3.4   Social Function Assignment

There are two ways to assign social functions: (1) through the creation of a new institutional relationship or (2) through the creation of an institutional contract.

(1) An *institutional relationship* is created between a number of institutional entities, two of which are institutional subjects, and at least one of which does not exist prior to the creation of the relationship. The new institutional entity is said to be *constituted* by the institutional relationship. When the relationship is created a number of rights are assigned. For example, when a household-ship is created, the household and its members have been recognized as institutional entities, it is also acknowledged that they have the right to claim income support from the municipality.

(2) Social functions could also be assigned through institutional contracts. An example of an institutional contract in the household case is the granted income support.

4 Conceptual Problems Found in the Case Study

In the social allowance welfare case from Sect. 2.2, the interaction between social welfare officers and the state agencies were analysed in the light of statute (SFS 2008:975), which prescribes how the interaction must be performed. When we investigated two of the most used case handling systems used in more than half of the municipalities, a number of conceptual ambiguities were disclosed.

Firstly, the case handling systems used the same identifier for the case, the household and one of the members of the household which was called "the leader of the registry". It was often the PID-number of the adult man that was used, and this caused a number of problems: (a) Decisions made by the social welfare officer using the case handling systems were only sent to the adult man and not to the adult woman of the household. (b) If the woman wanted information about the case she had to provide the PID-number of the man. (c) It was difficult to get the right statistics from the case handling systems because the clients were not distinctly identified within the household as its identity was mixed up with the identity of the adult man.

Secondly, the notion of an open case was ambiguous, and the municipalities had different opinions of what it meant. A new case was created only if the household had not been granted income support within three months before the application date. If the household earlier on had been granted income support within this period, the old case was just re-opened. However, when the law that regulates the case handling process (Förvaltningslag 1986:223) was scrutinized, we found out that there was no such case status (i.e. reopened case) defined in the law. So the notion of reopened case and how it was implemented in the case handling systems were not in line with the law.

5 Discussion

Below two models that solve the conceptual problems outlined above, as well as a number of ontological questions and modelling problems, are presented.

5.1 Identity Is Socio-Institutional, not Material, to Its Character

The model of Fig. 2 makes a clear distinction between a household, its clients (the household members), and the case. These concepts were not clearly separated in the case handling systems, because the same identifier was used for referring to the entities of all three classes. The model above shows that these are different classes and each class should provide its own principle of identity. This implies that the problems described above which were caused by the first conceptual ambiguity could be resolved. This also means that the identity of a household is not to be found by describing physical human beings or their properties it is something assigned by the municipality.

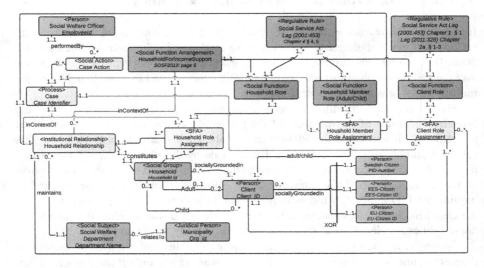

Fig. 2. A conceptual model that prescribe how the household relationship is constituted

Furthermore, the PID-number had also wrongly been chosen to identify the case. The Swedish law prescribes that every case should have a unique number, (which should not be mixed-up with a PID-number). The case is a process, which is composed of a number of social acts which have to be recorded according to the law. Thus, the case process should have its own principle of identity (see also Ågerfalk and Eriksson 2004). This indicates that the principle of identity in institutional reality is a matter of language rules rather than a rigid substantial property. This is an alternative view compared to the one that has been suggested e.g. in the UFO-ontology. According to UFO a process is a perdurant, which should be represented as an abstract class because it cannot provide a principle of identity since none of its temporal parts retain their identity through time (Guizzardi 2005, p. 211).

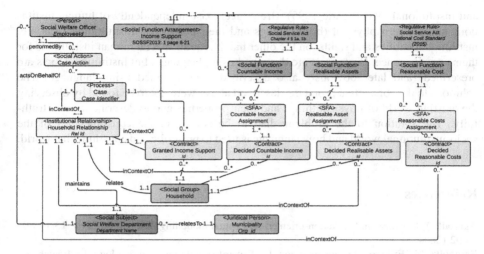

Fig. 3. A conceptual model prescribing how welfare contracts are constituted.

5.2 Institutional Relationships Should Be Modelled as Classes

The next model solves the second conceptual ambiguity problem because the model clearly distinguishes between the household institutional relationship and the case. The model in Fig. 3 shows that there could be several cases within the same household relationship. This draws from the fact that in the SMO institutional relationships are modelled as concrete classes with entities of its own. However, this is e.g. proscribed in the BWW-ontology where relationships should be modelled as mutual properties (Wand et al. 1999, p. 510). Based on this case and other case findings this should not always be prohibited, rather encouraged. This result is in line with e.g. (Guizzardi 2005, p. 267–268), which also warrants modelling mutual properties as (relator) classes.

5.3 Rights and Properties Are Ontologically Different

Another feature of the SMO is that rights are not modelled as properties of classes, but are relational, i.e. they do not appear in isolation but always in the context of institutional relationships that hold between classes, see Fig. 3. An example is the granted income support contract that exists within the relationship between the social service department and the household. This contract primarily consists of a duty for the municipality to cover household costs for the next month. In return, the household has a duty to inform about any changes which could affect the decided income, assets etc. of the household, which also are contracts within this institutional relationship.

5.4 Language as a Constituter of the Socio-Institutional World

The ontological difference between the material and socio-institutional is not yet well understood in conceptual modelling. It is important to make a distinction between brute and institutional facts (Searle 1995). Brute facts exist independently of human institutions and concern physical (brute) things and their properties. Institutional facts, i.e. institutional entities and rights, on the other hand, require special human institutions for their very existence. Brute facts are described using language, but institutional facts are prescribed (and later obviously also described) and assigned using language. The solutions to the conceptual problems described above were not to be found by observing the existing world of physical things and their properties and to describe it more truthfully. The solution to the problems had to be sought in the constituencies of the socio-institutional world and how language is used to prescribe and constitute that world.

References

Ågerfalk, P.J., Eriksson, O.: Action-oriented conceptual modelling. Euro. J. Inf. Syst. **13**(1), 80–92 (2004)

Bergholtz, M., Eriksson, O., Johannesson, P.: Towards a sociomaterial ontology. In: Franch, X., Soffer, P. (eds.) CAiSE Workshops 2013. LNBIP, vol. 148, pp. 341–348. Springer, Heidelberg (2013)

Eriksson, O., Goldkuhl, G.: Preconditions for public sector e-infrastructure development. Inf. Organ. **23**(3), 149–176 (2013)

Eriksson, O., Ågerfalk, P.: Rethinking the meaning of identifiers in information infrastructures. J. Assoc. Inf. Syst. **11**(8), 433–454 (2010)

http://www.notisum.se/rnp/sls/lag/19860223.htm

Gruber, T.R.: Toward principles for the design of ontologies used for knowledge sharing? Int. J. Hum. Comput. Stud. **43**(5), 907–928 (1995)

Guizzardi, G.: Ontological Foundations for Structural Conceptual Models, CTIT Ph.D. thesis Series, No. 05-74, Telematica Instituut Fundamental Research Series, No. 015 (TI/FRS/015) (2005)

Habermas, J.: What is Universal Pragmatics? In: Cooke, M., Habermas, J. (eds.) On the Pragmatics of Communication 1976, 1 edn. Massachusetts Institute of Technology, Cambridge (1984)

Henderson-Sellers, B., Gonzalez-Perez, C.: Granularity in conceptual modelling: application to metamodels. In: Parsons, J., Saeki, M., Shoval, P., Woo, C., Wand, Y. (eds.) ER 2010. LNCS, vol. 6412, pp. 219–232. Springer, Heidelberg (2010)

Hohfeld, W.N., Corbin, A. (eds.): Fundamental Legal Conceptions. Greenwood Press, Westport (1978)

March, S.T., Allen, G.N.: Toward a social ontology for conceptual modeling. Commun. Assoc. Inf. Syst. 34, Article 70 (2014)

National Standard of Expenditure, Riksnormen för försörjningsstöd. http://www.socialstyrelsen.se/ekonomisktbistand/riksnormen

Orlikowski, W., Scott, S.: Sociomateriality: challenging the separation of technology work and organization. Acad. Manag. Ann. **2**(1), 433–474 (2008)

Searle, J.: Speech Acts: An Essay in the Philosophy of Language. Cambridge University Press, Cambridge (1969)

Searle, J.: The Construction of Social Reality. Free Press, New York (1997)

Searle, J.: Making the Social World: The Structure of Human Civilization. Oxford University Press, Oxford (2010)

https://www.riksdagen.se/sv/Dokument-Lagar/Lagar/Svenskforfattningssam-ling/Socialtjanstlag-2001453_sfs-2001-453/

SFS (2008:975) In Swedish. Förordning om uppgiftsskyldighet i vissa fall enligt socialtjänst-lagen. https://lagen.nu/2008:975

Wand, Y., Storey, V.C., Weber, R.: An ontological analysis of the relationship construct in conceptual modeling. ACM Trans. Database Syst. **24**(4), 494–528 (1999)

Wand, Y., Weber, Y.: Research commentary: information systems and conceptual modeling—a research agenda. Inf. Syst. Res. **13**(4), 363–376 (2002)

Modeling and Utilizing Security Knowledge for Eliciting Security Requirements

Tatsuya Abe, Shinpei Hayashi[✉], and Motoshi Saeki

Department of Computer Science, Tokyo Institute of Technology,
Ookayama 2-12-1-W8-83, Meguro-ku, Tokyo 152-8552, Japan
{abe,hayashi,saeki}@se.cs.titech.ac.jp

Abstract. In order to develop secure information systems with less development cost, it is important to elicit the requirements to security functions (simply security requirements) as early in their development process as possible. To achieve it, accumulated knowledge of threats and their objectives obtained from practical experiences is useful, and the technique to support the elicitation of security requirements utilizing this knowledge should be developed. In this paper, we present the technique for security requirements elicitation using practical knowledge of threats, their objectives and security functions realizing the objectives, which is extracted from Security Target documents compliant to the standard Common Criteria. We show the usefulness of our approach with several case studies.

Keywords: Security requirements elicitation · Threat pattern · Common criteria

1 Introduction

Information systems deployed at different sites are being connected to each other through networks, and their users can obtain various services anytime and anywhere. In this situation, it is important to develop the information systems with functions that protect from so-called security threats to decrease damage. In order to develop secure information systems with less development cost, it is important to elicit the requirements to security functions (simply *security requirements*) as early in their development process as possible. The identification of the potentials of threats and their objectives (countermeasures to threats) are the first step of eliciting security requirements. However, there are two problems for requirements analysts to perform the above step; (1) Threats do not occur in the normal usage of information systems; rather they can be considered as exceptional events. It is more difficult to consider exceptional events rather than considering normal behavior of a business process, and as a result, it is not easy for even expert analysts to identify possible threats exhaustively in the earlier stage. (2) In addition to knowledge of a problem domain, the analysts are required to have security knowledge. For example, the security objective to an eavesdropping threat may be encryption, and the analysts should have this knowledge. To address these problems, accumulated knowledge of threats and

© Springer International Publishing Switzerland 2015
M.A. Jeusfeld and K. Karlapalem (Eds.): ER 2015 Workshops, LNCS 9382, pp. 236–247, 2015.
DOI: 10.1007/978-3-319-25747-1_24

their objectives obtained from practical experiences is useful, and the technique to support the elicitation of security requirements utilizing this knowledge should be developed. This technique suggests to the analysts the potentials of threats, their objectives, and furthermore security functions realizing the objectives.

In this paper, we present the technique for security requirements elicitation using practical knowledge of threats, their objectives and security functions. More concretely, we extract this knowledge from Security Targets (STs; explained in Sect. 2) documents and model the extracted knowledge so that we can use it at the stage of specifying behavior of business processes and information systems. In our approach, behavioral specification is represented with sequence diagrams as a set of scenarios. We have two types of scenarios; one is the scenarios of normal cases in enacting a business process or executing an information system, called normal scenarios, and the other is called negative scenarios representing how a malicious act is executed exploiting vulnerability points. STs are the documents compliant to the international standard Common Criteria (CC; ISO/IEC15408) [1]. The extracted knowledge from STs is modeled as transformation rules on scenarios to generate *negative scenarios* and to embed the executions of security functions into the original normal scenario Sect. 3. We call this resulting scenario where security functions are embedded *fixed scenario*. The transformation is automated with Attributed Graph Grammar (AGG) tool [8]. We extracted the patterns of 9 types of threats, their objectives and security functions from several STs and composed transformations rules. We applied these rules to 6 scenarios in case studies from two problem domains and could obtain successful results Sect. 4. We have already published similar work [2]. However, this previous work was for the identification of potentials of threats only and did not support the elicitation of their objectives or security functions at all.

2 Our Idea

In our approach, we identify the potentials of threats and the security functions that mitigate the threats from the normal scenarios. In describing scenarios, elements in the scenarios, their relationships and execution orders of the information passing events should be formally defined, and analysts who are not security experts should be able to understand the described scenarios easily. Thus, we take the technique of attaching stereotypes and tagged values to lifelines, objects, messages, information on messages, etc. of UML sequence diagram.

Suppose a simple example of an information system where its functions are available to users after they login to it. Its user knows his login password, and he inputs his password to the system. Figure 1 shows a normal scenario of this login process, and the stereotypes and the tagged values appearing in the figure will be mentioned in Sect. 3. It has potentials of eavesdropping threats to inputting and sending the password, and we can regard password encryption as an objective to the eavesdropping. To detect the potential of eavesdropping and derive its objective, we should have security knowledge like (1) passwords should be the information to be protected, (2) if we do not protect the information yet, there

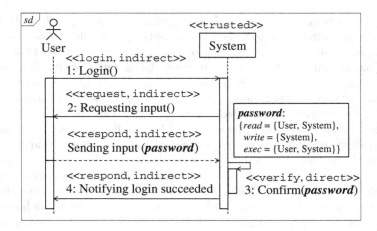

Fig. 1. Scenario example described as a sequence diagram with attributes.

are the risks of eavesdropping it, and (3) encryption is an effective way to mitigate eavesdropping.

We can apply transformation rules to this normal scenario, and produce negative scenarios and their *fixed* scenarios by using a technique of graph pattern matching on the sequence diagram.

To compose the transformation rules, in the same way of the technique [2], we use STs, because it describes threats, the objectives that can mitigate them, and the security functions that realize the objectives. STs are the documents whose structure such as chapter organization is specified by CC [1]. In an ST, objectives are realized by means of combining predefined security function components (SFCs). CC also provides a catalog of reusable SFCs, and they are defined in the form of templates having slots. A composer of an ST can choose several SFCs from CC and adapt them by filling their slots with suitable information, and combines the filled SFCs to realize objectives. For example, the SFC named "FCS_COP.1" defines the function of processing encryption with specified algorithm and the specified key length, and the composer fills the slots "specified algorithm" and "specified key length". The scenario of executing this SFC can be specified with sequence diagrams, and it can be embedded in the points in a normal scenario where eavesdropping may occur.

The technique how to extract the knowledge on threats, objectives and SFCs from STs is based on the approach proposed by Saeki et al. [7]. More concretely, we use the descriptions in Chapters 3.3 and 4 of STs, and matrices of Security Objective Rationale in Chapter 8.1 and of Security Requirements Rationale in Chapter 8.2. Figure 2 shows how these two rationales are used for extracting the relationships among threats, security objectives, and SFCs. The matrix of Security Objective Rationale in Chapter 8.1 shows which security objectives in a row of the matrix can mitigate which threats, such as "O.Communicate_Protection *mitigates* T.Intercept". Each security objective described in Chapter 4

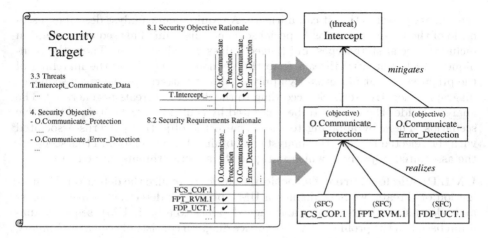

Fig. 2. Chained relationships among threats, security objectives, and SFCs.

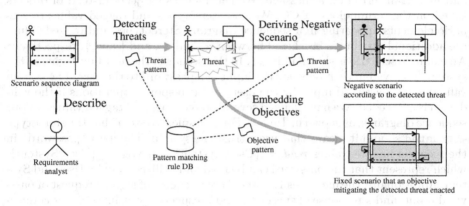

Fig. 3. Overview of our technique.

should be linked to the threats via this matrix to clarify its rationales on why it is necessary. Similarly, the Security Requirements Rationale in Chapter 8.2 specifies which SFCs can realize which security objectives, e.g. "the combination of FCS_COP.1, FPT_RVM.1, and FDP_UCT.1 *realizes* O.Communicate_Protection" in Fig. 2. The extracted relationships are used for specifying how to prepare the transformation rules to mitigate the detected threats in the given scenario.

3 Proposed Technique

The process of the proposed technique is shown in Fig. 3. In the technique, the user prepares the pattern matching rules for detecting threats (simply, *threat patterns*) and the rules of countermeasures for mitigating them (simply, *objective patterns*) extracted from STs in advance. An objective pattern is associated with the threats patterns that it can mitigate. A requirements analyst describes a scenario of the target system as a special sequence diagram. This sequence diagram includes special stereotypes and tagged values explained later. Then, the technique detects potential threats from this sequence diagram by the matching of the prepared threat patterns. By applying threat patterns to the given sequence diagram, a negative scenario according to the detected threats is generated. The analyst decides the threats to be mitigated by confirming the obtained negative scenarios. Then, by applying to the scenario the objective patterns associated with the selected threats, the analyst can obtain a fixed scenario. In this scenario, the associated objectives, which mitigate the selected threats, are enacted.

UML Profile for Threat Detection. In order to realize the detection and mitigation of threats, we have defined a UML profile for detecting security threats and added several stereotypes and tagged values to a basic UML sequence diagram based on the profile. A basic sequence diagram consists of *scenario elements*, which include *subjects* (lifelines), *messages* between them, their execution order, and *data* transferred on a message. We call lifelines subjects instead of objects based on the terminology of CC. We add stereotypes and tagged values to scenario elements appearing in a sequence diagram. Stereotypes and tagged values are additional attributes bracketed between ≪ and ≫, and { and }, respectively. An example scenario is shown in Fig. 1. In this scenario, the user first logins to the system. The system then requests the input of a password to the user. The system validates the password input by the user, and it responds operations if the validation is succeeded. We have defined several stereotypes and tagged values for our sequence diagrams, as shown in Table 1. For example, "System" has the stereotype ≪trusted≫, and it means that users trust the system. The data "password" in the scenario has the values $read = \{User, System\}$ and $exec = \{User, System\}$, which represent that the password can be read and utilized only by User and System. Additionally, the messages 1, 2, and 4 are a request of login, a request of password input, and a response of successful login respectively, using *indirect* connection with a user interface, whereas the message 3 is a verification of the correctness of the given password. So we attached the corresponding stereotypes, e.g., *login*, *request*, it respond, *indirect*, and *verify* to them.

Detecting Threats and Deriving Negative Scenarios. Next, potential threats are detected from the given scenario using threat patterns. Threat patterns can be prepared using the descriptions in Chapter 3.3 of STs. For example, consider a threat labeled T.Intercept_Communicate_Data, described in Chapter 3.3 of the smart card FeliCa's ST[1]. This chapter explains not only the threat but also the conditions when it can occur, e.g. an example scenario of the actual attacks in natural language. Based on this description, we can compose a pattern for detecting this threat as shown in Fig. 4. This figure shows a transformation rule of a sequence diagram, consisting of a threat pattern Fig. 4(a) as a left-hand side and a pattern of the resulting negative scenario Fig. 4(b) as a right-hand side. The threat pattern represents a pattern of the location of the potential threat on

---

¹ https://www.ipa.go.jp/security/jisec/certified_products/c0251/c0251_st.pdf.

Table 1. Stereotypes and tagged values.

Notation	Description
For subjects (lifelines):	
≪trusted≫	The subject has a security function
≪movable≫	The subject is movable and requires electronic power supply
For messages:	
≪direct≫	The message uses a wired connection for the data transfer
≪indirect≫	The message uses a wireless connection or UI
≪request≫	The message requests the opponent for data
≪respond≫	The message sends data as a response
≪modify≫	The message writes, modifies, or deletes data
≪verify≫	The message confirms the validity of data
≪login≫	The message logs in and starts a session
≪logout≫	The message closes a session
For data transferred on messages:	
$\{\,read = R \subseteq S\,\}^{*1}$	A set of subjects which are allowed to read the data
$\{\,write = W \subseteq S\,\}^{*1}$	A set of subjects which are allowed to modify the data
$\{\,exec = E \subseteq S\,\}^{*1}$	A set of subjects which are allowed to execute the data

^{*1} S = asetofgivensubjects ∪ {public}. The value "public" means every potential subjects.

the sequence diagram, and its occurrence is transformed into that of the pattern of the right-hand side. This threat pattern can match to the sequence diagram shown in Fig. 1 because we can associate the subjects S_1, S_2, the ≪respond≫ message, and the data d with User, System, Sending input, and the password, respectively. An example shown in Fig. 5 is to apply the transformation rule of Fig. 4 to the sequence scenario of Fig. 1. This negative scenario illustrates how the password is intercepted: a mis-actor installs a special device, and it intercepts the input of the password.

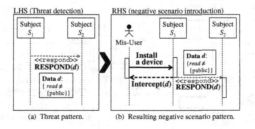

(a) Threat pattern.   (b) Resulting negative scenario pattern.

Fig. 4. Patterns for Intercept.

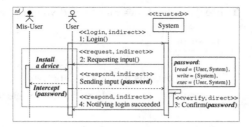

Fig. 5. Example negative scenario for Intercept.

Embedding Objectives: Generating Fixed Scenarios. After understanding the details of the threat with negative scenarios, we can mitigate the detected threats by enacting the associated security objectives. Since we may have more than one objective to a threat, the analyst selects the objectives that should be enacted. Figure 6 illustrates the application of an objective pattern obtained from the objective O.Communicate_Protection described in the ST. Based on the relationship between the objective and SFCs in the Chapter 8.2 of the ST, as shown in Fig. 2, this pattern is described as a combination of three SFC implementations: FCS_COP.1, FDP_UCT.1, and FPT_RVM.1. FCS_COP.1 is an SFC for performing cryptographic operations using the specified cryptographic algorithm. FDP_UCT.1 is for protecting user data to be exchanged. FPT_RVM.1 is for data protection to cover all objects in order to guarantee the non-bypassability. By combining these SFCs, a pattern shown in Fig. 6 represents "Ensuring to apply encryption before sending the data to be protected". Figure 6 is an example of the application result of this transformation. This is the fixed scenario where the O.Communicate_Protection objective is enacted on the example scenario shown in Fig. 1. Similar to generating the negative scenario as mentioned above, the threat pattern can be matched to the example scenario, and the target security objective is embedded by (1) inserting the ENCRYPT message just before the message "Sending input (*password*)" and the DECRYPT just after the message and (2) adding the KEY object as the encryption key.

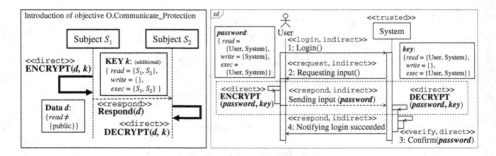

Fig. 6. Example of a fixed scenario with O.Communicate_Protection against Intercept.

Table 2. Prepared threat patterns and their source STs.

Threats	C251	C191	C229	1627	Total	# objectives
Violate Access (VA)				2	2	3
Abuse Command (AC)	1		1	1	3	4
Intercept (IC)	2	1	1	3	7	2
Powerdown (PD)	1	1			2	2
Spoofing (SP)	1	1			2	1
Skimming (SK)		1			1	1
Eavesdropping (ED)		1			1	1
Forgery (FG)			1	2	3	2
Hijack (HJ)				1	1	2
# covered threat occurrences	5	3	5	9	22	
# all of threats in ST	9	6	8	25	48	
Coverage	0.56	0.50	0.63	0.36	0.46	

4 Evaluation

For accessing the effectiveness of our technique, we conducted an evaluation using example scenarios. In this evaluation, we will answer the following evaluation questions (EQs): (1) To what extent does the proposed technique accurately detect threats in the given scenarios and introduce objectives based on the detected threats? and (2) Do the differences of the problem domains of the given scenarios affect the accuracy of the detection?

Prepared Patterns. We developed 9 threat patterns and 12 objective patterns associated with them. To obtain these patterns, we collected STs from two different domains: IC card system and client-server system for generality. From the former domain, we prepared three STs for: (1) "FeliCa" IC card system (C251), (2) an e-Passport system (C229)[2], and (3) a resident's card system (C191)[3]. From the latter domain, we prepared one ST for "Intel SOA Expressway v2.7.0.4 and Intel SOA Expressway v2.7.0.4 for Healthcare" (1627)[4]. Table 2 shows the prepared threat patterns and their source STs. In this table, each row indicates an extracted threat pattern and how many times it occurred in a specific ST. For example, the Violate Access threat occurred twice in the ST-1627, and we extracted three different objective patterns for this threat.

Scenario Preparation. One of the authors composed six scenarios for two systems, as shown in Table 3, and he intentionally embedded a couple of vulnerabilities to them. That is to say, the scenarios were recognized to have the

---

[2] http://www.ipa.go.jp/security/jisec/certified_products/c0229/c0229_st.pdf.

[3] https://www.ipa.go.jp/security/jisec/certified_products/c0191/c0191_st.pdf.

[4] https://www.commoncriteriaportal.org/files/epfiles/1627_ST-Version_1_9%20(2). pdf.

Table 3. Detection results.

Domain/Scenario	Size	TP	TP+	FP	FN	Fix Failure
S1: Gate/Enter	9	IC(2), PD	SK		SP	
S2: Gate/Exit	15	IC(2), PD(2), SK(2)			SP(2)	
S3: Gate/Issue	14	IC(3), ED	SP, SK		AC	
S4: e-Shop/Sign up	18	IC, ED	SK			SK
S5: e-Shop/Order	32	IC(9), ED(8), VA(3)	SK	SP	AC, SP(2), VA	
S6: e-Shop/Admin	13	IC(2), ED(2), HJ			SP, SK	HJ

possibility of threats and we call these threats intended ones. The table also shows the size of each scenario, which counts the number of messages and objects in the scenario sequence diagram. The scenarios S1, S2, and S3 are for an IC card gating system of train stations. S4, S5, and S6 are for a web application system of online shopping.

Results. We have automated transformation on sequence diagrams using AGG tool [8] and applied our scenarios. Table 3 shows the detection results. The columns TP, TP+, FP, and FN stand for true positives, additional true positives, false positives, and false negatives respectively. True positives (TP) are the intended threats that could be detected by our technique. Additional true positives (TP+) are the threats that the scenario author did not include but our technique could detect. Note that these threats were validated as correct ones. False positives (FP) are the threats that were not really threats but out technique incorrectly detected. False negatives (FN) are the intended threats that our technique failed to detect. The last column "Fix Failure" indicates the intended threats that were correctly detected but failed to apply the associated objectives to fix the given scenario. For example for the scenario S1: Gate/Enter, three intended threats: two of Intercept (IC) and a Powerdown (PD) were detected, and an unintended threat Skimming (SK) was additionally detected as a valid result. However, an intended Spoofing (SP) was not detected. The measured precisions, recalls, and F-measures are shown in Table 4.

Table 4. Precisions and recalls.

Domain	# oracles	# detected	# FP	Precision	Recall	F-measure
Gate	20	16	0	1.00	0.80	0.89
e-Shop	35	30	1	0.97	0.83	0.89
Total	55	46	1	0.98	0.83	0.89

Answering EQ. 1. As shown in Table 4, *the values of precision, recall, and F-measure are sufficiently high.* In 9 types of threats, we could correctly detect Eavesdropping, Hijack, and Powerdown. However, our technique failed to detect

Table 5. Detection failures and their reasons.

Type	Target	Reason
False negative	Spoofing	Gap between a pattern and a scenario
False negative	Abuse Command	Gap between a pattern and a scenario
False negative	Violate Access	Bug in a pattern
Not detected	Forgery	Not found in the target scenarios
False positive	Spoofing	Failed to capture logging in
Fix failure	Hijack	Bug in a pattern
Fix failure	Skimming	Incorrectly detected the location to embed

for the other types of the threats. We analyzed the reasons of detection failures. The reasons are summarized in Table 5. Most of the reasons were not due to the process of our technique but the insufficiency of the patterns, the attributes in the messages, and scenarios. All of the found bugs in the patterns were trivial so that we successfully corrected all of them.

Answering EQ. 2. The types of detected threats of the Gate system are different from those of the e-shopping system. For example, Powerdown was detected at many times from the Gate system, whereas Eavesdropping was frequently detected from the e-shopping system because the latter system uses many interactions with UI. In contrast, general threats such as Skimming and Intercept were detected from both of scenarios. Together with high values of precision and recall, we can conclude that *our technique could detect threats of high accuracy for both systems, which indicates its generality.*

5   Related Work

The authors' previous work [6] adopted two requirements elicitation methods; goal-oriented analysis and use case modeling. After identifying assets to be protected, an analyst attaches the attributes to it so as to characterize the assets. The analyst infers and derives the potentials of threats from the attribute values of the assets and from the threat catalog, by means of inference rules prepared beforehand. The threat catalog and the inference rules are developed from STs. The technique proposed by Kaiya *et al.* [5], an analyst develops an asset flow diagram, which is a variation of data flow diagram, to represent the movement of the assets between their source objects and sink ones. From the attached types of the assets, their sources and sinks, the analyst infers the potentials of threats to the assets. All of these techniques are similar to ours, in the sense that some attributes are attached to the elements of a business description (a use case diagram, a goal graph or an asset flow diagram, etc.) and then the potential of threats are deduced using the attributes. However, they did not consider the behavioral aspect of a business process. We consider that threats emerge in the execution sequences of business activities and have adopted scenarios as a starting point of identifying the threats. This is a contribution of our approach.

In [3], its authors compared three existing techniques to model vulnerabilities, e.g., i*, misuse modeling and CORAS, and tried to identify common concepts of vulnerabilities in order to develop an ontology or a set of vocabularies in a security domain. The obtained concepts and their relationships can be a meta model of vulnerability models for integrating different security requirements analysis methods, and the aim of this research is different from ours. Yoshioka *et al.* [9] surveyed various levels of security patterns from requirements analysis phases to implementation ones. Although the security patterns listed up in this literature can be knowledge sources to construct threat patterns in our approach, they did not consider automated supports of their utilization.

6   Concluding Remarks

This paper presented the technique to model threat and objective patterns and to apply them to the identification and mitigation of security threats during the development of a business model. Our approach transforms normal scenarios into the negative scenarios that realize the threats and into the fixed scenarios where the objectives mitigating the detected threats are introduced. Scenarios are described with sequence diagrams annotated with security-specific attribute values, and the transformation is based on a graph rewriting system considering sequence diagrams as graphs.

The future work can be considered as follows. We should make experiments of larger size and in various problem domains to get transformation rules of high quality, in addition to more elaborated evaluation. The development of an integrated supporting tool including the extraction of threat and objective patterns from documents and threat libraries such as STRIDE [4] and the other types of security patterns is desired. Also, the development of CASE tool for easily modeling our special sequence diagram is also needed.

Acknowledgments. This work was partly supported by JSPS Grants-in-Aid for Scientific Research (#15K00088).

References

1. Common Criteria : New CC Portal. http://www.commoncriteriaportal.org/
2. Abe, T., Hayashi, S., Saeki, M.: Modeling security threat patterns to derive negative scenarios. In: Proceedings APSEC, pp. 58–66 (2013)
3. Elahi, G., Yu, E., Zannone, N.: A modeling ontology for integrating vulnerabilities into security requirements conceptual foundations. In: Proceeding of the ER, pp. 99–114 (2009)
4. Hernan, S., Lambert, S., Ostwald, T., Shostack, A.: Threat modeling: Uncover security design flaws using the STRIDE approach (2006). http://msdn.microsoft.com /en-us/magazine/cc163519.aspx

5. Kaiya, H., Sakai, J., Ogata, S., Kaijiri, K.: Eliciting security requirements for an information system using asset flows and processor deployment. IJSSE **4**(3), 42–63 (2013)
6. Saeki, M., Kaiya, H.: Security requirements elicitation using method weaving and common criteria. In: Chaudron, M.R.V. (ed.) MODELS 2008. LNCS, vol. 5421, pp. 185–196. Springer, Heidelberg (2009)
7. Saeki, M., Hayashi, S., Kaiya, H.: Enhancing goal-oriented security requirements analysis using common criteria-based knowledge. IJSEKE **23**(5), 695–720 (2013)
8. Taentzer, G.: AGG: A graph transformation environment for modeling and validation of software. In: Pfaltz, J.L., Nagl, M., Böhlen, B. (eds.) AGTIVE 2003. LNCS, vol. 3062, pp. 446–453. Springer, Heidelberg (2004)
9. Yoshioka, N., Washizaki, H., Maruyama, K.: A survey on security patterns. Prog. Inform. **5**, 35–47 (2008)

Towards the Derivation of Secure Business Process Designs

Nikolaos Argyropoulos$^{(\boxtimes)}$, Haralambos Mouratidis, and Andrew Fish

University of Brighton, Brighton BN2 4GJ, UK
{n.argyropoulos,h.mouratidis,andrew.fish}@brighton.ac.uk

Abstract. Security is a critical aspect of business processes that organisations utilise to achieve their goals. Current works on secure business process design mainly focus on annotating existing process models with security related concepts. Meanwhile, little attention is given to the rationale and the alignment of such security choices to high-level organisational security goals. To that end, a goal-to-process transformation approach, with a clear security orientation, is introduced, as part of a wider framework. This transformation process, presented through an illustrative example, uses Secure Tropos goal models as an input to create intermediate, security-annotated process skeletons. These can be then refined, through a series of manual tasks, to create secure BPMN process models.

Keywords: Business process modelling · Business process security · Secure tropos · BPMN · Process derivation · Goal-to-process transformation

1 Introduction

Security is an important, non-functional characteristic of business processes, where critical information is exchanged between numerous participating organisations and individuals. According to the consensus of the requirements engineering (RE) literature [1,2], it is imperative for security concerns and organisational security regulations to be identified and elaborated, in the form of security requirements, during the early design stages of the information systems supporting such business processes. The development of *"secure by design"* business processes is considered highly beneficial [3], as information security breaches can impact organisations financially, due to unplanned downtimes and redesign, but also in terms of reputation and trust from the customer's side [4].

However, despite its apparent importance and its potential benefits, security is usually considered as an afterthought during business process development in practice [4]. Little attention is given by Business Process Management (BPM) approaches developed in research [5], most of which are limited to simple security-related annotation of already developed process models. Consequently, security choices at the process level are made based on arbitrary criteria and are often misaligned with higher-level strategic goals of the organisation. Therefore, the aim of this work is to cover the need for a structured approach for the

© Springer International Publishing Switzerland 2015
M.A. Jeusfeld and K. Karlapalem (Eds.): ER 2015 Workshops, LNCS 9382, pp. 248–258, 2015.
DOI: 10.1007/978-3-319-25747-1_25

derivation of secure business process designs from high-level, security-oriented goal models, which capture organisational goals and security requirements.

The rest of the paper is structured as follows; Sect. 2 explores related work on security during process design, Sect. 3 introduces a goal-to-process transformation approach through an example and conclusions are discussed in Sect. 4.

2   Related Work

Graphical process modelling standards alone are not fully equipped to capture the strategic rationale (e.g., high-level goals) which processes should achieve [6]. Thus, it is preferable to use goal-oriented approaches for elaborating on high-level organisational strategy [7]. Goal-oriented requirements engineering (GORE) approaches can capture and analyse the intentions of stakeholders and translate them to system requirements [8]. However, while goal models can provide an overall direction and encapsulate the rationale behind goals, they lack the ability to identify how such goals will be operationalised. Thus, GORE should be used more as an initial influence rather than a complete solution for the further development of business processes [9].

A number of approaches exist, utilising a variety of GORE frameworks as the starting point for the elicitation of process designs (e.g., KAOS in [10,11], Tropos in [12,13], i* in [6,14–16]). Such approaches support generic goal-to-process transformations, mapping organisational goals to activities at the process level. Nevertheless they are not sufficient in the context of security, as such mappings cannot capture the essence of security requirements, which act as restrictions on the means used for the achievement of goals. For such purposes specialised approaches have been developed. SecureBPEL [17] is a process specification language, emphasising the aspect of security by utilising Secure Tropos constructs to enforce delegation and trust in web services. The SecCo (Security via Commitments) framework [18] is based on the concept of social commitments between actors and elicits security requirements through the modelling and analysis of their objectives, roles and social interactions. Similarly in [19], transformation rules expressed in SecBPMN are used to introduce security requirements, identified using STS-ml, to already existing BPMN process models.

Security-oriented transformation approaches are scarce and often lack in maturity and practical validation. Additionally, they cannot cover the whole range of security requirements and also consider elements of risk management (e.g., threats). Moreover, the annotation of an already designed process model with elements of security, which they perform, is unable to capture and reflect the rationale behind such decisions. What is required in order to facilitate *"security by design"* is the creation of process skeletons, derived by security- and risk-aware organisational goal models. To achieve that, explicit concept mappings and strict transformation guidelines are required [20], allowing changes in the organisational goals, to also be reflected at the process level, and vice versa.

Security related aspects are also not natively supported by contemporary process modelling languages [21,22], including BPMN [23], the current "de-facto" graphical modelling standard [3]. Therefore, a number of BPMN extensions have been proposed, aiming to introduce security during the process design in a manner comprehensible by non-technical stakeholders [2,24]. Most of these extensions introduce new graphical elements, such as padlock symbols [24] and new sets of annotations [25] which can be used to denote various security requirements (e.g., integrity, confidentiality) at the process level. Other works extend already existing concepts of the BPMN meta-model in order to cover security aspects such as authorisation and separation of duty (SoD) [26,27].

Nonetheless, such approaches, often developed without taking into account existing extension mechanisms [28], do not facilitate the elaboration of security choices at the process level, as they are limited to simply annotating them on process models. Additionally, the lack of consensus on the definition and proper usage of BPMN's graphical notation [21,29] can introduce ambiguity [30], especially in the context of security [31]. Another issue is the complexity often introduced via large sets of new notation, which require particular domain knowledge for their interpretation [3,7], thereby overloading users.

3   Proposed Framework

A new framework for the derivation and evaluation of secure business process designs has been conceptualised, as illustrated in Fig. 1, in order to overcome some of the identified limitations. This framework aims to (i) provide rationale for security choices by connecting them to high-level organisational needs, (ii) introduce them at the process level via BPMN process models and (iii) validate their adherence to the initial requirements through formal model checking approaches.

The main components of a process skeleton (e.g., lanes, activities, resources) are automatically derived from a Secure Tropos goal model [32], which also

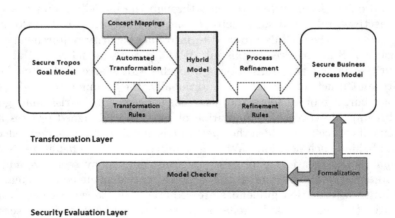

Fig. 1. An overview of the proposed framework

contains additional security related concepts (e.g., security constraints, security objectives, security mechanisms, threats). These security related concepts are mapped onto the derived process skeleton to create a hybrid model, which can be then manually transformed via a set of refinement rules to a secure business process model. The evaluation of the compliance of the produced BPMN process model to the initial security requirements, captured by the Secure Tropos goal model, will be performed at the security evaluation layer. In this layer, both the derived process model and the initial requirements will be formalised into a syntax compatible with one of the many available model checkers (e.g., SPIN, NUSMV), in order for the compliance checking to be performed.

In this paper we focus on the initial transformation layer, introducing the steps necessary for the derivation of a secure BPMN business process model, through an illustrative example. The outcome of this transformation should be a process design aligned to the strategic security goals of the organisation. It is important to produce a high quality process model as an output of the transformation layer, since it will be the basis for the rest of the analysis (i.e., security evaluation) supported by this framework.

3.1   Transformation Layer

To facilitate the initial transformation from the goal model to the hybrid process skeleton, concept mappings between Secure Tropos and BPMN concepts are proposed. Semantic analysis of the concept definitions and meta-models of Secure Tropos and BPMN [23,32] revealed conceptual similarities and facilitated such mappings. A transformation algorithm has been defined in Table 1, using these mappings and providing instructions on how they can be utilised for the derivation of the hybrid model.

In order to obtain a complete and secure process model some manual, process refinement tasks need to be performed on the derived hybrid model, which acts as an intermediate model between the goal and process models, containing elements of both. This manual refinement aims to provide the extra information needed for the creation of a complete process model, which cannot be derived from the goal model (e.g., ordering of activities, message exchanges) or cannot be directly mapped onto currently existing BPMN concepts (e.g., dependencies, threats).

The refinement process will lead to models illustrating activities and resources that need to be secured, along with tasks implementing the necessary security measures. Dependencies will also be transformed into message exchanges between process lanes and events will be used to represent threats. Certain choices during that refinement are left to the discretion of the analyst (e.g., how to break down a security mechanism into activities). Nevertheless, a set of refinement rules has been defined in order to provide some basic guidelines.

- Activities are ordered and interconnected and start and end events are added.
- Dependency links between lanes are transformed into message exchanges and connected to specific activities or events.
- Security constraint activities or resources are marked in order to be secured.

– Security mechanisms are translated into "secure" activities, connected to the corresponding security-annotated activities.
– Threats are transformed into events which may trigger alternate execution paths within the process.

Table 1. Transformation steps for the derivation of a hybrid process skeleton

Step 1	*For each* **actor** (a) of the goal model:
	Create a corresponding **lane** $l(a)$ in the hybrid model
Step 2	*For each* **root-level goal** (g) of the goal model:
	Create a corresponding **sub-process** $p(g)$ in the hybrid model
	For each of the **sub-goals** (g') of g:
	If it is a **leaf-level sub-goal**:
	Create a corresponding **task** $t(g')$, within $p(g)$
	Else: Create a corresponding **(sub-)sub-process** $p(g')$, within $p(g)$
Step 3	*For each* **resource** (r) of the goal model:
	Create a corresponding **data object** $d(r)$ in the hybrid model
Step 4	*For each* **dependency link** (dl) of the goal model, between two actors (a_d, a_D) for the achievement of a goal (g_D):
	Transfer it to the hybrid model, from the dependent activity ($p(g_D)$ or $t(g_D)$) of $l(a_D)$ to the dependee's lane $l(a_d)$
Step 5	*For each* **security constraint** (sc), **mechanism** (sm) or **threat** (t) connected to a goal (g) or resource (r) of the goal model:
	Transfer it to the hybrid model
	Connect it to the corresponding activities ($p(g)$ or $t(g)$) or data objects $d(r)$

3.2 Illustrative Example

The example Secure Tropos goal model presented in Fig. 2, built using the Sec-Tro tool [33], will be used as the starting point for the transformation process. The model illustrates a simplified version of the creation of a treatment plan for a patient by a medical practitioner, which is verified by a decision support software system. For the sake of simplicity the model only includes one security constraint, regarding the anonymity of the medical records transmitted by the medical practitioner to the decision support system for the verification of the treatment plan. It also includes one security objective which should be satisfied by complying with the constraint (i.e., confidentiality), one security mechanism to implement it (i.e., an encrypted communication channel) and one potential threat, concerning the malicious infiltration of the communication channel.

By applying our transformation rules to the example Secure Tropos goal model we can derive a basic process skeleton, illustrated by the hybrid model in

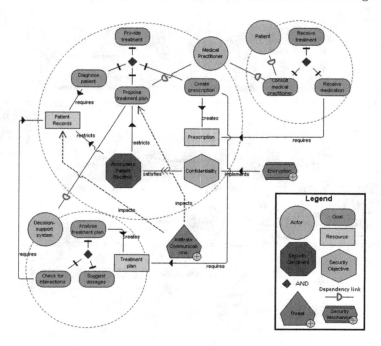

Fig. 2. Secure Tropos goal model of treatment plan creation

Fig. 3. Three process lanes are derived to match the actors of the goal model. The root-level goal of each actor leads to a sub-process, with the same name, within their lane (e.g. "Provide Treatment" for the Medical Practitioner lane), with each of its sub-goals transformed to an unordered task within that sub-process (e.g., "Diagnose Patient"). Dependency links, such as the one between the Patient and the Medical Practitioner for the achievement of the sub-goal "Consult medical practitioner", are transferred onto the hybrid model, beginning from the task corresponding to the dependant's sub-goal and ending at the dependee's main sub-process. The information resources (e.g., "Patient Records"), created or utilised by goals in the Secure Tropos model, are transformed into data objects, connected to the activities resulting from these goals in the hybrid model. The additional security-related concepts present in the model (e.g., constraints, mechanisms, threats) cannot be directly transformed into BPMN concepts but can be connected to specific elements of the hybrid model, which are derived from the initial goal model (e.g., the security constraint connected to "Patient Records" object and "Propose treatment plan" task).

By performing the refinement tasks on the hybrid model of Fig. 3, a complete version of a secure process model can be derived, as presented in Fig. 4. In the produced BPMN process model, the activities are manually ordered, starting and ending events are added in each lane and dependency links are refined into message exchanges (e.g., "Report Symptoms"). Finally, security constraint elements

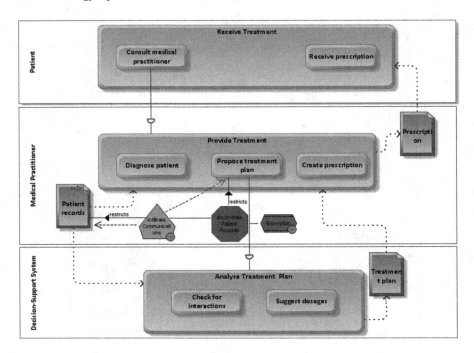

Fig. 3. Hybrid process skeleton model derived from Secure Tropos model

of the process are annotated with a red border (e.g. "Patient Records"), tasks or sub-processes enforcing security are elaborated by the analyst and denoted with a padlock symbol (e.g., "Encrypt data"), while threats are manually placed within the workflow as error events (e.g., "Communications Infiltration").

3.3   Discussion

Since the presented example is a rather simplified representation of a real-life, multi-agent system, solid conclusions regarding the scalability of our approach cannot yet be drawn. It also does not constitute a validation of the approach but it rather provides a proof of concept for the correctness of the defined concept mappings and rules, as they were able to connect elements of the goal model to conceptually similar elements of the derived process model. In the future, additional transformation rules will be developed, thereby reducing the manual effort required for the refinement of the hybrid model to a complete BPMN process model and keeping to a minimum the decisions left to the discretion of the analyst. Moreover, by explicitly defining such rules, using a formal definition language, ambiguities and potential misinterpretations can be avoided. As a result, larger parts of the transformation process will be able to be automated and integrated into tool support, which will also facilitate the use of model checkers for the security evaluation layer of our framework.

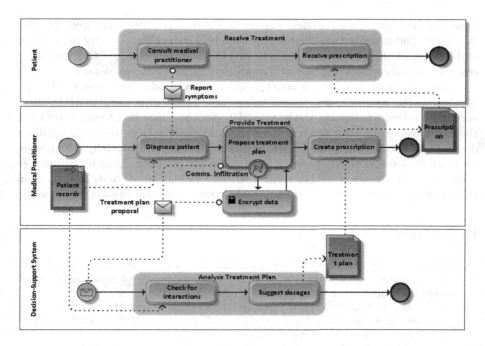

Fig. 4. Derived BPMN process model of treatment plan creation

The main contribution of the proposed approach lays in its ability to go beyond the simple security-related annotation of an already established process model, as it derives the main process skeleton directly from a security-oriented goal model. Thus security is considered from the early stages and throughout the process development, mapped from high-level organisational objectives to process-level activities. This mapping also facilitates the adaptability of the produced designs, as changes at the security requirements of an organisation can be traced and reflected to specific parts of its processes. Finally, Secure Tropos allows the expression of a wide range of security requirements and threats, most of which can be directly mapped to existing BPMN concepts. Therefore, a holistic approach towards security can be achieved by the proposed solution with only minimal concept extensions necessary, thus avoiding overly complex solutions.

4 Conclusion

The introduction of security to business processes requires structured and flexible approaches, able to encapsulate the rationale behind security choices, align it with high-level organisational objectives and facilitate well-informed and risk-aware decisions. To that end, a transformation method has been proposed, as part of a wider framework, for the derivation of secure business process designs from organisational goal models via intermediate, security-annotated, process skeletons. The contribution of such approach lays at its clear security orientation and ability to derive process designs, rather than annotate existing ones, via concept mappings between Secure Tropos and BPMN process elements.

Since this work is still at a conceptual stage, a number of issues need to be addressed. For example, which well-formedness constraints need to apply for a successful transformation of the goal model. Another issue is the transition from the high-level elaboration of security at the goal model to a more operationalised decomposition of security measures at the process level, especially when more abstract or non-functional security constraints are involved. In order to identify solutions to these issues further refinement and validation of the transformation rules will be required, which will be provided through case studies in future work.

References

1. Mellado, D., Fernández-Medina, E., Piattini, M.: A common criteria based security requirements engineering process for the development of secure information systems. Comput. Stan. Interfaces **29**(2), 244–253 (2007)
2. Altuhhova, O., Matulevičius, R., Ahmed, N.: Towards definition of secure business processes. In: Bajec, M., Eder, J. (eds.) CAiSE Workshops 2012. LNBIP, vol. 112, pp. 1–15. Springer, Heidelberg (2012)
3. Leitner, M., Miller, M., Rinderle-Ma, S.: An Analysis and evaluation of security aspects in the business process model and notation. In: 2013 IEEE International Conference on Availability, Reliability and Security. IEEE Press, pp. 262–267 (2013)
4. Neubauer, T., Klemen, M., Biffl, S.: Secure business process management: a roadmap. In: 1st IEEE International Conference on Availability, Reliability and Security, Vienna, Austria. IEEE Press, pp. 457–464 (2006)
5. Pavlovski, C.J., Zou, J.: Non-functional requirements in business process modeling. In: 5th Asia-Pacific Conference on Conceptual Modelling, vol. 79, Wollongong, Australia, pp. 103–112 (2008)
6. Decreus, K., Poels, G.: A goal-oriented requirements engineering method for business processes. In: Soffer, P., Proper, E. (eds.) CAiSE Forum 2010. LNBIP, vol. 72, pp. 29–43. Springer, Heidelberg (2011)
7. Ko, R.K., Lee, S.S., Lee, E.W.: Business process management (BPM) standards: a survey. Bus. Process Manage. **15**(5), 744–791 (2009)
8. Lapouchnian, A., Yu, Y., Mylopoulos, J.: Requirements-driven design and configuration management of business processes. In: Alonso, G., Dadam, P., Rosemann, M. (eds.) BPM 2007. LNCS, vol. 4714, pp. 246–261. Springer, Heidelberg (2007)
9. Horkoff, J., Li, T., Li, F.L., Salnitri, M., Cardoso, E., Giorgini, P., Mylopoulos, J., Pimentel, J.A.: Taking goal models downstream: a systematic roadmap. In: 8th International Conference on Research Challenges in Information Science. IEEE Press, pp. 1–12 (2014)
10. Koliadis, G., Ghose, A.K.: Relating business process models to goal-oriented requirements models in KAOS. In: Hoffmann, A., Kang, B.-H., Richards, D., Tsumoto, S. (eds.) PKAW 2006. LNCS (LNAI), vol. 4303, pp. 25–39. Springer, Heidelberg (2006)

11. Ghose, A.K., Narendra, N.C., Ponnalagu, K., Panda, A., Gohad, A.: Goal-driven business process derivation. In: Kappel, G., Maamar, Z., Motahari-Nezhad, H.R. (eds.) Service Oriented Computing. LNCS, vol. 7084, pp. 467–476. Springer, Heidelberg (2011)
12. Pistore, M., Roveri, M., Busetta, P.: Requirements-driven verification of Web services. Electr. Notes Theo. Comput. Sci. **105**, 95–108 (2004)
13. Guizzardi, R.S., Guizzardi, G., Almeida, J.A.P.A., Cardoso, E.: Bridging the gap between goals, agents and business processes. In: 4th International i* Workshop, CEUR, pp. 46–51 (2010)
14. Bleistein, S.J., Cox, K., Verner, J., Phalp, K.T.: Requirements engineering for e-business advantage. Require. Eng. **11**, 4–16 (2006)
15. Lo, A., Yu, E.: From business models to service-oriented design: a reference catalog approach. In: Parent, C., Schewe, K.-D., Storey, V.C., Thalheim, B. (eds.) ER 2007. LNCS, vol. 4801, pp. 87–101. Springer, Heidelberg (2007)
16. Ruiz, M., Costal, D., España, S., Franch, X., Pastor, Ó.: Integrating the goal and business process perspectives in information system analysis. In: Jarke, M., Mylopoulos, J., Quix, C., Rolland, C., Manolopoulos, Y., Mouratidis, H., Horkoff, J. (eds.) CAiSE 2014. LNCS, vol. 8484, pp. 332–346. Springer, Heidelberg (2014)
17. Séguran, M., Hébert, C., Frankova, G.: Secure workflow development from early requirements analysis. In: The 6th European Conference on Web Services. IEEE, pp. 125–134 (2008)
18. Paja, E., Giorgini, P., Paul, S., Meland, P.H.: Security requirements engineering for secure business processes. In: Niedrite, L., Strazdina, R., Wangler, B. (eds.) BIR Workshops 2011. LNBIP, vol. 106, pp. 77–89. Springer, Heidelberg (2012)
19. Salnitri, M., Giorgini, P.: Transforming socio-technical security requirements in SecBPMN security policies. In: 7th International i* Workshop, Thessaloniki, Greece, CEUR (2014)
20. Decreus, K., Snoeck, M., Poels, G.: Practical challenges for methods transforming i* goal models into business process models. In: IEEE International Conference on Requirements Engineering. IEEE Press, pp. 15–23 (2009)
21. Leitner, M., Schefer-Wenzl, S., Rinderle-Ma, S., Strembeck, M.: An experimental study on the design and modeling of security concepts in business processes. In: Grabis, J., Kirikova, M., Zdravkovic, J., Stirna, J. (eds.) PoEM 2013. LNBIP, vol. 165, pp. 236–250. Springer, Heidelberg (2013)
22. Ahmed, N., Matulevicius, R.: A taxonomy for assessing security in business process modelling. In: 7th IEEE International Conference on Research Challenges in Information Science. IEEE Press, pp. 1–10 (2013)
23. OMG: Business Process Model and Notation (BPMN) Version 2.0. Technical report, January 2011
24. Rodríguez, A., Fernández-Medina, E., Piattini, M.: A BPMN extension for the modeling of security requirements in business processes. IEICE Trans. Inf. Syst. **E90–D**(4), 745–752 (2007)
25. Salnitri, M., Dalpiaz, F., Giorgini, P.: Modeling and verifying security policies in business processes. In: Bider, I., Gaaloul, K., Krogstie, J., Nurcan, S., Proper, H.A., Schmidt, R., Soffer, P. (eds.) BPMDS 2014 and EMMSAD 2014. LNBIP, vol. 175, pp. 200–214. Springer, Heidelberg (2014)
26. Brucker, A.D., Hang, I., Lückemeyer, G., Ruparel, R.: SecureBPMN: modeling and enforcing access control requirements in business processes. In: The 17th ACM symposium on Access Control Models and Technologies. ACM, pp. 123–126 (2012)

27. Wolter, C., Schaad, A.: Modeling of task-based authorization constraints in BPMN. In: Alonso, G., Dadam, P., Rosemann, M. (eds.) BPM 2007. LNCS, vol. 4714, pp. 64–79. Springer, Heidelberg (2007)

28. Braun, R., Esswein, W.: Classification of domain-specific BPMN extensions. In: Frank, U., Loucopoulos, P., Pastor, Ó., Petrounias, I. (eds.) PoEM 2014. LNBIP, vol. 197, pp. 42–57. Springer, Heidelberg (2014)

29. van der Aalst, W.M.: Business process management : a comprehensive survey. ISRN Softw. Eng. **2013**, 1–37 (2013)

30. Indulska, M., Recker, J., Rosemann, M., Green, P.: Business process modeling: current issues and future challenges. In: van Eck, P., Gordijn, J., Wieringa, R. (eds.) CAiSE 2009. LNCS, vol. 5565, pp. 501–514. Springer, Heidelberg (2009)

31. Leitner, M., Rinderle-Ma, S.: A systematic review on security in process-aware information systems - constitution, challenges, and future directions. Inf. Softw. Technol. **56**(3), 273–293 (2014)

32. Mouratidis, H., Giorgini, P.: Secure tropos: a security-oriented extension of the tropos methodology. Int. J. Softw. Eng. Knowl. Eng. **17**(2), 285–309 (2007)

33. Pavlidis, M., Islam, S., Mouratidis, H.: A CASE tool to support automated modelling and analysis of security requirements. In: Nurcan, S. (ed.) IS Olympics: Information Systems in a Diverse World, pp. 95–109. Springer, Heidelberg (2012)

Goal-Oriented Requirement Engineering Support for Business Continuity Planning

Alvaro E. Arenas[1], Philippe Massonet[2(✉)], Christophe Ponsard[2],
and Benjamin Aziz[3]

[1] IE Business School, IE University, Madrid, Spain
alvaro.arenas@ie.edu
[2] CETIC Research Centre, Charleroi, Belgium
{philippe.massonet,christophe.ponsard}@cetic.be
[3] School of Computing, University of Portsmouth, Portsmouth, UK
Benjamin.Aziz@port.ac.uk

Abstract. Business continuity is a key management process that aims to maintain and rapidly recover an organizations key business functions in the face of serious incidents. The resulting business continuity plan must identify the key business functions that must be resilient, define recovery of critical business functions and define contingency measures when recovery is not possible. This paper argues that the process of business continuity planning can be efficiently supported by a goal-oriented requirements engineering approach. The main benefits of a modelling approach include taking a holistic approach when analysing the organisation, providing quality checks and related guidance across in all the elaboration phases, an supporting the generation of the continuity plan from a business continuity model.

1 Introduction

Business continuity management (BCM) is a management process to ensure the continuity of critical business functions in an organization after a business interruption [2]. The potential causes of business interruption include, among others, natural disasters, human errors, utility interruption such as power outages, or malicious threats from outsiders. Business continuity has become a topic of interest to organisations nowadays due to the recognition that any interruption in the continuity of the business for an extended period of time seriously affect the overall viability of the business, which is of paramount importance in today global economy and competitive environment. Simply recovering the business function is not enough; the business needs to resume as quickly and as efficiently as possible. Recovering the business function entails numerous corporate goals such as preservation of the customer base, restore IT systems, ensure cash flow, and maintain corporate image, among others.

There are several approaches for developing BCM, ranging from standards such as the ISO 22301 standard for business continuity management [8], international initiatives such as the European approach to business continuity led by EU Agency

© Springer International Publishing Switzerland 2015
M.A. Jeusfeld and K. Karlapalem (Eds.): ER 2015 Workshops, LNCS 9382, pp. 259–269, 2015.
DOI: 10.1007/978-3-319-25747-1_26

for Network and Information Security (ENISA) [6], practical approaches such as the three phases of business continuity planning [5], and academic proposals to continuity management [3,9,12]. All these approaches somehow address three interdependent objectives: (i) Identify major risks of business interruption; (ii) develop a business continuity plan (BCP) to mitigate or reduce the impact of the identified risk; and (iii) train employees and test the plan to ensure that it is effective.

A BCP can be seen as the document that defines the resources, actions, tasks and data required to manage the business recovery process in the event of a business interruption. A BCP seeks to eliminate or reduce the impact of a disaster condition before the condition occurs. A BCP should evolve as the business environment changes and its dependency on technology changes. However, BCM is criticised for no taking a holistic approach when analysing the organisation, and a lack of clear understating of the responsibilities of the BCP [7]. In this paper we advocate for the use of goal-oriented requirements engineering techniques (GORE) [14] to help in the development of a BCP with the aim of overcoming these limitations. We have used ENISA approach as our underlying business continuity approach [6].

This paper shows how goal-oriented requirements engineering concepts and analysis techniques (goal refinement, obstacle refinements) can strongly and systematically support the process to produce a high quality BCP, i.e. addressing relevant risks, identifying the critical assets and addressing them through adequate controls. Our work is more specifically anchored in the KAOS goal-oriented approach [14], although alternatives will be discussed.

This work contributes to the research and practice on business continuity management. On the research side, this study proposes a new approach to BCM, incorporating goal-oriented requirement engineering in the developing of continuity plans. We apply model-based techniques to provide quality assurance in the elaboration process, and to automate the generation/update of a BCP. The resulting document could then be completed by BCM specialists within the organisation. On the practical side, this study provides practitioners with a toolkit to analyse their main continuity requirements, to guide them to address key (risk) issues and to help in the generation of a BCP draft according to the needs of their organisations.

The structure of the paper is as follows. Section 2 presents the business continuity process to produce a business continuity plan addressing the right risks for critical assets through adequate controls, introducing a case study used as running example. Section 3 provides the required background on the KAOS goal-oriented methodology that will be applied in Sect. 4 for providing GORE support to the business continuity process. Section 5 will discuss related work. Finally, Sect. 6 will provide some conclusion and future work.

2   Business Continuity Process

2.1   ENISA Business Continuity Management for SMEs

Our underlying BCM model is the one proposed by ENISA [6], which is based on some elements from the OCTAVE ALLEGRO Risk Assessment Methodology [4] and tailored for the case of small and medium enterprises (SMEs). The ENISA approach consists of four phases, explained below.

Phase 1. Select Risk Profile. In this phase, main risks for the organisation are identified using a predefined set of qualitative criteria. Four risk areas as suggested: legal and regulatory, reputation and customer confidence, productivity and financial stability risks. Risks in each area are classified as high, medium and low. The output of this phase is an organisation risk profile.

Phase 2. Critical Asset Identification. In this phase, critical business functions are selected based on their relative importance to the organisation. Critical business functions are functions whose interruption will lead to an organisation suffering from serious financial, legal and/or other loss or penalty. For each critical business function, it is identified who is responsible for it and which assets are used in the function. An important step in this phase is the "Asset Continuity Requirements", concerned with the analysis of the continuity requirements of the identified assets. This phase comprises three steps: (i) Business Function Selection; (ii) Asset Type Selection, selecting the assets that each business function requires in order to be delivered; and (iii) Asset Continuity Requirement Analysis, concerned with the analysis of the continuity requirements of the identified assets.

Phase 3. Control Selection. Controls refer to measures defined to control the identified risks. Risk controls can involve the implementation of new polices and standards, physical changes and procedural changes that can reduce or eliminate certain risks within the business. The ENISA approach suggests two categories of controls: (a) organisational continuous controls, which are applicable to the organisation horizontally and are concerned with practices and management procedures; and (b) asset-based continuity controls, which are applicable to particular classes of critical assets. The approach includes a set of pre-defined controls in the form of control cards. This phase comprises three steps: (i) Select Organisational Continuity Controls; (ii) Select Asset-Based Controls; and (iii) Document List of Selected Controls.

Phase 4. Implementation and Management. In this phase, current continuity practices are evaluated and assessed the gaps between these practices and the selected controls. The output of this phase is the BCP.

In order to implement successful BCM within an organisation, it must first be initiated as a project, including well defined project structure, scope, objectives and deliverables. Once the Business Continuity project has been established, and in order to be able to commence development of the suite of BCP, it is essential to understand the organisation with respect to its mission critical activities or services, its organisational structure, roles and stakeholders. The ENISA approach exploit the existence of cards for assets and controls as a way of eliciting continuity requirements. We propose here to enrich phases 2 and 3 of the process with goal-oriented requirements engineering. We will exploit model-based technology to generate a draft of the BCP that would help in producing the final version in phase 4.

2.2   Running Case Study

We apply the ENISA approach extended with goal-oriented requirements to a case study presented in [6]. The case refers to a dental equipment supplier based in north England. The company supplies both the equipment as well as their maintenance. Most of the customers have contracts of annual maintenance. In addition a significant percentage of the customers have special contracts for expedited repair in case of equipment breakdown. These special contracts guarantee a repair of the equipment within the next business day of filing the request when no spare parts replacement is required.

In the case where spare parts need to be replaced then the required maximum time to repair is four business days to allow for the shipment of spare parts from the manufacturer. In general no other special limitations and hard requirements exist for this company. The company employs 8 persons full time including the owner. Financial matters are handled by the owner with the support of the secretary and an external accountant. In addition the IT needs of the company are covered with external support from a local IT expert who is engaged on-demand to resolve problems that may arise or implement new solutions upon request.

3   Goal-Oriented Requirements Engineering

Goal-oriented requirements models are structured into different sub-models: a goal model which is the driving model (the "WHY"), an object model to structure the domain description (the "WHAT"), an agent model to capture responsibilities (the "WHO") and an operation model for specification level (the "HOW" dimension); these models are elaborated using a method like KAOS [13,14].

A goal is a prescriptive statement of intent about some system (existing or to-be) whose satisfaction in general requires the cooperation of some of the agents. Agents are active components, such as humans, devices, legacy software or software-to-be components that play some role towards goal satisfaction. Some agents thus define the software whereas the others define its environment. Goals may refer to services to be provided (functional goals) or to quality of service (non-functional goals). Unlike goals, domain properties are descriptive statements about the environment, such as physical laws, organisational norms or policies, etc.

Goals are organized in AND/OR refinement hierarchies where higher-level goals are in general strategic, coarse-grained and involve multiple agents whereas lower-level goals are in general technical, fine-grained and involve fewer agents. In such structures, AND-refinement links relate a goal to a set of subgoals (called refinement) possibly conjoined with domain properties; this means that satisfying all subgoals in the refinement is a sufficient condition in the domain for satisfying the goal. OR-refinement links may relate a goal to a set of alternative refinements. Goal refinement ends when every subgoal is realizable by some individual agent assigned to it, that is, expressible in terms of conditions that are monitorable and controllable by the agent. A requirement and expectations are leaf goals respectively under responsibility of an agent in the software-to-be or the environment.

Goals refer to objects which are structured in models typically represented by UML class diagrams. Objects have states defined by the values of their attributes and associations to other objects. They are passive (entities, associations, events) or active (agents). In the above formalization, *finished* and *invoiceState* are attributes of the *Repair* entity declared in the object model. If the goal *InvoiceSent* is assigned to the *FinanceManager* agent, the latter must be able to monitor the attribute finished and control the attribute *invoice* of *Repair*.

Obstacles anticipate what could go wrong with the system design [15]. An obstacle is a pre-condition for the violation of a goal. Obstacles is the dual concept to goal and like goal then can be refined into sub-obstacles using a AND-OR refinement tree. An obstacle diagram for a given goal is a tree that shows how a root obstacle is refined into sub-obstacles. Example of obstacles for the case study are given in the next section.

Goals can be operationalized into specifications of operations to achieve them. In the scope of this paper, we will not consider the operation level.

4   GORE Business Continuity Process

In this section we show how goal-oriented analysis supports the different phases of the business continuity process described in Sect. 2. Main contributions of goal-oriented analysis are done in phases 2 and 3 of the ENISA approach. Table 1 summarises our business continuity process.

4.1   Select Risk Profile

Risk profile selection is a high level analysis. It targets four areas: legal and regulatory, reputation and customer confidence, productivity and financial stability risks. We assume that the risk profile selection has been done prior to modelling and that it is an input to the modelling process. Those risk areas are modelled as goals/obstacles and refined, risks related to regulation must be modelled as obstacles to goals for regulation and customer satisfaction.

4.2   Critical Assets Identification

Phase 2 involves 3 steps: "Business Function Selection", "Select Asset Types" and "Asset Continuity Requirements Analysis". The KAOS goal model has been used to model the first step. In this step critical business functions are identified as Goals because those function directly relate to key organisational objectives. Those can be refined down to atomic critical business operations, providing useful checks and related guidance such as refinement completeness and the existence of responsible agents.

Table 1. Mapping between business continuity and GORE concepts

BCM step	GORE model	Comment
PHASE 1: risk profiles selection		
Selection in available profiles	Generic strategic goal and risk driving the next phase	Specific model pattern for legal/regulatory/customer confidence can be used
PHASE 2. Critical asset identification		
Business function	Selection goal model	Critical business functions are modelled as goals and refined into sub-goals
Asset type selection	Object model	Assets used in critical business functions are modelled as entities
Asset continuity requirements	obstacle model	Identify obstacle to critical business functions
PHASE 3. Control Selection		
Select Organisation Controls	Obstacle resolution	Identify new requirements that provide organisational controls
Select Asset-Based Controls	Obstacle resolution	Identify new requirements that provide asset-based controls
PHASE 4. Implementation and management		
Gap between practices and controls	AS-IS vs TO-BE gap analysis	Same model can be used to just highlight the gap
BCP production	Report generation based on GORE model	Model-based generation enable easy update

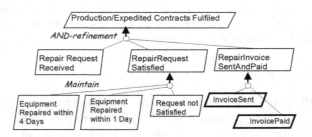

Fig. 1. Business continuity goal model fragment.

Figure 1 shows how the high level business continuity function "Production-ExpeditedService ContractsFulfilled" is refined into three main business sub-goals "RepairRequestReceived", "RepairRequestSatisfied", and "RepairInvoiceSent-AndPaid". The business critical goal "RepairRequestSatisfied" covers different cases and thus needs to be refined into three sub-goals "Equipment Repaired-Within 4 Days", "EquipmentRepairedWithin1Day", and "EquipmentCannot-BeRepaired".

The second step in phase 2 "Select Asset Types" has been modelled with the object model capturing all entities and relationships bound to critical business functions.

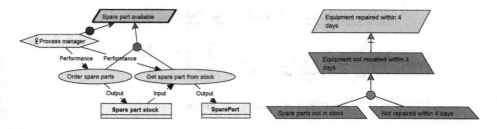

Fig. 2. Agent and operation model   **Fig. 3.** Obstacle model

Figure 2 shows the responsibilities in terms of agents, the operations and objects involved. The figure shows that the "Process Manager" agent is responsible for the requirement "SparePartAvailable", and that he can perform two operations to create state transitions to a state where spare parts are available. The operations cover the two cases where a spare part is available in the "SparePartStock" and the case where it is not and needs to be ordered via the operation "OrderSparePart".

To cover step 3 of phase 2 "Asset Continuity Requirement Analysis" we have used the KAOS obstacle model. In this model obstacles to critical business functions are identified and refined into sub-obstacles.

Figure 3 illustrates how the risk analysis for business continuity can be modelled using the KAOS concept of Obstacle. In the figure the critical business function that is to repair equipment within 4 days has been captured as a goal. The risk analysis identifies obstacles to the critical business function. This is captured as an obstacle "Equipment not repaired within 4 days" in the model. This obstacle is in turn refined into two sub-obstacles "Spare parts not in stock" and "Not repaired within 4 days".

4.3 Controls Selection

Phase 3 of the BC analysis involves 3 steps: "Select Organizational Controls Cards", "Select Asset Based Controls Cards" and "Document List of Selected Controls". The first two steps are modelled as obstacle resolutions. Obstacle resolution identifies new requirements that provide resolutions to the goal obstacles. Different tactics are available to identify resolutions to the obstacles. Step 3 of the phase corresponds to documenting the selecting controls and presenting the rationale for the selection. This documentation is generated from the model using a requirements report generator. This will be detailed in the next subsection.

Figure 4 shows how business continuity controls are identified to mitigate the risks to the business critical functions. This is captured in the requirements model by introducing a new requirement that resolves the obstacle. The figure shows that the goal "EquipmentRepairedWithin1Day" is obstructed by

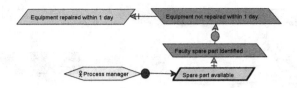

Fig. 4. Obstacle resolutions

the obstacle "EquipmentNotRepairedWithin1Day", which is itself refined into obstacle "FaultySparePartIdentified". This latter obstacle means that the spare part used to repair the equipment reveals itself to be faulty. This obstacle is resolved by a new requirement "SparePartAvailable" that describes state transition to a state where a spare part is available to replace the faulty spare part.

4.4   Implementation and Management - Creation of the BCP

For the BCP to be realisable, the proposed controls must be available. For this a specific gap analysis should take place with respect to the existing practices. GORE provide strong support to this because a classic activity is to compare the as-is with to-be situation. Both model generally share goals but could differ in more specific requirements and operationalisation. Typically some operationalisation could be missing or not achievable in the as-is situation. OR-refinement can be used to capture this in a single model and highlight the gap, e.g. specific controls to be added should be tagged with dedicated system alternative tag like "BCP".

Based on the rich GORE model, generating the BCP is just a matter of querying the appropriate information to feed the right section of the plan. Specific queries can easily be written to generate all the relevant table present in standard BCP template [6] such as: Critical Business Function List, BC Team Responsibility matrix, Business Function Protection Strategy, and Business Function Assets Recovery Actions.

We implemented the described mapping in the Objectiver GORE tool [11] which supports report generation both to text (RTF,ODT) and table format (XLS,ODS) using powerful queries [10]. For example here is the query that will automatically generate the Critical Business Function List presented in Table 2.

```
SELECT a.name AS Dept, g.name AS Function, g.Def AS Definition, g.Pri AS Priority
FROM Assignment AS ass, ass.parent AS g, ass.sons AS s, s.son AS a
ORDER BY g.Priority DESC
```

As the tool also support instance models, it is also possible to use instance level queries and generate tables specifying concrete roles and attribute, such as John Smith should be the *QualityControl* agent with cell phone +04 65 78 98 00.

5   Related Work

The literature on business continuity dates back to the 1980s. It is intertwined in a multi-disciplinary research area bringing together academics and practitioners

Table 2. Model-generated Critical Business Function List

Dept	Function	Definition	Priority
Production/Repair	Equipment repaired within 4 days	When spare parts need to be ordered then four business days is the defined maximum time to repair	High
Production/Repair	Equipment repaired within 1 day	The repairs must be performed next business day when no spare parts are required	High
Finance	RepairInvoiceSent AndPaid	Manage, store and process financial data generated by the commerce of medical equipment and services	Medium

from several disciplines such as organisational crisis management, information systems, and information and telecommunication technologies.

Most BCM approaches consists of a set of phases, and lack of tool support. For instance, in [3], Botha and Von Solms present a BCM methodology consisting of seven phases (project planning, business impact analysis, business continuity strategies, strategies implementation, continuity training, continuity testing, and continuity maintenance), and following a cyclic implementation approach comprising of four distinct cycles (back-up, disaster recovery, contingency planning, continuity planning). This exemplifies the limitation of current approaches: no taking a holistic approach when analysing the organisation, and being too prescriptive, which difficult traceability of continuity requirements. Our approach look to overcome these limitations by incorporating requirements engineering in the business continuity management process.

Recent approaches to BCM has concentrated on adding decision support to the continuity process [12] or automating the generation of a BCP [16]. Winkler and Gilani present in [16] a model-driven approach to generate a BCP using model-transformation chains to connect data across the different phases in BCM. Their approach is closer to ours in the generation of the plan, but our analysis is enriched by incorporating a well-established requirements methodology as it is the case of KAOS [14].

Another model-based approach has been proposed by Zambon [17]. It focuses on assessing and mitigating the risks related to the availability of the IT infrastructure. The starting point is similar as ours: the limitation of current Risk Management methodologies. The narrower scope also enable to consider specific domain properties, especially the dependencies linking the various constituents of the IT infrastructure are taken into account using incidents propagation model. Our approach is a more generic level but can however cope with domain specific reasoning to some extends, i.e. using the available concepts like domain properties, object model, goal and obstacle refinement semantics. However specific model like for incident propagation are beyond our current scope.

In relation to the use of goal-orientation in BCM, Asnar and Giorgini have used Tropos, another GORE methodology to analyse business continuity [1]. Their work is not related to any standard framework and business continuity process model like ENISA as in our case.

6   Conclusions

BC analysis is mostly a document intensive informal process driven by human analysts. The analysis produces a BC plan that aims to operationally guarantee that key business functions are resilient in the face of serious incidents. The BC plan is a document that identifies business critical functions and describes recovery procedures to make them resilient. This paper has investigated how a model-driven approach could be applied to BC analysis. In a model-driven approach the BC plan is derived from the model, thus improving its quality compared to a human-driven semi-informal BC process. The different steps of BC analysis were modelled in terms of a goal-oriented requirements engineering methodology. The risk analysis and the organisation risk profile was modelled as obstacles in an obstacle model. Critical business functions and processes were modelled as goals in goal models. Controls were modelled as obstacle resolutions in a goal model. The paper then showed how a BC plan could be systematically derived from the model. Such a BC plan could be shown to be complete for all obstacles to business critical functions. We argue that using a requirements modelling language provides higher level abstractions for modelling BC concepts.

A limitation in our work is the lack of empirical validation of the proposed approach. This is our next objective, and we are currently working with some European SMEs in the development of their BCP using our approach. Additional future work includes refining the mapping between BC concepts and RE concepts, and investigating how formalising some BC properties in terms of requirements could enhance the BC plan.

Acknowledgement. This work was partly funded by the SimQRI project (ERANET CORNET nr 1318172).

References

1. Asnar, Y., Giorgini, P.: Modelling risk and identifying countermeasure in organizations. In: López, J. (ed.) CRITIS 2006. LNCS, vol. 4347, pp. 55–66. Springer, Heidelberg (2006)
2. Blyth, M.: Business Continuity Management: Building an Effective Incident Management Plan. Wiley, New York (2009)
3. Botha, J., Von Solms, R.: A cyclic approach to business continuity planning. Inf. Manage. Comput. Secur. **12**(4), 328–337 (2004)
4. Caralli, R.A., Stevens, J.F., Young, L.R., Wilson, W.R.: The octave allegro guidebook, v1. 0, Software Engineering Institute (2007)
5. D'Amico, V.: Master the three phases of business continuity planning. Bus. Strategy Ser. **8**(3), 214–220 (2007)

6. ENISA, IT business continuity management. an approach for small medium sized organizations, European Network and Information Security Agency, ENISA Reports (2010)
7. Gallagher, M.: Business continuity management. Accountancy Irel. **35**(4), 15–16 (2003)
8. BS ISO, 22301, 2012. societal security. business continuity management systems. requirements, British Standards Institute, London (2012)
9. Järveläinen, J.: It incidents and business impacts: validating a framework for continuity management in information systems. Int. J. Inf. Manage. **33**(3), 583–590 (2013)
10. Ponsard, C., Darimont, R., Michot, A.: Combining Models, Diagrams and Tables for Efficient Requirements Engineering: Lessons Learned from the Industry, INFORSID 2015, Biarritz, France, June 2015
11. Respect-IT, Objectiver Requirements Engineering Tool (2005). http://www.respect-it.com
12. Sahebjamnia, N.: Integrated business continuity and disaster recovery planning: towards organizational resilience. Eur. J. Opera. Res. **242**(1), 261–273 (2015)
13. Van Lamsweerde, A.: Goal-oriented requirements engineering: a guided tour. In: Proceedings of Fifth IEEE International Symposium on Requirements Engineering. IEEE, pp. 249–262 (2001)
14. Van Lamsweerde, A.: Requirements Engineering: from System Goals to UML Models to Software Specifications. Wiley, New York (2009)
15. Van Lamsweerde, A., Letier, E.: Handling obstacles in goal-oriented requirements engineering. IEEE Trans. Softw. Eng. **26**(10), 978–1005 (2000)
16. Winkler, U., Gilani, W.: Model-Driven framework for business continuity management. Service Level Agreements for Cloud Computing, pp. 227–250. Springer, Heidelberg (2011)
17. Zambon, E., et al.: Model-based mitigation of availability risks. In: Proceedings of 2nd IEEE/IFIP International Workshop on Business-Driven IT Management, Munich, Germany, May 2007

Quality of Models and Models of Quality

Preface to the Second Workshop Quality of Models and Models of Quality

Information quality (IQ) and Information Systems (IS) quality have been long standing concerns for both researchers and professionals. They are today still hot and challenging topics requiring the strong implication of IS actors (analysts, designers, database designers, programmers) as well as business actors (customers, managers). This positions the research on quality at the intersection of a variety of disciplines such as Conceptual Modeling (CM), Software Engineering (SE), Web Semantics, Process Engineering etc. This active research encompasses theoretical aspects including quality frameworks and standards as well as practical/empirical aspects as tools, case studies and empirical research. Quality is also a cross-domains concern involving contribution from academic and practical fields such as universities, medical structures, commercial or governmental organizations.

As a consequence, research contributions are highly diverse but addressed issues share many common problems and solutions.

Our aim within this workshop is to offer an opportunity to cross-fertilization of ideas, research directions and methods by gathering researchers and practitioners from several disciplines and business domains. This will probably lead to envision new perspectives to the problem of evaluating quality in IS.

Quality has always been a topic of interest within the ER main conference through dedicated sessions and/or invited talks as well as in specific workshops.

This second edition of the Quality of Models and Models of Quality workshop held in conjunction with the 34th International Conference on Conceptual Modeling aims to promote research on quality in its several and diverse dimensions: data quality, information quality, system quality as well as models, methods, processes and tools for managing quality. For QMMQ 2015, submissions were solicited on a variety of topics, including but not limited to:

- Quality constructs, models and ontologies
- Quality measures and instruments
- Experiments for validating quality models, measures and instruments
- Methodological issues of research on IS quality
- Method and tool support for improving and monitoring quality
- Quality of requirements engineering artifacts and processes
- Quality of models and meta-models
- Quality of ontologies and reference models
- Data quality
- Big data quality

- Quality modeling languages
- Ontological analysis of conceptual modeling grammars
- Cost/benefit analysis of quality assurance processes
- Quality assurance practices : case studies and experiences
- Experiments and case studies on quality evaluation.

Out of 10 high quality papers submitted, the workshop international committee selected four papers for presentation and publication with an acceptance rate of 40%. The authors came from Australia, Brazil, France, UK and Uruguay.

We would like to thank all authors, presenters and reviewers for their work that helped bringing together the communities of Quality and Conceptual Modeling. We are also grateful to the 2015 ER workshop chairs for giving us the opportunity to organize this workshop.

Samira Si-Said Cherfi, CNAM, France
Charlotte Hug, Université Paris 1 Panthéon-Sorbonne, France
Oscar Pastor, Universidad Politècnica de Valencia, Spain

Data Currency Assessment
Through Data Mining

Sergio Pio Alvarez[✉], Adriana Marotta, and Libertad Tansini

Universidad de la República, Montevideo, Uruguay
{sergiop, amarotta, libertad}@fing.edu.uy

Abstract. The application of Data Mining (DM) techniques for DQ, often called Data Quality Mining (DQM), offers a wide range of possibilities for DQ assessment. The goal of this work is to propose a mechanism for data currency assessment using statistics and DM techniques. The proposed approach consists on estimating the validity period for the entities using a training set and then evaluating the probability of currency of the last known data value for each entity. The proposed scheme helps in two ways to lead to an always up-to-date database: it can warn if a certain data value is becoming obsolete, and it can inform the data manager about the best frequency for updating data.

Keywords: Data quality · Currency · Data mining · Clustering

1 Introduction

The importance of considering quality of data at the moment of data analysis is widely recognized. Data Quality (DQ) research area has significantly grown in the last two decades, addressing many important aspects such as dimensions and DQ management in general [1–4]. A great amount of techniques has been proposed for solving DQ assessment as well as data cleaning problems. However, very few works can be found that take profit of the existing knowledge in the area of Data Mining (DM) for addressing DQ problems. DM techniques allow the discovery of information that is not explicit in the datasets. We believe that this kind of techniques offer a wide range of possibilities for DQ measurement that have not been explored yet.

The approach of defining DQ in terms of its fitness for use [3, 4], and the idea that DQ is a subjective and context-dependent concept [3, 5] are widely accepted in the literature. Data values that are considered to be of good-quality in a certain context can turn to be of bad-quality in other contexts. The application of DM techniques for DQ assessment allows the consideration of the context, since it makes it possible to take into account the characteristics and behaviour of the data that is being evaluated.

Many different sets of DQ dimensions and definitions of them are proposed in the literature, with different degree of coincidence between them [6]. Currency is a DQ dimension that can deeply compromise the success of data-based tasks. Using obsolete data can lead to an idea of the real world that does not correspond to the present time [5, 7]. Although data currency was identified as one of the most important quality dimensions for data consumers, it was insufficiently treated [8]. Most works merely define the concept

© Springer International Publishing Switzerland 2015
M.A. Jeusfeld and K.Karlapalem (Eds.): ER 2015 Workshops, LNCS 9382, pp. 273–282, 2015.
DOI: 10.1007/978-3-319-25747-1_27

of currency and emphasize on its importance, while very few focus on the problem of analysing and assessing data currency [8, 9]. As is remarked in [3], timeliness is a context-dependent dimension, so it is also currency.

The purpose of DM is to discover hidden knowledge within large amounts of data. DM is not a new concept, but has been around since the seventies and it is considered a part of the process of Knowledge Discovery in Databases (KDD) [10]. Raw data, typically in databases, becomes information when users give it a meaning and turns into knowledge when domain experts can extract and model different behaviours from the data, thus giving it additional value.

The goal of this work is to propose techniques for data currency assessment. Our approach is to apply DM concepts and methods for the assessment, so that data context is taken into account. In this paper we present a first solution for performing the assessment based on DM concepts.

The rest of the document is organized as follows: in Sect. 2 we present the related work, in Sect. 3 we present the proposal for assessing data currency, in Sect. 4 we present an application of the proposal to a real dataset, and finally in Sect. 5 we present the conclusions.

2 Related Work

Data Quality Mining (DQM) is defined as the application of DM techniques to measure and improve data quality, especially for large databases [11–14]. The underlying concept is that the modelling of different behaviours within the data can not only be used to understand the data but also to detect anomalies, hence pointing out possible quality problems [13, 15, 16]. DQM is composed of two steps: modelling of the characteristics of the data and detection of deviations from that model.

The name DQM to the application of DM techniques with the aim of improving DQ was proposed in [12]. In particular they focus on finding association rules to detect records that do not satisfy those rules. Other authors propose the use of clustering algorithms to assess accuracy [17]. There is also work on comparing different methods to aid in the error detection process and cleaning of the data [18]. Machine learning has also been applied to improve DQ in different contexts [19] and even fuzzy techniques were explored [20]. In [21] authors apply entity resolution to identify records corresponding to the same entity and denial constraints to determine which of them is the most current when no time-related information is available.

It is worth pointing out that there is no significant work on DQM for currency.

3 Data Currency Assessment Through Data Mining

This work proposes a simple method to assess data currency of an evolving dataset (a set composed of snapshots of the state of some kind of homogeneous entities). The main idea is to determine the validity period of each entity, or set of entities, in order to be able to know if certain data are, or will be at some future point, still valid (not obsolete), and how frequently it should be updated to maintain it current.

To illustrate how it works, a practical case will be shown, based on determining how frequently each country raises its population at least 10 %. For some countries knowing its population from a few years back gives an accurate idea of its population at present, while for others even a two year-old record could be considered obsolete.

3.1 Previous Definitions

- *Object under study*: anything that can be understood by itself based on its properties. For example, the countries of the world can be an object under study and their population would be a property.
- *Entity*: a specific instance of the object under study that can be individualized by a subset of its properties. For example, each country is an entity, and can be identified by its name or its 2-letter ISO code, among others.
- *Record*: a snapshot taken at a certain moment of the evolution of a particular entity. For example, the population of Uruguay in 2013. A record is composed of attributes, each one representing one property, or a set of properties, of the corresponding entity. Three types of attributes are considered: identifiers (identify the entity), timestamps (when the observation was made) and data-values (properties values).

3.2 Basic Algorithm

The initial approach is to build a classification model using a set of data, known as the *training dataset*, which allows establishing the *validity period* for a particular data-value attribute of the study object as a whole. In order to do so, every change observed in successive snapshots of each entity, for that attribute, is accounted and the time elapsed between them is aggregated. The validity period for the attribute will be estimated as the total elapsed time between changes over the number of changes. Once the model is built, it can be used to determine if the last record of each entity can still be considered current or not. It is important to note that each data-value attribute of the same entity could have its own validity period. Each attribute should be analysed in a separated manner. Identifiers and timestamps are shared by all data-value attributes of the same record.

After the basic algorithm is described, some problems are discussed and some necessary improvements are proposed in the following Sections.

The basic algorithm is as follows:

1. Initialize a set of variables:
   - *TT (total change time)*. Integer variable for aggregating elapsed times between two consecutive snapshots of each entity, if the attribute value changed.
   - *CC (changes counted)*. Integer variable for counting the observed changes.
   - *CST (current state table)*. Table for registering the last value observed for each entity, together with its timestamp: CST(EntityId, CurrentValue, TimeStamp).

2. Sort records in the training set using their timestamps. It is not relevant if ascendant or descendant order is used.
3. Traverse the sorted set of records and for each one do the following:
    - If the record corresponds to an entity not observed yet, add an entry in the CST.
    - Else, check if the attribute value in the record is different from the value in the CST for the corresponding entity. If they are NOT equal, then it is a value change: add to the TT variable the difference between the timestamp of the record and the timestamp in the CST (in absolute value), increment the CC variable and update the CST with the new value and timestamp.
4. At the end, if the CC variable is equal to 0, then it means that the attribute is invariant (never changed its value for every entity). If the CC variable is greater than 0, then calculate the validity period (VP) of the attribute as $VP = TT/CC$.
5. If the attribute is invariant then its first value will always be current. Else, to determine if the last known value of each entity is still current, then check if the age of the last record corresponding to the entity (the elapsed time between the evaluation time and the record timestamp) is lower than the validity period. If it is the case that the age of the record is lower than the VP, then a probability of currency (PoC) for each record r can be estimated as $PoC(r) = 1- (age(r)/PV)$. Here, the concept of probability of currency is similar to that presented in [7].

The following Sections describe some improvements to the basic algorithm that can be made to overcome problems that arise in practical situations.

3.3   Ignoring Data Corrections

When the concept of "change" is mentioned, it is expected to mean a real change in the state of the entity. But there are changes that are just corrections made because of misspellings or typing errors detected immediately, or because of partial savings. Those changes should not be considered because the state of the real entity has not changed. A change may be considered a data correction when the time elapsed from the last observation is far less than an expected minimum interval (which must be established by the analyst). In this case, the TT and CC variables are not modified but the CST table is updated (value and timestamp) because the real value is the last one.

3.4   Ignoring Non-significant Changes

Another type of changes that should be ignored are non-significant ones. Non-significant changes are those where the current value and the new value are so close that are negligible. What a non-significant change means must be established by the analyst, and depends on the data type of the attribute. In case of numerical attributes it may be a kind of range (even fixed, such as ± 3px, or relative, such as ± 5 %), while in case of text some kind of distance function can be applied, such as edit distance or Levenshtein distance, and in case of dates different granularity can be considered (just the year, for example). When a non-significant change is detected, the same criteria than for data corrections can be applied.

This improvement can introduce a new problem that could be overlooked: if the successive value changes are "soft" (each new change is negligible with respect to the previous one), then no change would be accounted at all, even when the first value and the last one are completely different. To solve this inconvenience, the CST table must be modified to allow storing not only the current value but also the last accepted value (the last one that was not ignored). Then, in the algorithm, the record value must be compared to both, the current value and the last accepted value, accepting the change if at least one of the checks detects a real change.

3.5   Segregation by Affinity Groups

There is another detail that can be unnoticed if the analyst is unaware of the characteristics of the real world: although the object under study is the same, and the attribute is also always the same, not every entity behaves in the same way, and so the validity period for each one can be different. For example, some countries increase their population faster than others: for instance, Germany and the United Kingdom need more than 25 years to increase its population by 10 %, but Kenya and Niger need less than 4. If all cases where treated the same, probably the estimated validity period would not be useful neither for one case nor for the other. To overcome this situation, the clustering technique from DM shows useful.

Clustering consists in grouping the entities in affinity sets, called clusters, in such a way that all entities inside one cluster behave similarly, and distinct from the others [22]. Clustering differs from another DM technique called classification [11, 22], where the target groups ("classes") are predefined, while in clustering the clusters are not known a priori but are learned ("discovered") by applying some algorithm; usually, when applying clustering algorithms the analyst only establish the desired number of clusters, and/or the conditions expected to be satisfied by them (maximum or minimum number of elements per cluster, maximum distance between members of the same cluster, etc.) The clustering process also requires a notion of distance between the objects to be clustered. Given two objects some numerical value must be calculated that can be interpreted as the relative distance between them. In this case, the distance between entities must be calculated using the attributes modelling them.

The application of clustering to evaluate the data currency is as follows: instead of considering only one validity period for all entities, a validity period for each individual one should be considered. Then all entities are clustered based on their validity period assuming that entities with similar validity period behaves similar.

4   Application to Demographic Data

In this section an application of the proposed method to a real dataset is shown.

The fact that the global population is in growth is not under discussion. When certain worldwide organizations plan activities, knowing the population for target countries is important. It is not the same plan for a country with a few million people than for another with tens of millions, or for countries whose population is relatively stable as for fast-growing ones. Perhaps, for some countries a census from two, five or ten years ago, is pretty current, while for others it is not. What is proposed in this application case is to analyse how population evolves for each country, and then estimate a validity period for each one. Then, all countries will be clustered according to their change frequency. The results could be used to know if the last data value known for each country is still current, and even predict if it will be current at some future time.

Data for this experiment were taken from the World Data Bank [23]. They are composed by one record for each country, containing its name and the population for each year from 1960 to 2013 (for some countries there may be exceptions which were not considered), among other attributes. The Java programming language was used to build a data processor, and the Weka software [24, 25] for the clustering.

As an exercise, various alternatives were tried, although for space reasons only one of them is shown in this paper:

- Training datasets: the method was tested with three training datasets: a full dataset (containing all countries and all years for each one), a random dataset (containing all countries but only some random years for each one), and a periodic dataset (containing all countries but only one of each five years).
- Data similarity: different similarities were tested for populations values (whether the value in one record is equal or not to that of the previous record): 0 %, 1 %, 5 %, 10 % y 20 %.

In the rest of the section, the results shown correspond to the case where the whole dataset was used, and a similarity of 10 % was considered.

4.1 Procedure

First, a preprocessing stage must be applied to the data, transforming it from its original format (horizontal) to a more suitable format (vertical), in which each record contains the entity id (country name), the timestamp (year) and the attribute value (population for that entity in that year), as shown in Fig. 1.

Secondly, the described method was applied to the data, obtaining for each country p its total change time, $TT(p)$, its changes count, $CC(p)$, and its validity period, $VP(p)$.

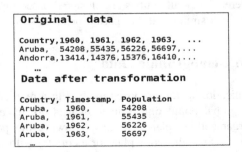

```
Original   data

Country,1960, 1961, 1962, 1963,  ...
Aruba,   54208,55435,56226,56697,...
Andorra,13414,14376,15376,16410,...
    ...
Data after transformation

Country, Timestamp, Population
Aruba,   1960,      54208
Aruba,   1961,      55435
Aruba,   1962,      56226
Aruba,   1963,      56697
    ...
```

Fig. 1. Data preprocessing

```
Entity,         TT,              CC,VP,              Description
Afghanistan,1640991600000, 11,149181054545,4 years 266 days
Albania,    1514761200000,  7,216394457142,6 years 314 days
Algeria,    1514761200000, 10,151476120000,4 years 293 days
Andorra,    1356998400000, 14, 96928457142,3 years 26 days
Angola,     1640991600000, 12,136749300000,4 years 122 days
...
```

Fig. 2. Results (TT, CC, VP) by country

This result was stored in a CSV file (comma separated value), as shown in Fig. 2 (TT and VP are expressed in milliseconds).

In third place, Weka (version 3.7.10) was used to cluster the entities based only on their validity period using the previous CSV file as input. The SimpleKMeans clustering algorithm (an implementation provided by Weka of the KMeans algorithm [22]) was chosen, establishing in 5 the number of desired clusters (leaving all other configuration parameters in their default values). The number of clusters is arbitrary (in most DM projects determining the best number of clusters is a problem in itself; in this case, 5 was chosen to represent five states: very stable, stable, normal, unstable and very unstable). Table 1 shows the obtained results after clustering. Note: the clustroid of a cluster is its "centre"; when a new item must be assigned to one of all available clusters, it will be assigned to that which has the smallest distance to its clustroid.

Table 1. Obtained results from clustering

Cluster #	1	2	3	4	5
Clustroid	2y 151d	5y 47d	9y 78d	14y 79d	27y 35d
Distribution	10 %	56 %	14 %	14 %	5 %
Sample members	Kenya, Niger, Qatar	Brazil, Haiti, India, Mexico, Somalia, Zimbabwe	Argentina, Australia, China, Cuba, United States	France, Italy, Japan, Russia, Switzerland, Uruguay	Germany, Sweden, United Kingdom

From the results shown in Table 1 it can be concluded that countries from cluster #1 raise its population by at least 10 % in about two years, so a record from three or more years ago is *probably* obsolete, while it is not the case from countries from other clusters. For Uruguay, for instance, which is in cluster #4, a census from even ten years ago is more or less accurate; in fact, its real estimated validity period is about 16 years. So, if the last know data value is from 2013 (two years ago), the probability of currency is PoC $= 1 - (2 /16) = 0.875$.

4.2   Obtained Results

As mentioned before, the experiment was executed with different combinations of datasets and various degrees of similarity. The question is: does the proposed method

Table 2. Partial comparison using 10 % similarity

Dataset	Cluster 1	Cluster 2	Cluster 3	Cluster 4	Cluster 5
Complete	2y 151d	5y 47d	9y 78d	14y 79d	27y 35d
Random	3y 62d	6y 98d	11y 82d	18y 217d	35y 190d
Periodic	9y 268d	13y 42d	18y 295d	27y 6d	42y 10d

behave in a consistent manner? Making a comparison of the clusters obtained with the three datasets under a 10 % similarity, the results are shown in Table 2.

It is not surprising that the clustroid of the clusters tend to show greater values and are more separated when less dense datasets are used. This corresponds to having bigger jumps between years, which produces that differences between timestamps are bigger and changes are fewer, so the validity period is greater. However, the validity period of each entity tends to be greater too, so the relation between the individual validity period and the cluster one remains almost constant.

For instance, an analyst could be interested in knowing if the last data value known for Uruguay (from 2013) was current in 2014 (age = 1), is still current in 2015 (age = 2) and will be current in 2020 (age = 7), considering a 10 % of similarity. These currency probabilities are shown in Table 3.

Table 3. Currency probability for uruguay at 10 % similarity

Dataset	VP of Uruguay	VP of cluster	Currency Prob. 2014	Currency Prob. 2015	Currency Prob. 2020
Complete	16y 3d	14y 79d	92,966 %	85,933 %	50,745 %
Random	18y 187d	18y 217d	94,623 %	89,245 %	62,343 %
Periodic	20y 5d	18y 295d	94,683 %	89,367 %	62,769 %

The probabilities are quite stable, even when the real values are more unstable.

4.3 Discussion

From the results in Table 3 it can be concluded that the currency probability (PoC) is more useful that the estimated validity period (VP), since it is more stable regarding the choice of training datasets. Hence, PoC es recommended to decide if a data value is current. It is worth noting that the VP is only useful if the new data, or target data, is sampled in exactly the same way as the training dataset, as it was shown in Table 3 that different ways of sampling affects the results.

It is important to note that, at first glance, it is better to collect or check the data as frequently as possible. As shown in Table 3, when every year data value was considered for each country, the validity period was more accurate. For example, consider the next sequence of values for some attribute/entity: {t1 = 'A',t2 = 'A',t3 = 'B'}. The validity period is (3-2)/1 = 1. But if only the first and last values are considered, the validity period is (3-1)/1 = 2. The entity and the attribute are the same, what changed was the sampling mechanism. This means that data should be collected periodically, even if there were no changes, precisely to stress that data do not change frequently.

Another important observation is about clustering. In the example case, the only attribute used in the clustering process was the validity period of each entity. This means that there are two ways to identify the cluster an entity belongs to: by finding the entity in one of the clusters, or knowing its validity period and looking for the clustroid with smallest distance to it. But what about new entities, which are not already in one of the clusters and whose validity period cannot be determined? For those entities the analyst can not determine if the only record known is current or not. To solve this, the clustering should be done using more properties of the entities. The determination of the set of attributes to be considered is a task the analyst must solve, but another technique from the DM area could be useful: the Association Rule Mining (ARM) [26, 27]. Rules between attributes could be found in the form $A \rightarrow B$ which means that when A holds, probably B also holds. This kind of rules could be used to detect which other attributes of the entity affect the evaluated attribute most significantly and then implement the clustering process using those attributes also. If a new entity appears, it could be "clustered" by examining these other attributes.

For records with more than one attribute some techniques should be evaluated for estimating the currency for the whole record based on the currency of each of the attributes. For example, it could be considered that the record is as current as its less-current attribute or assign a weight to each attribute an then calculate an average.

5 Conclusions

We have presented a novel approach for data currency assessment, where DM methodologies and techniques are applied. Our proposal is oriented to a dataset composed of snapshots of the state of homogeneous entities. This paper also presents the application of the proposed method to a real dataset as well as the obtained results.

The presented method helps in two complementary ways to lead to an always up-to-date database: (i) it can inform if a certain data value is (becoming) obsolete and should be updated, and (ii) it can give hints about the best frequency for updating data. Furthermore, we believe that the results are easily interpretable by non-experts.

We believe that the obtained experimental results show a promising path toward establishing a methodology for data currency assessment through DM techniques. However, the proposal should be validated over different kinds of datasets, applying quality measurements such as recall and precision.

References

1. Redman, T.C.: Data: an unfolding quality disaster. DM Rev. Mag. 8 (2004)
2. Scannapieco, M., Missier, P., Batini, C.: Data quality at a glance. Datenbank Spektrum 14, 6–14 (2005)
3. Strong, D.M., Lee, Y.W., Wang, R.Y.: Data quality in context. Commun. ACM 40(5), 103–110 (1997)
4. Pipino, L., Lee, Y.W., Wang, R.Y.: Data quality assessment. Commun. ACM 45(4), 211–218 (2002)

5. Wand, Y., Wang, R.Y.: Anchoring data quality dimensions in ontological foundations. Commun. ACM **39**(11), 86–95 (1996)
6. Scannapieco, M., Catarci, T.: Data quality under the computer science perspective. Arch. Comput. **2**, 1–15 (2002)
7. Heinrich, B., Klier, M.: Assessing data currency: a probabilistic approach. J. Inform. Sci. **37**, 86–100 (2011)
8. Peralta, V., Ruggia R., Kedad, Z., Bouzeghoub, M.: A framework for data quality evaluation in a data integration system. In: 19th Brazilian Database Symposium (SBBD) (2004)
9. Bouzeghoub, M., Peralta, V.: A framework for analysis of data freshness. In: IQIS, Maison de la Chimie, Paris, France (2004)
10. Firestone, J.: Data mining and KDD: A shifting mosaic. White Paper (1997)
11. Grüning, F.: Data quality mining: employing classifiers for assuring consistent datasets. In: Proceedings of the 3rd International ICSC Symposium, ITEE, Oldenburg, Germany (2007)
12. Hipp, J., Güntzer, U., Grimmer, U.: Data quality mining, making a virtue of necessity. In: Proceedings of the 6th ACM SIGMOD Workshop, California, EEUU (2001)
13. Grimmer, U., Hinrichs, H.: A methodological approach to data quality management supported by data mining. In: Sixth International Conference on Information Quality (2003)
14. Farzi, S., Dastjerdi, A.B.: Data quality measurement using data mining. Int. J. Comput. Theory Eng. **2**(1), 1793–8201 (2010)
15. Luebbers, D., Grimmer, U., Jarke, M.: Systematic development of data mining-based data quality tools. In: Proceedings of the 29th VLDB Conference, Berlin, Germany (2003)
16. Vázquez Soler, S., Yankelevich, D.: Quality mining: a data mining based method for data quality evaluation. In: Sixth International Conference on Information Quality (2003)
17. Dasu, T., Johnson, T.: Hunting of the snark: finding data glitches using data mining methods. In: Proceedings of the 1999 Conference on Information Quality, MIT (1999)
18. Maletic, J.I., Marcus, A.: Data cleansing: beyond integrity analysis. In: Proceedings of the 2000 Conference on Information Quality (2000)
19. Isaac, D., Lynnes, C.: Automated data quality assessment in the intelligent archive (2003)
20. Alizamini, F.G., Pedram, M.M., Alishahi, M., Badi, K.: Data quality improvement using fuzzy association rules. In: ICEIE (2010)
21. Fan, W., Geerts, F., Wijsen, J.: Determining the currency of data. ACM Trans. Database Syst. **37**(4), 1–46 (2012). Article 25
22. North, M.A.: Data mining for the masses. Free e-book published by Global Text Project (2012). http://globaltext.terry.uga.edu/booklist?cat=Computing
23. The World Data Bank - Population, total http://data.worldbank.org/indicator/SP.POP.TOTL. Accessed 15 February 2015
24. Hall, M., Frank, E., Holmes, G., Pfahringer, B., Reutemann, P., Witten, I.H.: The WEKA data mining software: an update. SIGKDD Explor. **11**(1), 10–18 (2009)
25. Machine Learning Group at the University of Waikato - Weka 3: Data Mining Software in Java - http://www.cs.waikato.ac.nz/∼ml/weka/. Accessed 15 February 2015
26. Agrawal, R., Imielinski, T., Swami, A.: Mining association rules between sets of items in large databases. In: Proceedings of the ACM SIGMOD Conference Washington DC, USA (1993)
27. Hipp, J., Gontzer, U., Nakhaeizadeh, G.: Algorithms for association rule mining: a general survey and comparison. SIGKDD Explor. **2**(1), 58–64 (2003)

Evaluating the Gap Between an RDF Dataset and Its Schema

Kenza Kellou-Menouer[(✉)] and Zoubida Kedad

PRISM, University of Versailles Saint-Quentin-en-Yvelines, Versailles, France
{kenza.menouer,zoubida.kedad}@prism.uvsq.fr

Abstract. An increasing number of linked datasets is published on the Web, using RDF(S)/OWL. The availability of the schema describing these datasets is crucial for their meaningful usage. A dataset may contain schema-related information, however, languages do not impose any constraint on their structure, and a gap may therefore exist between the schema and the actual instances. In this paper, we tackle the problem of evaluating this gap. We present an approach relying on both type and class profiles, as well as a set of quality metrics. We also present some experimental evaluations to illustrate the use of the proposed metrics.

Keywords: Schema quality · Semantic web · Linked data

1 Introduction

The Web has witnessed a proliferation of data expressed in RDF(S)/OWL referred to as linked data. This has transformed the Web from a collection of documents to a huge virtual database, enabling the design of intelligent applications capable of making sense of data. In order to exploit RDF datasets in a meaningful way, applications and users need their schematic description, which can be provided by the datasets themselves. However, the analysis of real RDF datasets [4] shows that many of them do not conform to their provided schema: entities of the same type may have different properties, and properties defined for a given class are not always the same as the ones specified for the instances of this class. Entities can be described by the *rdf:type* property, defining the types to which they belong, but most linked datasets are incomplete with respect to type information.

In this paper, we tackle the problem of evaluating the conformity between a dataset and its schema. We propose a set of metrics to assess different facets of conformity, as well as an evaluation methodology. Our approach uses the concept of type profile [9] associated to each type in the dataset. Assessing the conformity of a dataset to its schema relies on the comparison of type profiles and class definitions in the dataset. We have conducted some experiments on real datasets using our methodology and metrics.

The paper is organized as follows. A motivating example is presented in Sect. 2. Type profiles and class profiles are presented in Sects. 3 and 4 respectively. Metrics for evaluating the gap between the dataset and its schema are

© Springer International Publishing Switzerland 2015
M.A. Jeusfeld and K. Karlapalem (Eds.): ER 2015 Workshops, LNCS 9382, pp. 283–292, 2015.
DOI: 10.1007/978-3-319-25747-1_28

introduced in Sect. 5. Section 6 presents our evaluation methodology and the results achieved using real datasets. Related works are discussed in Sect. 7 and finally, a conclusion is provided in Sect. 8.

2   Motivating Example

A dataset includes both instances and some schema related information about them. This latter is not always provided, and when it is, it is not necessarily in adequacy with the described instances. Figure 1(a) shows an example of dataset related to the French National Library[1]. We can see that some entities are described by the property *rdf:type*, defining the types to which they belong. For other entities, such as "C2" and "E1", this information is missing. Two entities having the same type are not necessarily described by the same properties, as we can see for "W1" and "W2" which are both associated to the "Work" type, but unlike "W2", "W1" has not a "description" property.

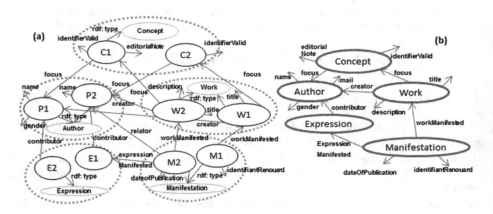

Fig. 1. A Dataset (a) and its schema (b).

Our goal is to evaluate the conformity between a dataset and its schema, and to provide a set of metrics to capture two kinds of mismatches: (i) schema information which is not defined for the entities of the dataset, and (ii) information defined for entities in the dataset, but not in the schema. In Fig. 1, the "gender" property is not defined for the entity "P2", however, it is defined for the corresponding class "Author". The property "relator", defined for some entities of the "Manifestation" type, is not described in the schema.

We define two kinds of profiles: type profiles, describing the entities of the dataset, and class profiles, corresponding to classes defined in the schema. These profiles are used in our quality metrics to evaluate the gap between the dataset and its schema. Their definition is provided in the following sections.

---

[1] BNF: http://datahub.io/fr/dataset/data-bnf-fr.

3   Type Profile

Consider the sets R, B, P and L representing resources, blank nodes (anonymous resources), properties and literals respectively. A dataset described in RDF(S)/OWL is defined as a set of triples $D \subseteq (R \cup B) \times P \times (R \cup B \cup L)$. Graphically, a dataset is represented by a labeled directed graph G, where each node is a resource, a blank node or a literal and where each edge from a node e_1 to another node e_2 labeled with the property p represents the triple (e_1, p, e_2) of the dataset D. In such graph, we define an entity as a node corresponding to either a resource or a blank node, that is, any node apart from the ones corresponding to literals. A group of entities having the same value for the *rdf:type* property corresponds to a type definition. Each type is associated to a profile defined as follows.

Definition. A type T in the dataset D is described by a profile TP composed of a set of properties, each property p is associated to a probability α and annotated by an arrow indicating its direction, and such that:

- If $(\exists(e, p, e') \in D$ and $\exists(e, rdf : type, T) \in D)$ then $(\overrightarrow{p}, \alpha) \in TP$.
- If $(\exists(e', p, e) \in D$ and $\exists(e, rdf : type, T) \in D)$ then $(\overleftarrow{p}, \alpha) \in TP$.

In a type profile $TP = \{(p_1, \alpha_1), ..., (p_n, \alpha_n)\}$, each p_i represents a property and each α_i represents the probability for an entity of T to have the property p_i. The probability α_i associated to a property p_i in the profile of the type T is evaluated as the number of entities of the type T for which p_i is defined over the total number of entities in T. The type profiles of the example in Fig. 1(a) are given in Table 1.

Table 1. Type profiles of the dataset in Fig. 1.

Type	Type profile
Concept	$\{(\overrightarrow{editorialNote}, 0.5), (\overrightarrow{identifierValid}, 1), (\overrightarrow{focus}, 1), (\overleftarrow{focus}, 1)\}$
Author	$\{(\overrightarrow{name}, 1), (\overleftarrow{creator}, 1), (\overleftarrow{relator}, 0.5), (\overrightarrow{focus}, 1), (\overrightarrow{gender}, 0.5), (\overleftarrow{contributor}, 1)\}$
Work	$\{(\overrightarrow{title}, 1), (\overrightarrow{workManifested}, 1)(\overrightarrow{creator}, 1), (\overrightarrow{description}, 0.5), (\overleftarrow{focus}, 1)\}$
Manifestation	$\{(\overrightarrow{workManifested}, 1), (\overrightarrow{dateOfPublication}, 0.5), (\overrightarrow{identifiantRenouard}, 0.5), (\overrightarrow{expressionManifested}, 0.5)\}$
Expression	$\{(\overrightarrow{contributor}, 1), (\overleftarrow{expressionManifested}, 0.5)\}$

We have introduced this notion of type profile in our previous works addressing the automatic generation of types from a dataset by grouping entities according to their similarity [9,10]. In this paper, we generate these profiles using *rdf:type* declarations in the dataset.

4   Class Profile

Beside type profiles, we consider a profile for each class defined in the schema of the dataset. The class profile will be considered as the gold standard for evaluating the conformity of a dataset to its schema, it is defined as follows.

Table 2. Class profiles of the schema in Fig. 1(b).

Class	Class profile
Concept	$\{editorial\overrightarrow{Note}, identifier\overleftarrow{V}alid, \overrightarrow{focus}, \overleftarrow{focus}\}$
Author	$\{\overrightarrow{name}, \overleftarrow{creator}, \overrightarrow{mail}, \overleftarrow{focus}, \overrightarrow{gender}, \overleftarrow{contributor}\}$
Work	$\{\overrightarrow{title}, \overleftarrow{workManifested}, \overrightarrow{creator}, \overrightarrow{description}, \overrightarrow{focus}\}$
Manifestation	$\{identifiant\overrightarrow{Renouard}, \overrightarrow{expressionManifested}, dateOf\overrightarrow{Publication}, \overrightarrow{workManifested}\}$
Expression	$\{\overleftarrow{contributor}, \overrightarrow{expressionManifested}\}$

Definition. A class C, in the schema of the dataset D is described by its profile CP composed of properties p, each one annotated by an arrow indicating its direction, and such that:

- If $\exists(p, rdfs : domain, C) \in D$ then $\overrightarrow{p} \in CP$;
- If $\exists(p, rdfs : range, C) \in D$ then $\overleftarrow{p} \in CP$.

The class profiles for the schema in Fig. 1(b) are presented in Table 2. The "mail" property belongs to the profile of the "Author" class, but does not belong to the profile of the "Author" type because no entity has this property in the dataset. The "relator" property is not in the profile of the "Manifestation" class as it is not declared in the schema. However, this property is in the profile of the "Manifestation" type (see Table 1) as it is defined for some of its entities.

5 Quality Metrics

The first criteria we are interested in is the completeness of a dataset with respect to its schema, i.e., to what extend do instances of a given class have values for the properties defined for this class in the schema. The second one is the accuracy of a schema with respect to its dataset, which can be stated as follows: are the properties of the instances in the dataset specified for some classes in the schema? The more properties are missing in the schema, the less accurate this schema is. Finally, we introduce a notion of conformity which reflects both completeness and accuracy.

Consider a dataset D, $T_D = \{T_i : i = 1, ...n\}$ the set of types in D, and $P_T = \{TP_i : i = 1, ...n\}$ the set of corresponding type profiles. S represents the set of classes in the schema of D, it is defined as $S = \{C_i : i = 1, ...k\}$. We denote $P_C = \{CP_i : i = 1, ...n\}$ the set of profiles corresponding to the classes in S. Note that n, the number of types in the dataset, can differ from k, the number of classes in the schema.

5.1 Dataset Completeness

To evaluate the completeness of the dataset with respect to its schema, we compare the properties of each type profile TP_i with the properties of the profile CP_i of the corresponding class. We use the probability of the properties in TP_i to evaluate the completeness of a property p as follows.

$$\forall p \in CP_i, PropertyCompleteness(p) = \begin{cases} \alpha & \text{if} \quad p \in TP_i \\ 0 & \text{otherwise} \end{cases} \quad (1)$$

In the above formula, α represents the probability associated to the property p in TP_i. We evaluate the completeness of a type T_i with respect to the corresponding class C_i in the schema as the average value of the completeness of properties in TP_i, as it is shown below.

$$TypeCompleteness(T_i) = \begin{cases} \dfrac{\sum_{\forall p \in CP_i} PropertyCompleteness(p)}{|CP_i|} & \text{if} \quad \exists C_i \in S \\ Undefined & \text{otherwise} \end{cases}$$

$$(2)$$

We evaluate the completeness of a dataset D with respect to its schema S as the average value of their type completeness, as follows.

$$DatasetCompleteness(D) = \frac{\sum_{\forall T \in T_D} TypeCompleteness(T)}{|S|} \quad (3)$$

5.2   Schema Accuracy

To evaluate the accuracy of the schema with respect to its dataset, we compare the properties of each class profile CP_i to the ones of the corresponding type profile TP_i. We consider the probability of the properties in TP_i to evaluate the accuracy of a property p in the schema as follows.

$$\forall p \in TP_i, PropertyAccuracy(p) = \begin{cases} \alpha & \text{if} \quad p \in CP_i \\ 1 - \alpha & \text{otherwise} \end{cases} \quad (4)$$

We evaluate the accuracy of a class C_i with respect to the corresponding type T_i in the dataset as the average of the property accuracy values considering their respective profiles CP_i and TP_i as it is shown below.

$$ClassAccuracy(C_i) = \begin{cases} \dfrac{\sum_{\forall p \in TP_i} PropertyAccuracy(p)}{|TP_i|} & \text{if} \quad \exists T_i \in T_D \\ Undefined & \text{otherwise} \end{cases} \quad (5)$$

We evaluate the accuracy of a schema S with respect to its corresponding dataset D as the average value of the accuracy of its classes, as follows.

$$SchemaAccuracy(S) = \frac{\sum_{\forall C \in S} ClassAccuracy(C)}{|T_D|} \quad (6)$$

5.3   Conformity Between a Dataset and Its Schema

We introduce the notion of conformity between the dataset and its schema which relies on both the completeness of the dataset and the accuracy of the schema. We first evaluate the conformity of a property p in TP_i or CP_i, as follows.

$$PropertyConformity_i(p) = \begin{cases} 0 & \text{if } p \notin TP_i \wedge p \in CP_i \\ \alpha & \text{if } p \in TP_i \cap CP_i \\ 1-\alpha & \text{if } p \in TP_i \wedge p \notin CP_i \end{cases} \quad (7)$$

We evaluate the conformity between a type T_i in the dataset and its corresponding class C_i in the schema as the average value of the conformity of their properties considering their respective profiles TP_i and CP_i as shown below.

$$Conformity(T_i, C_i) = \frac{\sum_{\forall p \in \{TP_i \cup CP_i\}} PropertyConformity(p)}{\sum_{\forall p \in \{TP_i \cup CP_i\}} 1} \quad (8)$$

The conformity of a type (resp. class) in the dataset (resp. schema) has a value of zero if it has no corresponding class (resp. type) in the schema (resp. dataset). The conformity between a type and its corresponding class is calculated as follows: $Conformity(T_i, C_i) = Min\{TypeCompleteness(T_i), ClassAccuracy(C_i)\}$. The conformity between a dataset D and its schema S is the average value of the conformity of their types and classes:

$$Conformity(D, S) = \frac{\sum_{\forall (T_i, C_i) \in (D \times S)} Conformity(T_i, C_i)}{|T_D| + |S| - \sum_{\forall (T_i, C_i) \in (D \times S)} 1} \quad (9)$$

6   Experiments

This section presents some experimentation results using our approach with different real datasets. We have generated type profiles for each dataset and evaluated the quality metrics defined in the previous section.

6.1   Datasets

We have used three datasets: the Conference[2] dataset, about several Semantic Web related conferences and workshops; the BNF[3] dataset, which contains data about the French National Library (Bibliothèque Nationale de France) and a dataset extracted from DBpedia considering the following types: Politician, SoccerPlayer, Museum, Movie, Book and Country.

6.2   Metrics and Experimental Methodology

We have first listed the types existing in the dataset to build their profiles. We have then compared the type profiles to the schema of the dataset when it was provided, as for the BNF dataset. If no schema was provided, such as for the Conference and DBpedia datasets, we have manually designed it.

---

[2] Conference: http://data.semanticweb.org/dumps/conferences/dc-2010-complete.rdf.
[3] BNF: http://datahub.io/fr/dataset/data-bnf-fr.

We have extracted the existing class definitions from our datasets and considered them as a gold standard. We have built for each class C_i its class profile CP_i as described in Sect. 4 and we have generated the types T_i from the dataset. We have compared the properties of each generated type profile TP_i to the ones of the corresponding class profile CP_i. Using the metrics defined in Sect. 5, we have evaluated the completeness, accuracy and conformity between a type T_i and its corresponding class C_i. Finally, we have evaluated the completeness of the dataset, the accuracy of the schema and the conformity between the dataset and the schema.

6.3 Results

Figure 2 shows the completeness, the accuracy and the conformity of the properties of the "Person" type in the Conference dataset (a) and the "Manifestation" type in the BNF dataset (b). For the Conference dataset, we do not present graphically the other types and give their profiles because the probability value of their properties equals 1. Some entities of "Person" do not have all the properties declared in the schema. The accuracy and conformity of the "mail" property are equal to zero, and its completeness is undefined, because this property is declared in the schema but not defined for any of its entities in the dataset. For the BNF dataset, the results for the "Manifestation" type are shown graphically; for the other types, the probability of each property is shown in the class profiles in Table 3. The properties of the "Manifestation" type do not all conform to the declared schema; the "relator" property is defined for some entities but not in the schema, its probability is therefore 0.8, its completeness/conformity value is 0.2 (1–0.8) and its accuracy is undefined. As the number of properties for a class in DBpedia is very hight (150 on average), we do not present the results graphically; we give instead an overview of the type profiles in Table 4.

Figure 3 shows the completeness, accuracy and conformity between the types of the Conference (a), BNF (b) and DBpedia (c) datasets and their schema. For the Conference dataset, the completeness and conformity of the untyped classes are equal to zero, and the accuracy is undefined because these classes are not declared in the schema. However, the entities of these untyped classes have homogeneous sets of properties. For the "Person" type these metrics are not maximum because the corresponding entities have heterogeneous sets of properties. For the BNF and DBpedia datasets, these metrics vary from one type to another.

Table 3. Type profiles for the BNF dataset.

Type	Profile
Work	$((\overleftarrow{focus}, 0.71), (\overrightarrow{subject}, 1), (\overrightarrow{creator}, 1), (\overrightarrow{language}, 0.85), (\overrightarrow{date}, 0.57),...)$
Concept	$((\overrightarrow{prefLabel}, 1), (\overrightarrow{editorialNote}, 0.71), (\overrightarrow{focus}, 1), (\overrightarrow{FRBNF}, 1), (\overrightarrow{identifier}, 0.28))$
Person	$((\overleftarrow{creator}, 1), (\overrightarrow{languageOfThePerson}, 1), (\overrightarrow{placeOfDeath}, 0.6), (\overrightarrow{auteur}, 0.2),...)$
Expression	$((\overleftarrow{expressionManifested}, 0.5), (\overrightarrow{contributor}, 1))$
Manifestation	$((\overrightarrow{date}, 1), (\overrightarrow{relators}, 0.8), (\overrightarrow{auteur}, 0.8), (\overrightarrow{identifiantRenouard}, 1),...)$

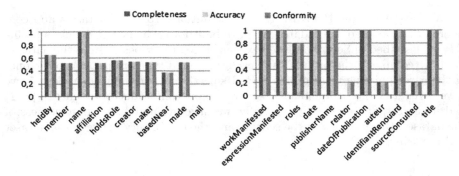

Fig. 2. Completeness, accuracy and conformity of the properties of the person type for the conference dataset (a) and the manifestation type for the BNF dataset (b).

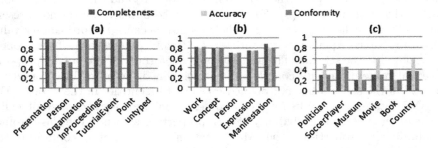

Fig. 3. Type completeness, class accuracy and type/class conformity for the conference (a), BNF (b) and DBpedia (c) datasets.

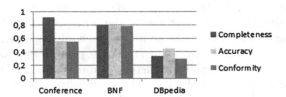

Fig. 4. Dataset completeness, schema accuracy and conformity for the conference (a), BNF (b) and DBpedia (c) datasets.

Figure 4 shows the completeness, accuracy and conformity between the Conference (a), BNF (b) and DBpedia (c) datasets and their schema. We can see that the DBpedia dataset is the least complete and it does not conform to its schema, because of the high number of properties declared of each type. The accuracy of the Conference schema is low because there are four types in the dataset which are not declared in the schema.

Table 4. Type profiles for the DBpedia dataset.

Type	Profile
Country	$((\overrightarrow{name}, 1), (\overrightarrow{capital}, 0.8), (\overleftarrow{deathPlace}, 0.2), (\overrightarrow{lat}, 0.2), (\overrightarrow{long}, 0.2),...)$
Politician	$((\overrightarrow{name}, 1), (\overleftarrow{primeMinister}, 0.2), (\overleftarrow{party}, 0.73), (\overrightarrow{children}, 0.21),...)$
Soccer player	$((\overrightarrow{name}, 1), (\overrightarrow{height}, 0.46), (\overrightarrow{deathDate}, 0.06), (\overleftarrow{currentMember}, 0.8),...)$
Movie	$((\overrightarrow{writer}, 1), (\overleftarrow{created}, 0.05), (\overleftarrow{previousWork}, 0.11), (\overrightarrow{subTitle}, 0.05),...)$
Book	$((\overrightarrow{author}, 1), (\overrightarrow{language}, 0.71), (\overrightarrow{successor}, 0.07), (\overrightarrow{title}, 0.92),...)$
Museum	$((\overrightarrow{name}, 1), (\overrightarrow{numberOfVisitors}, 0.26), (\overrightarrow{director}, 0.26), (\overleftarrow{city}, 0.06),...)$

7 Related Works

Information quality has been the topic of many research works (see [2] for a survey). Quality is described through a large number of quality factors [15,16], quality models including these factors have been proposed [3,13], as well as approaches for evaluating these factors [14]. Some works have addressed quality issues for data sources in the semantic web. In [1], IBM ILOG CPLEX solver is used to refine classes in order to achieve a better structure homogeneity. In [5], generic SPARQL queries are presented to identify missing or illegal values and functional dependency violations. In [6], the SPARQL query language and the SPARQL Inferencing Notation (SPIN) are used to identify data quality problems. An ontology for data quality management is presented in [8], allowing the standardized formulation of data quality and data cleansing rules, the classification of data quality problems, and the computation of data quality scores for Semantic Web data sources. SWIQA [7] is a framework for information quality assessment of Semantic Web data which classifies data quality problems and calculates information quality (IQ) scores for different dimensions. In [12], a taxonomy of common quality problems is proposed and used for the evaluation of individual resources via crowdsourcing. A methodology for quality assessment of Linked Data is presented in [11]; SPARQL query templates are proposed and instantiated into concrete quality test queries. Our work is a contribution to the definition of metrics to handle a specific quality problem, the one of the conformity of entities in a dataset to the corresponding schema.

8 Conclusion

We have proposed an approach to evaluate the conformity of a dataset to its schema. To this end, we have built a profile for each type consisting of a vector where each property is associated to a probability. We have also built the profile of each class declared in the schema. We have proposed a set of metrics along with an evaluation methodology. Our experiments have highlighted the existing mismatches between three datasets and their schema. In future works, we will focus on the identification of quality improvement actions in order to increase both accuracy and completeness which will result in improving the conformity.

Acknowledgements. This work was partially funded by the French National Research Agency through the CAIR ANR-14-CE23-0006 project.

References

1. Arenas, M., Díaz, G., Fokoue, A., Kementsietsidis, A., Srinivas, K.: A principled approach to bridging the gap between graph data and their schemas. In: VLDB (2014)
2. Batini, C., Scannapieco, M.: Data Quality: Concepts. Methodologies and Techniques. Springer Science & Business Media, New York (2006)
3. Berti-Équille, L., Comyn-Wattiau, I., Cosquer, M., Kedad, Z., Nugier, S., Peralta, V., Cherfi, S.S.-S., Thion-Goasdoué, V.: Assessment and analysis of information quality: a multidimensional model and case studies. IJIQ **2**(4), 300–323 (2011)
4. Duan, S., Kementsietsidis, A., Srinivas, K., Udrea, O.: Apples and oranges: a comparison of rdf benchmarks and real rdf datasets. In: SIGMOD (2011)
5. Fürber, C., Hepp, M.: Using semantic web resources for data quality management. In: Cimiano, P., Pinto, H.S. (eds.) EKAW 2010. LNCS, vol. 6317, pp. 211–225. Springer, Heidelberg (2010)
6. Fürber, C., Hepp, M.: Using SPARQL and SPIN for data quality management on the semantic web. In: Abramowicz, W., Tolksdorf, R. (eds.) BIS 2010. LNBIP, vol. 47, pp. 35–46. Springer, Heidelberg (2010)
7. Fürber, C., Hepp, M.: Swiqa-a semantic web information quality assessment framework. In: ECIS (2011)
8. Fürber, C., Hepp, M.: Towards a vocabulary for data quality management in semantic web architectures. In: Workshop on Linked Web Data Management (2011)
9. Kellou-Menouer, K., Kedad, Z.: Discovering types in RDF datasets. In: 12th European Semantic Web Conference, ESWC. Springer (2015, poster paper)
10. Kellou-Menouer, K., Kedad, Z.: Schema discovery in RDF data sources. In: Jeusfeld, M., Karlapalem, K. (eds.) ER 2015. LNCS, vol. 9382, pp. XX–YY. Springer, Heidelberg (2015)
11. Kontokostas, D., Westphal, P., Auer, S., Hellmann, S., Lehmann, J., Cornelissen, R., Zaveri, A.: Test-driven evaluation of linked data quality. In: WWW (2014)
12. Kontokostas, D., Zaveri, A., Auer, S., Lehmann, J.: TripleCheckMate: a tool for crowdsourcing the quality assessment of linked data. In: Klinov, P., Mouromtsev, D. (eds.) KESW 2013. CCIS, vol. 394, pp. 265–272. Springer, Heidelberg (2013)
13. Moody, D.: Theoretical and practical issues in evaluating the quality of conceptual models: current state and future directions. In: Data & Knowledge Engineering (2005)
14. Pipino, L., Lee, Y., Wang, R.: Data quality assessment. Commun. ACM **45**(4), 211–218 (2002)
15. Redman, T.: Data Quality for the Information Age. Artech House, Boston (1996)
16. Wang, R.Y., Strong, D.M.: Beyond accuracy: what data quality means to data consumers. J. Manage. Inf. Syst. **12**(4), 5–33 (1996)

Modeling Stories for Conceptual Model Assessment

Bernardo F.B. Braga[✉] and João Paulo A. Almeida

Ontology and Conceptual Modeling Research Group (NEMO),
Federal University of Espírito Santo (UFES), Vitória, ES, Brazil
{bfbbraga, jpalmeida}@inf.ufes.br

Abstract. Conceptual modeling is a challenging activity and assessing the quality of conceptual models is key to ensure that they may be used effectively as a basis for understanding, agreement and construction of information systems. Stories have always been used as means of communicating complex affairs and we argue that they may be used effectively to assess models and reveal modeling decisions to those that cannot understand the modeling language. This paper proposes an approach to assess conceptual models by creating narratives about a subject domain. These narratives employ concepts of the conceptual model and are formalized as abstract stories. These stories guide model simulation, supporting the validation of the conceptual model. Contrasting simulation with the intended conceptualization is the basis for model assessment.

Keywords: Conceptual modeling · Storytelling · Model assessment · Ontology

1 Introduction

In a broad perspective, conceptual modeling has been characterized as "the activity of formally describing some aspects of the physical and social world around us for purposes of understanding and communication" [12]. These formal descriptions are called conceptual models and are built using artificial modeling languages.

Conceptual models may be used as basis for information systems such as the semantic web and its applications. Therefore, assessing their quality is key to ensure they may be effectively put to use. Assessing model quality is a challenging activity, in particular assessing whether the model corresponds to the modeler's original intention, and whether it reflects accurately the conceptualization of a subject matter expert. This is aggravated by the fact that frequently subject matter experts do not know the modeling language and modelers know little or nothing beforehand about the subject matter. Helping communication between these parties motivated our efforts into building tools and techniques for conceptual model assessment.

Here, we build on previous efforts by approaching model assessment using model transformation and a lightweight formal method. In our previous approach [1, 3, 9], an ontology-based conceptual model is translated to the Alloy logic-based language [11] that presents valid instances of the model or may search for assertion counter examples.

© Springer International Publishing Switzerland 2015
M.A. Jeusfeld and K. Karlapalem (Eds.): ER 2015 Workshops, LNCS 9382, pp. 293–303, 2015.
DOI: 10.1007/978-3-319-25747-1_29

This allows the inspection of model instances (in what could be considered a model "simulator") and therefore allows the assessment of the consequences of modeling choices. So far, the generation of model instances in this approach is based purely on a random strategy. This means that the modeler cannot control the validation process. While this is useful to detect problems in the conceptual model (e.g., "edge cases" [18]), the simulation still has an overwhelmingly large number of possible instantiations. In order to control the model assessment process, we explore in this paper a technique that allows the modeler to guide the simulation through storytelling.

The rest of this paper is organized as follows: in Sect. 2, we position storytelling and conceptual modeling as complementary means to transfer knowledge about reality. In Sect. 3, we present our approach to creating stories and formalizing them, using as a running example a model in the software configuration domain. In Sect. 4, we discuss some related work, and, finally, in Sect. 5, we present conclusions and topics for further investigation.

2   Relating Storytelling and Conceptual Modeling

According to [7], "there is little doubt that narrative thought developed earlier in human history than scientific and logical thought". The ability to narrate gives us the possibility to reenact real-world events eliciting the imagination of the listeners, giving them experiences that they never had themselves. Early in the history of mankind, oral storytelling culture produced collective, standardized narrative versions of reality, particularly of past events; having become what we call the dominant "myths" of a society. Myths reflect the earliest form of integrative thought. In contrast with myths, theories are "very large, externally nested cultural products" which only emerged much later, as our culture allowed the externalization of memory [7].

Similarly to storytelling, conceptual modeling is also used for transferring knowledge. Nevertheless, the concrete representation of this knowledge takes a very different form. Although a conceptual model also represents a view of some subject matter, it does so in a very structured manner, using a formal language to describe the categories of entities that are assumed to exist in a subject matter and how these entities relate to each other. We take ontology-based conceptual models to be a particular means to represent a theory about a subject domain, formally capturing admissible states of affairs [10] using invariants i.e. logical assertions or rules that are held to always be true.

Our approach in this paper aims to leverage the value of storytelling as means for transferring knowledge, not substituting but enriching ontology-based conceptual modeling. In this approach both subject matter experts and modelers create natural language narratives using the concepts that appear in the conceptual model. The modeler translates these natural language narratives into Formal Stories using a story specification language that makes explicit reference to the concepts in the conceptual model. These formal stories constrain the generation of valid instances of the model to generate Formal Narratives (simulations) that conform to the specified formal story. By complementing a natural language narrative with a formal narrative, one can exemplify how the domain was modeled. That means modelers may assess whether their intentions were correctly expressed in the model by exemplifying model features and "testing" their correctness with a subject matter expert. Also, this allows subject matter experts to assess the content of a model regardless of their knowledge of the modeling language: guiding which elements of a natural language narrative correspond to formalized knowledge. This helps to bridge the communication between modelers and subject matter experts. We integrate the support for story modeling in the model assessment tool ecosystem developed at our research group. We thus assume models are defined using the ontologically well-founded OntoUML profile [10], which provides a clear semantics for a fragment of UML class diagrams.

3   Creating Stories for Model Assessment

Our approach aims to validate existing conceptual models using a mix of informal and formal storytelling. In Fig. 1 we summarize our approach, showing three of its elements: (i) the natural language narrative, (ii) the formal story (anchored in the conceptual model) and (iii) the formal narratives (roughly a simulated story). Typically, natural language narratives about the subject matter are recorded. These natural language narratives are partially formalized regarding their semantic content (including the specification of which classes are instantiated from the conceptual model), using in this activity the specification language we defined. The product of that activity is called a formal story, which may partially define valid instantiations of the model. Formal stories are used to constrain the model simulation, resulting in what we call a formal narrative (a.k.a. model simulation).

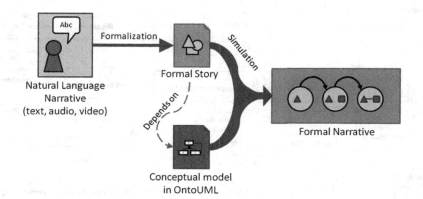

Fig. 1. An overview of the approach

In order to demonstrate the application of the technique, we introduce a running example in the domain of Software Configuration Management. We use as a starting point a previously published conceptual model for this domain extracted from [4]. This model is presented briefly in Sect. 3.1. In Sect. 3.2, we discuss the development of natural language narratives, providing a narrative for our running example. In Sect. 3.3, we present a Story Specification Language and the informal narrative of our example is represented as a formal story. This formal story is simulated in Sect. 3.4, demonstrating how formal narratives may support model assessment.

3.1 Running Example

We use as running example a fragment of a model extracted from [4]. The diagram in Fig. 2 specifies different kinds of **Items** that can be versioned: **Software Tools** and **Artifacts** such as **Source Code**, **Document** and **Diagram**. Classes stereotyped as Kinds are classes that apply necessarily to their instances and define a principle of identity for them. Categories (e.g., **Item**) are classes that also apply necessarily to their instances (i.e. are Rigid), but subsume instances with different principles of identity. An Item that has been selected by a **Configuration Manager** assumes the role of a **Configuration Item**. Configuration Manager is the role a **Person** assumes in the context of that selection. Roles are Anti-Rigid (a.k.a. dynamic) classes i.e. they apply contingently to instances. The relationship between the Configuration Manager and the Configuration Item is reified as a **Configuration Selection.** The Person class is omitted from the diagram and appears in italics on the top classes that specialize it.

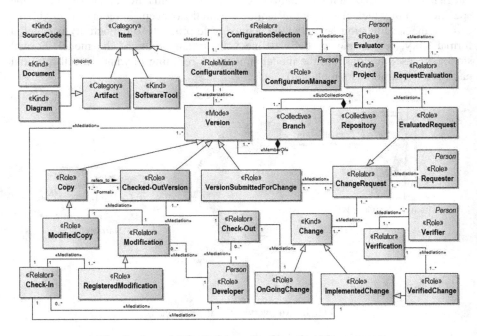

Fig. 2. A model for Software Configuration Management

Each Configuration Item is characterized by some **Version.** Version is stereotyped as Mode, meaning they are existentially dependent and inhere in the thing they characterize. In this case, Versions can only exist in Configuration Items. Versions are part of some **Branch.** Branches, on the other hand are part of some **Repository.** Stereotyped as Collectives, their instances are collections formed by uniform parts. Versions can be **submitted for change**, when **requested**. A **Developer** is a **Person** that may **Check Out** versions, **modify** them and **Check In Modifications** (a checked-in modification is called a **Registered Modification**). Versions that are checked out are **Checked-Out Versions** and generate **Copies.** A **Copy** that has been modified assumes the role of **Modified Copy**, and when checked-in, makes the requested **change implemented**. A **verifier** may assess an **implemented change**, making it **verified**.

3.2   Natural Language Narrative

Producing some natural language narratives about the domain can be the first step in our approach. The activity of creating these narratives and validating them is done between subject matter experts and modelers. Either of them may create the narrative. With regard to the scope of a narrative, in the case of modeler-authored narratives, the modeler may exercise fragments of the model he/she suspects may be incorrect i.e. he/she imagines a real-world scenario where the concepts of such fragment are instantiated. In the case of subject matter expert authored narratives, the subject matter expert narrates real life events about a fragment of the model requested by a modeler. The narratives help the modeler to understand how these concepts are exercised in their real context.

Drawing from our running example, we produced the following natural language narrative. It exercises the classes of the model presented in Fig. 2. Whenever a class is used in the narrative, it is highlighted in bold. This narrative is the basis for the formal story presented in Sect. 3.3 which will in its turn be used to generate formal narratives (simulations) in Sect. 3.4.

*"John, Mary, Fred and Thomas work at OntoSoft company as **developers**. They are working on an information system for a bakery to manage its finances and supply-chain processes. The system they are producing already manages the finance aspects, and currently they are developing new **artifacts** (such as **diagrams**, **documents** and **source code**) to manage the supply-chain processes. Thomas is the **Configuration Manager** and he **selects** some of the **artifacts** they created to be part the project's repository, where they are **version**-controlled.*

*As the team focuses efforts on the bakery's supply-chain processes, Fred finds a deadlock in a process diagram for buying raw materials and files a **change request** for it, describing the problem he found and the **change** that should be implemented. John **evaluates** the request and **checks out** the **diagram** in the version control system to **modify** it. After doing the necessary adjustments, he **checks in** the **modified version** and Mary is assigned to **verify** whether John has met the **change request**.*

*Mary **verifies** the **code** and notices that John's modifications introduced bugs in the already-approved finance processes. These **changes** have a deep impact in the approved parts of the software so Mary rejects the **version** and asks John to **branch** the **project** and try again from a different angle."*

3.3 Formal Stories

Stories are abstract representations of a narrative. Elsewhere, these concepts are alternatively called *Fable* and *syuzhet* [15], respectively. Here, Formal Stories are abstract representations of both Natural Language Narratives, discussed in the previous section, and Formal Narratives, which will be discussed in the next section.

There are two ways to create such stories. In the first case, they may be based on an existing Natural Language Narrative. In this alternative, the modeler captures what happens in the story using the concepts present in the conceptual model. When formalizing an existing natural language narrative much detail is lost since formal stories only contain semantic aspects of the narrative that are relevant to the conceptual model. However, this process may create information that is more precise than their natural language counterparts. Inconsistencies, ambiguities and suppositions are removed in this stage, making the modeler commit to a certain interpretation of the story's semantic content. The formal story acts like an explanation, revealing the elements involved in the story and its unfolding.

In the second case, a modeler may take the reverse approach: first create formal stories and posteriorly elaborate a natural language narrative based on it. By narrating this story to a subject matter expert, the modeler may validate his understanding of the domain. This is especially helpful for checking edge cases, as it is common practice in the testing of computer algorithms [18].

Formal Stories are model instances of our special-purpose language, whose metamodel is presented in Fig. 3. In this language, the user may specify *nodes* and *links* between *nodes*. Each node may be assigned to instantiate some Rigid classes from the conceptual model, while links instantiate Associations. Individuals (nodes and links) can be present in *worlds* and a world sequence represents the unfolding of the story (the world sequence is represented using "next" and "previous" relations). A world is a snapshot of the story, capturing the state of things in a particular point in the story. As the story progresses, elements may be created, changed or destroyed. Change is represented as classification statements that may be made about the nodes, which specify contingent characteristics of it, i.e., the Anti-Rigid classes a node instantiates.

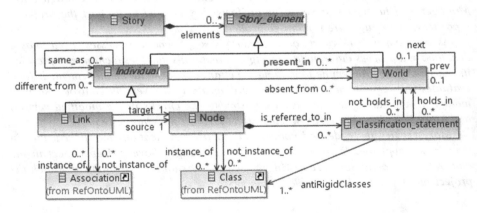

Fig. 3. Metamodel of the formal story language

The relations in this model capture the "facts" that the modeler asserts about the story. The modeler can assert a fact (e.g., "John" is an instance of "Developer") or assert its negation (e.g., "Mary" is not an instance of "Developer") by using the appropriate relations. Whenever the model is silent with respect to a particular choice, e.g., when nothing is said about whether "John" is a developer, the simulator will allow both options, meaning either case can appear in a formal narrative of such story. This is useful to partially formalize a narrative and simulate to see the possible rearrangements of states of affairs generated by the simulator. Later, a story may be revisited to constraint it further, specifying more details.

Formalizing our running example, John and his peers are represented as Nodes that are **instance of** Person and each **is referred to in** a classification statement (Developer). The Items are also nodes and their classifications statements specify they are Configuration Items. All of those statements **hold in** every world of the story. A classification statement about Fred instantiating Requester, does **not hold** in the first world of the story and **holds in** the last two worlds exemplifying dynamic classification. That statement enforces that, in every simulation, John will always be instance of Requester in the last two worlds and will never be in the first. Other nodes defined include a selection and a check-out. To specify that these are actually Thomas' selection and John's checkout, we must specify links between Thomas and the selection, as well as between John and the checkout. We could specify the type of link instantiated but in this case there is only one type of relationship between person and each of these classes, meaning the simulator will assert the correct type of link, so there is no need for specifying it in the formal story.

Figure 4 is a screenshot of the prototype application, showing part of the formal story we just described. The tool represents this formal story internally as an instance of the abstract syntax metamodel presented in Fig. 3 (using code generated by EMF). The tree table specifies the story elements (Nodes and Links) in each row and the Worlds on the columns. Each field determines if the element exists (a checkmark), does not exist (an x), or if it is left unspecified (an empty box); for each world column. The classes each story element instantiates, as well as the anti-rigid classes for the classification statements, can be defined in the list below the story elements panel.

3.4   Formal Narrative Generation

The generated narratives allow the assessment of what is possible according to the model's constraints, confronting the modeler and the stakeholders with the consequences of modeling choices. Counter-intuitive simulations of the story hints to modeling issues. Here we discuss a small sample of the issues that were identified in the simulation of our story and concern the quality of the conceptual model of Fig. 2.

Figure 5 shows the first world in a simulation of our story. It shows not only those elements explicitly mentioned in the natural language narrative but also reveals other elements which are required to exist given the conceptual model. We have noticed that, similar to Fig. 5, every single simulation of the story had in its first world simultaneous check-ins, check-outs and modifications. Inspecting the model closely, we found that the minimum cardinalities of several relations create a cycle of mandatory entities. This

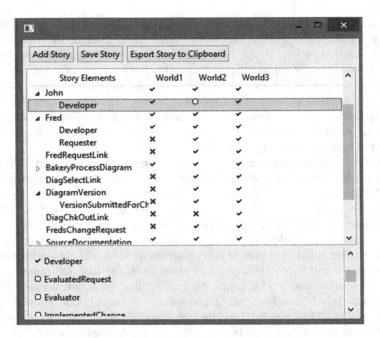

Fig. 4. The Formal Story Specification interface

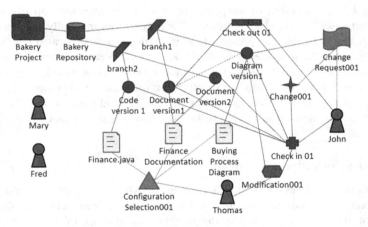

Fig. 5. The first world (snapshot) of a simulation

means that any check-in must be associated with a check-out. As a consequence, a brand-new repository with no check-outs cannot be represented in this model. Note that it is not the *story* that requires check-outs in the first world, but these elements were included in the formal narrative by *logical necessity* by the Alloy Analyzer in order to show as a simulation of the story that is conformant with the conceptual model. The cycle in the model was most likely not detected by the authors of [4]. Identifying this by inspecting the conceptual model directly is not trivial as it involves 10 classes and requires navigation of several relationships. Relaxing the minimum cardinalities would break the cycle.

Other issues concern role interaction. In Fig. 5, Thomas's modifications were checked in by John. Is this possible in the domain? If not, then the model is under constrained, which could be fixed by requiring the modifier of a checked-in version to be the same person that checked it out (e.g., we could write a temporal OCL invariant [9] reflecting this domain rule). Further, in Fig. 5, Thomas selects the configuration items but it is John who checks them in. Again, if needed, invariants could be required to specify that a person who selects items is the same who checks them in for the first time. Finally, in Fig. 5, the set of items that were selected together and checked-in together, have versions belonging to different branches, a situation which could be presented to domain experts in order to assess validity.

4 Related Work

There are many applications of storytelling and narratives in computer science, with many purposes different than ours (which is a posteriori assessment). [15] reviews some of these approaches. E.g. there are symbolic annotation tools [8], metadata for news stories [14] and means of assessing database systems [6]. One particular approach, Cucumber [16], share some of our goals by aiming to bridge communication between subject matter experts and developers. Differently from our approach, their technique consists of elaborating short stories that exemplify systems features with the purpose of driving development. The technique shows a promising direction for future work in expanding our approach to use stories to guide model development (and not only a posteriori assessment).

Other model transformations have been defined for OntoUML to other languages besides Alloy, including transformations to OWL [17] and SVBR [5]. The Alloy transformations were specified initially in [1, 3], and later merged and improved in [13]. We build on these previous approaches by allowing the modeler to guide the simulations and inspect them intentionally.

5 Final Considerations

We have presented a technique to incorporate storytelling in an existing model validation approach to improve communication between modelers and experts, as well as facilitating model assessment. Formalizing natural language narratives allows the simulation of the model for validation. Natural language narratives have details which are not represented in the conceptual model and the process of formalizing natural language narratives or interpreting formal narratives in terms of a natural language narrative adds detail to the interpretation of the theoretical logical constructs. Analyzing examples allows an intuitive understanding of the model and the consequences of abstract definitions. To analyze the model by itself one must unfold in their own mind the possibilities and interactions between classes. The mental workload of performing this analysis is offloaded to the Alloy Analyzer, shifting the focus of the modeler to the validation task.

While we have applied the approach on a number of models and performed qualitative evaluations, there is still work to be done on systematically evaluating the approach and specifying quality criteria that could be quantitatively measured.

Currently, there are limitations with respect to the scalability of the analysis, given that the approach based on the Alloy Analyzer becomes intractable when the size of the model grows. The tool we use allows the modeler to select fragments of a larger model for assessment to cope with that. However, further investigation is required to assess whether fragments of models are a sound basis for overall model assessment.

While the Alloy instance visualizer does provide customization of elements using different shapes and colors, further work is required to incorporate visualization techniques described in [2] to generate better diagrams. Further work also includes a reverse transformation from formal narratives to formal stories, allowing the use of a simulation as a template for the definition of a formal story.

Acknowledgments. This research is funded by the Brazilian Research Funding Agencies CNPq (grants number 311313/2014-0, 485368/2013-7 and 461777/2014-2) and CAPES/CNPq (402991/2012-5).

References

1. Benevides, A.B., Guizzardi, G., Braga, B.F.B., Almeida, J.P.A.: Validating modal aspects of OntoUML conceptual models using automatically generated visual world structures. J. Univ. Comput. Sci. **16**, 2904–2933 (2011)
2. Braga, B.F.B.: Cognitive effective instance diagram design. Graduation Thesis, Federal University of Espírito Santo (2011)
3. Braga, B.F.B., Almeida, J.P.A., Guizzardi, G., Benevides, A.B.: Transforming OntoUML into Alloy: towards conceptual model validation using a lightweight formal method. Innovations Syst. Softw. Eng. **6**, 55–63 (2010)
4. Calhau, R.F.: Uma Abordagem Baseada em Ontologias para a Integração Semântica de Sistemas, Master Thesis, Federal University of Espírito Santo (2011)
5. Carraretto, R.: A modeling infrastructure for OntoUML. Graduation Thesis, Federal University of Espírito Santo (2010)
6. Ciarlini, A.E.M., Furtado, A.L.: Understanding and simulating narratives in the context of information systems. In: Spaccapietra, S., March, S.T., Kambayashi, Y. (eds.) Conceptual Modeling - ER 2002. Proceedings 21st International Conference on Conceptual Modeling (ER), vol. 2503, pp. 291–306. Springer, Heidelberg (2002)
7. Donald, M.: Origins of the modern mind: Three stages in the evolution of culture and cognition Cambridge. Harvard University Press, MA (1991)
8. Elson, D.: Scheherazade. http://www.cs.columbia.edu/~delson/software.shtml
9. Guerson, J., Almeida, J.P.A.: Representing Dynamic Invariants in Ontologically Well-Founded Conceptual Models, 20th EMMSAD, Sweden (2015)
10. Guizzardi, G.: Ontological Foundations for Structural Conceptual Models. Telematica Instituut, The Netherlands (2005)

11. Jackson, D.: Software Abstractions-Logic, Language, and Analysis. The MIT Press, Cambridge (2012)
12. Mylopoulos, J.: Conceptual Modeling, Databases, and CASE: An Integrated View of Information Systems Development; Conceptual Modeling and Telos. Wiley, New York (1992)
13. Sales, T.P.: Ontology Validation for Managers, M.Sc. Thesis, Federal University of Espírito Santo, UFES (2014)
14. Wilton, P., Tarling, J., Mc Ginnins, J.: Storyline Ontology. http://www.bbc.co.uk/ontologies/storyline
15. Winer, D.: Review of ontology based storytelling devices. In: Dershowitz, N., Nissan, E. (eds.) Choueka Festschrift 2014, Part II. LNCS, vol. 8002, pp. 394–405. Springer, Heidelberg (2014)
16. Wynne, M., Hellesoy, A.: The cucumber book: behaviour-driven development for testers and developers. Pragmatic Bookshelf (2012)
17. Zamborlini, V., Guizzardi, G.: On the representation of temporally changing information in OWL. In: 14th IEEE International Enterprise Distributed Object Computing Conference Workshops (EDOCW), pp. 283–292. IEEE (2010)
18. Zimmerman, J.: Unit Testing. Principles of Imperative Computation (2012)

Improving Model Quality Through Foundational Ontologies: Two Contrasting Approaches to the Representation of Roles

Sergio de Cesare[1]([⊠]), Brian Henderson-Sellers[2], Chris Partridge[1,3], and Mark Lycett[1]

[1] Brunel University London, London, UK
{sergio.decesare, chris.partridge,
mark.lycett}@brunel.ac.uk
partridgec@borogroup.co.uk
[2] School of Software, University of Technology Sydney, Ultimo, Australia
brian.henderson-sellers@uts.edu.au
[3] BORO Solution Ltd., London, UK

Abstract. Several foundational ontologies have been developed recently. We examine two of these from the point of view of their quality in representing temporal changes, focusing on the example of roles. We discuss how these are modelled in two foundational ontologies: the Unified Foundational Ontology and the BORO foundational ontology. These exhibit two different approaches, endurantist and perdurantist respectively. We illustrate the differences using a running example in the university student domain, wherein one individual is not only a registered student but also, for part of this period, was elected the President of the Student Union. The metaphysical choices made by UFO and BORO lead to different representations of roles. Two key differences which affect the way roles are modelled are exemplified in this paper: (1) different criteria of identity and (2) differences in the way individual objects extend over time and possible worlds. These differences impact upon the quality of the models produced in terms of their respective explanatory power. The UFO model concentrates on the notion of validity in "all possible worlds" and is unable to accurately represent the way particulars are extended in time. The perdurantist approach is best able to describe temporal changes wherein roles are spatio-temporal extents of individuals.

Keywords: 3D and 4D ontologies · Metaphysical choices · Endurantism · Perdurantism · Presentism · Eternalism · Foundational ontology · Representation of temporality · Roles · BORO · UFO

1 Introduction

Traditional conceptual and design modelling, especially that using the object-oriented approach, uses class icons to represent classes of things in the real world. These include general types of things, such as roles, which repeatedly appear in models. For example, there will be many models with a class icon for the role Student. However, there is little

© Springer International Publishing Switzerland 2015
M.A. Jeusfeld and K. Karlapalem (Eds.): ER 2015 Workshops, LNCS 9382, pp. 304–314, 2015.
DOI: 10.1007/978-3-319-25747-1_30

infrastructure to support these general types of thing. In this paper, we focus on one example, the modelling of roles, which will illustrate the modelling of modality (how individual objects can possibly differ) and temporality (how individuals can change over time).

Foundational ontologies, which provide a complete list of the most general kinds of things, can provide this infrastructure. One way of characterising the foundational structures is metaphysical choices, and two choices that are relevant to modelling roles are the endurantist-perdurantist choice and the closely associated presentist-eternalist choice [1]. We also consider the 'modally extended versus unextended individuals' choice [1]. These choices have an impact on another important choice– what identity criteria there are.

The endurantist-perdurantist choice dictates whether, and how, particulars (individual things) are temporally extended. In endurantism (or 3D) an individual thing (e.g., John Smith) endures through time and is regarded as totally present at any moment in its lifetime. In perdurantism (or 4D) an individual thing perdures through time and is extended in time, and so can be said to be only partially present at any moment in time (e.g., the whole of *John Smith* extends over time from his birth to his death). The 'modally extended versus unextended individuals' choice considers, as the name suggests, whether and how they are extended across many possible worlds. We also look at spatial extension. The presentist-eternalist choice dictates whether and how objects exist in different ways in the past, present and future. The choice of identity criteria determines how one decides whether one is modelling one or more objects (for example, whether '*John as a child*' is the same object as '*John as an adult*'). Many modelling approaches, including UML, take no account of these (and the other) choices– and hence allow models that mix the choices in arbitrary and unstructured ways, with a detrimental effect on quality.

The paper examines two foundational ontologies that have made different clear choices and so mandate a particular way of modelling roles, in particular, and modality and temporality, in general. This provides two contrasting examples on how a foundational approach can raise the quality of role modelling.

UFO-A makes an endurantist choice [2], in which particulars are 'individual concepts' that are regarded as outside space, time and modality. These are then related to snapshots that are temporally and modally unextended– though they are spatially extended. To clarify, the snapshot is world-bound (i.e. in a particular world at a particular point in time). In contrast, a perdurantist approach such as BORO considers all particulars as having a temporal as well as a spatial extent, often referred to as 4D (e.g. [3–6]).

Both ontologies make an eternalist choice - adopting what McTaggert [7] calls the Series B view of time. This choice is noted to give context to the frameworks. As the two ontologies make the same choice, there is nothing to compare.

In modelling domains with no infrastructure for change over time, one particular contentious kind of entity is the role or roletype; this is intended to capture where a particular temporarily acquires one or more characteristics and may later shed them.

There are two broad choices, illustrated by the two sample ontologies, of an entity that might be regarded as a rigid basekind in an endurantist ontology. In traditional approaches, like UML, roles are essentially labels attached to a class representation – either as an end of association label (UML), as a class that is a specialization (in the OO sense) of a basekind (using UFO terminology) or as a class linked to a basekind with an association (e.g. [8]). Detailed discussions of various means of doing this are to be found in, for instance, [2, 9–11].

These choices are intimately related to the identity criteria issue [8]. This can be illustrated by considering the identity of collections. If one regards, for example, being a person as belonging to the collection of persons and being a student as the person belonging to the collection of students then, as in Fig. 1, the collections change over time. So in this approach, the membership of a collection is not fixed and so cannot simply be its identity criteria.

A different approach would be to regard being a person as belonging to the collection of persons and being a student as belonging to the collection of students – where student is a state of a person – a different object from the person. In this approach the collections are more like sets, and the identity criteria of the collection-set can be its members.

The two sample ontologies illustrate these choices. UFO takes the first approach where the person is a student. BORO takes the second approach, where a person has a (different) student state – and hence can adopt an extensional criterion of identity.

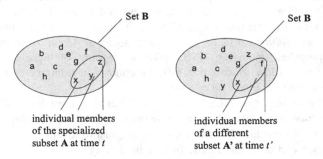

individual members
of the specialized
subset **A** at time t

individual members
of a different
subset **A'** at time t'

Fig. 1. Temporal changes in set members requires the creation of a new set (after [12])

Both endurantist and perdurantist approaches are arguably successful and acceptable philosophically. Some authors claim to need the adoption of one of these two approaches to the exclusion of the other, whilst other authors show more equanimity by accepting that the choice of approach depends upon the problem to be solved. Here, we discuss and compare two different ontological approaches: one predominantly endurantist (UFO) and one perdurantist (BORO).

In Sect. 2, we provide a brief overview of these ontological approaches. In Sect. 3, we describe a problem that is frequently encountered in information systems design and, in Sect. 4, apply each of the ontological approaches in turn to this problem. Our conclusions are then presented in Sect. 5.

2   Overview of the Two Foundational Ontologies

2.1   The Unified Foundational Ontology

The Unified Foundational Ontology (UFO) [2] has a number of parts, labelled UFO-A, UFO-B and UFO-C. We focus on UFO-A as it contains a class roles – though UFO has other types of roles. UFO-A is a 3D or endurantist foundational ontology. UFO-B contains perdurantist aspects mostly targeted at agent-oriented modelling; whilst UFO-C takes a first step towards a socially-focussed foundational ontology. UFO-A is depicted in Fig. 2, which shows the Kind and Role classes used to characterise roles.

Each of these classes in UFO represents some ontological aspect and leads to a particular commitment within a modelling approach. In particular, it means that we could have in our domain model classes such as Person:Kind, Student:Role and StudentPresident:Role.

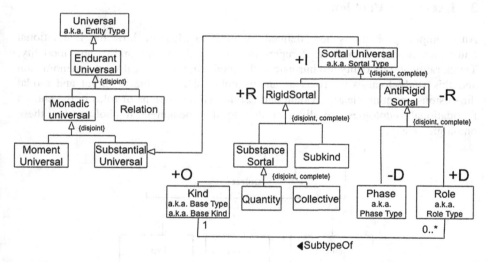

Fig. 2. The UFO-A hierarchy of Universals, focussing on the subtypes of Endurant Universal (adapted from diagrams in [2]) where I, R, D and O refer to the metaproperties (as defined in [13]) of identity condition, rigidity, external dependency and identity provision

In UFO, Kind and Role classes obtain identity criteria in different ways. Instances of Kind supply identity. Role types (instances of RoleType) carry identity and not supply it [2], they obtain their identity from Kinds. In UFO a Student obtains identity, by specializing a base kind such as Person. We take this model as most representative of UFO as practised [2, 11]. This is the representation that will be examined in the case of our exemplar in Sect. 4.

2.2 Boro

BORO [3] is an extensionalist 4D foundational ontology, which has been used extensively for software applications [14, 15]. The relevant subset (for the example) is visualised in Fig. 3 using UML.

The top object within the BORO foundational ontology is Object (a.k.a. Thing), which has everything that exists as instances. The ontology has three major ontological categories: Element, Type and Tuple. Every object belongs to one and only one of the three categories, which have their own identity criteria. For example, an element is a particular/physical entity whose identity is given by its spatio-temporal extent. A type is a collection (set) of objects (playing a similar role to universals). A type can collect any type of object (in other words, objects of any of the three categories). Tuples relate objects. For the example, the key relationship is *temporalWholePart*; this relates an individual with its temporal parts (states and/or events).

3 Exemplar Problem

An exemplar problem is here defined in order to illustrate how the foundational ontologies described in Sect. 2 represent roles, and so temporality and modality. Temporality and modality are intrinsic to the modelling of any real world phenomenon and this study focuses on roles as an exemplar since (1) the temporal and modal dimensions are quite clearly evident and (2) the representations of roles in the chosen foundational ontologies are different due to the metaphysical choices that these ontologies make.

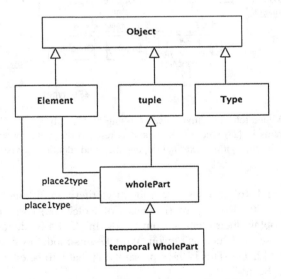

Fig. 3. BORO foundational ontology (partial view).

Role, as defined by the Oxford Advanced Learner Dictionary, is "the function assumed or part played by a person or thing in a particular situation". Examples include president, student, employee, patient, parent, spouse and so on. A role normally initiates with a specific event and terminates with another event. These events can occur on the basis of laws (e.g., election of members of Parliament), agreements (e.g., contract of employment) or natural events (e.g., the birth of a child). Roles can even be played by non-humans, for example a software system responsible for carrying out a specific task in a business process (e.g., a credit scoring system). Moreover, a person or a thing can play several roles at once (e.g., mother, employee and student).

The exemplar problem has been defined to focus on the key characteristics of roles and is described as follows:

"John enrols as a university student in Chemistry and graduates three years later. He is elected President of the Students Union (PSU) during his degree serving for one year."

The following section will present models of this exemplar problem with the chosen foundational ontologies, identifying their strengths and weaknesses.

4   Problem Analysis

4.1   Representation of the Student Role

4.1.1   UFO

Utilizing the UFO, as an underpinning foundational ontology to model the problem statement of Sect. 3, results in the model described in Fig. 4. In UFO, roles are modelled as subtypes of an instance of Kind. In this problem, both Student and the PSU (President of the Student Union) are role types. These roles obtain their identity from Person – the base kind in this model. Initially we focus on Student, which is represented in Fig. 4.

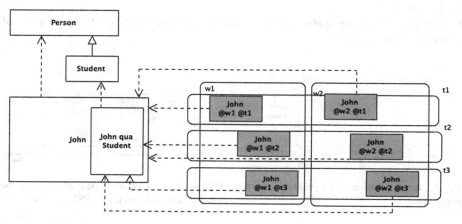

Fig. 4. Representation of the problem statement according to UFO (Legend: @w_1 means 'at possible world 1'; @t_1 means 'at time t_1')

In the fragment of the example shown in Fig. 4, John is an individual that obtains its identity by virtue of being an instance of the base kind Person. He also is an instance of the role Student – note that as discussed in Sect. 1, the same thing is both a person and a student. The way in which these differ is that John is always an instance of Person, but only an instance of Student at some times in some worlds – because it is possible that John was never a student, and even in worlds where he was a student, there will be some times where he was not a student. For any world and time, one can ask and so determine whether John is a student [2] (p. 276) – another way of expressing this is that there are some world-bound time-slices of John that are snapshot instances of John qua Student, and others that are not. We have tried to illustrate this in Fig. 6 above by having a 'John qua Student' box inside the 'John' box. This is not intended to imply that there are two entities – John and John qua Student – but to have an owner for the snapshot instantiations of John qua Student.

To illustrate how this works, consider how one would determine the duration of the John's studentship. One would first have to fix a world (as the duration could be completely different in different possible worlds – in one world he could be student early in life in another late in life). Then, within that world, one would determine the times when John was a student, and the lower and upper bounds of the times would give the duration.

As UFO makes an eternalist choice, there is no distinction made between the past, present and future 'versions' of John and John qua Student. As it makes an endurantist choice, John is not temporally extended. In this approach, it makes no sense to ask about the temporal extent of John, nor about the modal and spatial extents. The question makes more sense for the world-bound snapshot timeslices. These have a spatial extent, but no temporal or modal extent. One result of this is that there is only one entity John; there is no separate John qua Student entity. Hence, John can inherit identity criteria from Person; and John qua Student, as the same entity, has the same identity criteria.

4.1.2   BORO

In BORO elements are spatio-temporal extents; roles are (types of) temporal parts of elements – often called states.

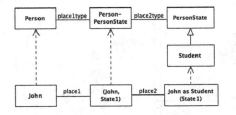
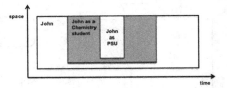

Fig. 5. Representation of the problem statement using BORO

Fig. 6. Example space-time map showing the role student and additional PSU subrole

Figure 5a exemplifies this for John. Here Student is a subtype of PersonState and Person is related to PersonState. John is an instance of Person and there is a state (temporal stage) of John that is an instance of Student.

Since BORO elements are extended in space and time, they can be visualised in a space-time map, where each element's spatial extent is depicted on the x-axis and temporal extent on the y-axis. Figure 5b provides an example based on our scenario. As the space-time map makes clear, the duration of John's studentship is determined by the temporal boundaries of John's Student state.

As BORO (like UFO) makes an eternalist choice, there is no distinction made between the past, present and future 'versions' of John or of the Student state. As it makes a perdurantist choice, John is temporally extended, as well as spatially extended. John is not modally extended, but world-bound to a particular possible world. In BORO modality is handled through a counterpart relation.

Note that as discussed in Sect. 1, in BORO, there are two entities, John and John's Student state. This enables the use of spatio-temporal extents as identity criteria.

4.2 Subroles Versus Subtypes

The metaphysical choices described above also lead to less obvious differences in the ways which roles are modelled. This can be illustrated with the second part of the example, in which John is President of the Student Union (or PSU Occupation). In this example, only a person who is a student can be elected as PSU. It is a case of a role of roles. The following subsections compare UFO and BORO. The former considers PSU Occupation as a subtype of the Student role, whereas the latter represents it as a subrole (with temporal whole-parts). In both examples, PSU Occupation is compared to the role of being a Chemistry Student, where Chemistry Student is a sub-type (rather than sub-role) of Student. What is at issue here, is that (as far as the example is concerned), if one is a Chemistry Student, then one is always a Chemistry Student when one is a student. However, while one is a Student one can sometime be a PSU and sometimes not.

4.2.1 UFO

Figure 6a is the UFO representation of PSU Occupation and Chemistry Student. Both roles are subtypes of Student and, like Student, they are anti-rigid sortals whose principle of identity is inherited from the base kind Person. The subtyping of a rigid sortal by an anti-rigid sortal is permitted in UFO but not when adhering to the OCL constraints specified in the UML. Furthermore, as seen in Fig. 6a, the introduction of a (true) subtype of Student, say ChemistryStudent, utilizes the same subsumption notation – but (presumably) with different semantics to that of the PSU-Student relationship.

Architecturally, this is because the qua mechanism is between rigid and anti-rigid classes, and so an anti-rigid class cannot be, so to speak, anti-anti-rigid (or a quaQuaIndividual. A different mechanism is needed.

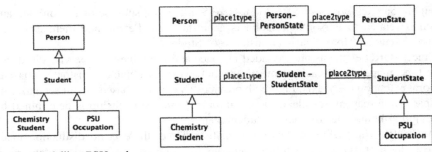

Fig. 7. Modelling PSU and ChemistryStudent in UFO

Fig. 8. Modelling PSU and ChemistryStudent in in BORO

4.2.2 BORO

Figure 6b is the BORO representation of PSU Occupation and Chemistry Student. These two roles are not modelled in the same way. Since individual objects (elements) are spatio-temporally extended in BORO, we must consider the extension of the elements that instantiate the type. In fact, as Fig. 5b illustrates, John-as-PSU is spatio-temporally contained within John as a Chemistry Student (see also Fig. 5b). John as a Student and John as a Chemistry Student are the same extent since John is a Chemistry student during his whole studentship. Hence, while the type ChemistryStudent is a subtype of Student, since all instances of the former are always instances of the latter, PSUOccupation is a subtype of StudentState and related to Student via a whole-part relation. Therefore PSUOccupation is modelled as a subrole of the role Student. BORO can take advantage of the different types of relation (sub-type and temporal part) to characterise the difference between sub-types and sub-roles of roles.

4.3 Comparative Analysis

BORO's and UFO's choices lead to quite a different account of what entities exist. If one applies that basic ontological test of counting and comparing entities, one gets very different answers. In UFO there is just John (who is identical to John qua Student and John qua PSU), in BORO there are three elements with their own identity (spatio-temporal extents) John, John's Student state and John as PSU.

In UFO, the instance of Person and Student is the same object - John – across all possible worlds in which John exists. John, his studentships and his presidencies in this world and across possible worlds and times are characterised through the use of world- and time-bounded snapshots. Given there are an infinite number of worlds and times to play with, there are an infinite number of snapshots.

In BORO John, his studentships and his presidencies are all distinct objects. They have counterparts in other possible worlds. As there are an infinite number of possible worlds (as noted above), there are an infinite number of counterparts.

UFO builds upon the intuition that a student is a way of being rather than a different thing – so John qua Student is John being a Student. BORO builds upon the intuition that the same thing cannot be different at different times, and so John's student stage is not exactly the same as John, but a temporal-part. One can start to see a connection between these two positions if you regard Armstrong's view [16] that parthood is partial identity (and temporal parthood a strong form of partial identity. So the states of John are partially, but not completely identical to John.

However, as illustrated in the second part of the example, UFO's architectural choices make it less easy to characterise sub-roles (roles of roles). Moreover the explanatory power of BORO is enhanced by the temporal whole-part relationships that underpin its mereology. As shown in Sect. 4.2.2, roles of roles are modelled simply by adopting the whole-part pattern of the foundational ontology. In UFO, since PSUOccupation is merely modelled as a subtype of Student, then the representation lacks in being able to show that being a PSU is the state of a student and not a student.

This analysis is not aimed at establishing the superiority of one approach over the other, but instead the superiority of making explicit the meta-ontological choices made. If this is done, then it is possible for conceptual modellers to create more understandable models and better quality modelling languages because there is an agreed common grounding which modellers can refer to. As a consequence, conceptual models are more self-explanatory, hence higher quality. Where the meta-ontological choices are known, then the model is capable of expressing much more of its own semantics to the reader, without recourse to the authors.

5 Summary and Conclusions

We have examined the way in which two foundational ontologies improve the model quality by providing a general architectural infrastructure for roles. We have characterised the architectures in terms of key metaphysical choices [17]. We used an illustrative example, to show how roles are modelled in quite different ways in the Unified Foundational Ontology (endurantist) and the BORO foundational ontology (perdurantist). Our running example is in the university student domain, wherein one individual is not only a registered student but also, for part of this period, the President of the Student Union. By examining the PSU role, we have shown how quite subtle differences can emerge between the choices by looking at how both ontologies handle the requirement for a role of a role. Given the need for conceptual modelling to improve its quality with more general infrastructure for things such as roles, hopefully this paper has raised awareness of the need to architect this infrastructure using, for example, metaphysical choices and to be aware of the consequences of these choices. As an aside, where there is no architecting, these choices are still being made, but in a heterogeneous and random way, so there is no management of the consequences of the choices and a consequent reduction in quality.

Acknowledgements. The work was supported by the UK Engineering and Physical Sciences Research Council (grant EP/K009923/1).

References

1. Partridge, C.: Note: A Couple of Meta-ontological Choices for Ontological Architectures. Technical Report 06/02, LADSEB-CNR, Padova, Italy (2002)
2. Guizzardi, G.: Ontological Foundations for Structural Conceptual Models. CTIT Ph.D. Thesis Series, No. 05–74, Enschede, The Netherlands (2005)
3. Partridge, C.: Business Objects: Re-Engineering for Re-Use. Butterworth-Heinemann (1996)
4. Sider, T.: Four-Dimensionalism: An Ontology of Persistence and Time. Oxford UniverCity Press, Oxford (2002)
5. West, M.: Roles: a four-dimensional analysis. In: Borgo, S., Lesmo, L. (eds.) Formal Ontologies Meet Industry, pp. 45–55. IOS Press (2008)
6. Zamborlini, V., Guizzardi, G.: On the representation of temporally changing information in OWL. In: Proceeding of the 14th IEEE International Enterprise Distributed Object Computing Conference Workshops, pp. 283–292. IEEE Computer Society Press (2010)
7. McTaggart, J.E.: The unreality of time. Mind **17**(4), 457–474 (1908)
8. Henderson-Sellers, B., Eriksson, O., Agerfalk, P.J.: On the need for identity in ontology-based conceptual modelling. In: Saeki, M., Kohler, H. (eds.) Proceedings of the 11th Asia-Pacific Conference on Conceptual Modelling (APCCM 2015) Sydney, Australia. CRPIT, 165. ACS, pp. 9–20 (2015)
9. Wieringa, R., de Jonge, W., Spruit, P.: Using dynamic classes and role classes to model object migration. Theor. Pract. Object Syst. **1**(1), 31–83 (1995)
10. Steimann, F.: On the representation of roles in object-oriented and conceptual modelling. Data Knowl. Eng. **35**, 83–106 (2000)
11. Guizzardi, G.: Agent roles, qua individuals and *the Counting Problem*. In: Garcia, A., Choren, R., Lucena, C., Giorgini, P., Holvoet, T., Romanovsky, A. (eds.) SELMAS 2005. LNCS, vol. 3914, pp. 143–160. Springer, Heidelberg (2006)
12. Henderson-Sellers, B., Eriksson, O., Gonzalez-Perez, C., Ågerfalk, P.J.: Ptolemaic metamodelling? The need for a paradigm shift. In: Garcia Diaz, V., Cueva Lovelle, J.M., Pelayo García-Bustelo, B.C., Sanjuán Martínez, O. (eds.): Progressions and Innovations in Model-Driven Software Engineering. IGI Global, Hershey, PA, USA, pp. 90–146 (2013)
13. Guarino, N., Welty, C.A.: A formal ontology of properties. In: Dieng, R., Corby, O. (eds.) EKAW 2000. LNCS (LNAI), vol. 1937, pp. 97–112. Springer, Heidelberg (2000)
14. IDEAS Group: The IDEAS Model. http://www.ideasgroup.org/foundation/. 22 May 2015
15. de Cesare, S., Foy, G., Partridge, C.: Re-engineering Data with 4D ontologies and graph databases. In: Franch, X., Soffer, P. (eds.) CAiSE Workshops 2013. LNBIP, vol. 148, pp. 304–316. Springer, Heidelberg (2013)
16. Armstrong, D.M.: Universals. An Opinionated Introduction. Westview, Boulder (1989)
17. Partridge, C., Mitchell, A., de Cesare, S.: Guidelines for developing ontological architectures in modelling and simulation. In: Tolk, A. (ed.) CAiSE Workshops 2013. ISRL, vol. 44, pp. 27–57. Springer, Heidelberg (2012)

Conceptual Modeling Education

Preface to the 3rd Symposium on Conceptual Modeling Education (SCME 2015)

The 3rd Symposium on Conceptual Modeling Education (SCME 2015) provides a forum for discussing the education and teaching of concepts related to conceptual modeling, methods and tools for developing and communicating conceptual models, techniques for transforming conceptual models into effective implementations, case studies of interesting projects, and pedagogies of modeling education for our next generation.

We received six papers in response to the call for papers, each of which went through a thorough review process with two reviews from the SCME chairs. Four of the submissions were selected for inclusion in the workshop proceedings:

- "Challenges in Teaching Conceptual Modeling for Architecting", Gerrit Muller.
- "Effects of Simulation on Novices' Understanding of the Concept of Inheritance in Conceptual Modeling", Gayane Sedrakyan and Monique Snoeck.
- "The Importance of Teaching Systematic Analysis for Conceptual Models: An Experience Report", Elda Paja, Jennifer Horkoff and John Mylopoulos.
- "Reuse of Simulated Cases in Teaching Enterprise Modelling", Ilia Bider, Martin Henkel, Stewart Kowalski and Erik Perjons.

In addition, the symposium also included an invited keynote "The Role of Ontological Analysis in Educating to Conceptual Modeling", presented by Nicola Guarino (University of Trento, Italy), a leading expert in conceptual modeling.

We would like to thank all authors who submitted papers to SCME 2015 for their efforts in promoting education in conceptual modeling. Our most sincere appreciation also to Nicola Guarino for accepting to give the keynote. Finally, we are also grateful to the ER General Chairs, Paul Johanesson and Andreas Opdahl, and to the ER 2015 Workshop Chairs, Manfred Jeusfeld and Kamalakar Karlapalem, for their help in organizing the Symposium and for their advice in the difficult task of attracting submissions.

We do hope that the interesting contributions of SCME 2015 to conceptual modeling education have raised the reader's interest to have a closer look at the workshop proceedings as well as to foster the contribution for future editions of the SCME Symposium.

Giancarlo Guizzardi
Ernest Teniente
Program Co-Chairs
SCME'15

Challenges in Teaching Conceptual Modeling for Systems Architecting

Gerrit Muller[✉]

HBV, Kongsberg, Norway
Gerrit.muller@hbv.no

Abstract. Systems architecting requires systems architects that are able to understand, reason, communicate and make decisions about system specification and design. Systems architects use multiple views on a system and its context to achieve that. Systems architecting uses conceptual modeling as tool for understanding, reasoning, communication and decision making.

After ten years of teaching, we reflect on the challenges of teaching the conceptual modeling ability to practitioners in companies. We find that we have to stretch participants multifold to let them evolve from designer into systems architect and conceptual modeler.

Keywords: Systems architecting · System context · Competence · Teaching

1 Introduction

Many companies need systems architects who are able to lead development projects to ensure that specifications, design, and implementation satisfy stakeholders' needs and expectations. In the past ten years, we have taught systems architecting courses in companies and at universities. These systems architecting courses teach conceptual modeling as means for systems architecting.

Many of these companies realize that the systems architecting competence requires hard and soft skills and significant experience. Typically, these companies compose an educational program consisting of some technical depth, systems architecting methods and mindset, and soft skills. Systems architecting courses teaching conceptual modeling typically fit in such broader program.

We observe that the entire systems architecting training program continuously stretches the majority of participants. We have to challenge participants to get them out of their comfort zone and out of their original mental paradigms.

In this paper, we discuss the challenges of teaching conceptual modeling in this context. Section 2 explains the broad meaning of systems architecting. Section 3 elaborates how conceptual modeling supports the systems architecting efforts. Section 4 discusses the teaching challenges.

© Springer International Publishing Switzerland 2015
M.A. Jeusfeld and K.Karlapalem (Eds.): ER 2015 Workshops, LNCS 9382, pp. 317–326, 2015.
DOI: 10.1007/978-3-319-25747-1_31

2   Systems Architecting and Systems Architecting Challenges

Rechtin and Maier [1] provide a foundation for Systems architecting in the book "The Art of Systems Architecting". The systems architecting activity has as purpose to create and maintain an systems architecture that ensures that systems and their designs fulfill stakeholder needs and expectations. Figure 1 visualizes a top-view on systems architecture, where we decomposed stakeholder needs in customer value proposition and business proposition. These propositions drive the system requirements that in turn drive the system design. Vice versa, design and requirements enable customer value and business propositions.

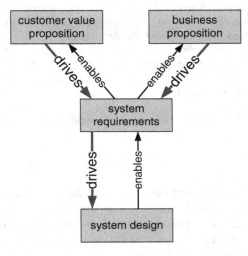

Fig. 1. Systems architecture top-view, relating customer value and business proposition to system requirements to system design

TRIZ [2] positions the system of interest in a 3 by 3 matrix, as shown in Fig. 2 right-hand side. In this matrix, the vertical direction is the system scope. The system of interest is part of a larger super system (shown above). The system-of-interest itself is partitioned in subsystems (shown below). The horizontal dimension I the time axis, running from past to future. Figure 2 adds at the left-hand side the organization that dominates the system scope. For the system-of-interest that is the developing organization, while the customer organization owns and operates the super system.

A typical challenge in developing systems is that we have knowledge from past systems that we like to re-use for future systems. However, innovation may require other and new knowledge than the knowledge from the past.

Figure 3 overlays Fig. 2 with systems architecture that captures and guides past, current, and future, and super system, system, and subsystems. All organizations contribute to the systems architecting activity, with the systems architect as owner and conductor of the systems architecting activity.

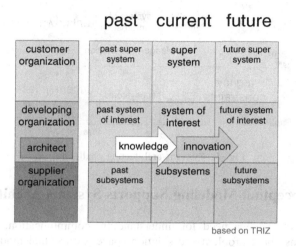

Fig. 2. The current system of interest in broader perspective

Figure 4 annotates Fig. 2 with challenges for the systems architecting activity. The past systems bring legacy constraints. The broad context of the system in the super system and its related organizations are complex and large; size and complexity are significant challenges for systems architecting. The broader world of super systems is heterogeneous in stakeholders, and their concerns and needs. These stakeholders tend to express themselves ambiguous. Moving into the future opens a new unknown world full of uncertainties.

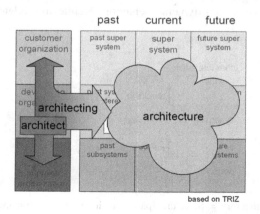

Fig. 3. The systems architecture as overarching description

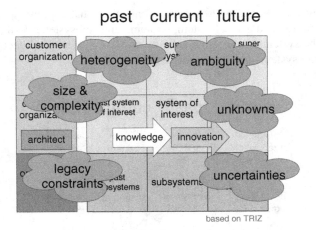

Fig. 4. Systems architecting challenges

3 How Conceptual Modeling Supports Systems Architecting

Systems architects have a need for understanding, communication, reasoning, and making decisions about problem and solution space. Conceptual modeling is a good tool to support these needs [3, 4]. Bonnema [5] describes how systems architecting benefits from modeling, using key drivers and quantified technical budgets. Borches [6] combines the use of conceptual modeling with A3 s to create compact A3 Architecture Overviews. Muller, Wee, and Moberg [7] describe an example of the results of teaching conceptual modeling and A3 s.

Bonnema [5] and Borches [6] describe three core views in systems architecture descriptions: parts, dynamics (functionality), and quantified characteristics, see Fig. 5. We observe that many stakeholders in the developing organization think and act on the structure (the parts and the interfaces). However, the prime interests of customers are the capabilities they get from the system. Capabilities are (quantified) performance characteristics and the related dynamic behavior. Architecture relates these views.

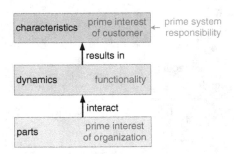

Fig. 5. Systems architecture = Structure (parts and interfaces) + dynamics + characteristics; Conceptual Modeling captures these relations

Since 2005, we have been teaching courses in architectural reasoning at companies and universities. Figure 6 shows the core principle, objectives, and recommendations in these courses. The main principles behind the approach are feedback (do we move in the proper direction, does our solution solve the problem) and being explicit (make issues tangible by being explicit, for example by quantifying).

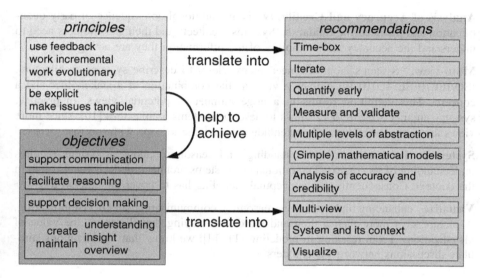

Fig. 6. Recommendation for Conceptual Modeling

These principles help to achieve our main objectives of understanding, communication, reasoning, and decision making. The principles and recommendations translate into a concrete set of recommendations.

Time-box and Iterate. We translate the principle of feedback is into an approach where modelers spend a limited amount of time on a topic. However, they revisit the topic many times (iteration) to include insights gained from other topics; see [8].

Quantify Early. We translate the principle of being explicit into early quantification. The idea is that quantification forces designers to be explicit; discussing a number brings sharpness in the discussion. However, stakeholders should be aware of the limitations of quantification in early phases. Numbers may and probably will change, and they need validation.

Measure and Validate. The early quantification benefits from measurements (what is current practice) and validation (what evidence and arguments do we have for the numbers).

Multiple Levels of Abstraction are countermeasures for size and complexity. In fact, abstraction is the core of conceptual modeling. However, a challenge is to connect high-level abstractions to lower-level abstractions, such that the systems architecture offers concrete guidance to designers and engineers.

Simple Mathematical Models are instrumental for being explicit and for understanding and reasoning about problems and solutions. Mathematical formulas capture relations between parts and components in such way that we can reason about these relations.

Analysis of Accuracy and Credibility is an additional consequence of early quantification and the need for validation. Systems architects and their stakeholders need to understand the accuracy and credibility of the information they are acting on.

Multi-view. Systems architects need many views to describe systems architecture. ISO/IEC/IEEE 42010 [9] defines a view as the combination of a stakeholder and a concern. This definition results in a large number of potential views. In practice, systems architects use 8 to 12 views to describe systems architecture [10], since more views are not manageable and stakeholders are unable to cope with too many views.

System in its Context. Understanding and reasoning about a system requires understanding of its context. The rationale of systems architecture decisions is often in the context. Consequently, the conceptual modeling has to cover the context too.

Visualize enhancing understanding, reasoning, communication, and decision-making. A picture says more than a thousand words is a saying that illustrates the value of visualizations. From research in modeling [11–14], we know that visualizations stimulate discussions between stakeholders.

4   The Current Educational Approach

The course format has evolved over the past 10 years. The core of the format, however, has stayed the same over all these years. The course primarily stimulates participants to experience the views and various modeling techniques by applying them in the classroom with guidance from the teacher. The teacher offers small nuggets of theory followed by an assignment of 15 to 40 min (time-boxes). The participants preferably use a case from their daily work environment, since these cases suffer from "real-world" complexity as shown in Fig. 4. The only exception is the first assignment, where we use an elevator example explaining essential aspects of conceptual modeling, as described in [15], such as the need for complementary models. Figure 7 shows the various conceptual models and visualizations that we use in this elevator example. The parts, dynamics, and (quantified) characteristics are all present.

The assignments guide the participants through three iterations for their case to let them experience the growth and evolution of their case insight. The first iteration, covering supersystem, system, and subsystem level, makes 6 steps of 15 min to explore the "playing field" with a focus on the current situation. Following two iterations make 5 to 6 steps of 20 to 40 min with a focus on extending the system in functionality or performance. These longer time-boxes allow some elaboration per model. The participants work during all assignments on flip charts, which they attach to the wall. In this way, the case "grows" on the wall, helping participants to see all views and the increasing insight in many related aspects; see Fig. 8 for a typical classroom setting.

The final step is integration and convergence of all steps into a limited set of lines of reasoning, to create overview. This last step is quite challenging for the participants. All earlier steps create some information or insight. After so many steps and 3 iterations, the amount and variety of information tends to overwhelm participants. In this last step, they have to recover the overview by selecting the most relevant information form systems architecting perspective.

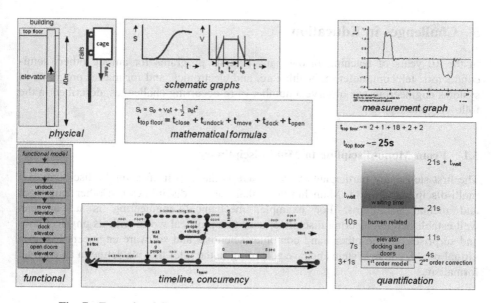

Fig. 7. Example of Conceptual Models and Visualizations from an Elevator

Fig. 8. A typical class room during the course

In the homework after the course, participants elaborate the models they made in the classroom. However, outside the classroom, they can easier access knowledge in their company and validate or correct earlier assumptions. They transform most models from flip chart to electronic diagrams, for example in PowerPoint or Visio. Again, the most challenging step is ordering the models in a "T-shape" presentation. A T-shape presentation is a presentation that guides the audience top-down through the case, starting broad in setting the context, explaining solution options in depth, and concluding broad by showing impact and recommendations. The challenge in this last is to make the mental shift from chaotic divergence to structured convergence.

5   Challenges in Education

In the 10 years of teaching in company specific programs for among others semi-conductors, telecom, defense, health care, and electronics, and for master programs in systems engineering, we observe a number of re-occurring challenges, described in the following subsections.

5.1   From Mono-discipline to Multi-disciplinary

The first step many participants have to take is the step from a single discipline to a multi-disciplinary world. Main hurdle is that various disciplines use other languages and mental paradigms. For example, mechanical engineering is a concrete, well-established engineering discipline, used to a physical world with its physical laws and surprises. At the other hand computer scientists and software engineers live in a virtual world, where systems behave according to the rules that we define in an abstract formalism.

5.2   From Multi-disciplinary to System

Initially, engineers have the impression that systems are simply the sum of the various contributing disciplines. However, once they have experienced emergence of behavior and properties, they start to see that systems engineering is a discipline in itself with its own methods and techniques.

5.3   From System to Customer and Life Cycle Context

Next step is that designers and engineers have to zoom out further and enter the context of the system. We distinguish the customer context (the context where the system is in operational use) and the life cycle context from conception to decommissioning. The evolution of a system throughout its lifecycle tends to be a revelation. The exploration in the customer context brings a confrontation with all non-technical aspects, especially human factors.

5.4   From Static to Dynamic

Many stakeholders with the developing organization think about the system in static terms: its structure of parts and interfaces. For some of them the static understanding is sufficient, e.g. for purchasing. However, for anyone who needs to understand merging system behavior and performance, the dynamic interaction is crucial. We experience that understanding and reasoning about dynamic behavior is challenging for a significant amount of the participants.

5.5   From Qualitative to Quantitative

Many participants hesitate to quantify. Uncertainty (we do not know yet) partially drives the hesitation. Partially, fear for misuse by stakeholders drives the avoidance of quantification. Participants have to learn to make assumptions (and validate them later) to make progress in understanding and reasoning. Participants who stay qualitative may discover too late that they have been working in the wrong direction.

5.6   From Well-Defined to Ill-Defined

Every step from designer to systems architect decreases the degree of certainty in the problem definition. Mentally, participants need to grow an acceptance to act in a problem and solution space that is ill defined in many aspects.

5.7   From Technical to Human and Nature

When moving from the world of technical design to the context with humans and physical environment, humans and nature confront the participants with major surprises. Especially the humans open a world where participants need other (softer) methods and techniques.

5.8   From Reactive to Proactive and Critical

Lastly, the role of systems architect (and conceptual modeler) requires a proactive and critical attitude. Good systems architects are obsessed with the need to understand and the ability to reason. Systems architects need to challenge assumptions and question requirements. Additional challenge is to be critical in a constructive way, such that guides and leads the team.

6   Conclusions

Conceptual modeling is a natural tool for systems architecting. Systems architecture descriptions consist of a collection of conceptual models. Teaching conceptual modeling to (potential) systems architects is necessary. However, participants have to take many hurdles to make the step from designer to systems architect and conceptual modeler.

References

1. Rechtin, E., Maier, M.: The Art of Systems Architecting. CRC Press, Boca Raton (1997)
2. Altshuller, G.: The Innovation Algorithm; TRIZ, systematic innovation and technical creativity. Technical Innovation Center, Worcester, MA. Translated, edited and annotated by Lev Shulyak and Steven Rodman (2000)
3. Robinson, S.: Conceptual Modelling: Who Needs It? SCS M&S Magazine 2010/n2 (April). http://www.scs.org/magazines/2010-04/index_file/Files/Robinson.pdf
4. Davies, I., Green, P., Rosemann, M., Indulska, M., Gallo, S.: How do practitioners use conceptual modeling in practice? Data Knowl. Eng. 4(1), 4–13 (2005)
5. Bonnema, G.M.: FunKey Architecting - An Integrated Approach to System Architecting Using Functions, Key Drivers and System Budgets, Ph.D. thesis University of Twente (2008)
6. Borches, D.: A3 architecture overviews: a tool for effective communication in product evolution, Ph.D. thesis University of Twente (2010)
7. Muller, G., Wee, D., Moberg M.: Creating an A3 Architecture Overview; a Case Study in SubSea Systems, INCOSE 2015 in Seattle
8. Muller, G.: System and context modeling – the role of time-boxing and multi-view iteration. Syst. Res. Forum 3(2), 139–152 (2009)
9. ISO/IEC/IEEE 42010:2011 - Systems and software engineering - Architecture description Iso.org. 2011-11-24. Retrieved 2013-08-06
10. System Architecture Forum whitepaper: Architectural Descriptions and Models (2006). http://architectingforum.org/whitepapers/SAF_WhitePaper_2006_2.pdf
11. Engebakken, E., Muller, G., Pennotti, M.: Supporting the system architect: model-assisted communication. Syst. Res. Forum 4(2), 173–188 (2010)
12. Rypdal, R.W., Muller, G., Pennotti, M.: Developing the Modeling Recommendation Matrix: Model-Assisted Communication at Volvo Aero, INCOSE 2012 in Rome
13. Polanscak, E.: Supporting Product Development: A3 as a tool to capture and visualize Architecture knowledge sharing/A3-assisted Communication and Documentation, master project paper at HBV (2011)
14. Stalsberg, B., Muller, G.: Increasing the value of model-assisted communication: Modeling for understanding, exploration and verification in production line design projects. In: Proceedings of the INCOSE 2014, Las Vegas, July 2014
15. Muller, G.: Teaching conceptual modeling at multiple system levels using multiple views, CIRP 2014 in Milano

Effects of Simulation on Novices' Understanding of the Concept of Inheritance in Conceptual Modeling

Gayane Sedrakyan[✉] and Monique Snoeck

Management Information Systems, Katholieke Universiteit Leuven,
Naamsestraat 69, 3000 Leuven, Belgium
{gayane.sedrakyan,monique.snoeck}@kuleuven.be

Abstract. In this paper we present our experience in the experimental development and use of simulation instrument for learning object-oriented conceptual modeling in a master level course on analysis and design of information systems. The focus of our research is on the teaching of one particular topic in object-oriented conceptual modeling - *inheritance*. The results from the pilot experimental study (with a student sample N = 32), demonstrate a positive effect of simulation-based learning method on the understanding by novice business analysts of the concept of inheritance when applied in a conceptual model.

Keywords: Teaching conceptual modeling · Object-oriented analysis · Inheritance · Simulation-based learning · Automated feedback

1 Introduction

Modern software engineering builds largely on object-oriented (OO) paradigm [1, 2] that aims to incorporate the advantages of modularity and reusability. In the OO approach requirements are organized around cooperating objects that belong to hierarchically constructed classes which encapsulate both structure and behavior [3, 4]. The possibility of software reuse during the development lifecycle being not just a matter of reusing the code of a subroutine, but also encompassing the reuse of any commonality expressed in class hierarchies [5], was among the important reasons promoting the rapid growth of this paradigm during the last decades. Consequently object-oriented analysis (OOA) and design (OOD) have emerged to support the use of object-oriented paradigm throughout the entire software engineering lifecycle [2]. This has been supported by the introduction of a unified notation and OO modeling (OOM) language (the Unified Modeling Language (UML)) being currently heavily used in OOA and OOD activities.

One major advantage introduced by the object oriented paradigm is the conceptual continuity across all phases of the software development lifecycle, i.e. the conceptual structure of the software system remains the same, from system analysis down through implementation [5]. Therefore when the object-oriented paradigm is used, the design phase is linked more closely to the system analysis and the implementation phases because designers have to deal with similar abstract concepts (such as classes and

© Springer International Publishing Switzerland 2015
M.A. Jeusfeld and K. Karlapalem (Eds.): ER 2015 Workshops, LNCS 9382, pp. 327–336, 2015.
DOI: 10.1007/978-3-319-25747-1_32

objects) throughout software development phases [5]. Conceptual structures are represented through a conceptual model – the first artifact produced in OO analysis. Clearly, the quality of the conceptual model is the foundation of consistency between the requirements and the final software. At the same time continuous efforts are made in the area of OO conceptual modeling, in order to provide reliable and productive software production environments [6].

Teaching requirements formalization through conceptual modeling however has been proven to be challenging [7, 8]. Amongst the factors affecting learning outcomes of novice requirements engineers and business analysts are 1. the complexity of industry tools being "noisy" with various constructs which can result in misusing concepts and creation of unintended models, 2. the lack of domain experience as a result of absence of trial and error rehearsals, 3. the lack of validation techniques and tool support for testing/validating models. Additionally, several researchers correlated novices learning achievements in system's analysis with 4. the lack of technical insights considering the absence of technical components (such as computer-assisted learning) from education as a major contributing factor to the lack of preparedness of their skills [9].

Computer-based simulation has been proven to be an excellent technique assisting juniors in understanding complex systems by allowing them to "learn by experiencing" [10–12]. Simulated environments are also known to promote successful transfer of the skills learned in classroom to real-world environments by allowing to simulate real-life situations where learners improve their technical and problem-solving skills. In the domain of conceptual modeling the use of simulation-based teaching is hampered by at least two shortcomings introduced by the existing standards for simulation technologies. The major disadvantages include being too complex and time consuming to be achieved by novice modelers whose technical expertise is limited [13]. Another important disadvantage is connected with the difficulty of interpreting the simulation results. Our previous work presents significant positive effects on learning achievements of novices for conceptual modeling when using a simulation that is 1. adapted to limited technical expertise of novices using easy and fast ("single-click") approach to achieve simulation 2. adapted to conceptual modeling goals in which constructs irrelevant for conceptual modeling goals are filtered away, and 3. is enhanced with feedback that links simulation results to their causes in a model design [14–16].

The work presented in this paper builds on our previous research on simulation-based teaching/learning of conceptual models by extending it with OO concepts. While the OO development approach is defined by one of its founders as a *"hierarchy of reusable classes united via inheritance relationships"* [2, 3], this perspective is largely neglected in literature on simulation-based teaching of OO system analysis and modeling. More specifically, in this work we target at a simulation technique that allows novices to master the concept of *reusability that can be exploited by means of class inheritance* – a key OO concept, the semantics of which is among the most challenging to be mastered by novices [17, 18], while inheritance being also often avoided [19] and/or a misapplied modeling construct [20, 21]. The effectiveness of proposed method is evaluated with respect to comprehension by novices of the concept of *inheritance when applied in a conceptual model*. The results of the experimental study show a positive impact of the proposed technique on learning outcomes of novices.

The remainder of the paper is structured as follows. The second section describes the educational context and assumptions used within this paper. Section 3 gives a brief overview of the simulation environment subsequently highlighting the learning benefits of the proposed method. Section 4 describes the experimental study targeting to measure the effects of the proposed simulation technique on the learning outcomes of novice modelers, followed by the data analysis and subsequently reports on the results. Finally, Sect. 5 concludes the work proposing some future research directions.

2 Educational Context

The proposed simulation method has been developed and validated within the course "Architecture and Modeling of Management Information Systems"[1] over a 5-years period of teaching, with participation and constant feedback from 500 students overall. The course targets at master level students with heterogeneous backgrounds from the Management Information Systems program. The goal of the course is to familiarize the students with modern methods and techniques of Object-Oriented Analysis and Design for Enterprise Information Systems, to let them understand the relation between an information system and the organizational aspects of an enterprise, and to let them acquire sufficient skills of developing an enterprise model as basis of an enterprise information system. During the course students have to formalize business requirements into conceptual domain models using an adapted for conceptual modeling and simulation environment JMermaid[2]. The methodology uses the UML as modelling language, but underneath it relies on the concepts of MERODE[3], an Enterprise Information Systems engineering methodology developed at the university of Leuven, which follows the Model-Driven Architecture and Engineering approach. In MERODE a conceptual model integrates both structural and behavioral views of a system to be engineered using a restricted class diagrams with regular binary associations, multiple interacting state charts and an interaction model. Throughout a modeling process self-regulated activities, such as testing and validation of models, are promoted through model simulation using MERODE's semantic prototyper [16] which allows simulating model solutions using a "one-click" approach. In this paper we will refer to simulation of a conceptual model as a process of generating prototype applications using a conceptual model as an input. We will therefore use the terms "simulated model" and "prototype" interchangeably. The simulation effects on the learning outcomes of novice modelers are measured with respect to *understanding of model semantics* as defined in the Conceptual Model Quality Framework [22].

---

[1] The course page can be found on http://onderwijsaanbod.kuleuven.be/syllabi/e/D0I71AE.htm.

[2] http://merode.econ.kuleuven.ac.be/mermaid.aspx.

[3] MERODE is an Object Oriented Enterprise Modeling method. Its name is the abbreviation of Model driven, Existence dependency Relation, Object oriented DEvelopment. Cfr. http://merode.econ. kuleuven.be.

3 Extending Simulation Model with the Concept of Inheritance

MERODE's model simulation environment has been extended to support the key concepts of object-oriented approach. 1. classes are created in hierarchies, and *inheritance* allows the *structural features (attributes)* and *behavioural features (methods)* to be passed down the hierarchy 2; this is realized through the concepts of *concrete classes* (classes which can be instantiated) and *abstract classes* (classes that have no instances but are used for creating other classes via *inheritance*).

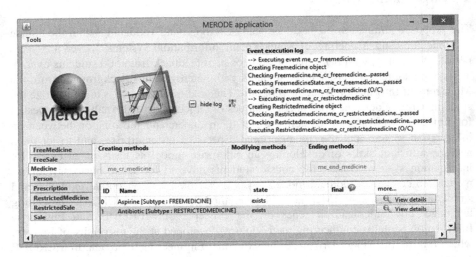

Fig. 1. Interface showing a tab for an abstract superclass

Understanding the interface (input and output models) of the generated prototype is quite intuitive. The graphical interface of a prototype application includes a main window and a set of input/output popup windows. Business entities are presented across tabbed views in the main window each containing corresponding properties of object instances (such as attributes and associated objects) presented in a tabular format. Each view of a tab panel also contains buttons corresponding to the business events that can be triggered for a particular class. MERODE prototypes offer basic functionality like triggering the creating and ending of objects, and triggering other business events that returns the output to a user in a passed/failed format. The tabs representing abstract classes are in disabled mode except for viewing buttons. An attempt to trigger any business event for this class is followed by an explanation message about the concept of 'abstract class'. The list of instances has an indication of the subclass name for each subclass instance. Figure 1 shows the main interface of the prototype: the tab for abstract class "Medicine" with disabled functionality includes instances "Aspirine" that belongs to the subtype "FreeMedicine" and "Antibiotic" that belongs to the subtype "RestrictedMedicine".

Inherited (from a supertype) and specialized (further extended by a subtype) methods are defined by a modeler in JMermaid environment. Inherited methods are those methods that have been inherited from a supertype without changing their signature, whereas specialized methods are new methods that "extend" the subclass with additional features. Tabs for subtype classes show buttons both for the inherited and specialized methods (see Fig. 2).

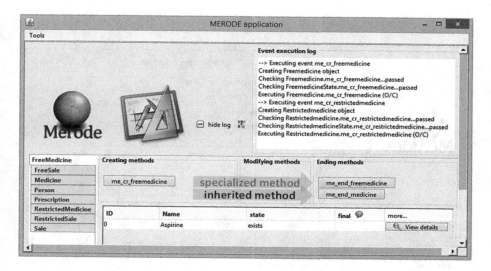

Fig. 2. Interface showing a tab for an subclass with inherited and specialized methods

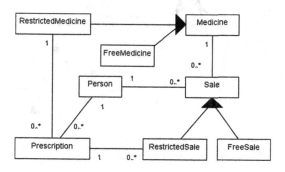

Fig. 3. Sample erroneous model

The entire interaction process is guided by user-friendly messages in case of an invalid input or a failure of an event execution (e.g. creating, ending or modifying object instances) thus ensuring maximum transparency between a prototype and its design model. A sample erroneous model and validation scenario is described in Fig. 3. Notice that in the diagrams abstract classes have been graphically represented by a black filled triangle rather than by the textual keyword {abstract} as in UML.

An example of a modeling task would be to validate a given model solution for the requirement *"To buy a restricted medicine a customer needs to have a prescription. However a prescription is not required for buying a free medicine. Registering a buyer's identity is not required for selling a free medicine. Both free and restricted sale can have a shared behavior, e.g. undergo a promotion, ... Likewise free and restricted medicine can both be out of stock, removed from sale, have a delivery request, expire,..."*.

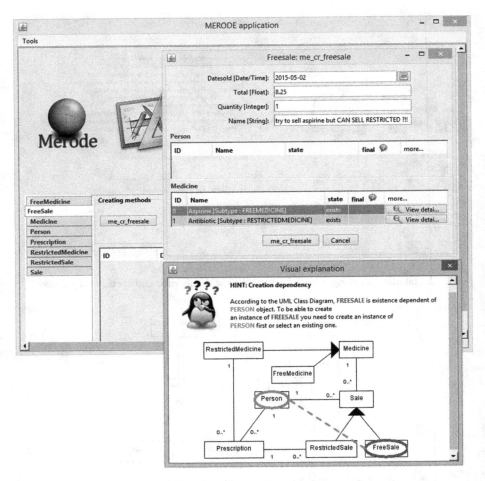

Fig. 4. Validation through a simulated model with a sample feedback on mandatory one rule violation for an association linked to the supertype class

When testing a model's prototype a student will be confronted with the following scenario: trying to register a free sale for "Aspirine" (according to a designed model this will be by means of triggering a creating event of a 'FreeSale') a popup window will request an input for the attributes specified in the model as well as to choose instances of the associated mandatory objects "Medicine" and "Person". As a result, a first problem that the prototype will allow to discover is that the selling of a free medicine requires a person to be associated with it as a result of the mandatory relationship between its superclass "Sale" and the class "Person" (cardinality of [1..1]). This is clearly in contradiction with the requirement that registering a buyer's identity is not required for selling a free medicine. A second problem that the student will discover, is that -as a consequence of the Liskov principle of substitutability- while choosing the medicine to associate with the newly created instance of the "FreeSale" object also instances of the subtype "RestrictedMedicine" will be available as potential substitutes for the supertype "Medicine", thus enabling an unrestricted sale for a restricted medicine. Through such testing, a student's analytical problem-solving ability is stimulated to pursue a correct design solution in order to fix the detected error in the model. While iteratively improving a model solution and testing with a simulated model a student is involved in a self-regulative learning process through what-if scenarios and trial and error rehearsals that allows him/her to not only achieve better but also allowing to gain knowledge that emerges from own practice. The generated feedback facilitates the process of achieving the intended behavior by explaining the reasons each time the execution of intended behavior is refused as illustrated in Fig. 4.

4 Evaluation Method

Our research goal was to assess the effectiveness of such feedback-enabled simulation in improving the novices understanding of the semantics of inheritance in a conceptual model. We opted for an experimental study with a pre/post-test control group experimental design.

Procedure: The experiment was conducted in two parts. In the first part students had to answer the set of TRUE/FALSE questions without the use of the model's prototype, so only by means of manual inspection of a given model solution. The goal of this part was to establish a baseline model validation capability level to measure the simulation effects in the second cycle. Then, in the second part of the experiment, analogous questions about a similar model had to be answered again, this time with the use of the generated prototype. The answers had to be recorded on an answer sheet. We will further refer to cycles without simulation (a paper exercise by means of manual inspection of a given model to answer the test's questions) as "withoutPT", and cycles with the use of simulation (students were required to use laptops to run a simulated model of a given model solution to answer the test's questions) as "withPT". The effectiveness of the proposed simulation method was measured by means of comparison of the test results of students between experimental cycles (without and with a use of a simulation).

Observable Dimensions: Assessing the semantic correctness of a model requires a combination of model understanding and comparing model statements with requirements. Model-reading knowledge specifically for inheritance can be assessed at different levels of understanding. In this pilot study we target at understanding of the semantics of a single level inheritance, hidden dependencies through chain of associations and parallel paths via subclass and superclass:

Level 1: Understanding the difference between the concepts of abstract and concrete classes.

Level 2: Understanding the basic concept of inheritance: that attributes and methods are inherited by the subtype from the supertype. This includes understanding the direction of the inheritance relationship.

Level 3: Understanding a single inheritance hierarchy (inheritance of associations): through inheritance and the Liskov principle of substitution, objects of the subclass can participate in associations defined at the level of the superclass (e.g. in Fig. 4, a subclass "FreeSale" inherits the association to "Person" from supertype "Sale").

Level 4: Understanding complex models with more than one inheritance hierarchies connected with a single (chain of) association.

Level 5: Understanding complex models with more than one inheritance hierarchies connected with multiple parallel (chains of) associations (e.g. in Fig. 4, the hierarchy of "Sale" and the hierarchy of "Medicine" are directly connected via the association between "Sale" and "Medicine" classes, but also through "Person" and "Prescription").

Minimum 2 questions per each dimensions have been included in the tests.

Table 1. Summary of sample demographics

Gender	*Male*	59 %
	Female	41 %
Age distributions	*Min age*	22 y.
	Max age	42 y.
	Mean age	24.6 y.
Previous knowledge of data modeling	*No knowledge*	19 %
	Little knowledge	28 %
	Moderate knowledge	38 %
	Extensive knowledge	15 %

Participants: Students who participated in the experiments were final year master students from Management Information Systems programs at KU Leuven. Overall 32 students participated in the experiment. Analysis of the pre-experimental test for basic data modeling skills and the context information from the post-study questionnaire resulted in the demographics presented in Table 1. The normality of distributions of pre-experimental knowledge as well as the experimental test scores were confirmed.

Data Analysis and findings: Data has been analyzed by means of statistical comparison of mean scores among the experimental cycles. The effectiveness was assessed based on the relative average advantage (positive correction). The results of the paired T-Test comparing mean scores of withoutPT and withPT experimental cycles ($\bar{X}_{withoutPT} = 6.04$, $\bar{X}_{withPT} = 8.37$, $\bar{X}_{difference} = 2.33$, p-value = 0.000) provide evidence that the prototyping method was effective in producing positive correction with regard to students' understanding of the concept of inheritance applied in a conceptual model. At individual test level the corrections in scores varied from 0 up to 9 (out of total 12). Despite a tool's usefulness, insufficient user acceptance can however be another factor affecting learner performance (Venkatesh, et al., 2003) such ease of use (EU) referring to the required effort to interact with a system and perceived usefulness (PU). The ratings collected in a post-study questionnaire used to assess students perceptions on a 6-point Likert scale reflect positive perceptions (Mean EOU = 4.7/6, Mean PU = 5.15/6) on the simulation environment. Students also reported a high perceived utility on the inclusion of feedback to execution failures in the prototype (5.75/6).

5   Conclusion and Future Work

The work reported on experimental extension of a feedback-enabled simulation of conceptual models with the concept of OO inheritance. The results of our pilot study described in this work show a positive effect of the proposed learning method on novices understanding of the concept of inheritance when applied in a conceptual model. While the simulation environment presented in this work uses regular binary associations in a class diagram, expanding the simulation environment with other concepts such as associative classes, composition/aggregation as well as broader coverage for inheritance with more advanced concepts such as multi-level inheritance are in the domain of future research. Among possible further directions of this research a replication experiment in the context of other university study programs with an improved experimental design (e.g. factoral 4 group experiment) is considered. In addition extending feedback framework specifically for inheritance can be another direction for this research. Yet further research must be conducted towards methodologies allowing better consistency between different abstraction levels used in a conceptual model and more detailed design models used for lower level specifications and code implementation.

References

1. Vazquez, G., Pace, J.A.D., Campo, M.: Reusing design experiences to materialize software architectures into object-oriented designs. Inf. Sci. **259**, 396–411 (2014)
2. Booch, G.: Object Oriented Analysis & Design with Application. Pearson Education India, Redwood (2006)
3. Booch, G.: Object-oriented development. IEEE Trans. Softw. Eng. **2**, 211–221 (1986)
4. Northrop, L.M., Object-Oriented Development. Encyclopedia of Software Engineering (1994)
5. Capretz, L.F.: A brief history of the object-oriented approach. ACM SIGSOFT Softw. Eng. Notes **28**(2), 6 (2003)
6. Pastor, O., Insfrán, O., Pelechano, V., Ramírez, S.: Linking object-oriented conceptual modeling with object-oriented implementation in Java. In: Tjoa, A.M. (ed.) DEXA 1997. LNCS, vol. 1308. Springer, Heidelberg (1997)

7. Siau, K., Loo, P.-P.: Identifying difficulties in learning UML. Inf. Syst. Manage. **23**(3), 43–51 (2006)
8. Erickson, J., Keng, S., Can UML be simplified? practitioner use of UML in separate domains. In: Proceedings of the 12th Workshop on Exploring Modeling Methods for Systems Analysis and Design (EMMSAD 2007), Held in Conjunctiun with the 19th Conference on Advanced Information Systems (CAiSE 2007), Trondheim, Norway (2007)
9. Barjis, J., et al.: Innovative teaching using simulation and virtual environments. Interdisc. J. Inf. Knowl. Manage. **7**, 237–255 (2012)
10. Kluge, A.: Experiential learning methods, simulation complexity and their effects on different target groups. J. Educ. Comput. Res. **36**(3), 323–349 (2007)
11. Damassa, D.A., Sitko, T.: Simulation technologies in higher education: uses, trends, and implications. EDUCAUSE Center for Analysis and Research (ECAR), Research Bulletins (2010)
12. European Commission, Opening up education: Innovative teaching and learning for all through new technologies and open educational resources. Communication from the commission to the European parliament, the council, the European economic and social committee and the committee of the regions (2013)
13. Sedrakyan, G., Snoeck, M.: A PIM-to-Code requirements engineering framework. In: Modelsward 2013-1st International Conference on Model-driven Engineering and Software Development-Proceedings (2013)
14. Sedrakyan, G., Snoeck, M.: Lightweight semantic prototyper for conceptual modeling. In: Indulska, M., Purao, S. (eds.) ER Workshops 2014. LNCS, vol. 8823, pp. 298–302. Springer, Heidelberg (2014)
15. Sedrakyan, G., Snoeck, M.: Technology-enhanced support for learning conceptual modeling. In: Bider, I., Halpin, T., Krogstie, J., Nurcan, S., Proper, E., Schmidt, R., Soffer, P., Wrycza, S. (eds.) EMMSAD 2012 and BPMDS 2012. LNBIP, vol. 113, pp. 435–449. Springer, Heidelberg (2012)
16. Sedrakyan, G., Snoeck, M., Poelmans, S.: Assessing the effectiveness of feedback enabled simulation in teaching conceptual modeling. Comput. Educ. **78**, 367–382 (2014)
17. Liberman, N., Beeri, C., Kolikant, Y.B.-D.: Difficulties in learning inheritance and polymorphism. ACM Trans. Comput. Educ. (TOCE) **11**(1), 4 (2011)
18. Hadar, I., Leron, U.: How intuitive is object-oriented design? Commun. ACM **51**(5), 41–46 (2008)
19. Sedrakyan, G., Snoeck, M., De Weerdt, J.: Process mining analysis of conceptual modeling behavior of novices empirical study using jmermaid modeling and experimental logging environment (accepted). Comput. Hum. Behav. **41**(2), 486–503 (2014)
20. Rumbaugh, J.: Disinherited-Examples of misuse of inheritance. J. Object-Oriented Program. **5**(9), 22–24 (1993)
21. Deligiannis, I.S., et al.: A review of experimental investigations into object-oriented technology. Empir. Softw. Eng. **7**(3), 193–231 (2002)
22. Nelson, H.J., et al.: A conceptual modeling quality framework. Softw. Qual. J. **20**(1), 201–228 (2012)

Reuse of Simulated Cases in Teaching Enterprise Modelling

Ilia Bider, Martin Henkel[✉], Stewart Kowalski, and Erik Perjons

Department of Computer and Systems Sciences,
Stockholm University, Stockholm, Sweden
{ilia,martinh,stewart,perjons}@dsv.su.se

Abstract. Case-based teaching/learning is widely used in Information Systems (IS) education in general, and in teaching/learning modeling, in particular. A case presents to the students a real or imaginary business situation asking them to build a model of it, or showing how such model can be built. In situations where a business case is presented in a text form, reusing it as is, or with modification in the same or a different course does not constitute much of a problem. However, using textual description for presenting cases has drawbacks on its own, as it does not help the students to acquire the skills of dissecting analyzing and analyzing the reality when building a model. The latter can be better achieved when a case is presented in a multimedia form, e.g. recorded interviews, website of a company, etc. As the previous works of the same authors show, such case presentations gives the students better understanding of the essence of modeling, which is appreciated by the students. The dark side of the multimedia presentation is that such a case presentation requires more time to build compared to using a textual form, and it is not easy to change it. This paper is a preliminary inquiry into the problem of reusing of cases presented with the help of multimedia. It presents a conceptual model of the domain aimed at discussing the potential of reuse of the whole case or its parts, and concludes with considerations on reusability that need to be covered when building multimedia presentations of cases.

Keywords: Case based learning · Modeling skills · Information systems · IS · Simulation · Education · Multi-media · Reuse

1 Introduction

One of the important skills that practitioners in the field of Information Systems, need to possess is the skill of modeling different aspects of organizational structure and behavior in order to provide proper IT solutions for businesses and public offices. This topic, which is often referred to as business or enterprise modeling, is of special importance for the university programs in Information Systems (IS), and other IT-related fields such as Computer Science and Software Engineering. Its importance for the IT professionals is well understood, and is discussed in the literature related to university teaching in IT-related fields, see, for example, [1–3].

One of the accepted methods of teaching modeling skills is a case-based teaching/learning, which is widely used in the majority of IS courses the department of

© Springer International Publishing Switzerland 2015
M.A. Jeusfeld and K. Karlapalem (Eds.): ER 2015 Workshops, LNCS 9382, pp. 337–346, 2015.
DOI: 10.1007/978-3-319-25747-1_33

Computer and Systems Sciences (DSV) at Stockholm University where the authors are engaged in teaching. A case presents to the students a real or imaginary business situation asking them to build a model of it, or showing how such model can be built. Cases are used in lectures, seminars, exams, etc.

The most important usage of the cases in teaching/learning modeling at DSV is in project work, which constitutes an essential part of each course that includes in its learning objectives the students acquiring modeling skills. A project is carried out in groups where each group gets a case presentation and needs to build a solution of the same kind as the suggested solution. However, there is no requirement that the students' solution should be exactly the same as the suggested one. Deviations are allowed as case presentation, usually, allows different interpretations. A student group can include from 2 to 5 students depending on the course and the number of enrolled students. Each group gets tutoring during the project, including milestones reviews with the teacher. The project is graded, often just on the basis pass/failed. The goal with the project is not so much examination, but learning (acquiring modeling skills) through doing.

The most spread way of presenting a case to the student, at least for the ordinary bachelor courses, is in text form [3]. This method is widely used when teaching modeling skills at DSV. The advantage of such presentation is that it is relatively easy to create for a teacher, and relatively easy to analyze by a student when building a model. The drawback is that this kind of modeling does not exist in the reality. Nobody will give to the students after graduation a full text to build a model. The information needed is to be extracted from various sources, documents, Internet, interviews with the stakeholders, etc.

Acquiring skills on how to extract knowledge from the unstructured reality of business life is a different skillset from getting knowledge on the syntax and semantics of modeling languages. While the latter is quite suitable for teaching in the classroom of a university, the former is not, as it belongs to the area of tacit knowledge [4] or Ways of Thinking and Practicing (WTP) [5]. The best known solution for acquiring WTP is apprenticeship where the students follow and help a modeling master in a real business case. However, in a university classroom setting this is difficult to arrange, if even possible.

As has been shown in our previous works [6, 7], a good approximation to the situation of real apprenticeship could be achieved via simulation using a multimedia case presentation. In such kind of simulation, the students follow a modeling master and help him/her to do some part of the work on building models. More specifically, the master chooses the information sources to be used for building a model, and hands the work of building the model to the students. Such sources may include (but are not limited to): (a) interviews with stakeholders, e.g. CEO, CIO, (b) samples of relevant documents, e.g., meetings protocols, forms for managing orders, (c) web-based sources, e.g. a company web site, results of twitter search on company name.

The trials with a simulated multimedia case presentation performed at Stockholm University [6, 7] completed in 2013–2014 showed positive results both in student engagement and the exam results. Though building a multimedia case representation took a relatively small amount of resources (55 person-hours according to [6]), spending that much resources for each business case used in the multitude of courses related to modeling might be impractical. The question arises whether one business case can be reused for different purposes and different courses.

When all cases are presented in a text form, reuse of them with or without modification does not constitute a major problem, and is often occurs in courses taught at DSV. However, when the case presentation is a multimedia simulation, the possibility of reuse becomes problematic, and may need special measures taken when designing the presentation. This is especially true if the case needs to be modified, even slightly. What is easy to change in the text, may require redesign of a number of parts in a multimedia presentation.

This paper is devoted to developing a conceptual model of the domain aimed at discussing the potential of reuse of the whole case or its parts, and requirements on reusability that need to be observed when building multimedia presentations of cases. This goal is achieved in the subsequent sections according to the following structure. Section 2 gives an overview of our previous work on apprenticeship simulation to give the reader some understanding of what kind of problems may arise with reusing a multimedia presentation of a case as a whole, or some of its part. In Sect. 3, we make an overview of the literature on representation of modeling cases and the educational modeling related to reuse of "learning objects". In Sect. 4, we present and discuss our conceptual model aimed at understanding the problems and finding solutions for building reusable multimedia case presentations. Section 5 concludes the paper.

2 An Example of Simulated Case Presentation

To illustrate the main concepts of the conceptual model to be built in the next section, we will be using a simulated case representation described in our previous works [6,7]. The simulated presentation has been built for an introductory course in IS for the first year students, the course *IT in organizations* (ITO). One of the main learning activities in the ITO course is a project assignment that requires the students in groups to build different types of enterprise models of an imaginary company presented to them. In earlier occasions of the course, the company was presented in form of a text description. The simulator substituted the text description with a web site that contained multimedia sources of information as described above and a number of modeling assignments left to the students by the master. The site also contained some tips on what sources to use when completing particular assignments via links made from assignments to these sources. The simulator has been used in two course occasions and got positive feedback from both the students and teachers engaged.

Besides working with the simulator on their own, the students meet a teacher three times during the project, two of them for consultations, and one for presentation of the results to the teacher and peers. In the two first meetings, the teacher plays the role of modeling master, which makes the setting more close to the real apprenticeship.

The multimedia sources included in the case presentation are listed in Table 1. The course was artificially created around the situation in an imaginary organization called AFFE that were engaged in the development of a business game. Therefore all sources listed in Table 1 where artificially constructed, not taking from the reality, including the interviews where the teachers played roles of both system analysts and stakeholders.

Table 1. Multimedia sources of the AFFE case (adapted from [6])

Source type	Case sources
Video recording	*Interview 1* with game development manager (simulated)
	Interview 2 with sales manager (simulated)
	Interview 3 with CEO (simulated)
Web-based sources	*Website* of the company (AFFE) (simulated)
	Twitter feed containing customer opinions (simulated)
	Financial info from http://www.proff.se/ (simulated)
	IT systems in use – links to real system vendors websites
Document-based sources	*Excel sheet 1*- sales leads management template (simulated)
	Excel sheet 2 - customer management template (simulated)
	Protocol of internal management meeting (simulated)

3   Overview of Related Research

Our main theme of reuse of simulated case representations is related to two general topics in the educational literature. Firstly, it is the topic of case-based teaching/learning in the IT-related disciplines, and secondly, it is the area of educational modeling (EML) that deals with representation of courses contents in the form of modules. The former is related to the case presentation, while the latter covers the topic of content structuring and reusability.

Case-based teaching/learning techniques, where a student builds a model of a real or imaginary case, are often used in IS teaching. The case be represented in various ways, the simplest for is a textual description of the organization [3], which is often used at DSV. Furthermore, role playing cane be used to represent a case by letting students acts as representatives for an organization [8]. Some courses at DSV use readily available real-life cases, such as Amazon, for project assignments. This approach, using real-life cases, is similar to the one presented in [9]. One filed where simulation has been successfully used in teaching is in the medical filed where a patient can be simulated, see for example [10]. In our case simulating and enterprise would be a difficult task. Thus we focus on simulating an apprenticeship situation, where an apprentice follows master analysts who gather information about an organization.

The representation of course material in a structured form has been of interest for achieving the goal to efficiently support education, and associated administration, with IT systems. The research has led to the creation of Educational Modeling Languages (EMLs). One well known example of an EML is SCORM [11]. SCORM defines the structure in form of activities, assets, "sharable objects" and the sequencing of activities in a course. SCORM also includes detailed definitions of the XML structures needed to export/import content into learning management systems. Other languages, such as PALO [12], also includes pedagogical ontologies to describe the contents of a course. A central target for these modeling languages is the description of learning objects (referred to as "knowledge objects" in PALO and "sharable content object" in SCORM). The use of learning objects is a way for organizations to create, manage, and update learning materials [13]. According to the IEEE Standard for Learning Object

Metadata [14], a learning object is defined as any entity, digital or non-digital, that may be used for learning, education, or training. In this paper we specialize the concept of learning object to specifically handle digital learning objects that deal with a case based approach to learning modeling within the field of information systems. Since our focus is on case presentation, we do not include aspects such as teaching activities, assignments and grading. These aspects are covered by SCORM and PALO.

4   A Model for Case Representation Reuse

In this section we will present a set of concepts that can help structuring case representation used within the IS field. A conceptual model aimed at analyzing the potential of reuse the whole or parts of case presentation is presented in Fig. 1. Some concepts are illustrated in Figs. 2, 3 and 4. Below, we give working definitions for these concepts and show how they are connected to each other. We also give examples of how the concepts relate to the example course described earlier in Sect. 2.

Note in Fig. 1 the relationship *learning objective* between a *learning object* and a *modeling technique* can be derived from the relationships *built with* and *intended output*. The redundant relationship was introduced for clarity sake.

A **modeling technique** is a set of principles of building a model representing some aspect of organizational behavior and/or structure. Examples of modeling techniques are *Data (conceptual) modeling, Functional modeling, Business process modeling,* Goal modeling, etc. A modeling technique may be specified with more or less precision. For example *Data modeling* is a technique of data modeling in general, while *Data modeling with UML class diagrams* is more specific as it uses a particular language to depict the model. The same relationships exist between such pairs as

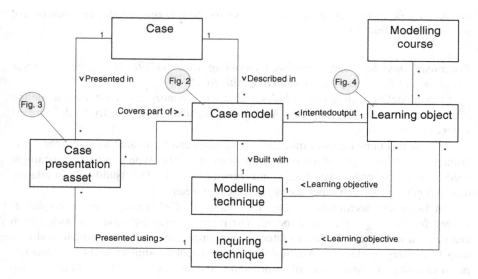

Fig. 1. Conceptual model for case presentation reuse

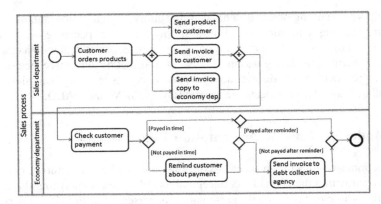

Fig. 2. A partial case model drawn using the BPMN technique, from the ITO course

Fig. 3. Example of two case *presentation assets* from the ITO course, video interview (a) and fictitious Twitter feed (b)

Functional modeling and *Functional modeling with IDEF0*, or *Business process modeling* and *Business process modeling with BPMN*.

Each modeling techniques includes a number of concepts, one or more modeling languages, and modeling patterns. A language includes some constructs defining its syntax and semantics.

As was mentioned above, modeling techniques can be related to each other, e.g. through the general- specialized type of relationships. Other type of relationships might need to be introduced as well (this is not shown in Fig. 1). This could help in relating different courses to each other and share cases between them.

An **inquiring technique** is a set of principles of obtaining information that is needed for building a particular model. The range of such techniques is wide– from analyzing a textual description to interviewing employees and management, and running facilitating workshops. Applicability of a particular inquiring technique depends on availability of certain kind of information sources, e.g. textual description of the business activity prepared by some business consultant, people agreeing to be interviewed, meetings minutes, etc.

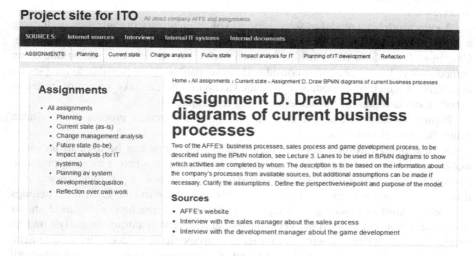

Fig. 4. A representation of a learning object in the ITO course, note links to assets/sources

In the course held at DSV we used two basic inquiring techniques; interviews, and document analysis. Document analysis consisted of both internal documents (such as protocols from meetings) and external documents, such as web sites. Other inquiring techniques include for example observation and facilitating workshops.

A **modeling course** is a course at a university that include teaching/learning at least one modeling technique as part of the course objectives. The example course *IT in organizations* (ITO) at DSV includes introduction to a number of modeling techniques, such as process modeling, goal modeling, etc. The same modeling technique could be included in several courses, for example one course takes it on the introductory level, the next takes it on the advance level, and the third course takes it on the expert level.

A modeling **course learning object** is a relationship between (a) a *modeling course* (b) a *modeling technique* that the *course* is supposed to teach and (c) *inquiring techniques* that the students are supposed to learn for the purpose of creating models with the given *modeling technique*. The expected result from the learning object is that students learn how to create a *case model*. The *course* may have other objectives than teaching modeling techniques, but we will disregard them for the sake of this discussion. The *course* may include several *learning objects* that are related to different *modeling techniques*. The *learning object* should describe which *modeling techniques* are included and which inquiring techniques will be used for building a *case model*. An introductory course may include only the analysis of a text description prepared by a business consultant, while the advanced course may also include interviewing employees and management.

Figure 4 contains an example of a presentation of a learning object from the course. The intended output is a process model, drawn using the BPMN technique. The learning object is linked to three *case presentation assets*: a website, and two interviews.

A **case model** is a model of some aspect(s) of an imaginary organization built using a given *modeling technique*. A *case model* represents only one modeling technique. *Case models* can have relationships between each other, the most important one being compatibility. Two *case models* considered as compatible if it is possible to imagine an organization which both models represents. Compatibility can take a form of inclusion if both models represent the same modeling technique.

Figure 2 shows an example case model from the course, a process model drawn using the BPMN technique.

A **case presentation asset** is a multi-media object that can be used as an information source for one or more *case models*. An asset can be a text, a meeting protocol, a recorded interview. A *case presentation asset* is said to *cover* a part of a *case model* if it contains enough information for building this part of the model. Each asset belongs to a certain kind of *inquiring technique*, i.e. *interviewing employees*. Figure 3 shows two presentation assets from the ITO course— an interview featuring an analyst and an employee, and a document with Twitter feeds from the fictitious company's customers.

A **case** consists of a case model, and a set of *case presentation assets* that *covers* all parts of the case model. Each case represents one aspect of an imaginary organization. We assume that the name of this organization, "Seven wonders", or "Military hospital", is included in at least one of the presentation fragments of the case. It also can be included in some elements of a case model.

5   Discussion - Reusing Learning Objects

We intend to use the conceptual model from Sect. 4 in an empirical study (already started) of the possibility to reuse the case presentation from the ITO course (described in Sect. 2) in other courses at DSV. The aim of the study is to determine whether *learning objects* and *assets* created in one course could realistically be used in another, and how much adjustment might be needed for this end. However, based on our experience with the ITO course and similar courses at DSV, we can tentatively identify three areas that need to be addressed in order to make reuse possible:

Technical considerations. Reusing parts of cases is a common practice at DSV. However, current reuse is in the form of copying and partially modifying textual descriptions. Obviously, it is more difficult to change a video interview, or even a pdf document, compared to plain text. To make such changes in a cost effective manner will, probably, require planning for reuse when building assets and learning objects.

Level of reuse considerations. In the ITO course we have identified several learning objects that include the use of presentation assets. An ongoing question is if it is more effective to reuse whole learning objects (for example an assignment) or just the assets (for example a video recording). As pointed out in [15] the choice here lies between reusing small assets without contextual information— or including more of the context, such as the desired modeling techniques.

Management considerations. Initial discussion of the possibility of reusing case presentations within DSV has raised some questions on the level of course management. Besides the need to create a variation of the case to adjust to the goal of another course, there is an issue of plagiarism that need to be handled. The latter may require changing the learning objects from year to year even in the same course. This can be done by changing the case assets, or by changing the assignment in the learnings objects and corresponding case model, for example requesting using some additional features in BPMN that were not required in the previous year assignment. The latter solution, probably, is more cost-efficient.

6 Conclusion

In this paper we have presented a preliminary conceptual model describing the core concepts of case based learning within the field of teaching enterprise modeling in IS courses. We specifically focused on the use of *apprenticeship simulation* to make a presentation of a case. This focus entails presenting a case in the way a master analyst would present a case to an apprentice, e.g. by gathering documents and performing interviews. The model presented in this paper will be used in an already started case study that examines how case representations can be shared among modeling courses.

The main contributions of this paper are as follows. Firstly, to the best of our knowledge, the idea of using apprenticeship simulator of the sort presented in [6, 7] has not been discussed in the literature devoted to education in IS and other IT related disciplines. Therefore the problems related to reusability of multimedia case presentations were not formulated and discussed before. Secondly, we have suggested an initial conceptual model that could help with investigating and solving the reusability problems. The model is capable to cover our simulated case, which gives it some validity. The next and more essential test of this model usefulness will be made through using it in our already started empirical investigation.

Acknowledgments.   The project was sponsored by Stockholm University's program "Future Learn". The authors are grateful to our colleagues Jelena Zdravkovic and Anders Thelemyr who participated in interview recording.

References

1. Bezivin, J., France, R., Gogolla, M., Haugen, O., Taentzer, G., Varro, D.: Teaching modeling: why, when, what? In: Ghosh, S. (ed.) MODELS 2009. LNCS, vol. 6002, pp. 55–62. Springer, Heidelberg (2010)
2. Engels, G., Hausmann, J.H., Lohmann, M., Sauer, S.: Teaching UML is teaching software engineering is teaching abstraction. In: Bruel, J.-M. (ed.) MoDELS 2005. LNCS, vol. 3844, pp. 306–319. Springer, Heidelberg (2006)
3. Fenstermacher, K.D.: If I had a Model, I'd Model in the Morning. In: Proceeding of OOPSL 2004, pp. 88–89 (2004)
4. Polanyi, M.S.: Knowing and Being. University of Chicago, Chicago (1969)

5. McCune, V., Hounsell, D.: The development of students' ways of thinking and practising in three final-year biology courses. High. Educ. **49**(3), 255–289 (2005)

6. Bider, I., Henkel, M., Kowalski, S., Perjons, E.: Teaching enterprise modeling based on multi-media simulation: a pragmatic approach. In: Proceedings of the 6th MCETECH Conference on e-Technologies. LNBIP, vol. 209, pp. 239–254. Springer (2015)

7. Bider, L., Henkel, M., Kowalski, S., Perjons, E.: Simulating apprenticeship using multimedia in higher education: a case from the information systems field. Interact. Technol. Smart Educ. **12**(2), 137–154 (2015)

8. Costain, G., McKenna, B.: Experiencing the elicitation of user requirements and recording them in use case diagrams through role play. J. Inf. Syst. Educ. **22**(4), 368–382 (2011)

9. Recker, J., Rosemann, M.: Teaching business process modelling: experiences and recommendations. Commun. AIS **25**, 379–394 (2009)

10. Ellaway, R., Poulton, T., Fors, U., McGee, J.B., Albright, S.: Building a virtual patient commons. Med. Teach. **30**, 170–174 (2008)

11. Jesukiewicz, P.: Sharable content object reference model (SCORM), 4th Edition Content Aggregation Model, Advanced Distributed Learning (2009)

12. Maíllo, M.F.V., Rodríguez-Artacho, M.: Modeling educational content: the cognitive approach of the PALO language. Educ. Technol. Soc. **7**(3), 124–137 (2004)

13. Lee, L., Tono, D.: Learning objects: implications for instructional designers. Int. J. Instr. Media **38**(3), 253–260 (2011)

14. IEEE, IEEE Standard for Learning Object Metadata, The Institute of Electrical and Electronics Engineers, New York, IEEE Std 1484.12.1-2002 (2002)

15. Agrawal, M., Banchuen, R., DiBiase, T., Gahegan, D.: Building rich, semantic descriptions of learning activities to facilitate reuse in digital libraries. Int. J. Digit. Libr. **7**(1–2), 81–97 (2007)

The Importance of Teaching Systematic Analysis for Conceptual Models: An Experience Report

Elda Paja[1]([✉]), Jennifer Horkoff[2], and John Mylopoulos[1]

[1] University of Trento, Trento, Italy
{paja,jm}@disi.unitn.it
[2] City University London, London, UK
horkoff@city.ac.uk

Abstract. In this paper, we report on our experience in teaching conceptual modeling at a master-level course at the University of Trento. We use our experiences to argue that systematic model analysis is an important factor that influences learning and understanding of conceptual modeling techniques. In particular, we have observed this effect with the i^* goal-oriented language. In previous years students were required to perform only modeling as part of their projects, while in the last year they were also required to apply systematic analysis. We observe that i^* analysis not only allows students to evaluate the satisfaction of goals in their model, but also to better understand their models, helping to refine models until they are more meaningful and more likely to fulfill their intended purpose.

Keywords: Conceptual modeling · Models · Analysis · Education

1 Introduction

For conceptual models to be used in practice, conceptual modeling languages and techniques must be taught through university and professional courses. Currently they are taught, often at the undergraduate level, as topics in the syllabus of courses such as database design (ER modeling), software engineering (UML), requirements engineering (goal models), and business analysis (BPMN). As instructors, it is our aim that students, at the end of their learning experience, are capable of building useful conceptual models that add value to their future work. But, how do we achieve this goal? The main thesis of this paper is that the teaching of conceptual models should be coupled with one or more types of systematic analysis techniques. It is through analysis that students understand whether their models are meaningful and fulfill their purpose. It is such analysis that makes students appreciate the benefits of models and modeling.

Our thesis has been tested with a qualitative study involving a masters-level course at the University of Trento. The course is titled "Organizational Information Systems"and has been offered for more than 10 years with 20–35 enrollments per year. The course covers enterprise modeling, strategic objectives modeling and analysis with i^* [12], business process modeling and simulation

© Springer International Publishing Switzerland 2015
M.A. Jeusfeld and K. Karlapalem (Eds.): ER 2015 Workshops, LNCS 9382, pp. 347–357, 2015.
DOI: 10.1007/978-3-319-25747-1_34

with Adonis [6]. Course requirements include a course project worked on in teams involving modeling and analysis of an enterprise of each team's choice.

In the past, course projects required students to draw i*, or other types of goal models, but did not explicitly require the application of any type of systematic goal model analysis. In order to keep course topics in line with conceptual modeling advances, in the 2014 offering of the course, systematic analysis procedures for i* and BIM (Business Intelligence Modeling) [2] were added to the course syllabus and projects. We observed that these additions, particularly the addition of i* analysis, had positive effects on the students' use of the models within their course projects, allowing students to better link the models to the project analysis and recommendations.

The rest of the paper is structured as follows. In Sect. 2 we present the methods taught and used for the projects, while providing more details about the course syllabus and the student projects requirements. Section 3 illustrates i* and i* analysis with the help of a running example, while Sect. 4 summarizes course project results. Section 6 reviews related work and Sect. 7 concludes.

2   OIS Course Syllabus

The Organizational Information Systems (OIS) course is taught at the master level with the objective of (i) teaching students basic concepts about modeling business organizations and business processes; (ii) teaching information system technologies and architectures used to support the operation of organizations; (iii) understanding how to manage organization information systems and to ensure information assurance; and (iv) introducing new trends in organizational information systems. Students are required to have general knowledge of software engineering, including knowledge of UML, as well as general knowledge of databases and information systems.

The course is organized as follows. First, it provides an introduction to organizations and organizational information systems, organizational structures, and organizational business processes. Second, it presents students with modeling approaches for organizations, standards and reference architectures. Among others, it presents approaches for organizational modeling such as i* [12] and strategic business modeling such as BIM [2]. Emphasis is placed on teaching systematic analysis for both i* and BIM [2,5]. Third, the course covers modeling and analysis approaches for business processes, based on Adonis[1]. Fourth, it discusses OISs Management - plan, implement, deliver, monitor, evaluate, and improve organizational information systems. Finally, the course discusses information assurance, presenting methods for IT Goal-Risk-Compliance [1], and Information Security, e.g., [9].

Over the years the syllabus of the course has been continuously updated to accommodate new and emerging techniques. Although many goal model analysis procedures exist [4], we have chosen to teach the students qualitative, interactive analysis [5], as this type of analysis is relatively simple, does not require detailed domain information, and comes with relatively stable tool support.

---

[1] http://www.boc-group.com/it/products/adonis/.

Student evaluation is done through a course project, to be completed by teams of two or three. Students choose their own teammates, and are required to play interchangeably the roles of the requirements analyst and stakeholders, in order to capture both perspectives when building and analyzing the models. Students have interacted directly with real stakeholders and customers in only a few cases. The project is discussed in a final oral exam.

Project Description. Student projects are divided into two assignments. The first assignment is focused on modeling, while the second focuses on analysis, intended to support the improvement of the organization. The first two rows of the Zachman framework [13] are followed to determine what to model.

A1. In the first assignment, students report on the problem by initially describing the organization in natural language (English/Italian). This description provides an overview of the organization (sector, size, location, services, etc.), specific features (what makes it different from competitors), and hypothetical plans about the future of the organization. Students should define the scope of the project (especially for big organizations), i.e. the parts of the organization for which they will design an information system that will support the future developments.

In the rest of the first assignment students are required to model the existing organization (within the defined scope), representing important actors, their goals and interdependencies. This modeling is typically performed with i*, although students are free to use state-of-the-art tools of their choice. Moreover, an important step of the modeling activities involves capturing strategic goals of the organization, including relevant situations and indicators, typically represented with BIM models. In representing the organization's services and products, students are required to model a class diagram. Finally, students are required to identify business processes through which the organization delivers services or conducts its business, to then model at least three complex business processes with BPMN or Adonis. They should account for events affecting the business processes of the organization. The students should report on the problem, models and the rationale behind their design choices.

A2. The purpose of the second assignment is twofold: (1) to analyze the chosen organization in order to identify weaknesses, bottlenecks, and underperformance. Emphasis is placed on the instruction of strategic analysis for i* and BIM, as well as business process analysis and simulation with ADONIS; (2) to improve the current organization by designing part of an organizational information system. Ideally, the system will overcome the identified limitations. This should be demonstrated using further analysis.

To achieve these objectives, students should analyze their i* models and BIM models to determine goal satisfaction or denial. The analysis results help them understand what organizational changes can be made to better achieve goals. Most importantly, they are required to describe how these changes affect the identified business processes.

From the business process view, students are required to execute: (i) consistency queries for all the models, to show that the models are syntactically correct and complete; moreover, they should run some queries to elicit useful information from the business processes; (ii) path analysis; and (iii) capacity analysis. Students should report and interpret the results of the queries, describing their conclusions.

3   Background: *i** and *i** Analysis

Before reporting on our course observations, we provide some background *i** and qualitative i* analysis, using a small running example of a hardware/software wholesaler (HSD) for illustration. HSD wants to provide high quality products to retailers and ensure very competitive prices. In order to do so, it buys goods from producers. HSD must maintain success via efficient logistics and low cost. To do so, it can either use a just-in-time order policy, or store items in their warehouse. We illustrate the goals and alternatives for HSD using *i**.

The *i** framework [11,12] was developed by *Eric Yu* to model and reason about organizational environments and their information systems. It addresses the need to model and analyze the motivations behind stakeholders requirements during early-phase requirements engineering. The basic constructs offered by the *i** language are: *actor*, together with its associations; *intentional elements* (goals, tasks, and resources), *strategic dependencies* among actors, and internal relationships among intentional elements (*decomposition links*, *means-end links*, and *contribution links*). We start with the identification of the main actors for HSD. Actors represent organizational units, such as *Purchase department*, *Sales department*, *Logistics departments*, and identified roles, such as *Supplier*, *Customer*, *Sales agent*, *Supplies manager*, *Sales campaign manager*, *Complaints responsible*, and *Warehouse worker*.

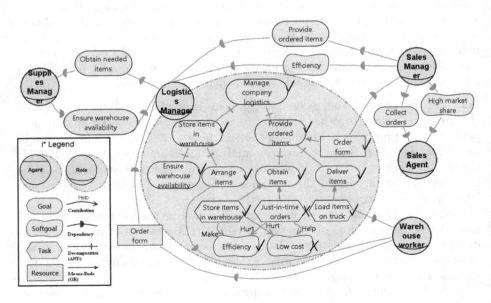

Fig. 1. Partial *i** model for HSD Example

i^* modeling emphasizes dependencies between actors. For instance, for the HSD company, (Fig. 1) shows that the *Sales manager* depends on the *Logistics manager* to *provide ordered items*, while achieving *efficiency*.

i^* also allows one to capture the internal rationale of actors, in terms of intentional elements—goals, tasks, resources, softgoals. By making knowledge about an actors' rationality explicit, such models are useful to reason about actors' behavior. Figure 1, shows the rationale of actor *Logistics Manager*. To *Manage company logistics*, the *Logistics Manager* stores items in the warehouse and provides ordered items. To store items in the warehouse, he should ensure warehouse availability and arrange items, while in order to provide ordered items he needs order form, and he should obtain items and deliver them. To deliver items, he should load items on truck, for which he depends on the *Warehouse worker*. Similarly, we could expand the internal rationale for the Supplies Manager, to understand how she achieves her main goal.

The i^* language comes with associated analysis techniques, such as [5], to answer "What if?" or "Is this achievable?" questions. These procedures allows users to explore the meaning of the connections within their models, understanding the consequences of alternative selection. Such analysis is intended to help find problematic areas in the model, and to help choose the best mitigation or alternative for such problems. Similar analysis procedures have been introduced for complementary frameworks, such as the Business Intelligence Model (BIM) [2].

For example, in the HSD case, we can ask: "what if we store items in the warehouse and do not implement just-in-time ordering?" How does this effect goals in our model? Is this a viable alternative? To answer these questions we place initial qualitative labels on the leaf elements which reflect this question (Fully satisfied (check) on Store Items in Warehouse and Fully denied (cross) on just-in-time ordering). Tool support will propagate these labels automatically, using the semantics of i^* as defined in [5], asking the user for input in situations with conflicting or partial evidence. For example, Low cost receives partial negative evidence via store items in warehouse and the denial of just-in-time orders. Using their knowledge of the domain, do users judge this goal to be fully or partially denied? Propagation continues until all connected elements are given values representing their level of evidence, and the results are interpreted to determine if the alternative is viable, see Fig. 1 for the full analysis results. In this case, the alternative satisfies efficiency and denies low cost. Other alternatives can be similarly evaluated in order to compare results and guide final recommendations.

Similarly, users can perform "backward" analysis of goal models, in this case placing desired labels on important goals (e.g., manage company logistics and low cost should be satisfied) and asking the tooling to find a solution (set of implemented elements), if such a solution exists (in this case, just in time orders).

4   Results and Lessons Learned

As mentioned, the course has been continuously reshaped to accommodate new emerging state-of-the-art techniques. While it initially focused on enterprise architecture and business process modeling and analysis, using goal models only to describe the chosen organization, in the last two course instantiations, we have required students to make more use of systematic analysis techniques to assess their goal models. We report on our observations of how the use of goal model analysis influenced students' understanding, with a focus on 2014. Although the same teaching methods were used for the current course instance (2015), we do not yet have the results (the exam is to take place in the end of June).

OIS'14 results. We noticed qualitatively that the outcomes of the projects were much improved in the 2014 course instantiation. During the oral exam, we observed that students demonstrated a better understanding of goal models after applying analysis, which allowed them to iteratively and incrementally build goal models that adequately capture the intended domain and fulfill their purpose.

We can summarize the results for OIS'14, a class of size 17, as follows:

- Out of the 9 projects, 8 performed extensive goal analysis over i^* and BIM models, and only 1 (team with a single student) failed to do so.
- Of the 8 projects who performed goal analysis, all 8 teams made suggestions for model improvement after applying analysis. 6/8 teams went further, re-running analysis over the improved models.
- Roughly half of the projects' marks fell in the 28/30 range (very good). Those teams with very good marks performed extensive analysis, improvement, reiteration, and supported their decision-making using analysis.

We have observed that the results of the goal-analysis help students to understand what organizational changes can be made to better achieve goals. Moreover, they have used BIM analysis to identify the strategies that support those goals.

With respect to BIM modeling and analysis, as compared to i^* analysis, students performed only one round of analysis and simulation. This may be due to the immaturity of the BIM analysis tool, or to the nature of BIM analysis, aimed for business intelligence, which requires quantitative input from real or realistic KPIs (Key Performance Indicators). Such information was not readily available to students.

We provide excerpts from a representative student project which applied analysis to iteratively improve and/or decide on the best alternatives captured in the model.

The students have applied both forward and backward analysis, running analysis over 4 different scenarios for forward analysis and 2 for backward analysis, respectively. The forward scenarios evaluated included: *"What if they invest in training?"*, *"What if they invest in recruitment?"*, and *"What if we invest in recruitment but we are not able to setup production facilities?"*. Figure 2 shows part of the i^* model and the results of the forward analysis for the last scenario.

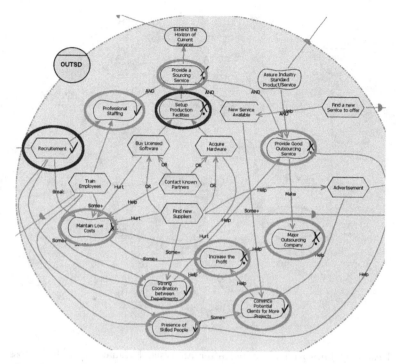

Fig. 2. i^* forward analysis: What if we invest in recruitment but we are not able to setup production facilities? (Color figure online)

The highlights on this figure were added by the students to show initial (blue circle) and resulting (green circle) analysis labels.

Upon analysis results, the students reported: *"As expected, there would be more skilled people and a good coordination between departments, allowing the organization to convince more partners for more projects, but it would not be able to provide a sourcing service, and so all would be useless."* Thus, we see that students are able to interpret the results over the model in a reasonable way, in this case ruling out a particular alternative for re-design.

In this project, running backward analysis allowed the students not only to find potential solutions (sets of tasks which satisfy desired goals) in the model, but also encouraged them to improve their goal models, see Fig. 3 for a version of the model after such improvements. The students report: *"The first thing a manager would probably know is how to maintain low costs. Surprisingly, running more times the analysis did not seem possible to find a satisfiable scenario. This was very interesting and allowed us to understand why; the reason was the semantics of the OR decomposition (Find new suppliers OR Contact known partners) and made us understand that there was too much detail in our model. In particular, distinguishing between Buy Licensed Software and Acquire new Hardware was not worth it, because satisfying one or the other has the same*

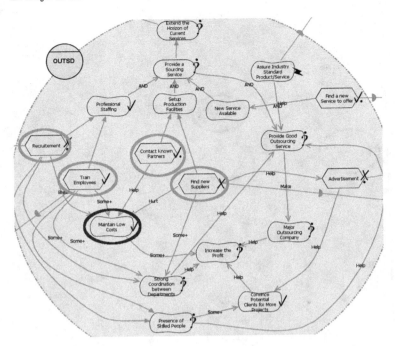

Fig. 3. Resulting improved i^* model after analysis; Evaluation of: Is it possible to maintain low costs?

consequences and also because we are not able to predict for instance whether it costs more to obtain a software license or some hardware equipment. We reviewed our model, obtaining the final diagram presented in Fig. 3. The analysis gave the expected results; it is better to train employees than recruiting new ones, and it is better to contact new partners instead of finding new suppliers.

In this case, the student group observed that the model analysis conflicted with their perception of reality (there was no solution, when there should be). The students refined the model to remove elements which prevented the discovery of a solution, justifying this removal by observing that the two alternatives had identical effects in the model, and were thus indistinguishable. In another case, the disconnect between the model and the students' perception of the domain could lead to the students learning more about the organization, discovering some new trade-off. In processing future assignments, we should look specifically for these various classifications of model changes (model improvement vs. learning).

Previous Years Results. In order to better understand the impact of teaching analysis techniques for i* models, we compared the course projects for 2014 with those for two previous years (2009, 2010) when the course was taught without covering analysis techniques. For those editions of the course, students were asked to conduct simulation of the business processes they model using the ADONIS tool provided by BoC. The results were as follows, for classes of size 18 and 24 respectively:

– About a third of all projects did not perform much analysis (simulation or otherwise), while another third did some simulation without drawing any conclusions. Only the top third of the class (roughly, with marks in the range 28–30/30) did substantial simulation and analysis;
– There was very good correlation between how much analysis a project did and what mark it got;
– Roughly a third of the marks for the two classes fell in the range 28/30 (very good), with another third falling below what we'd consider satisfactory performance, while in the 2014 offering, roughly half of the student marks fell in the "very good" range.

5   Threats to Validity

Although our experiences have been revealing, our study has several threats to validity. In terms of internal validity, many of the conclusions reported in our study are based on our personal experiences, with limited ability to perform more quantitative analysis and measures. This is, in part, because our access to past assignments is now limited, and also because we did not plan the course and assignments in such as way that they could be easily measured and compared. Despite this, we think the conclusion drawn from our experiences – the importance of analysis – is useful for conceptual modeling education. In the future we plan to include more precise measurements over assignments into the course design.

It is also possible that the particular class of students may have been exceptionally skilled, as compared to previous years. However, we believe that the experience and skills of the students were very much in line with students registered for the course in past years.

Considering external validity, we have only had the opportunity to test our hypothesis concerning the benefits of analysis with one course in one university. However, we believe that the course registrants are representative, in terms of experience and background, of Master-level students in Europe undergoing a technical degree. Future studies should test our hypothesis in different courses with different student demographics.

In the 2014 OIS course instantiation, the method designer, specifically the designer of i* qualitative, interactive analysis as per [5], was the method teacher. Although this situation is not generalizable, we make the slides specific to the analysis procedures used in the course available online[2].

6   Related Work

Although pedagogy has been a subject of interest in technical fields such as Computer Science (via the SIGCSE conference) and Software Engineering (via the

---

[2] http://www.cs.toronto.edu/~jenhork/Presentations/11-AdvancediStarBIM.pdf.

CSEE&T conference), interest in Education specifically for conceptual modeling has been only recently reflected in academic venues, via the first and second Conceptual Modeling Education Symposiums. In a similar track, the MODELS conference has held an Educational Symposium (EduSymp) traceable back to 2008. Looking through available papers, we do not find papers related to (a) goal model education or (b) the benefits of model analysis for teaching purposes.

A new initiative has started the iStar Teaching Workshop (iStarT), co-located with the Conference on Advanced Information Systems Engineering (CAiSE), to be held in June, 2015. An earlier, less-detailed version of this paper will appear in iStarT'15 [10].

Related work can be found in other venues. In [3], the authors evaluate use of i* in academic assignments and research papers in order to find the most frequent deviations from recommended i* syntax, making recommendations concerning the language and tooling. Such error lists are helpful in guiding goal-oriented teaching practices.

In [7], Koch and Landes apply i* to understand pedagogical goals, but do not teach goal modeling directly to students. Monsalve et al., use i* modeling to capture teaching goals, aiming for increased pedagogical transparency [8]. Neither approach make use of i* analysis.

The i* analysis procedure used in the course [5] was originally introduced not only to support evaluation of goal satisfaction, but to help interactively improve the quality of early, high-level models through interactive exploration. The positive effect on model quality was demonstrated as part of a large, real case, but more controlled class-room style experiments on smaller, more artificial models did not confirm these results. The authors concluded that in order to improve their models, modelers must be motivated by realistic factors. In the OIS course, working on large, realistic cases, analysis motivated many, but not all students to improve their models. This helps to confirm the initial conclusions in [5], the benefits of analysis are tied to the level of realism of the model domain.

7   Conclusions

We have described our experience in teaching conceptual modeling, and in particular goal-modeling techniques at a graduate level course. We observed that the use of goal model analysis offered students a deeper understanding of the activities they performed, in some cases allowing them to make improvements to their models. The presented results are from the previous two course instances; we plan to further test our hypothesis on course assignments for the current year, as well as future course offerings.

Acknowledgements. This research was partially supported by the ERC advanced grant 267856, 'Lucretius: Foundations for Software Evolution', www.lucretius.eu. Jennifer Horkoff is supported by an ERC Marie Skodowska-Curie Intra European Fellow-ship (PIEF-GA-2013–627489) and by a Natural Sciences and Engineering Research Council of Canada Postdoctoral Fellowship (Sept. 2014 - Aug. 2016).

References

1. Asnar, Y., Giorgini, P., Mylopoulos, J.: Goal-driven risk assessment in requirements engineering. Requirements Eng. **16**(2), 101–116 (2011)
2. Horkoff, J., Barone, D., Jiang, L., Yu, E., Amyot, D., Borgida, A., Mylopoulos, J.: Strategic business modeling: representation and reasoning. Softw. Syst. Model. **13**(3), 1015–1041 (2014)
3. Horkoff, J., Elahi, G., Abdulhadi, S., Yu, E.: Reflective analysis of the syntax and semantics of the i* framework. In: Song, I.-Y., Piattini, M., Chen, Y.-P.P., Hartmann, S., Grandi, F., Trujillo, J., Opdahl, A.L., Ferri, F., Grifoni, P., Caschera, M.C., Rolland, C., Woo, C., Salinesi, C., Zimányi, E., Claramunt, C., Frasincar, F., Houben, G.-J., Thiran, P. (eds.) ER Workshops 2008. LNCS, vol. 5232, pp. 249–260. Springer, Heidelberg (2008)
4. Horkoff, J., Yu, E.: Analyzing goal models: different approaches and how to choose among them. In: Proceedings of the 2011 ACM Symposium on Applied Computing, pp. 675–682. ACM (2011)
5. Horkoff, J., Yu, E.: Interactive goal model analysis for early requirements engineering. Requirements Eng. **97**, 1–33 (2014)
6. Karagiannis, D., Junginger, S., Strobl, R.: Introduction to business process management systems concepts. In: Business Process Modelling, pp. 81–106. Springer, Heidelberg (1996)
7. Koch, M., Landes, D.: Modeling software engineering education with i. In: Proceedings of iStar 2014 (2014)
8. Monsalve, E.S., Liete, J.C.S.d.P., Werneck, V.M.B.: A case study to evaluate the use of i* for helping pedagogy transparency. In: Proceedings of iStar 2014 (2014)
9. Paja, E., Dalpiaz, F., Giorgini, P.: Managing security requirements conflicts in socio-technical systems. In: Ng, W., Storey, V.C., Trujillo, J.C. (eds.) ER 2013. LNCS, vol. 8217, pp. 270–283. Springer, Heidelberg (2013)
10. Paja, E., Horkoff, J., Mylopoulos, J.: The importance of teaching goal-oriented analysis techniques: an experience report. In: Proceedings of iStarT 2015 (2015)
11. Yu, E.: Modelling strategic relationships for process reengineering. Ph.D. thesis, University of Toronto, Canada (1996)
12. Yu, E., Giorgini, P., Maiden, N., Mylopoulos, J.: Social Modeling for Requirements Engineering. MIT Press, Mylopoulos (2010)
13. Zachman, J.: The zachman framework for enterprise architecture. Zachman International (2002)

Author Index

Printed in the United States
By Bookmasters